Norman Garstin

Irishman & Newlyn Artist

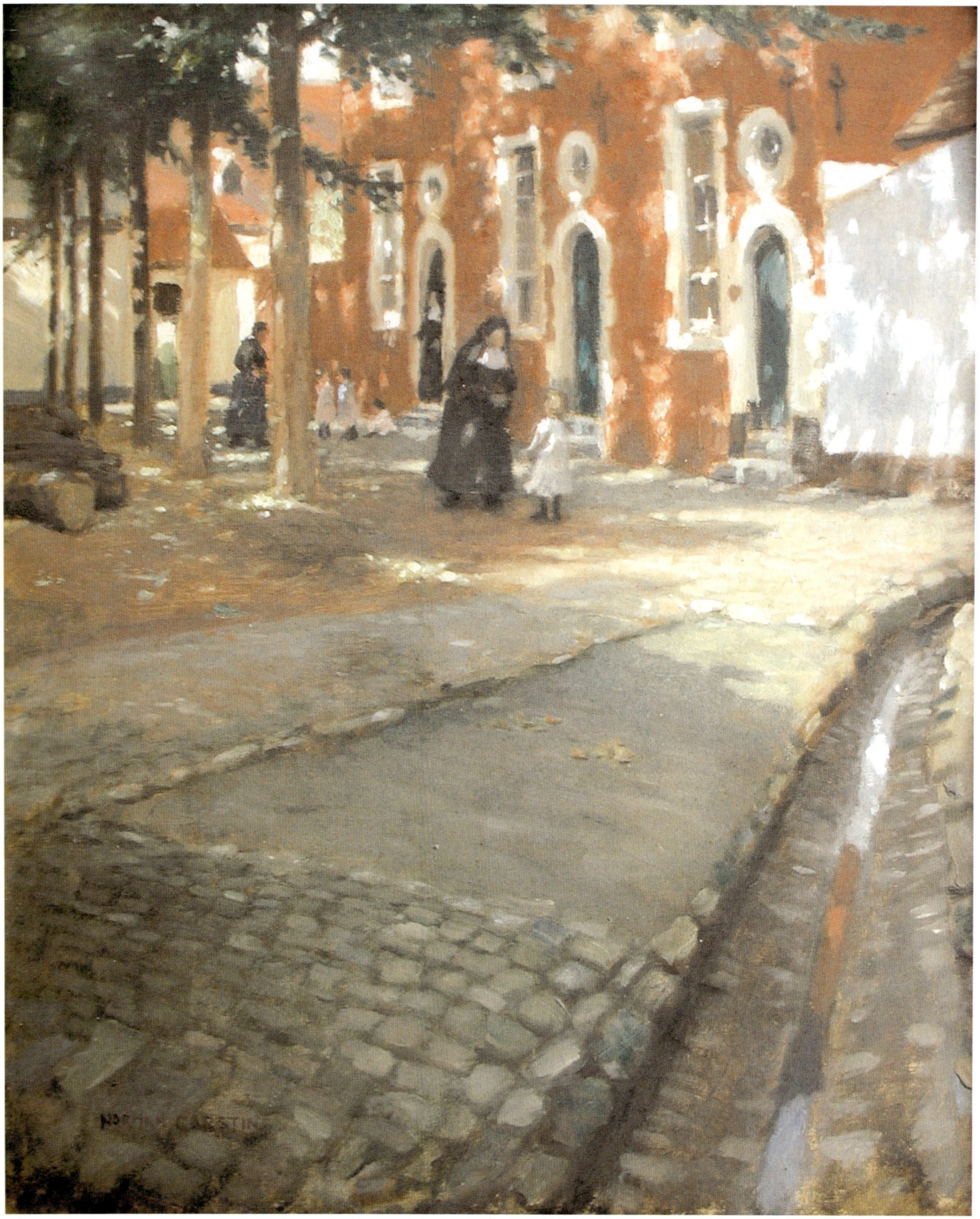

Norman Garstin
Irishman & Newlyn Artist

Richard Pryke

Spire Books Ltd
PO Box 2336, Reading RG4 5WJ
www.spirebooks.com

Spire Books Ltd
PO Box 2336
Reading RG4 5WJ
www.spirebooks.com

CIP data:
A catalogue record for this book is available
from the British Library
ISBN 0-9543615-9-8

Designed and produced by John Elliott
Copy editing by Geoff Brandwood and
Christopher Webster
Text set in Adobe Bembo

Printed by Alden Group Ltd
Osney Mead
Oxford OX2 0EF

Opposite title page:
Plate 1 *The Red Houses*, 1912, oil, 23.5" x 19" (private collection).

Opposite:
Plate 2 *Temptation*, 1888, oil, 32" x 25" (private collection, auctioned as *Seamstress Thinking).*

Opposite Contents page:
Plate 3 *Earthenware*, 1912, oil, 10.5" x 8.25" (private collection).

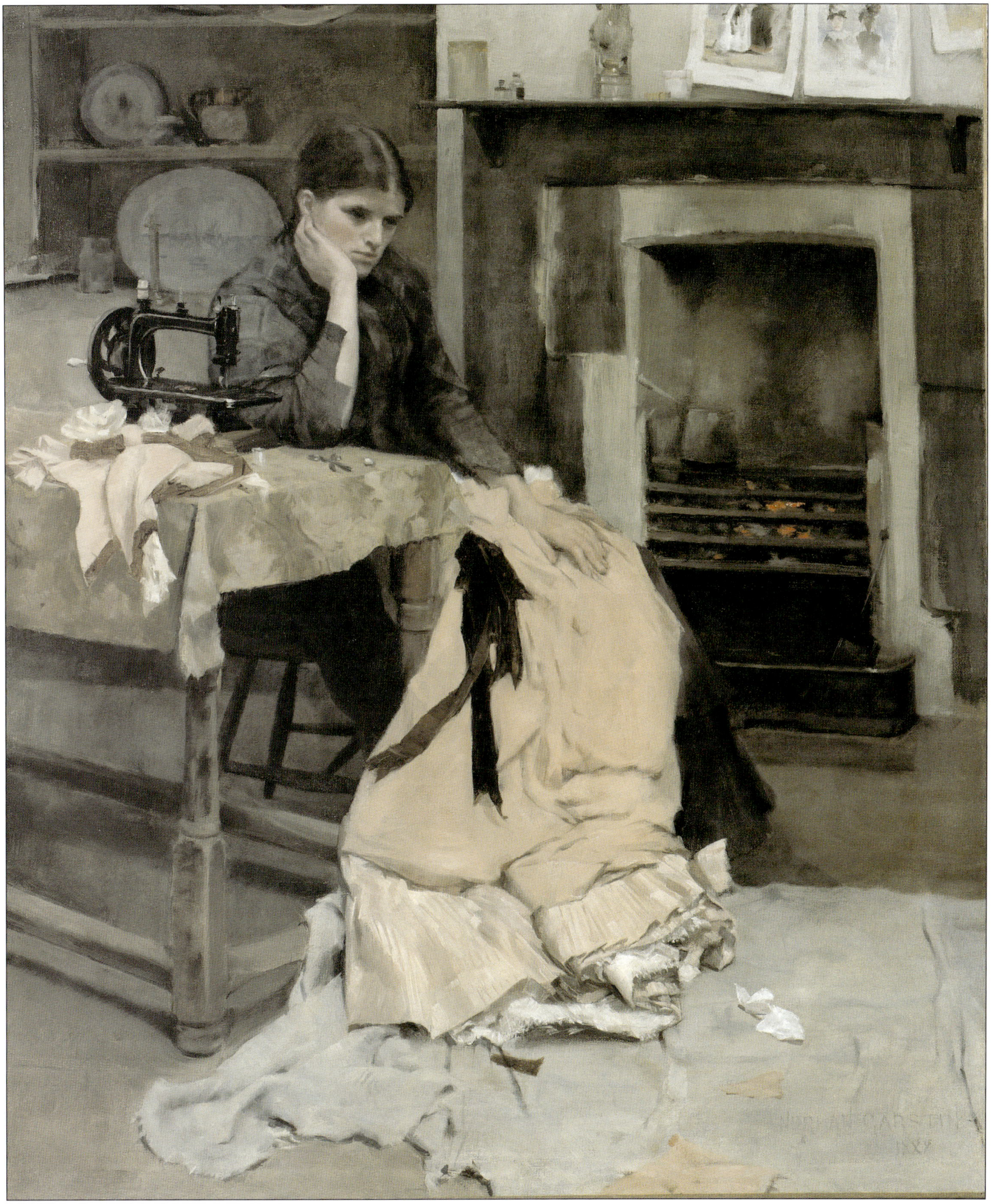

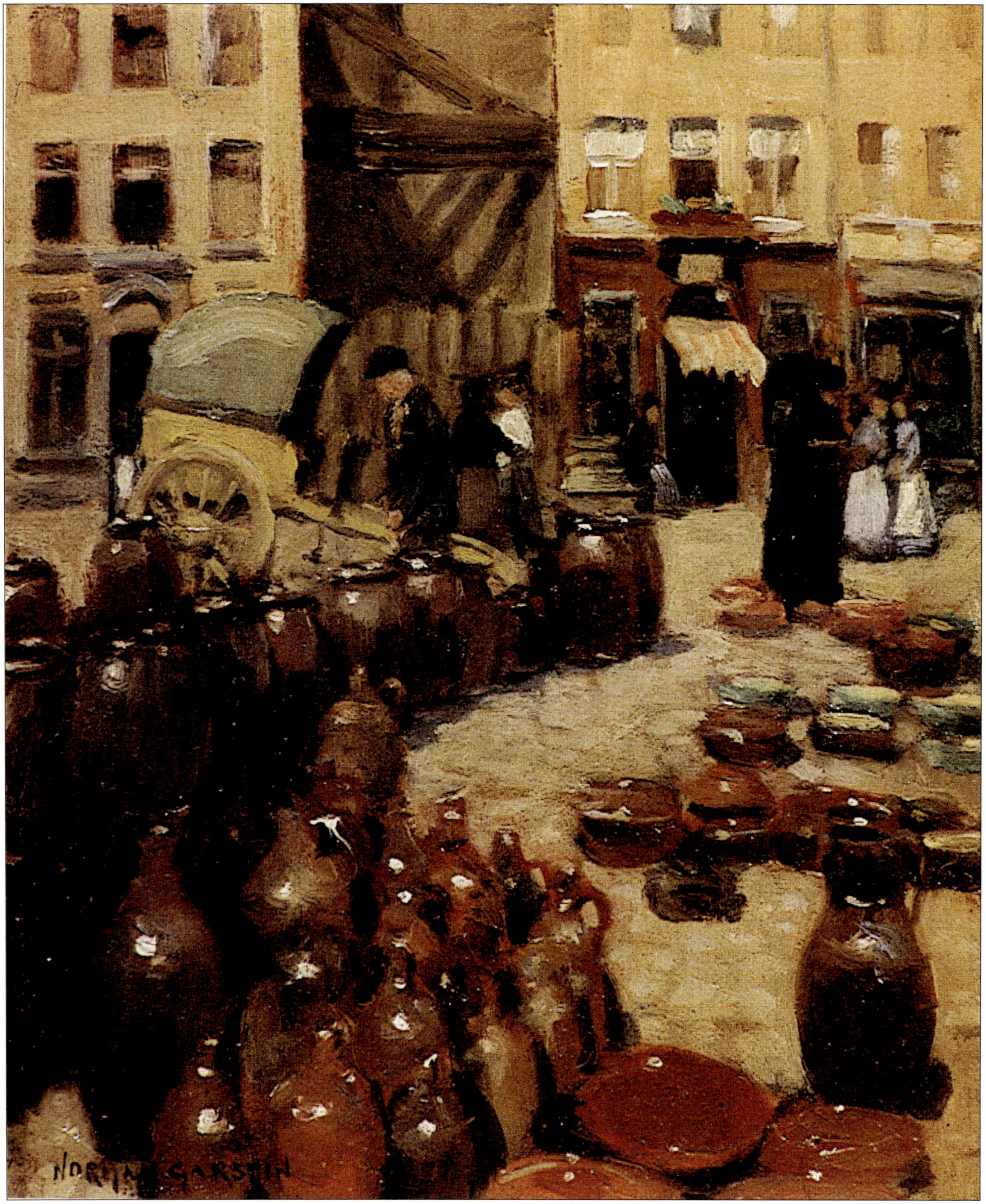

Contents

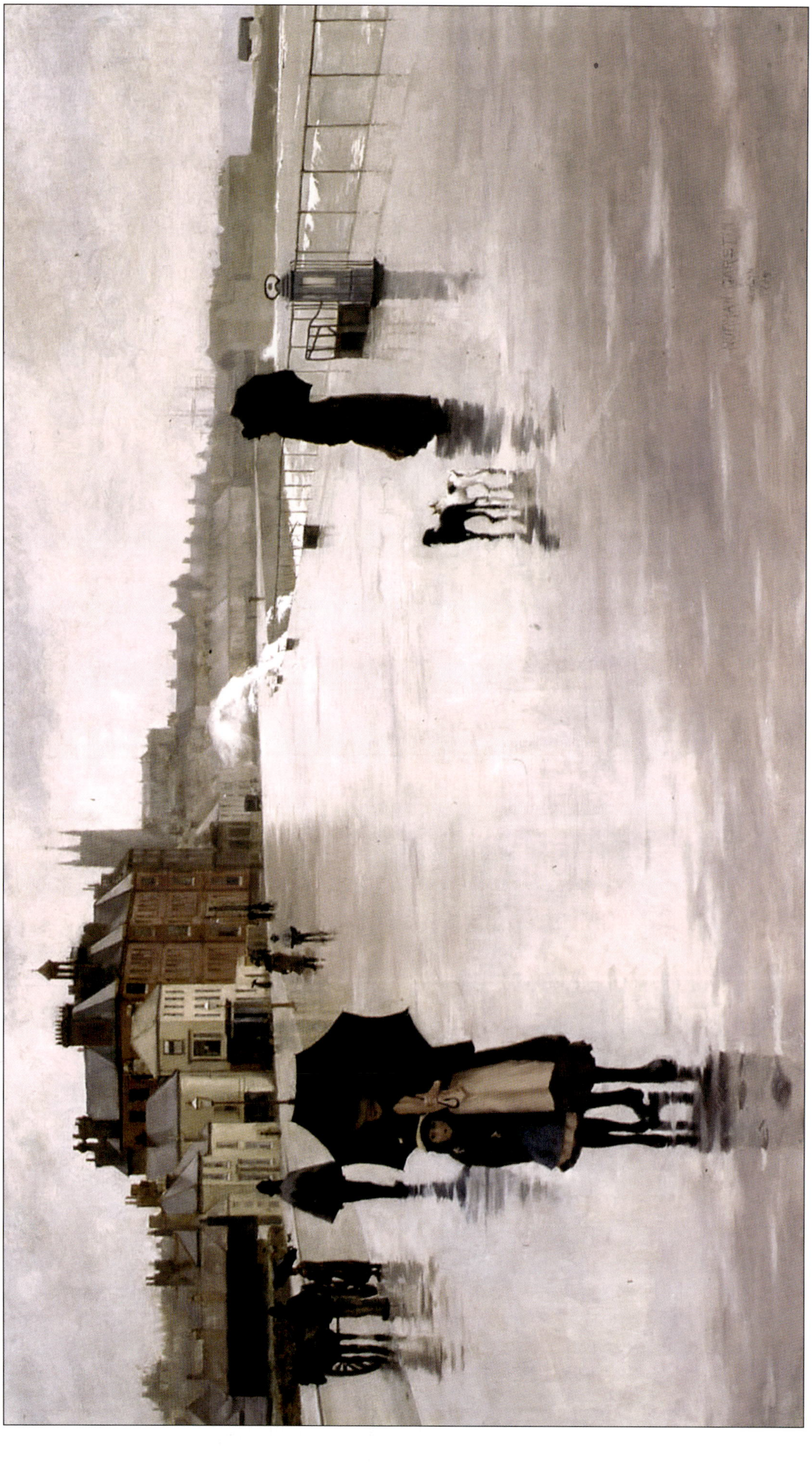

Preface

Biography is not my favourite form of literature. All too often biographers seem unable to escape from a strictly chronological treatment, and become obsessed with the minutiae not only of their subject's life and doings but also of attendant topics. I now understand how this comes about. One becomes so fascinated by the process of unearthing obscure facts, and so pleased at one's occasional successes, that the biographer cannot forbear to tell the reader about what has been discovered. I hope I have avoided this pitfall. If I have, it is largely due to the advice of my friend Peter Walters. When I was embarking on this project, I asked him whether he had any counsel. He promptly and succinctly replied, 'Try to answer the big questions about Garstin's life and work'. This I have earnestly tried to do, and Peter deserves pride of place in the long list of those I must thank.

The biggest question about Norman Garstin concerns his status as an artist. Was he, as I believe, a major artist of the Realist Movement, or merely a minor figure? In order to answer this question it will be necessary to say something not only about his life and work but also about the developments that were taking place when he was painting and, in particular, about Realist art and its characteristics. However, in order not to overload the text background material is somewhat schematic. To evaluate the work of Garstin, or any other artist, necessarily involves making judgments about their pictures. It may be felt that such judgments are subjective and should therefore be avoided. This is an impossible requirement.

All statements concerning perception and emotional response are in some sense subjective and, even if this were not the case, judgment is absolutely unavoidable where one is trying to answer questions about artistic worth and value. What is illegitimate is not judgment as such but *ex cathedra* pronouncement: the failure to explain why a particular conclusion has been reached. This I have done my best to avoid and all judgments about the quality of important pictures are, to the best of my knowledge, preceded or followed by supporting reasons.

Opposite:
Plate 4 *The Rain it Raineth Every Day*, 1889, oil, 37" x 64" (Penlee House Gallery, Penzance).

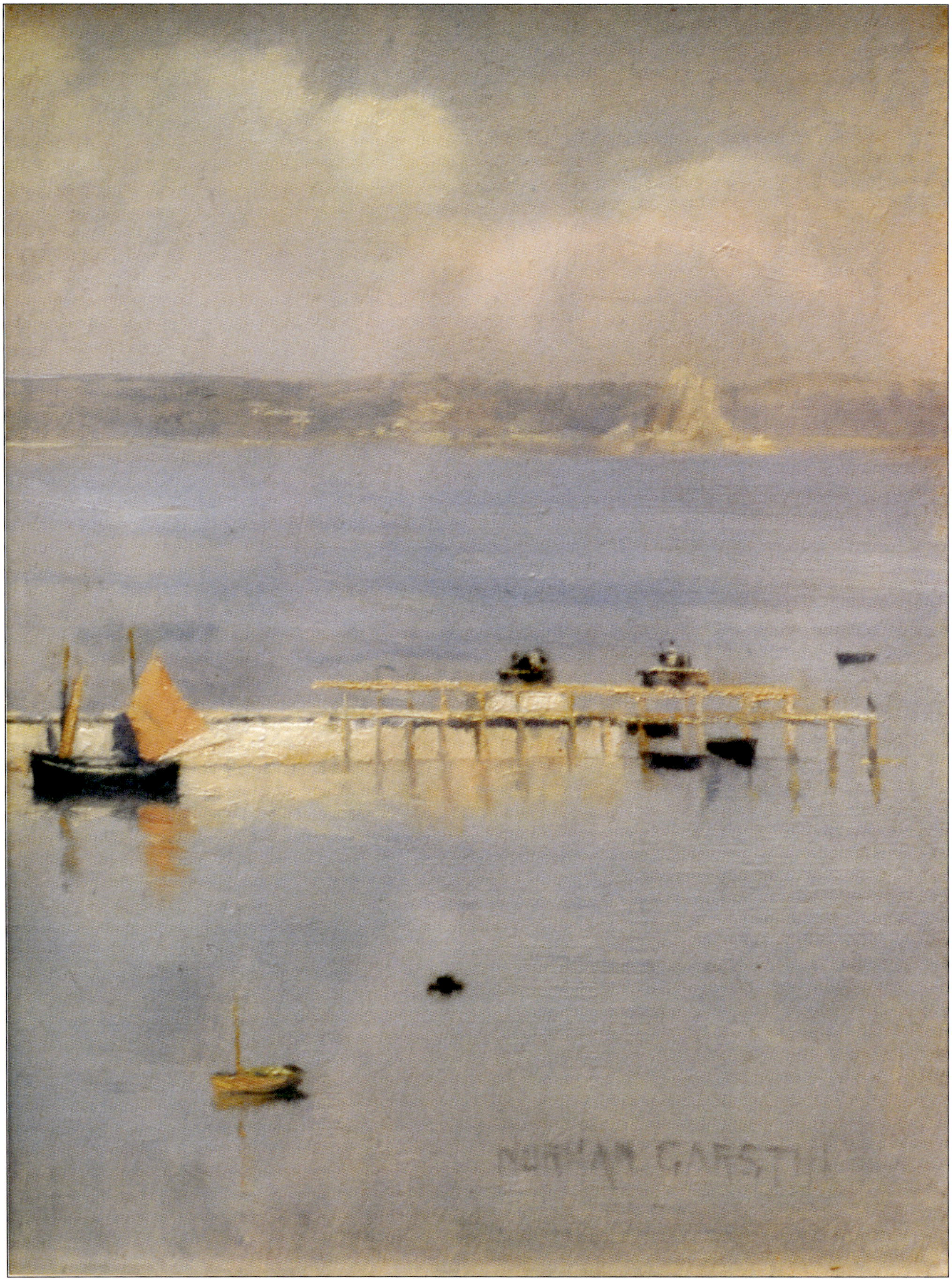
NORMAN GARSTIN

I have, in general, avoided qualifying my judgments with 'it appears to be true that', or 'it seems likely that', as this would serve no good purpose, but only the bad one of creating a false impression of academicism. Where I say 'seems' or 'appears' this means that I am particularly uncertain. Except where uncertainty turns into ignorance, I have not hesitated to tell the reader what conclusions I have reached. Nothing is more annoying in a biography than a parade of facts that seem to imply something but which, because the author fails to reach a conclusion, leave the reader puzzled as to what he or she thinks. The author is, or should be, the expert on the subject and hence one wants his verdict, if only to provide an anvil on which to forge a contrary view.

At various points in the text I say that my comments on a Garstin picture are based only on a black and white reproduction. This is not because of any lack of effort on my part. I have viewed all the pictures by Garstin that are in public collections, have discovered the whereabouts of many pictures that are in private hands, have scoured auction catalogues, and badgered auctioneers for additional colour images. Nevertheless the whereabouts of many Garstins remains unknown, and some must have been destroyed.

I have in the endnotes given the sources of quotations; the book to which reference is being made where authorities are mentioned in the text; and the places, if particularly important or obscure, from which information was mined. Other items from the Garstin Papers of which use was made are listed at the end of the Notes.

Valuable help has been received from numerous persons, including Judith Abbs; Maureen Attrill; Joan Bartholomew; George Bednar; Noel Channan; Professor Anne Crookshank and the Knight of Glin; John de Vere White; Melissa Hardie; Geoffrey Hassall; Philip Hills; Pat Hourigan; Alex Kitson; Dominic Milmo-Penny; Barbara Kirk at David Lay; Patrick O'Driscoll; Mark Pomeroy; Alex Robertson; Peyton Skipwith; Margaretta Gee; Lochlan Quinn; Mary Shackleton; Joseph Sharples; David Tovey; Fanny Underhill; Jane Wallis; Tina Wilkinson; and Alan Yarrow.

The following libraries (and librarians) have also been especially helpful: City of London Library; Cornish Studies Library and in particular Kim Cooper; Lambeth Palace Library; Morrab Library (Annabelle Read and Jan Ruhrmund); the Representative Church Body Library, Dublin; the Royal Academy; Société Jersaise; the Witt Library.

I am also most grateful to the individuals, firms and galleries that have so kindly provided many of the reproductions that appear in this book, and for their permission to publish. They include James Adam, Dublin; Bonhams; the Bridgeman Art Library; Bristol City Museum and Art Gallery; Christie's; de Veres Art Auctions, Dublin; Crawford

Opposite:
Plate 5 *Mount's Bay in June*, 1897, oil, 10" x 7.5" (Penlee House Gallery, Penzance, where it is known as *A View of Mount's Bay with the North Pier*).

Art Gallery, Cork; The Fine Art Society; Linda Gill; the Gorry Gallery, Dublin; Richard Green; the Hugh Lane Gallery, Dublin; Jorgensen Fine Art; Kelvingrove Art Gallery and Museum, Glasgow; Thomas Mawer; Messum's, 8 Cork Street, London; Milmo-Penny Fine Art; the Molesworth Gallery; the Morrab Library, Penzance; The National Gallery of Ireland; Penlee House Gallery, Penzance; Plymouth City Museum and Art Gallery; Pyms Gallery, 9 Mount Street, Mayfair; Royal Cornwall Museum; the Royal Pavilion Libraries and Museums, Brighton and Hove; Sheffield Galleries and Museums Trust; Sotheby's; the Tate Gallery; University of Hull; June Stanier; V & A Picture Library; York City Art Gallery.

Finally, I would like to acknowledge the particular help I have received from Mrs Robina Graze and from Alison Bevan; and the generous hospitality and assistance received from Lady Pickthorn and from Gerald and Peggy FitzGerald of Grenfell, Saskatchewan. Nic Hale kindly permitted me to use the Garstin Papers at the Morrab Library. Julian Campbell deserves thanks for reading through a draft and making valuable comments, and Keith Freeburn for his great help with photography.

My debt to Jo, my wife, is of a superlative order. Not only has she been a constant source of encouragement and advice, but she has also been of mighty assistance in research on the Garstin Papers.

Richard Pryke
Chester
September 2004

Introduction: A Necessary Re-appraisal

The greatest of the uncelebrated British artists of his era, and the outstanding painter of the Newlyn School; the British artist with the most interesting and exciting life, certainly during his generation; the wittiest and most articulate painter of his period, Whistler excepted; an elegant essayist; the kindest and most generous of men. Biographers must beware of overenthusiasm. Nevertheless a powerful case can be made for each of these claims about Norman Garstin, although some are less far reaching than they appear: the artists of his own generation were typically dull dogs with boring lives.

Without risk of exaggeration, it can be claimed that Norman Garstin was an artist of distinction, and one of the most important Realist painters of his time.[1] Yet he received little recognition during his life, and the subsequent reassessment of his work has been tardy, patchy and, often, plain wrong. During the long period when Victorian art was an object of derision, he was, like his contemporaries, ignored. It was not until the late 1950s that Garstin and the other Newlyn artists were rediscovered. In 1973 there was a perceptive, although unpublished, thesis in which Garstin was placed in the context of the Realist Movement.[2] The first, and only, extensive exhibition of his works took place in 1978. In the catalogue, Patrick Heron provided a laudatory appreciation of his work, and Michael Canney a short but useful biography.[3]

This was an auspicious start, but the appraisal of Garstin's work took the wrong turning. Heron began the process by describing him as an Impressionist, and Caroline Fox, the major writer on the Newlyn artists, discerned in his work a 'conflict of attitude: superlative small landscapes, rather strained exhibition pieces, the single impressive compromise *The Rain it Raineth Every Day* ... and, in his later work, an indecisiveness of direction'.[4] The impression was conveyed by Fox and others that from the mid-1890s Garstin painted little except sentimental costume pieces, trivial scenes of upper-class life, and anecdotal subjects. That Garstin was almost incapable of painting anything other than small works, and rapidly became degenerate, has been parroted ad nauseam. Although he has been seen as an Irish artist by Julian Campbell (and as an orientalist painter by James Thompson), Garstin has not gained recognition as a son of Ireland, although other artists, such as Roderick O'Connor who did not even go back, have been appropriated.[5]

A full life of Garstin, and re-appraisal of his work, is more than overdue.[6] Such an evaluation will come at a favourable time: during a period when previously discredited artists, such as Tissot and Leighton, have been re-habilitated, and virtually unknown figures, such as Frank O'Meara, have been discovered. That so much re-evaluation is taking place is no accident. It is partly due to the normal ebb and flow of reputation, but it has also occurred because of the great thawing in the ice cap of Modernism. During a long and dark era, artists who worked from around 1874 – the year of the first Impressionist Exhibition – were evaluated according to the contribution they made, or did not make, to the movement that was to culminate in Abstract Art. If it was thought that they made a contribution of significance, they were beatified, and if they did not they were damned. This form of evaluation reflected the belief that it is possible to identify those artists (and writers) that form part of the canon, and are on the artistic (or literary) high road, and those that are not.

Although they are still widespread, such beliefs no longer hold undisputed sway, and it has become possible to evaluate painters, including it is to be hoped Norman Garstin, regardless of their stylistic associations and by the intrinsic quality of their work.

Chapter 1

Vicarage, Veldt and Vocation, 1847-79

Norman Garstin was born on 28 August 1847 at the vicarage in Caherconlish, Co. Limerick. His mother, Mary, was the daughter of the vicar, Matthew Moore, and his father was Captain William Garstin of the 83rd Foot, an Irish regiment in the British army.

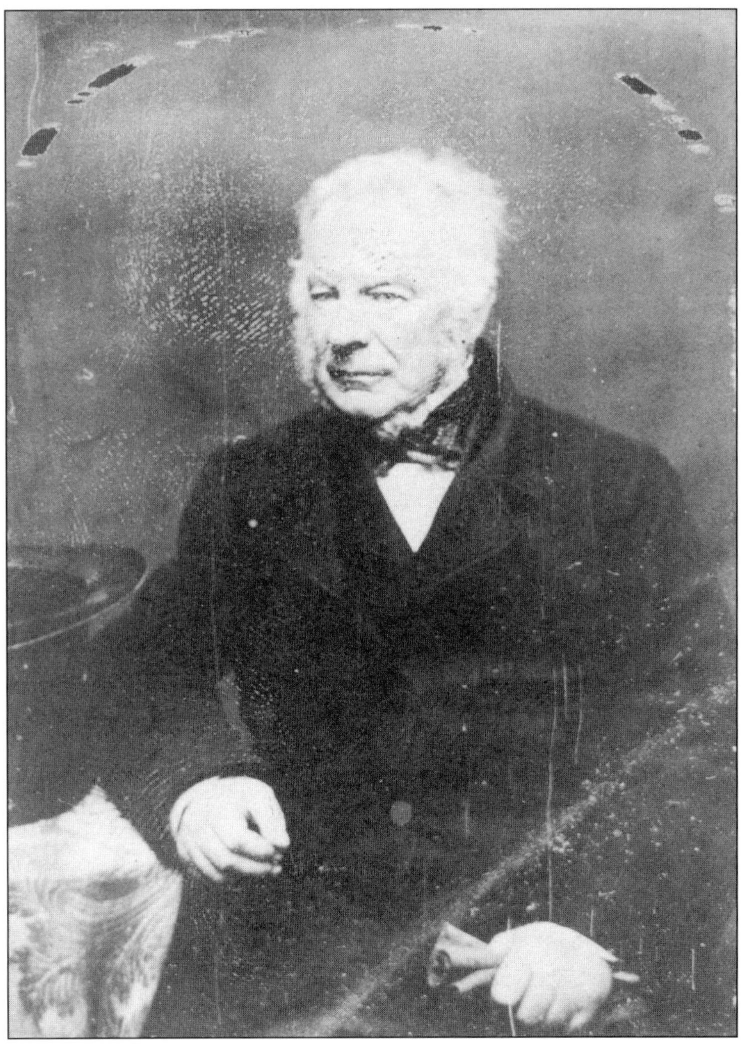

The Rev. Matthew Moore.

A Scion of the Anglo-Irish Establishment

Norman's parents belonged to the Anglo-Irish ascendancy, the network of Protestant families that originally came from England, and exercised power and influence in Ireland. The Garstins, who had settled during the reign of Elizabeth, were the beneficiaries of the seizures that, between 1641 and 1703, reduced the proportion of cultivable Irish land in Catholic ownership from nearly 60 per cent to less than 15. In 1654, Major James Garstin received Braganstown in Co. Louth, together with other lands, in return for his military services and financial assistance to the Protestant cause. At James' death, in 1677, the estate passed to Norman Garstin, the son of yet another Cromwellian. He then profited from the further confiscation of Catholic estates after the Revolution of 1688. This Norman was our Norman's great-great-great grandfather.[1]

Garstin's mother was descended from another landed family that had obtained land confiscated during the seventeenth century, namely the Moores of Mooresfort, Co. Tipperary. Around 1715 Edward Moore acquired the bulk of the Mooresfort estate, although only by leasing. On

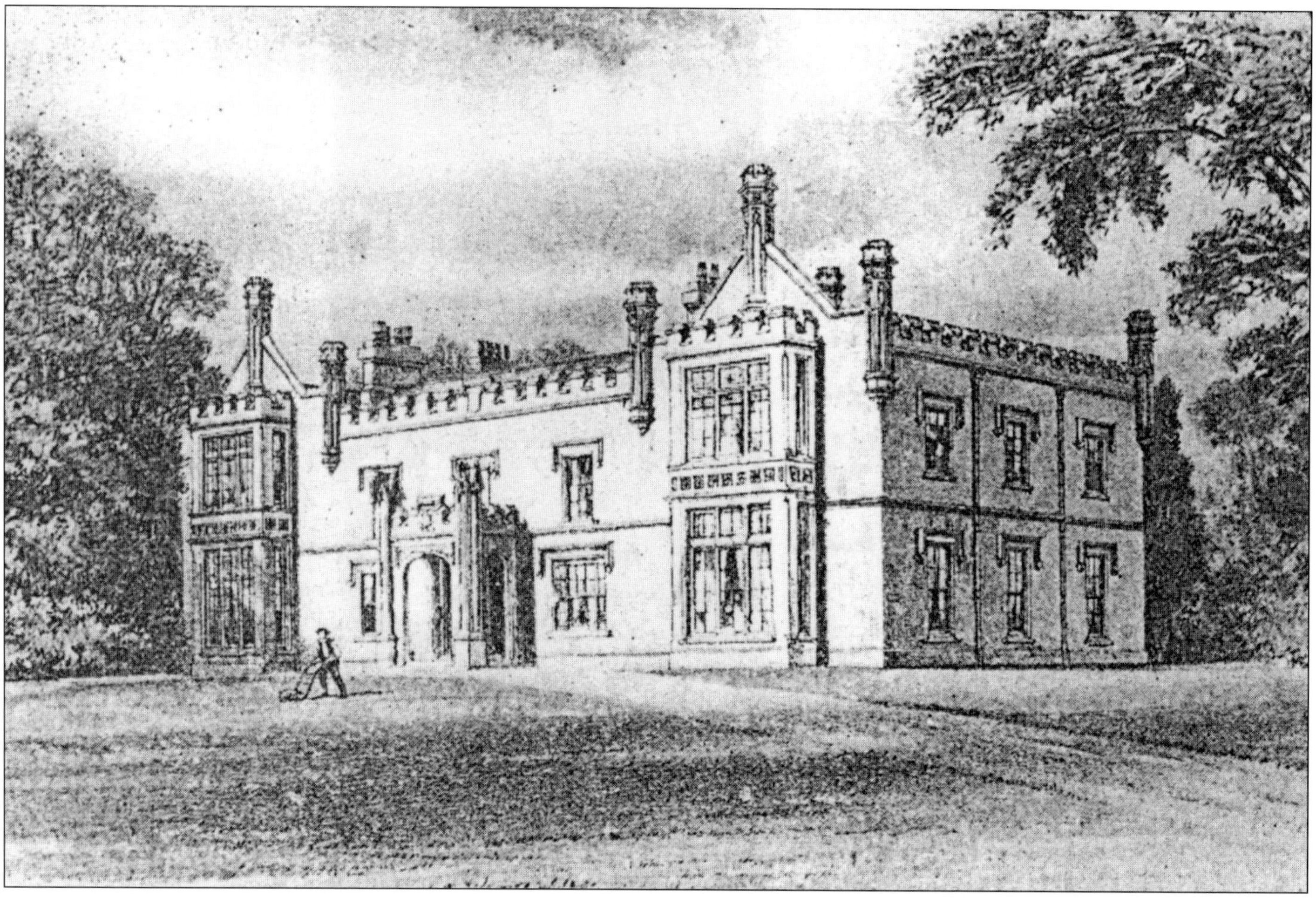

Braganston, Co. Louth; now owned by Mr Larry Goodman.

both sides, Garstin was descended from the younger sons of those who had inherited the family land. But his connection with these estates was relatively close: both of his grandfathers – Norman Garstin and Matthew Moore – were brought up in the big houses.

Because Norman Garstin was so firmly rooted in the Anglo-Irish gentry, the occupations pursued by his forebears, and his close relations, were extraordinarily restricted. If we consider the Moores and Garstins from whom he was descended, together with his uncles by blood, there was in this group of eleven, stretching back as far as the original Norman, only one man who was not a landowner, an army officer, or a vicar in the established church. In some cases, the church and the army were combined in the role of chaplain, as with grandfather Norman. Apart from the army and the church, there was almost no connection with the professions, and there was certainly none with trade, as there might well have been if the family had been English gentry. Many of those who were landowners or clergymen went to Trinity College, Dublin: the seat of higher education for the Protestant establishment. Although he repudiated many of its views and values, Norman was never in any doubt about belonging to what he referred to as, 'my own Class'.[2]

Grandfather Norman became Senior Colonial Chaplain in Ceylon, where he died (in 1830) long before Norman was born. William Garstin, Norman's father, was born in 1806, and entered the army in 1824. From 1845 his regiment was stationed in Limerick. There was a small barracks at Caherconlish, and it seems likely that this was how William became acquainted with the vicar's daughter.[3] Mary and William were married in 1846, when he was 40 and she was an exceedingly pretty young woman of 22.

Within a few years of Garstin's birth in 1847 Mary was struck down by paralysis so severe that she was unable to speak, and Norman had no brothers or sisters and no recollection of his mother's voice. Either because of his wife's condition, or because the 83rd Foot was posted to India, William Garstin retired from regimental service in the spring of 1849, and was placed on half pay. He transferred to the administration of the pensions system that the army provided for other ranks, serving in quick succession at a number of places – Chester, Waterford, Cavan, Sheffield and Limerick – until his final retirement in 1860, as a Colonel. Seven months later, in 1861, he committed suicide. Obviously William was, until he retired fully, unable to care for his wife or bring up his son.

Mother and child went to live at the vicarage in Caherconlish, and it seems likely that Mary was looked after by her younger sister, Elizabeth. At the end of 1851, Elizabeth married John Frend, the descendant of yet another Cromwellian officer, and the son of a local landowner. However, the vicarage was large enough to accommodate the whole family, or possibly the Frends lived in a house nearby. What is certain is that the Frends were still living at Caherconlish in 1862–3, that Mary lived at the parsonage between 1864 and 1867, and that Norman was living there in 1867, which was the year in which grandfather Matthew Moore died.

Norman appears to have been largely brought up not by Elizabeth, who must have had her hands full, but by Anne FitzGerald. She was his great-aunt's stepdaughter, or to be more precise the stepdaughter of the sister of his maternal grandmother. Unfortunately very little is known about her, except her dates and that she was devout. She was born in 1812, never married, and died at Grenfell, Saskatchewan, in 1896. However, there is one fact of great significance: the portrait of her that Garstin painted at Grenfell, in 1891, has a label on the back that declares, 'She was a second mother to me when I was a boy in Caherconlish'.[4] In an earlier portrait Anne is looking upward and her face occupies most of the space, which is a way of conveying an impression of intimacy. It may be significant that in his picture of Elizabeth (Plate 6) she is sitting upright, is dressed in black, is not looking at the artist, and has a somewhat severe expression.

Love is a star

Love is a star
The human heart knows it is ever there,
Shining behind the clouds of black despair,
And when the clouds break as they always
  do,
Love, like the star, comes smiling brightly
  through:
Guiding our stumbling feet where darkness
  hid the way,
Strengthing the faltering heart and driving
  doubt away
Lifting our sight to those high places far
Where love does reign supreme, – Love is a
  star.

William Garstin

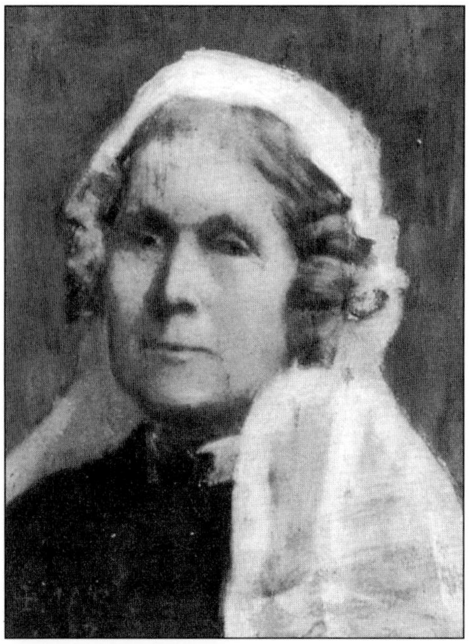

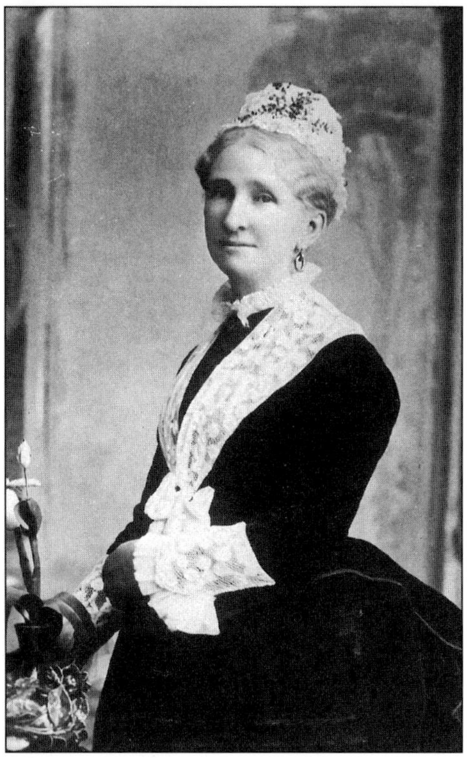

Above:
Norman Garstin portrait of Anne FitzGerald, 1887, oil, 7.75" x 6" (private collection).

Below:
Margaret Fulton (née Twiss).

Anne was not the only relation to have been a mother figure. At her death in 1910, Garstin said that Margaret Fulton, 'had been quite a mother to me ever since I can remember', and he later praised her 'generous spirit'.[5] Margaret was the daughter of another sister of his maternal grandmother, and lived with her sisters at Birr, Co. Tipperary. Norman said that he 'owed so much to the aunts in every way', and he was their favourite young relative. In view of his close relationship with Anne and Margaret, it would be wrong to jump to the conclusion that, just because his mother was paralysed and his father absent, Garstin must have been starved of affection. His late marriage, and the emotional coolness of his pictures, might seem to suggest that this was the case. However, the direct evidence of what he said about his childhood, together with his close relationship with his wife and children, do not suggest that he was emotionally scarred.

Of Norman's early schooling nothing is known, but he was almost certainly tutored by his grandfather. In August 1858 he went to Victoria College, Jersey having previously attended St Aubin's school - also in Jersey - for perhaps two years. St Aubin's was a small school with a good reputation, which took boys of all ages and had been established by Philip Le Maistre. This may seem a curious choice but, at that time, Garstin suffered from delicate health, and his uncle, the Rev. Norman Garstin, lived in St Helier. During term time Garstin appears to have lived with his aunt and uncle, who had young children. Victoria College had the advantage that its fees were lower than they would have been in England. William Garstin may also have been attracted by the 'special classes for Military Instruction', mentioned in the Prospectus.[6] In 1855 the Queen had presented commissions to two pupils, and a substantial proportion of pupils went into the army. Norman probably stayed at Victoria College until he was eighteen, because, if he had left earlier, there would be an unaccountable gap in his career.

The Influence of Family, Class and Public School

Although it has been possible (after much effort) to disinter the dry bones of Norman's early life, there is not much flesh. We know, for instance, very little about the character of either Matthew Moore or William Garstin, and nothing about Norman's time at Victoria College. With the inspiration of Sherlock Holmes and his deductive method, it is nevertheless possible to say something about the influence exerted by Garstin's early life.

Although he repudiated many of the beliefs and values of his class, Norman Garstin was a gentleman. He was, as we shall see, courteous, kind and generous, and lived by high standards. No doubt, this was partly his natural disposition, but it must also have been due to his upbringing, and to the family and class from which he came. He believed in a code of gentlemanly conduct and that the family name stood for something. On hearing that their little boy had slapped a relation with whom he was staying, Garstin's wife wrote in reproach, 'Dada says gentlemen and big boys never do such naughty tricks'.[7] When his second son came of age, Garstin exhorted him to, 'keep up the name'.[8]

Until he moved to Limerick in 1856, William Garstin cannot have seen much of Norman, and at about that time Norman went away to school in Jersey. The Rev. Matthew Moore and the family at Caherconlish must have been a more formative influence. The household was probably both cultured and tolerant, as Matthew was a graduate of Trinity, and owned a considerable and valued collection of books. During the period when Moore was vicar, an important evangelical movement arose within the Church of Ireland, of which his bishop (Dr Daly) was the 'Protestant Pope'. Its members were, at once, dedicated, bigoted, rabidly anti-Catholic, and proselytizing. However, there were not many sectarian clergymen around Caherconlish, and Matthew, who was born in 1790, belonged to an earlier generation that was untouched by 'enthusiasm'. It did its best to keep on good terms with the Catholic priest and to help, but not convert, his flock.[9] Matthew ran a soup kitchen in co-operation with two priests during the Famine, and, after Moore's death, Catholics subscribed to the memorial window in the new Protestant church at Caherconlish.

Garstin turned out to be tolerant, reluctant to quarrel, and non-judgemental. This was both precept and practice. 'I hold', he declared, when telling the story of a wife who had left her husband for another man, 'that no one ever knows enough to judge anybody else'.[10] An impressive reluctance to take offence is shown by his reaction when, in 1899, Stanhope Forbes broke an important arrangement. Garstin along with Forbes, who was the leading artist in Newlyn, had agreed to set up an art school when Garstin returned from France, where he was conducting a sketching class. Before his return, Forbes went ahead and established his own school, attracting some of Garstin's pupils in the process. Garstin never referred to this incident, and, not long after, wrote a generous appreciation of Forbes' work and character. Reading between the lines, he attributed Forbes' high-handed behaviour to his social background: he came, Garstin says, from a great railway family where it was second nature to take charge.[11] Garstin regarded Forbes in the same way that his grandfather may well have viewed the local Catholic priest: he was the product of upbringing and environment.

The Church of Ireland had pathetically few members, especially in the south and west and, in 1861, Moore had only 108 parishioners, which represented about 20 families. Like other ministers of the established church, he can have had very little to occupy him (which was one reason why so many turned to the conversion of Catholics). In a short story about a child in a Church of Ireland vicarage, Garstin pictures the clerical grandfather as playing whist in the afternoon. Matthew Moore was certainly a dedicated fisherman. Although Caherconlish was not an especially rich benefice, Moore received an exceptionally large income, by Irish standards, and he lived in what was, by any standards, a fine, large house with retinues of servants. A painting of it by Garstin is reproduced in Plate 7. The vicarage was fronted by an ornamental lake, and approached by an avenue of copper beeches and horse chestnuts. There was a lodge, spacious stables, and a big orchard.

The contrast between the affluence and leisure of the vicarage and the poverty and toil of the Catholic peasantry in their cabins would have been stark, even though Caherconlish was not a particularly poor place. Garstin cannot have failed to notice the chasm, and it probably contributed towards his political radicalism. He did not believe in 'the good old days', which he regarded as an Irish myth.[12] Despite, or more likely because of, his upbringing in an Irish vicarage, Garstin became a non-believer.

Victoria College would have reinforced many of the tendencies imparted by family background. Established as a public school only a few years earlier, in 1852, it had something over 200 pupils when Garstin entered in 1858. William Henderson, the headmaster until 1862, was a forceful man with liberal views, who did not use corporal punishment and was on the committee of the Early Closing Association, which campaigned that all shops in a town should close at lunch time one day each week. Garstin's progressive attitudes may have owed something to Henderson. One certain consequence of Garstin's attendance at Victoria College was a thorough grounding in French. Classes in French occupied twice as much time as those in English, and the teaching was of a high order. This, together with the presence of French speaking boys, must explain Garstin's proficiency with the language.[13] He was able, as part of his art training, to enter a Parisian atelier, where it was compulsory to speak French and, later on, to take painting parties to the Continent.

It seems doubtful whether Garstin would have received much tuition in drawing. Pupils can only have had about two hours of art each week, and some of the time appears to have been devoted to planning, mapping and military drawing. On the other hand, the drawing master from 1859 was Thomas Berteau, who studied in Paris, was a notable Jersey artist, and produced accomplished portraits in pencil and pastel.

1866-72: Moving Sideways

Garstin's relations wanted him to enter the army, or the church. He wished for neither, and desired to become a painter. Instead he was sent to Cork to live and study with the Professor of Engineering at Queen's College, with the intention that he would enter this profession. The year is uncertain, but, working backwards, it seems likely that this was in 1866. Garstin soon pronounced himself a failure in engineering because of his weak mathematics, and the Professor, having noticed that his drawings were more accurate than his calculations, advised him to try architecture. This suggestion was adopted as a compromise by Garstin's relatives, who recognised that he had an artistic temperament, but were still opposed to his becoming an artist.

There is obviously no full answer to the question of why Garstin wanted to become an artist, but there were probably three contributory influences. Perhaps the most important, albeit the one that is most speculative, was that Caherconlish was a beautiful and romantic place. There was a fine view across to the Slieve Felim Mountains, there were many interesting ruins and standing stones nearby, and, close to the vicarage, stood the splendid old castle of O'Farrell's Rock. Garstin was fascinated by the picturesque, and believed that the purpose of art was to create beauty. In addition he regarded painting as a gentlemanly activity: painting was not trade, and trade was ungentlemanly. Garstin drew a firm distinction between businessmen who provided goods that consumers wanted, and artists who painted as a form of self-expression. He did not say this until 1921, but the belief that painters were engaged in a special and high activity went back much further.[14] Finally, it may well be that he was predisposed towards art because he was in mild reaction against a conservative and stuffy family background.

That his family was conservative, unadventurous and conventional is shown by his relatives' continued opposition to a painting career. Hostility of this type was certainly not unknown. The widowed mother of one future artist (A. S. Hartrick) was influenced by the opposition of the housemaster, and headmaster, at his public school, Fettes. They regarded artists as dull dogs, and an uneducated lot. On the other hand, some parents thought that only gentlemen with independent means could afford to take up painting. The biographer of Sir John Lavery reports that many parents, 'believed that painting and sculpture were pastimes for the well-to-do, not callings for any youngsters who had their bread to earn. Art was a candidate for the workhouse'.[15] But where there was opposition it did not usually last long (as for Hartrick and for Garstin's friend Henry Scott Tuke), or seems to have been readily accepted by the young man (*vide* Alexander Mann, another friend). In some cases parents welcomed

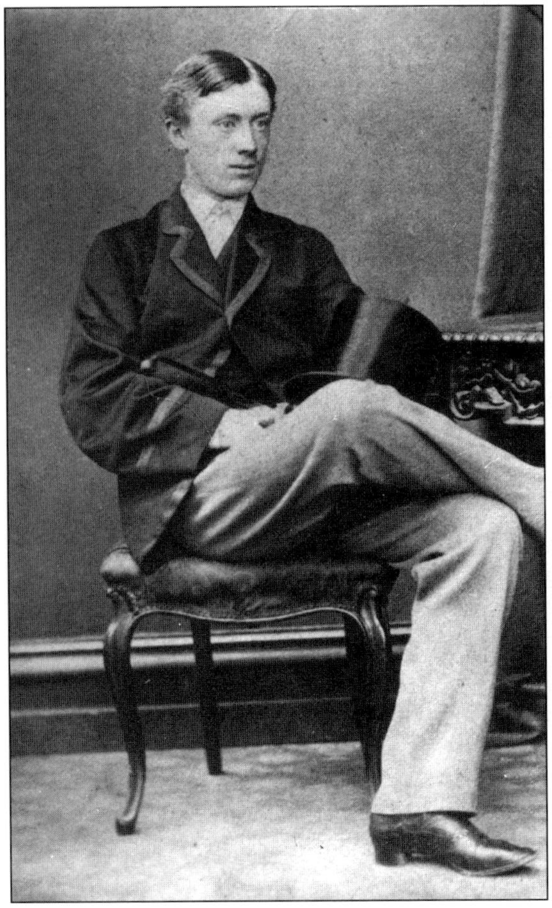

Norman Garstin about 1870, photographed by F. H. Mares, Dublin.

their son's desire to become a painter. When Jacomb-Hood – yet another friend – said that he wished to become an artist, his father gave him the encouraging news that he hoped to leave him an income of two or three hundred a year.

Garstin was placed with the architect Benjamin Ferrey, probably in 1867 or 1868. The firm was in Charing Cross in central London, and Ferrey was an architect of considerable distinction. He was one of A. C. Pugin's pupils and was mainly engaged in the design of churches. Garstin, as an unqualified beginner, was, of course, only engaged on routine work, and he later complained that he, 'detested the detail of measuring stairs and things'.[16]

His lack of enthusiasm was compounded by his enjoyment of what appears to have been his first serious training as an artist. This took place at classes held at the Whitefriars Glassworks by Thomas Graham Jackson, a distinguished architect who undertook design work for the owner, James Powell. When working on stained glass windows, Jackson felt that he needed to improve his figure drawing, and, from January 1870, organized life classes. These were attended not only by some of Powell's draftsmen but also by Garstin. They were serious affairs, and included lectures on artistic anatomy. Jackson reported that the life classes taught him a great deal.[17]

Garstin did not persevere with architecture, nor, more surprisingly, with art training. He met an old friend who was one of the first pioneers at the newly discovered diamond diggings at Kimberley in South Africa: 'Fascinated by his tales of diamonds and the glittering stones he showed me I turned my T-square into a pickaxe and sailed away to seek my fortune'.[18] It seems unlikely that this is the full story. His mother had died early in 1871, and Garstin was now free to go abroad. He would have inherited whatever she possessed, and those who had charge of the family investments would no longer have needed to pay for Mary's keep. As he was now 24, his guardians would, almost certainly, have decided to pay him this income without question.

If, however, he had financial resources, as he must have done in order to become a digger, it is surprising that he did not train as an artist instead. It seems clear that his desire to become an artist cannot have been very strong: he had not yet found his vocation He might conceivably have been hoping to make a fortune so as to able to retire to a life of painting, but he himself said that adventure was his only motive.[19]

At Kimberley with Rhodes

At the end of March 1872 Garstin arrived at Kimberley. Years later he provided vivid descriptions, although they were very similar to what he had written in the London *Standard* at the time:

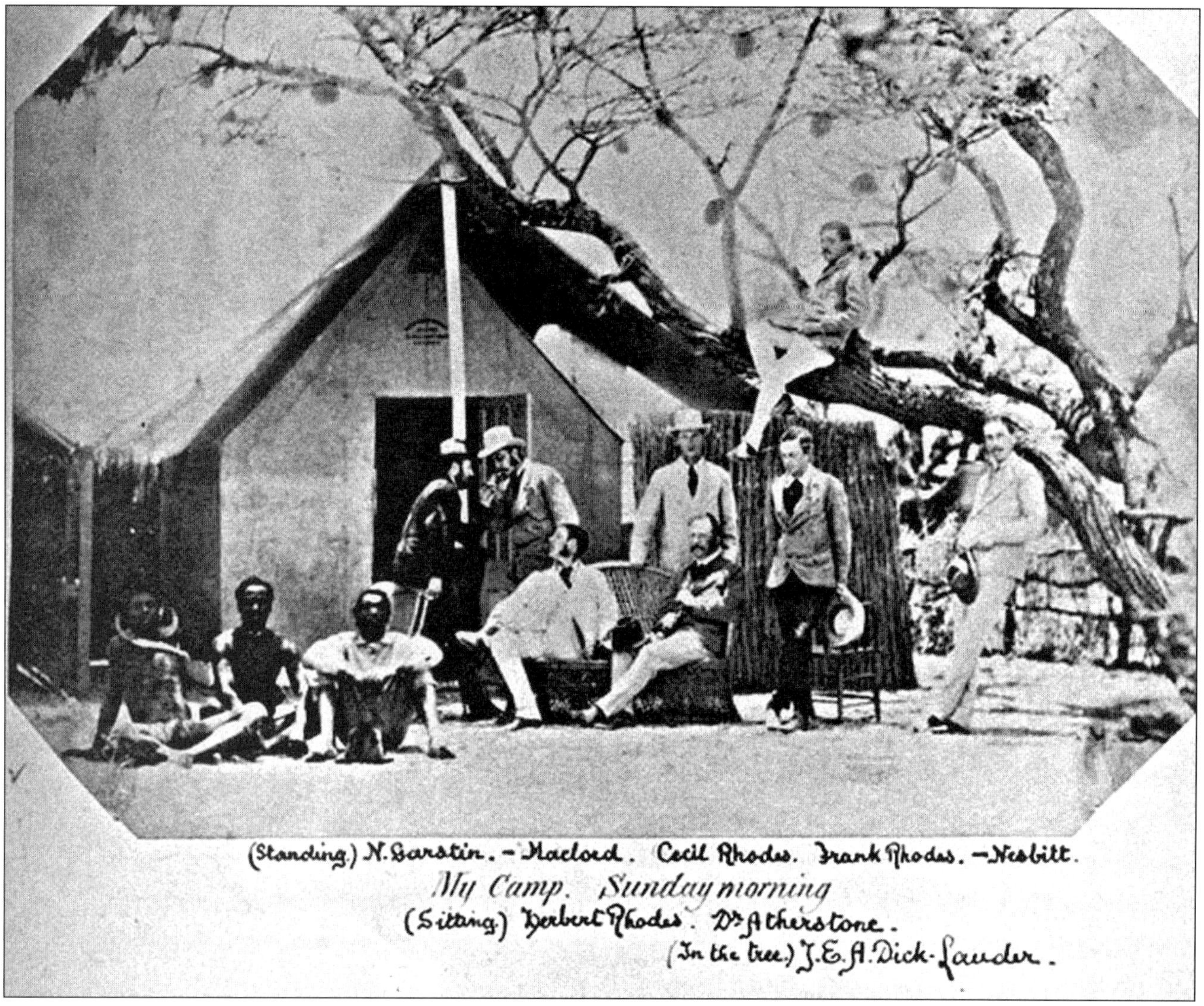

Garstin, Rhodes and colleagues at Kimberley.

The New Rush, as Kimberley was called in 1872, was a chaos of tents and rubbish heaps seen through a haze of dust. I had tumbled, numbed and sleepy, out of the coach that for twelve days and nights had jolted on over mountain and veldt … Having a friend at 'The rush' I set out at once to find him, but it was a puzzling business … for the whole place was a heterogeneous collection of tents, waggons, native kraals, and debris heaps, each set down with cheerful irresponsibility and indifference to order. At length, however, after following many distracting directions, I lit upon a little cluster of tents and beehive huts, set around an old and gnarled mimosa tree.[20] Towards the centre the streets had crystallized into a sort of irregular form; and grimy canteens, stores for the sale of old uniforms, shoddy blankets, suicidal muskets, groceries and digging implements – with the small canvas offices of the diamond buyers – constituted the business quarter of the camp. The mine itself was a vast chasm of some nine acres, spanned by perilous rickety causeways left by the order of the Mining Inspector. Along these terrible pathways, with precipices at times seventy feet deep on either hand, passed carts and

> waggons – drawn by spans of oxen, mules, or horses – loaded with the precious gravel to be sorted round the lip of the mine. These lumbered on, jostling each other, indifferent to their own safety or that of the hurrying crowds of diggers and niggers who dodged in and out amongst them. The roads being of the same stuff as the rest of the mine, and readily acted upon by the atmosphere, gradually slipped down into the adjacent claims. Sometimes an odd wagon would fall, and then a great shout would rise from the thousands of workers who seemed like black ants in and around the earth scar. A ring of dust that rose slowly round the mine denoted the positions of the tables and the sieves of the diamond sorters, where all day long, in the blinding sun and the even more blinding particles, the baas, with perhaps three or four Africans, sat squatting on their heels, having little iron scrapers in their hands. With these the gravel was swept into thin layers on the table, glanced at and quickly swept to the ground. It is not hard to understand that many diamonds were lost in this casual unscientific method of search.[21]

Cecil Rhodes and his brothers, Herbert and Frank, occupied a large tent by the mimosa tree. To begin with, Garstin and his friend and partner, Tommy Townsend, did not belong to the same mess as the Rhodes brothers but he was, from the beginning, on intimate terms with Cecil Rhodes, and before long did become a member. The mess was a colourful set and, together with visitors, included several who were to attain future distinction. One, Jacob Barry,

Kimberley Mine, 1873.

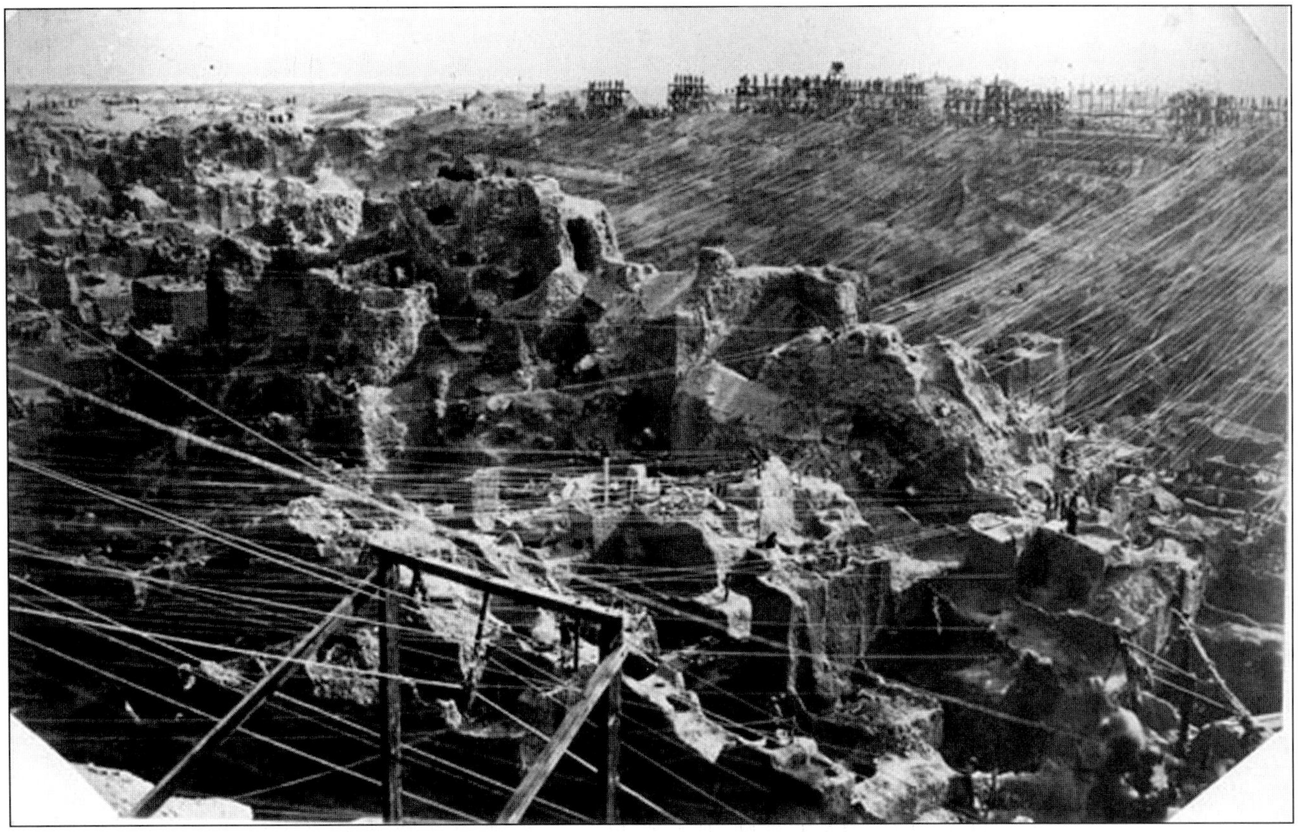

became a South African judge and another, J. X. Merriman, a South African statesman. There was also William Scully, then a boy, who messed with Garstin and Townsend, and was to become a notable South African writer. The future eminence of so many of Garstin's colleagues was not altogether surprising: the early diggers included many who were well educated and from good families.

Garstin later gave a vivid picture of most notable member of the mess: the great empire builder of the future:

> As I search my memory for the Rhodes of the early seventies, I seem to see a fair young man, frequently sunk in deep thoughts, his hands buried in his trouser pockets, his legs crossed and possibly twisted together, quite oblivious of the talk around him; then without a word he would get up and go out with some set purpose in his mind which he was at no pains to communicate. The same dual qualities that were to go with him through life were discernible now. He was a compound of moody silence and impulsive action. He was hot and even violent at times, but in working towards his ends he laid his plans with care and circumspection. He was fond of putting the case against himself. 'You will probably think so and so', he would say, then he would balance his own contention against the view that he felt the devil's advocate would take; this habit of seeing the other side probably helped him in his career. Few men are adequately aware of what the other side thinks. The duality of his nature, the contemplative and the executive, had a curious counterpart in his voice, which broke, when he was excited, into a sort of falsetto, unusual in a man of his make: his laugh also had this falsetto note. In all his wide range he had no place for personal appearance; of this he was contemptuously indifferent. I remember the laughter he evoked by describing how, on his first return home, during the voyage his one pair of trousers gave out in an important detail, and he had to stay in his berth until a sailor had patched them with a piece of sail-cloth ... Very simple in his tastes and wanting few things, he determined only to trouble himself about the most important, but for the attainment of these he spared neither himself nor others.[22]

> He was a born financier, but he acted as one who plays a game more for the fun of playing it than for the stakes. I remember his saying to me in the confidences of a shooting expedition that he would not mind losing his money, since what he liked was the excitement of making it, more than anything it could buy.[23]

These descriptions are of interest for their own sake: they and other material provide what is by far the best pen picture of the young Rhodes. However, they deserve quotation here because they show Garstin to have been an artist with words as well as with paint. He had a painter's eye for the telling and stimulating detail and for its place in the broad picture. He observed that fleas increased in size and vigour the nearer one approached the diamond fields!!

1872-6: Digger, Colonial Official and the Cape Times

Garstin quickly found the reports of riches from diamond digging to be wildly exaggerated. As he explained in *The Standard*, those who arrived first did well, but costs soon rose and the price of diamonds slumped. He showed that, with average finds, there was now very little to be made, and that 'the brilliant vision conjured up by the words "diamond digging" fades ... under the cruelly destructive force of arithmetic'.[24] Moreover the job was unpleasant and the environment harsh. A life sorting gravel from breakfast till dark, under a miserably hot sun and with persecuting summer insects, was not his idea of pleasure. However, he persevered until around April 1873, when he gave up digging.

But he did not leave Kimberley. In an article Garstin described how, having survived homesickness and disgust at early disappointments, the newcomer forms friendships, and becomes less fastidious and more charmed with the freedom of his new life. Friendship and the camaraderie of the mess were probably of particular importance. His messmates were not only colourful but also high-spirited. Scully tells how one night, when returning with the Rhodes brothers, Garstin and others, he was thrown onto the roof of a church and forced, under stress of pelting stones, to ring the discordant bell.

Garstin had a gift for friendship, and was to retain the affection of both Scully and Rhodes. Scully wrote a brief account of him, which contains a glowing tribute and a fascinating, though irrelevant, fact:

> One of my most intimate friends was Norman Garstin, a man whom to know was to love. Once he nearly frightened me to death. He had a habit of sleeping with his eyes wide open, but of this I was quite unaware. Returning home late one night I struck a match and saw him lying on his back, his eyes fixed and glassy. I seized him by the shoulders and, much to his disgust, dragged him into a sitting posture. Garstin was an accomplished draughtsman. His caricatures, which were never ill-natured, and his black and white 'parables' brought him wide popularity in the days when we foregathered.[25]

Garstin found a job as the secretary of a government commission to enquire into the working of the diamond mines, but it did not last long. He then moved into the local civil service, and spent two years in the office of John Blades Currey, who was Secretary to the Government of Griqualand West, the new Crown colony established in 1873 for the Kimberley region. Currey gathered about him some of the most promising young men in Kimberley, and Garstin was one

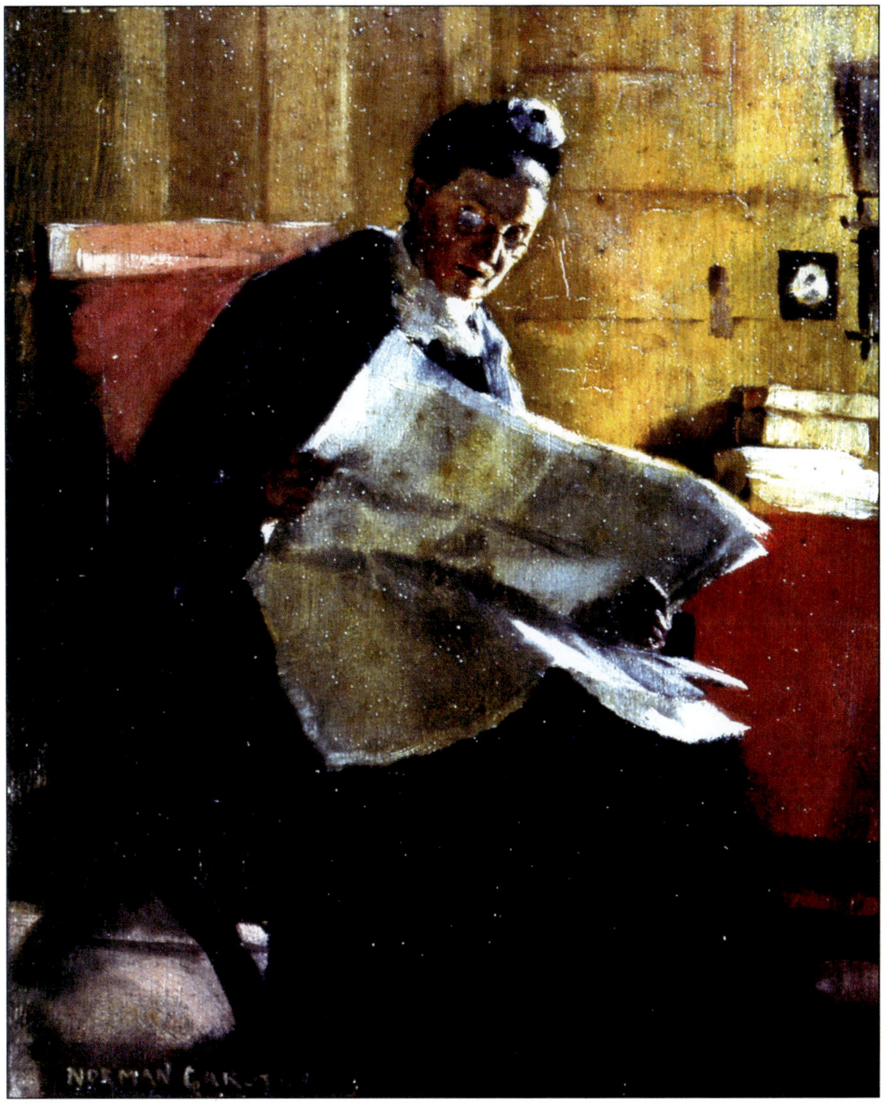

Plate 6 *Elizabeth Frend*, 1891, oil, 10" x 8.5" (Tate Gallery where it is known as *A Woman Reading a Newspaper*).

of them. Garstin's wife believed that he acted as secretary to the Governor, Sir Henry Barkly. The latter was also Governor of Cape Colony; and hence his principal office was at Cape Town, and Garstin's position was probably less exalted than it may sound. Garstin (as fellow philatelists will be delighted to hear) was also reported to have designed a stamp for the new colony but, due to shortage of funds, it was never produced![26]

Presumably using money saved from his employment in the civil service, Garstin went back for a larger but even more dismal venture at the mine. Finally, he became a member of the Mining Board for Dutoitspan, which was another Kimberley mine. The Board was elected by claimholders and had the power to make byelaws for its management, and to levy rates for work that the government-appointed Surveyor had either proposed or approved. Hence the post of secretary, which Garstin must have held, was a relatively important

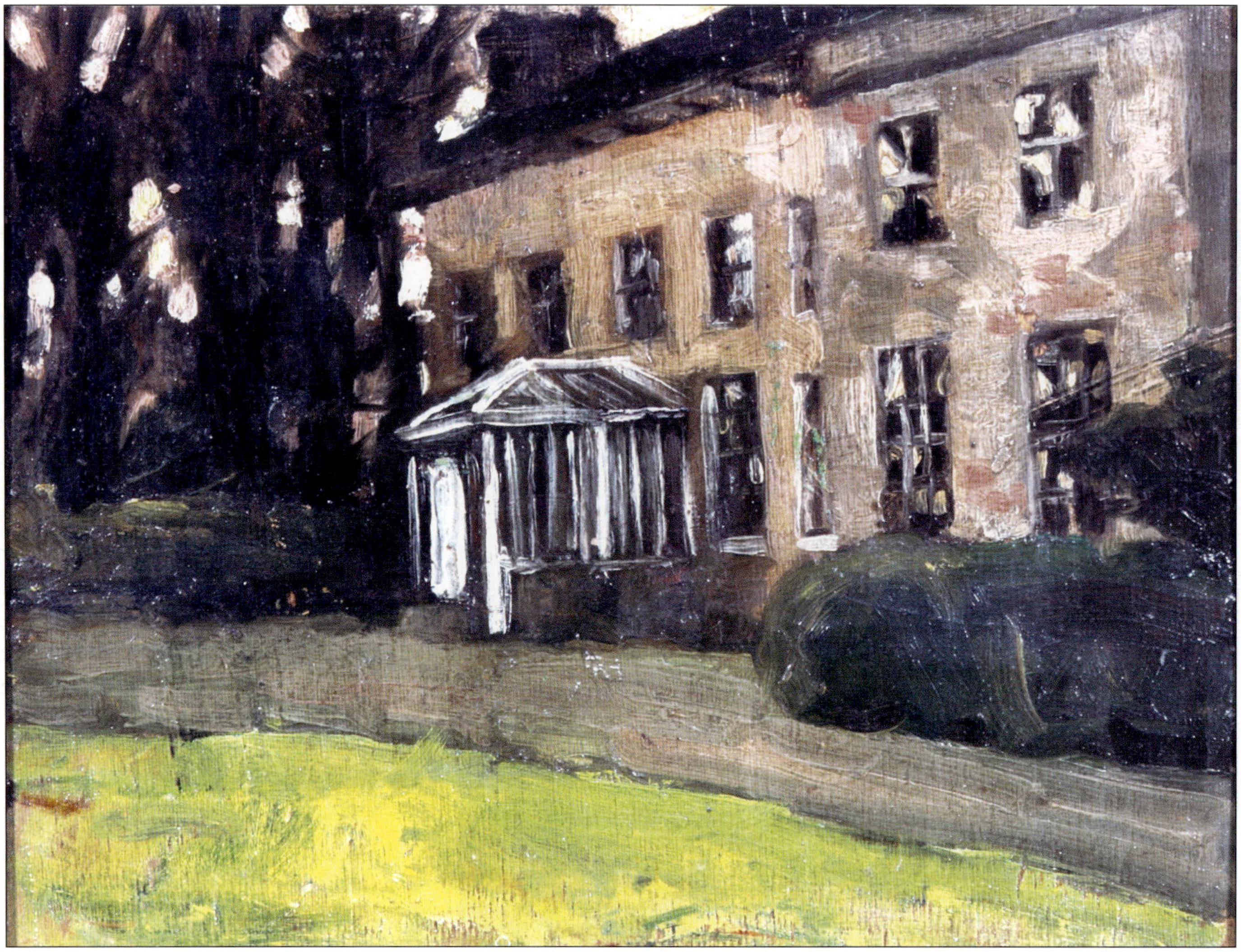

Plate 7 *The Old Parsonage*, 1915, oil, 8.25" x 10.75" (private collection, auctioned as *Artist's Home, Cahereconlish*). The house is now a ruin.

Opposite:
(above)
Annsgift, Co. Tipperary, now owned by the Coolmore Stud.

(below)
Ada FitzGerald, née Frend.

one; the more so because the diggers were a quarrelsome group who were jealous of their privileges. Ultimately, some of them staged a minor rebellion, troops had to be called, and Currey was dismissed.

In August 1875 Garstin left Kimberley for Cape Town, where he spent the next eighteen months. It is possible that Garstin's departure was connected with Currey's dismissal, as he went to Cape Town with him. There Garstin worked at the *Cape Times* under Frederick York St Ledger, who had previously edited a Kimberley paper. As Garstin is believed to have written for a local paper, he may well have become friendly with St Ledger. After Garstin had helped to set up the *Cape Times*, he became assistant editor, but he found the work extremely demanding and threw up his job.

1877-9: Hunting and Sketching in Ireland

At the beginning of 1877, Garstin returned to Ireland. He went back to live with the Frends at Annsgift, near Fethard in Co. Tipperary. This was the house to which his aunt Elizabeth, his uncle

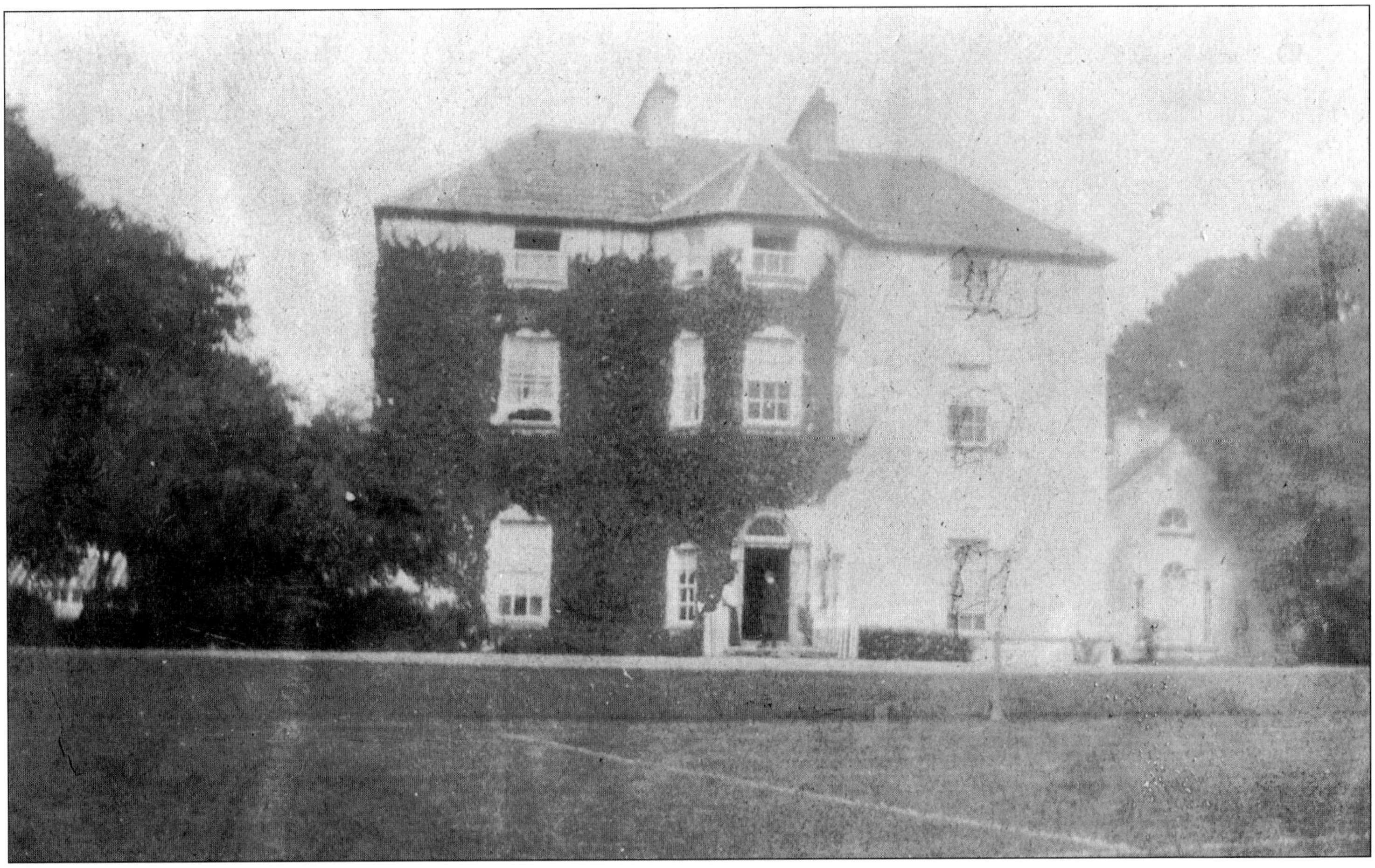

John and their daughter Ada, had moved after Matthew Moore's death in 1867; it was where Garstin's mother had lived until her death; and it was where Garstin had himself lived when he was at home. Annsgift was an attractive place to be. Ada who, in 1877, was a young woman of 24, became a life-long friend; and Annsgift was situated in quiet lush countryside with mountains to the south. It was a fine three-storeyed Georgian mansion, with the front door set in an interesting half-hexagonal bay. A letter from Garstin's wife to their young son is revealing: 'We went one day [in 1891] to see Dada's old home called Annsgift, it was so pretty such a big garden, and a little pinewood and a river called the Silver stream with a plank across … and Dada felt sad because strangers live in the old house'.[27]

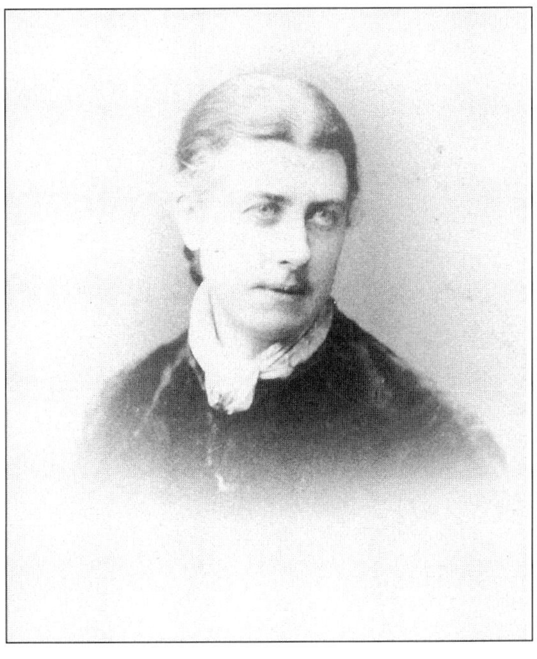

'Now', Garstin was to recall, 'came a period of hunting in winter, sketching in summer'.[28] As he asked a London friend to send him some paints, his artwork must have been slightly more serious than the word sketching suggests. He also devoted a substantial amount of time to journalism. Before leaving Cape Town, he had arranged to write for *The Lantern*, a weekly journal, but he then waited nearly a year before writing his first article, which appeared in December 1877. After publishing at least sixteen pieces over the next twelve months, he abruptly stopped writing. As he only had a small income from trust funds, there must have been a good reason for this.

The most likely explanation was a serious accident while hunting. In his first article in *The Lantern* he had reported that he had been out hunting on the first meet of the season, and that, 'owing to the lateness of the summer the fences were very blind and difficult and many fresh pinks were duly christened'.[29] Perhaps the fences were also a hazard the following year, because it is known that, while out hunting, he came into conflict with a thorn bush, and was blinded in his right eye. Garstin's partial loss of sight was to have a most surprising and important consequence but, before considering this, it is desirable to glance at his articles.

Radical Journalism in The Lantern

They are the work of an intellectual; with the intellectual's keen interest in general problems and love of paradox. Garstin was fascinated by the way in which agrarian outrages were most frequent in those parts of Ireland colonised most thoroughly by the English, and were almost unknown in the purely Celtic regions of the far west. The theory of there being an essential English element in such outrages possessed, he said, the charm of not being superficially obvious.[30] Among the general problems in which he was interested was the position of women in a society where one in four could not expect to marry.[31] There is a close link between Garstin's writing and his painting: he turned out to be the most cerebral of artists.

Garstin had little sympathy for Anglo-Irish landlords. After Lord Leitrim's murder, which was an agrarian crime, he pointed out that his lordship had spent years in constant litigation with his tenants and was in the process of evicting 80 of them. Garstin regarded Leitrim, with his views about the rights of property, as an anachronism.[32] This would have been less surprising if Garstin had not himself been a junior member of the same class. Garstin's doubts about property rights were not confined to landownership in Ireland: he was sceptical about a system of inheritance that could lead to a shower of undeserved wealth landing in the lap of a fortunate descendant.[33]

The articles show that Garstin already had progressive views. He was in favour of votes for women, and protested against their exclusion from higher education and the professions, though permitted to do laborious and low paid work. 'This', he wrote, 'is a hard sentence, and I think an unjust one, because it is passed on those who ask nothing, but to be allowed a fair chance in the race for life'.[34] In support of his position, Garstin argued not only that there were surplus women but also – and interestingly – that married men were no longer prepared to support their wives' unmarried sisters.

Such forward-looking social and political attitudes were to be matched by Garstin's progressive views on painting.

Half-Blind but Resolved to Paint

One of the most striking facts of Garstin's life is that it was after becoming half-blind that he decided to train as an artist. He himself says laconically, 'I met a painter-sportsman who seriously advised me to take up Art as a profession. After a lot of thought I determined to have a good try and so started for Antwerp …'.[35] There is no mention of his accident. However, Michael Canney in his short biography, which was based on interviews with Garstin's daughter, declares that, 'The partial loss of his sight seems to have provoked a crisis in his life. It was a turning point'.[36] This rings true: Garstin was now well over 30, and his partial blindness must have raised the question of what he was to do with his life. Unlike some other defects in vision, the loss of sight in one eye is unlikely to have a marked effect on the type or quality of work that a painter will produce.

Garstin's training did not begin until the summer of 1880. The delay may have been due to a long period of treatment and recovery after his accident, and it is possible that he went to Antwerp earlier. He left Ireland in 1879, but it is not known when. However, the real puzzle is why Garstin did not start training as an artist before his accident. He cannot just have been having a holiday: his period of relaxation was far too long and it was only after his accident, and a great deal of thought, that he at last decided to start training. Before that, he was content to vegetate. This may seem surprising but Irish gentlemen were, as a decaying class, prone to inactivity. This is the picture of the Irish gentry that is given in one novel after another. *A Drama in Muslin* by George Moore is a particularly good example. The ineffectual and self-mocking Arthur Barton is a dilettante artist, who devotes his time to painting kinky pictures, but takes little interest in his estate. Garstin's grandfather would have provided Norman with a fine role model of idleness.

This seems the likely explanation for his behaviour, given that Annsgift was a pleasant place to be, and he was having an enjoyable time painting and hunting. He referred later to having spent many happy years in that part of the country, and, as he said at the time, 'I don't … object to this sleepy existence, on the contrary I like it'.[37]

An Inauspicious Start

Garstin was nearly 33 when, at last, he began to train as an artist. Hitherto his life had been varied and stimulating, but desultory. He had started training as an engineer and then as an architect but gave up; he had worked as a colonial civil servant and on a newspaper but quit. He had displayed considerable talent as a freelance journalist, but this was not to be his principal career. There had also been long periods of quiescence, during one of which he had lost the sight of an eye.

This was an inauspicious beginning. Unless he was to continue painting into old age, Garstin's late start suggested that his output of pictures would never be large. His apparent lack of staying power made it doubtful whether he would ever produce great work. On the other hand, his experience was much wider than that of most other artists; he now had the capacity for independent judgement; and he had not, at an early age, either passed through the restrictive academic training of the time, or been steeped in painting of the sentimental or anecdotal variety. This meant that he was unlikely to become a traditional academic painter, and would be more open to new influences than many of his contemporaries. It was to be expected that his pictures would differ from those of the other Newlyn painters, and that he would be reluctant to paint works of a sentimental or trivial type.

Some of these predictions were to be borne out by events but, as we shall see, others were not.

Chapter 2

Training and Grand Tour, 1880-6

Garstin's period of formal art training lasted from the summer of 1880 to the summer of 1884. He began by spending a year at the Royal Academy in Antwerp, and went on to spend the autumn of 1881 painting in the country with Théodore Verstraete. This was a short but probably formative period. Then, like so many of his contemporaries, Garstin went to Paris, the artistic Mecca of the world. He joined the atelier of Carolus-Duran, which was small but notable. Here he completed his training as a tonal painter, and began to exhibit his own works in the leading British galleries. Garstin then made a Grand Tour through Italy, Morocco and Spain to broaden his artistic horizons and paint. Information on this period of his life is far from plentiful, but fortunately Duran and his studio are well documented, and there are letters about the Grand Tour.

At the Antwerp Academy, 1880-1

In June 1880, Garstin enrolled at the Antwerp Academy, which was a less surprising choice than it may seem. There were numerous art schools in the British Isles, but the training they provided was long, laborious and limited. More advanced tuition could be had at the Slade or the Royal Academy Schools. However, the training at the latter was very conservative, and was criticised even by an academic artist like Poynter; and, although the Slade was more highly regarded, it was fee paying and there were few places. The Antwerp Academy had the advantages of being free, while the cost of living was low. It had received glowing reports, and was becoming increasingly popular.[1]

Students from Britain entered the *Antiek* class or the more advanced *Natuur*, where students painted models. In *Antiek* students drew from a plaster cast or some famous piece of classical sculpture. This was the routine form of training for beginners, though at

Antwerp stress was placed on the overall picture and purely mechanical work was discouraged. At British art schools stippling – shadowing by means of dots – and a high degree of finish were customary.

Garstin was (like Vincent Van Gogh a little later!) placed in *Antiek*, probably because of his lack of previous training. What is more puzzling is his failure to gain promotion, despite a good mark at the end of the winter term. Garstin said that he studied under Charles Verlat, who taught the *Natuur* class. The explanation may be that, although he never officially belonged, he was allowed to attend. Though too conservative to spot the originality of Van Gogh, Verlat was a relatively good teacher who encouraged a bold approach and had a close relationship with his pupils. Garstin's pictures were in a very different style from those of Verlat. Hence Garstin is unlikely to have gained anything more than good advice, which, as Verlat was an indifferent painter, was just as well.

While he was in Antwerp, Garstin became acquainted with the Belgian artist Théodore Verstraete and, during the last six months of his stay in Belgium, he painted in the country with him. This was probably during the summer and autumn of 1881. In May Garstin had, once again, been placed in the Antiek class. This ended in August and he may not have completed the term.

Realism, Naturalism and Plein Air

Verstraete was almost certainly an important mentor, and perhaps the most significant formative influence on Garstin. He was both a realist and a *plein air* painter.[2] To understand his impact it is necessary to look briefly at the developments that were taking place in the world of painting.

When Garstin became a student, academic painters, such as Leighton and Alma-Tadema, still occupied the centre of the stage, but the Realists were increasingly pushing their way forward. According to Linda Nochlin, the aim of the Realist movement, that started in the 1840s, 'was to give a truthful, objective and impartial representation of the real world, based on meticulous observation of contemporary life'.[3] There had been realist artists since the early Renaissance, but one distinguishing feature of these nineteenth-century Realists was that they were interested in ordinary people and the poor. They were not (like the arch-realist Velázquez) mainly concerned with princes, prelates or palaces, but with picnics, parks, plages and prostitutes.

By the time that Garstin began painting with Verstraete the early leaders of the Realist tendency were dead – Courbet in 1877 and Millet in 1875 – and Realism had divided into two broad groups. There were Impressionists and there were the Naturalists.[4] The first

Impressionist Exhibition had been held in 1874. However, Monet, Sisley, Pissarro, Renoir and the other French Impressionists were, even by 1881, only just starting to be recognised. They were, at least to begin with, primarily concerned with bright colour and tended to use unmixed paint. As they themselves explained, they tried to capture, 'the fugitive phenomena of light'.[5] They painted with small dabs of paint, and their pictures lacked finish.

The other group of Realists were the Naturalists, although naturalism is a very slippery word, which has had many different uses. While they have subsequently been eclipsed (and engulfed) by the Impressionists, the Naturalists seemed the more important grouping at the time. The pioneer was the German Adolf Menzel, but, in 1881, the best known was Bastien-Lepage, with his *Haymakers* of 1878. The most famous was to be Degas, who called himself a Naturalist and rightly denied being an Impressionist. In its pure form Naturalism was everything that Impressionism was not. The Naturalists painted in muted colours and half tones. They favoured grey light and avoided bright sunshine. Their pictures have a high degree of finish and their use of paint tended to be smooth and economical, frequently applied with square brushes. Degas commended some sketches by Walter Sickert for being painted like a door ('comme une porte'), and was fond of saying that 'Nature is smooth' ('La nature est lisse').[6] Although the Naturalists were not simply engaged in description, their paintings have a photographic quality, and some of them made extensive use of this medium.

Impressionism and Naturalism are alternative ways of viewing the world, each of which corresponds to a different section of our field of vision. The centre of the field will be in focus and the image will be precise, but outside, and away from the centre, the image will be progressively more and more out of focus and increasingly blurred. The Naturalists painted the whole scene in focus, as if it were in the centre of the field, whereas the Impressionists painted it out of focus, as if it were on the periphery. Though it is necessary to qualify this by saying that the Naturalists, and especially Bastien-Lepage, often painted their backgrounds in a more impressionistic fashion in order to convey the notion of recession. Another caveat is that many of the Impressionists, including Monet, Renoir and Pissarro, were short-sighted and refused to wear long-distance spectacles. Hence, even in the centre of the field, they would not have seen clearly. Because Impressionism and Realism correspond to different parts of the field of vision neither has a greater *a priori* claim to be realistic: both are right and each is wrong.

Plein air painting was the other big development taking place. There was nothing new in painting directly from nature: landscape artists had long made studies in the countryside, although they were rarely exhibited. What was new was that painting in the open air now became a movement, and was elevated into a doctrine. Such painting was facilitated by the introduction of portable equipment and paint in lead tubes. The Impressionists are often thought to have been responsible for the development of *plein air* painting, but this is incorrect. The Barbizon School initiated the movement, and Bastien-Lepage was its most popular exponent. That Lepage was both a Realist and a *plein air* painter is, of course, no accident. It was believed that only by working on the spot was it possible to paint a picture that provided an accurate depiction, and was therefore sincere.

Théodore Verstraete

Although Verstraete was somewhat younger than Garstin, having been born in 1851, he had, as far back as 1867, entered the Royal Academy at Antwerp. He began exhibiting in 1873 and by the early eighties was already an established artist with a mature style. For most of his short career Verstraete, who went blind in 1896, was an archetypal Naturalist and a dedicated *plein air* painter. After the Academy, he went into the countryside and lived in a caravan with

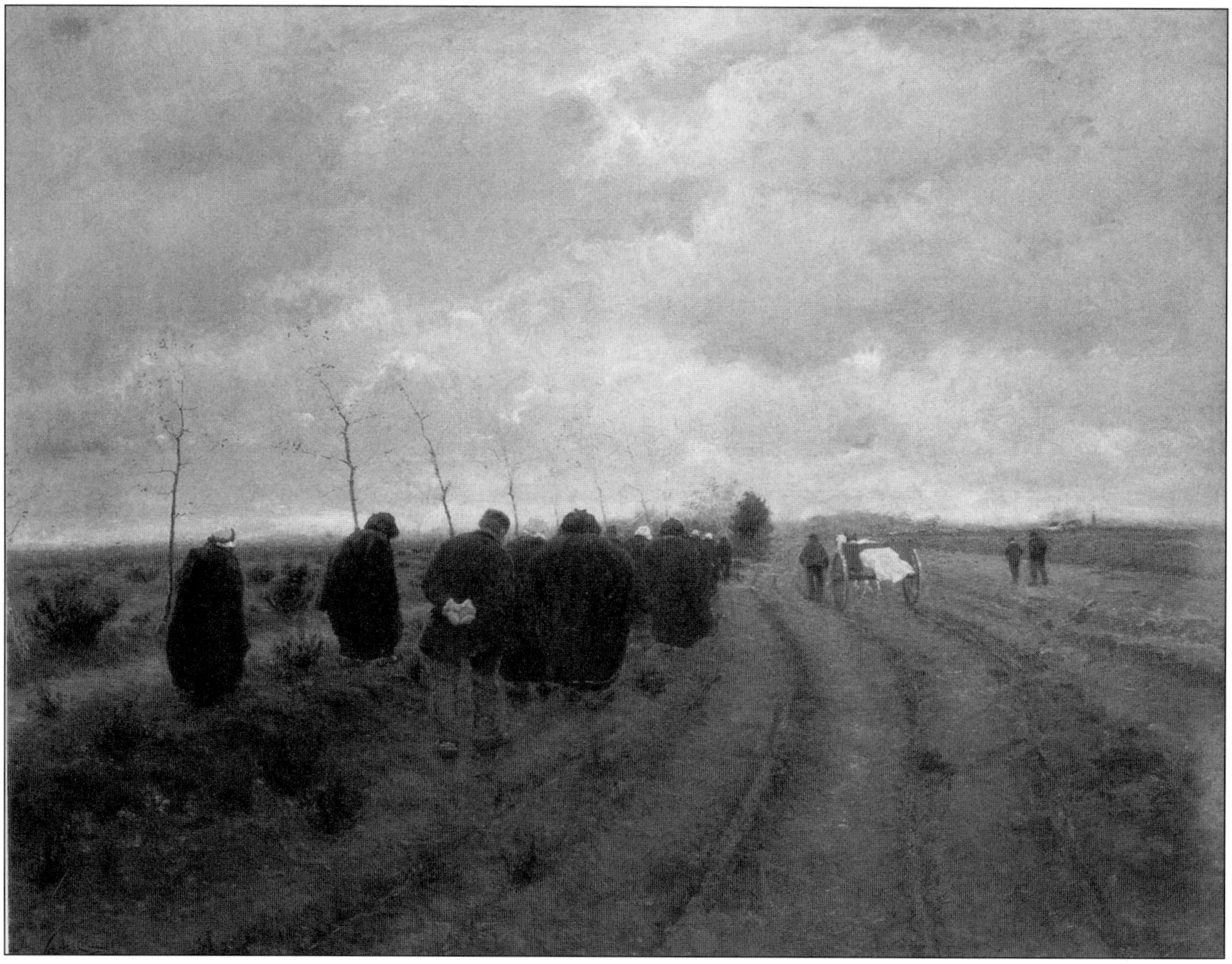

Théodore Verstraete, *Burial in the Campine*, 1888, oil (Musée des Beaux-Arts de Tournai).

large windows in which he could continue to work even when the weather was bad. He painted ordinary unromantic countryside, under overcast skies, inhabited by common folk. Even when they were engaged in exceptional activities, such as funeral processions, there is a total absence of theatre. The emotional temperature is very low, but, as with a cold wind, sometimes intense. When he painted figures, he typically used a back or side view. His colours are generally muted, harmonious and melancholy: greys, browns, dull yellow-gold, and black predominate. Despite this, his pictures contain areas of striking luminosity, as shown, for instance, by his masterpiece *Burial in the Campine* (1888).

Verstraete's glowing effects were due to the use of a wide range of tones. Although his colours were for the most part dark and dull, he used some brighter colour. As a result they appear exceptionally bright, just as they do in the chiaroscuro work of Caravaggio and Rembrandt. This is because the eye is sensitive not only to absolute levels of brightness, but also to relative effects. The Impressionists, who in most of their early pictures used a high-keyed palette, and avoided black, tended to employ a narrow tonal range. This was because of their observation that in bright light even the shadows have colour and their desire to achieve an absolute match between the tones of their pigments and those of the shadows they observed. Because Verstraete, like other Naturalists, was not preoccupied by bright sunlight, or by absolute matching, he was able to employ a wide tonal range, and to paint pictures which seem to glow.

Except that, prior to 1900, he did not paint the working classes very frequently, Garstin's pictures have the same hallmarks as those of Verstraete. For instance, his figures are often seen from the back or in profile. There is a small Garstin picture of 1883, known as *The Shelter*, which appears to be extraordinarily similar to Verstraete in technique and, on this occasion, subject matter. It shows a husbandman at rest with his face in profile. Unfortunately, only a black and white reproduction is available (despite a thorough search), but the subject matter strongly suggests that the colours are muted.[7] But the most important way in which his pictures are similar to those of Verstraete is that Garstin employed a wide tonal range and that his pictures often have a striking luminosity.

There is no account of the period that Garstin spent with Verstraete but, although it was important for his career, he would have experienced the frustrations of painting out of doors. A few years later he was to describe the perils and pains of *plein air* in terms which, despite their humour, betray real feeling. What he wrote may well have been inspired by his first extended period of working in the open air.

Hey! Ho! For the wind and the rain! What memories will these words evoke in the mind of every landscape painter – of hopes and fears; of eagerly-scanned skies; of consultations with unconscientious barometers; of debates with still less conscientious peasants or marine prophets; of the almost human malignity of the wind, always taking advantage of your preoccupation to buffet your work and knock it over with some sly, sudden gust; of the ominous little cloud that rapidly covers all the blue; of the first few drops that we can hardly believe in ; of the ingenious devices wherewith to defy nature; of defeat, of retreat , of despair. Hey! Ho! For the wind and the rain; and when peradventure by some strange chance these do not afflict us, then may be heard the voice of the culex family, lest you should forget them and be happy … The open-air painter finds everything leagued against him, from the sun in heaven, which thinks it not undignified on the part of a great luminary to perpetually shift and change the poor man's light and shade, so that the landscape one hour gives the lie to its representation the next, down to the very colours in his box, which, with a littleness of soul perhaps more comprehensible on their part, take a childish delight in hiding from his hand.

(Norman Garstin, 'Apology' in *Gnats* by Alexander Mann, 1884.)

Opposite:
Carolus-Duran, *The Lady with a Glove*, oil, 1869 (Musée d'Orsay, Paris).

The Parisian Art Student, 1882-4

Garstin appears to have left Belgium for Paris during the late autumn of 1881. He was certainly living there by early 1882, because he gave a Parisian address when, in mid-March, he exhibited a picture at Southport. This was notable as it was his first known exhibit. What was even more important was that he was now studying in Paris, the artistic capital of the world to which flights of students were moving from Britain and America.

Garstin entered the atelier of Carolus-Duran and went to live at the Hôtel St Malo, which was quite close. This is a smallish hotel, now called the Berkeley, in the Rue d'Odessa. It was one of a large number of establishments in Montparnasse that provided cheap accommodation for students. In an interview Garstin said

> I was one of a group of young painters who made their headquarters the Hotel St. Malo, and there we always dined. There were a lot of Bulgarian students there, mostly from the Sorbonne, big blond sort of men, and they gave us 'singing nights' sometimes. We were an enthusiastic crew, and used to have eternal discussions about art over little restaurant tables.[8]

These conversations were no doubt very similar to those that took place, around the same time, at another café frequented by British students. According to Alexander Roche, who was one, 'ardour and tobacco were burned freely before the shrines of Puvis de Chavannes and Jules Bastien-Lepage. Between these extremes [for Chavannes was no realist] the talk went to and fro on some evenings, but, as a rule, the favourite topics were Bastien-Lepage and *plein air*'.[9] From time to time Garstin may well have been a participant. The café was not far from Duran's atelier, and one of his great friends, Thomas Millie Dow, was a member of the group.

During 1883 Garstin may have moved from the St Malo to the Hôtel Béranger in the Rue Vavin, which is the other side of the Boulevard de Montparnasse. Still later he appears to have rented a studio. 'I remember', recalled a friend, 'a studio, on the fifth floor of a white building in the Latin Quarter of Paris, with a large hole in the floor through which the canvasses, rolled up, were let down into the street below. There Mr. Garstin spent many an evening after long hours at the schools'.[10] Though his residence may have changed, he continued, while in Paris, to do little else except paint and discuss painting. 'I seem to live in a world', he told his future wife in 1884, 'where people paint, paint, talk, paint and think. I know of nothing else and my days have nothing else in them'.[11]

Carolus-Duran and his Atelier

The merits of Duran's atelier, and they were considerable, did not

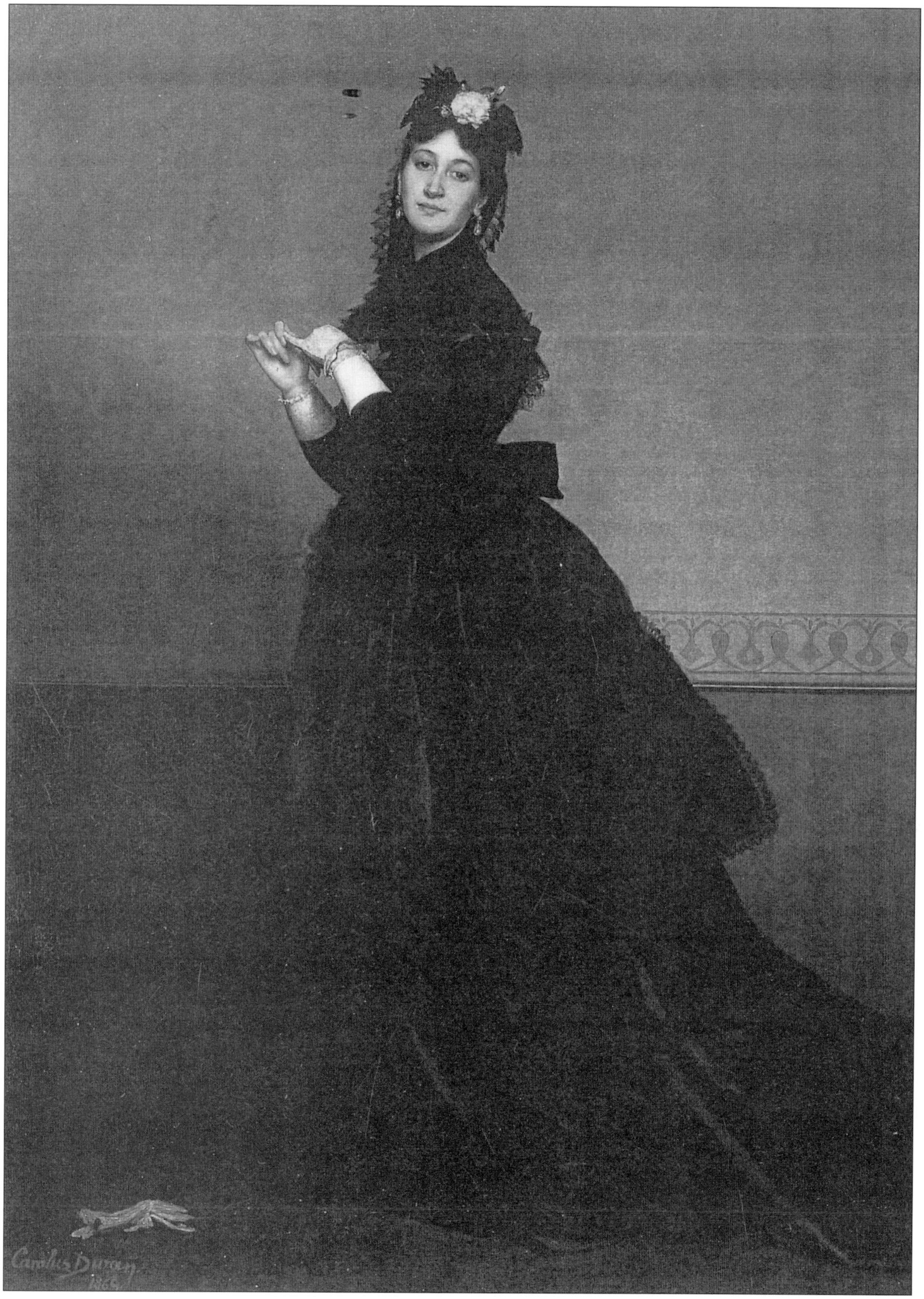

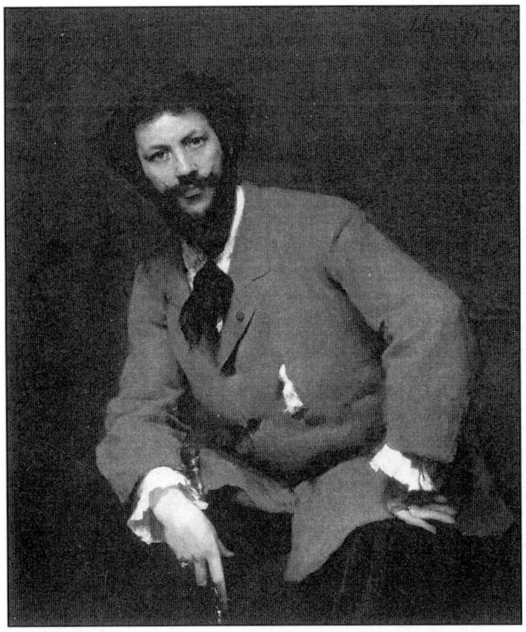

Singer Sargent, *Portrait of Carolus-Duran*, oil, 1879, oil (Sterling and Francine Clark Art Institute, Williamstown, U.S.A.).

include the studio itself: Garstin later recalled, 'the old grimy school in the Boulevard Port Royal'.[12] But it was small and intimate, with only about 40 students. In contrast, Julian's student factory had several hundred. Although most of those at Duran's studio were British or American, French was the only language permitted, and those who infringed the rule were fined. Thanks to his schooling in Jersey this was not a regulation that would have caused Garstin any difficulty. Carolus-Duran and other artists with ateliers provided their services free of charge, but with a small levy to cover the cost of running the studio and providing models, which could, at least for Duran's studio, be greatly reduced by signing up for a full year.[13] At the commercial studios, such as Julian's, the fees were higher, while at those that were financed by the state (Cabanel, and Gérôme) there was no charge. Duran visited his atelier twice a week to inspect his students' work and sometimes gave impromptu lectures; on another day the class would visit Duran's studio to watch the Master at work.

Duran's atelier was almost certainly the most distinctive and stimulating in Paris. Lavery only recalled receiving one piece of advice during his three years at Julian's; and Eliot Gregory, who was one of Duran's former students, commented that the change from his former sleepy teaching environment, 'to the vivid enthusiasm and dash of Carolus-Duran's studio was like stepping out of a musty cloister into the warmth and movement of a market-place'.[14] Gregory attributed this not to its intimate size and its especially dedicated group of students, though they must have helped, but to Carolus-Duran and the impetus imparted by his success.

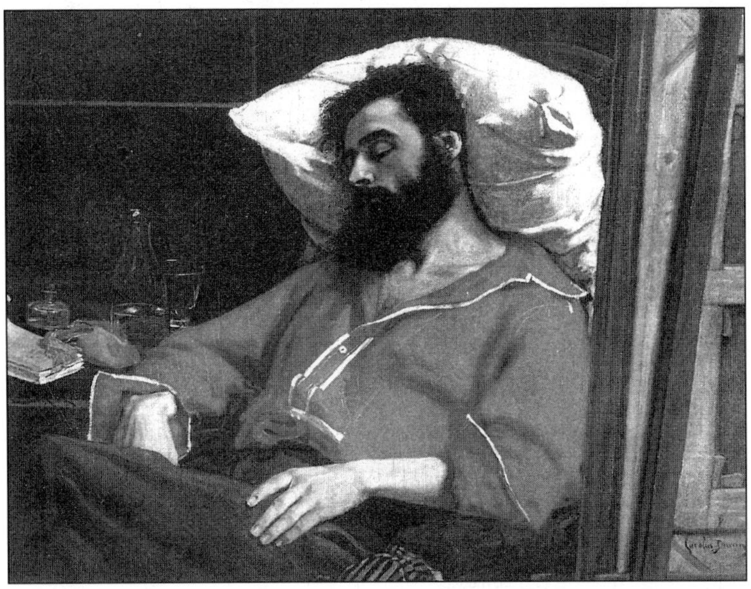

Carolus-Duran, *The Convalescent, c.*1860, oil, (Musée d'Orsay, Paris).

Opposite:
Carolus-Duran, *Portrait de Madame Sainctelette*, 1871 (Musées Royaux des Beaux-Arts, Brussels).

Carolus-Duran (1838-1917) had a fairytale life. He began as an impoverished artist, at one stage almost starving to death, but became a wealthy and celebrated society painter. His persona was as dramatic and diverse as his career. He dressed elegantly to impress; he had the reputation of being a brilliant swordsman; in the words of one former student, who liked him, he was sometimes 'the very embodiment of high-strung pride'; he was nevertheless capable of great restraint in the face of provocative behaviour; he relished wealth but, according to another former student, would often dip into his own pocket to 'smooth the path of some improvident pupil'.[15] With such a character, Carolus-Duran was either admired or despised. To the uncharitable Kenyon Cox, who quickly left his atelier, Duran was a vulgar and childish snob.[16] But most of his students stayed and were fiercely loyal.

Duran began as a strict Realist and an admirer of Manet. His *Convalescent* , painted about 1860 and showing a sick and totally self-absorbed painter, is a promising piece of Realism. In 1869 he made

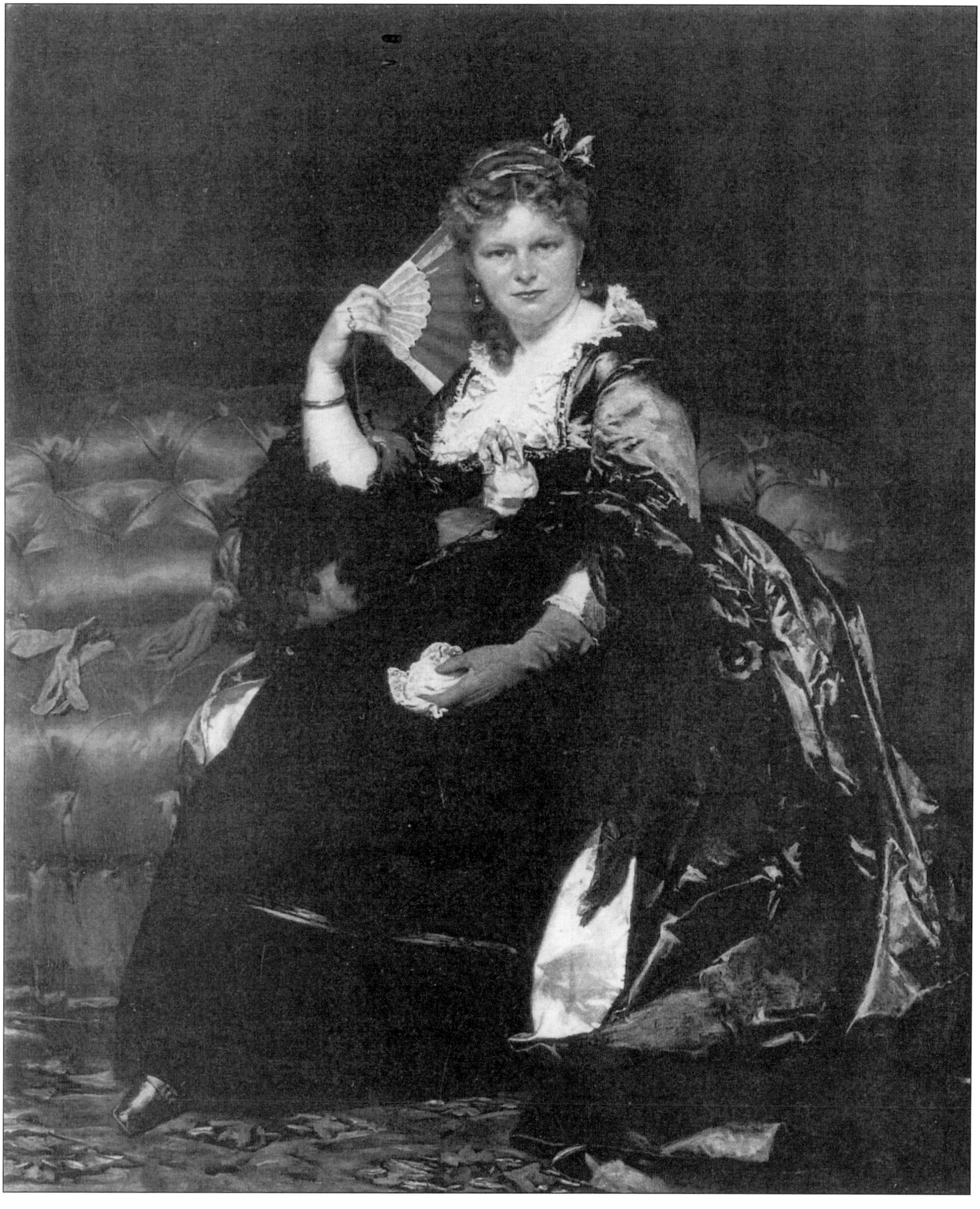

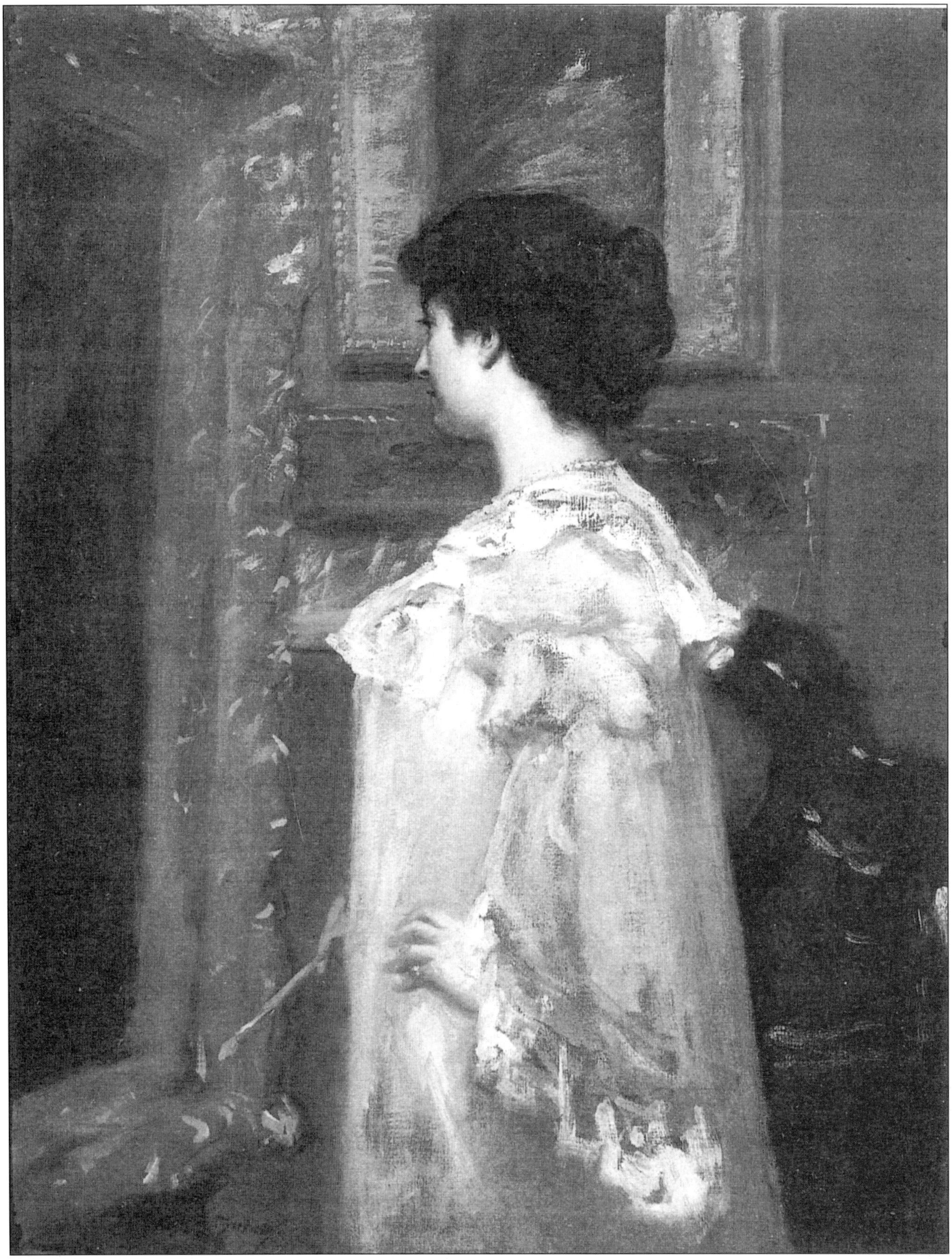

his name, with *The Lady with A Glove*. This is an elegant and striking portrait of his wife in a style inspired by Gainsborough and Velázquez, whom Duran had studied during a trip to Spain. He went on to paint a series of society portraits, which command attention by the way in which the subjects seem to project themselves from the canvases, or by the use of rich and glowing colours for backgrounds or clothes. However, Duran was not just a fashionable artist. He also produced landscapes of some merit, and, above all, he painted pictures of servants and women that were affectionate (*le Jardinier de l'artiste*) or tender and erotic. *Study for Lilia* and *Artist in her Studio* are pictures of women facing away, or in profile, who appear vulnerable. It cannot, on the other hand, be denied that Duran's work was uneven, that some of his portraits were flashy, and that a few of his later pictures would have disgraced a biscuit box (Consuelo Vanderbilt at Blenheim), but this was in the future.[17]

At the time, most of his pupils had a high regard for his painting, and Garstin shared their admiration, later describing Duran's technique as 'brilliant'.[18] His weaknesses were probably overlooked because of his success; because his work compared favourably with that of other Parisian teachers; and because he was an excellent teacher, which was his students' main concern. 'He couldn't do it himself, but he could teach it', was the eventual but over-harsh verdict of Sargent, Duran's most distinguished student.[19]

The Gospel according to Duran

What would Garstin have been taught by Duran? Perhaps the most important lessons would have dealt with the practical aspects of painting. Sargent, for instance, was taught to begin by painting the middle tones, then to work towards the darker tones, and, finally, to paint the brightest values. As Duran was a master of technique, his practical instruction is likely to have been exceptionally valuable. Garstin would also have learned a number of important general precepts. Duran stressed the desirability of avoiding mere charm and of suppressing the inessential. 'In art all that is not indispensable is harmful', and 'express the maximum by means of the minimum', were two of his favourite slogans. These were lessons that Garstin was to take to heart. Above all, he would have been taught to paint what he saw and, when doing so, to seek out the appropriate half tone (the shade between the lightest and darkest value). 'Look for the half tone' was reinforced by the advice to emulate Duran's hero, Velázquez.[20] But, except in exercises, students were not to copy other artists: 'When you go out into the fields you will not see a Corot; paint what you see'.[21]

Garstin would have received much the same advice about the importance of values at the other Parisian ateliers. What was

Opposite:
Carolus-Duran, *Artist in her Studio*, *c.*1880, oil (La Salle University Art Museum, Philadelphia).

distinctive was Duran's method of instruction. The conventional method was for the student to start with drawing and, only when this had been mastered, to begin painting; although, even then, the picture would be drawn out in detail on the canvas. Duran would have none of this. The beginner was thrown straight into painting, and all that was permitted, by way of preparation, was a slight sketch in charcoal to indicate proportions. The student was expected to paint the main planes of the subject onto an unprepared canvas, and to fill in the gaps in this crazy paving with smaller planes. It was forbidden to fudge by brushing one surface into another, or by indicating boundaries and contours with lines.

All too often this form of instruction proved too difficult, and, according to Will Low, a former pupil, many of Duran's students found themselves 'floundering in colour and shapeless form'.[22] Many left for training of a more orthodox type; that Garstin remained and flourished reveals both his perseverance and his ability. Those who survived, instead of being taught, in the conventional manner, to draw a dark object on white paper, were forced to recognise that what they are looking at, and trying to paint, is a light object against a background that is often darker. Perhaps even more important, Duran's students became, due to the absence of detailed drawing and modelling, especially conscious of the importance of the overall structure and balance of a painting. One of the features of Garstin's pictures was their asymmetrical balance, although this must have owed something to his study of Whistler and Chinese art. Duran's method would also have made Garstin particularly aware of the need to observe the precise and delicate relationship between different colours and patches of light. Garstin's ability in this respect is, once again, demonstrated by his paintings. Although it would be wrong to imagine that Garstin would not have gradually learned the same lessons elsewhere, they were unavoidable at Duran's atelier.

'I think', Garstin wrote, 'the impulse given by Carolus-Duran [to Alexander Mann] was perhaps, the strongest and most enduring of his artistic education, and though in the years to come he used his powers in various directions, yet he never lost the style which became his method of expression in these days'.[23] It seems likely that Garstin would, if he had been asked, have said the same about himself.

Garstin on Manet: A Mixed Verdict

The period that Garstin spent in Paris was notable for other reasons apart from his formal training. He began to write about art. In 1884 Garstin produced an article about Manet for the *Art Journal.* He had obviously been to the great retrospective exhibition for Manet in January, which contained paintings from Manet's late

Impressionist period. Garstin described Manet as an 'impressionist' and says that there was a 'delicious brightness and happiness in his work ... He lets in air and light. Pictures like his later ones amongst the brown bitumen canvases of the average exhibition seem like patches of sunlight on a prison wall. It is hardly possible to overestimate the value of Manet's work upon outdoor painting'.[24]

Although Garstin found much to praise in Manet's work he also found much to criticise. Manet, he wrote,

> did not see far, and his hand had little cunning. There is no subtlety in his work and rarely any delicacy ... His taste is worse than questionable – it is often revolting. How seldom can we stand in front of even his best-painted canvasses without asking, 'but why was it painted at all?'... In his later work there seems to be little or no choice [of subject], fragments of the world around him, pictures that seem like portraits without the *raison d'être* of portraiture, and whose personality is often as unpleasant as its colour. What is known as ugliness so far from being repellent was to him positively attractive.[25]

These are, at first sight, puzzling criticisms. Except for his brief Impressionist period, Manet's palette was characterised by white, grey, black and dark tones. Hence Garstin appears, at one and the same time, to be praising Manet's later pictures for their delicious brightness and criticising them for their unpleasant colour. His attack on Manet for his lack of taste may, at first sight, appear equally surprising. Very few of the pictures in the retrospective exhibition seem open to this criticism. Was Garstin, like conservative critics, offended by *Le Déjeuner sur l'Herbe* and by *Olympia*, which shows a courtesan?

The explanation for Garstin's contradictions on Manet's colour is probably that, although he could see that Manet had let in air and light, his colours appeared unsophisticated to somebody who had been drilled in the use of half tones and subtle shades. Because Impressionism has become so familiar it is now extremely difficult to realise how crude it then looked not only to the aged critic but also to the art student. Garstin's strictures on Manet's taste may be explained by his conviction that art was about beauty, a topic to be examined later. Garstin may not have regarded a strained and chilly looking prostitute as beautiful. His puzzlement at the pictures' subject matter is easier to understand since many of Manet's pictures are indeed somewhat bewildering. *Le Déjeuner sur l'Herbe* is, for instance, a very strange picture, if only because of the absence of any relationship between the figures.

Garstin's reaction to Manet helps to explain why Impressionism had such a limited impact on Garstin, although, as we shall see, it did influence some of his early paintings. Many of his contemporaries,

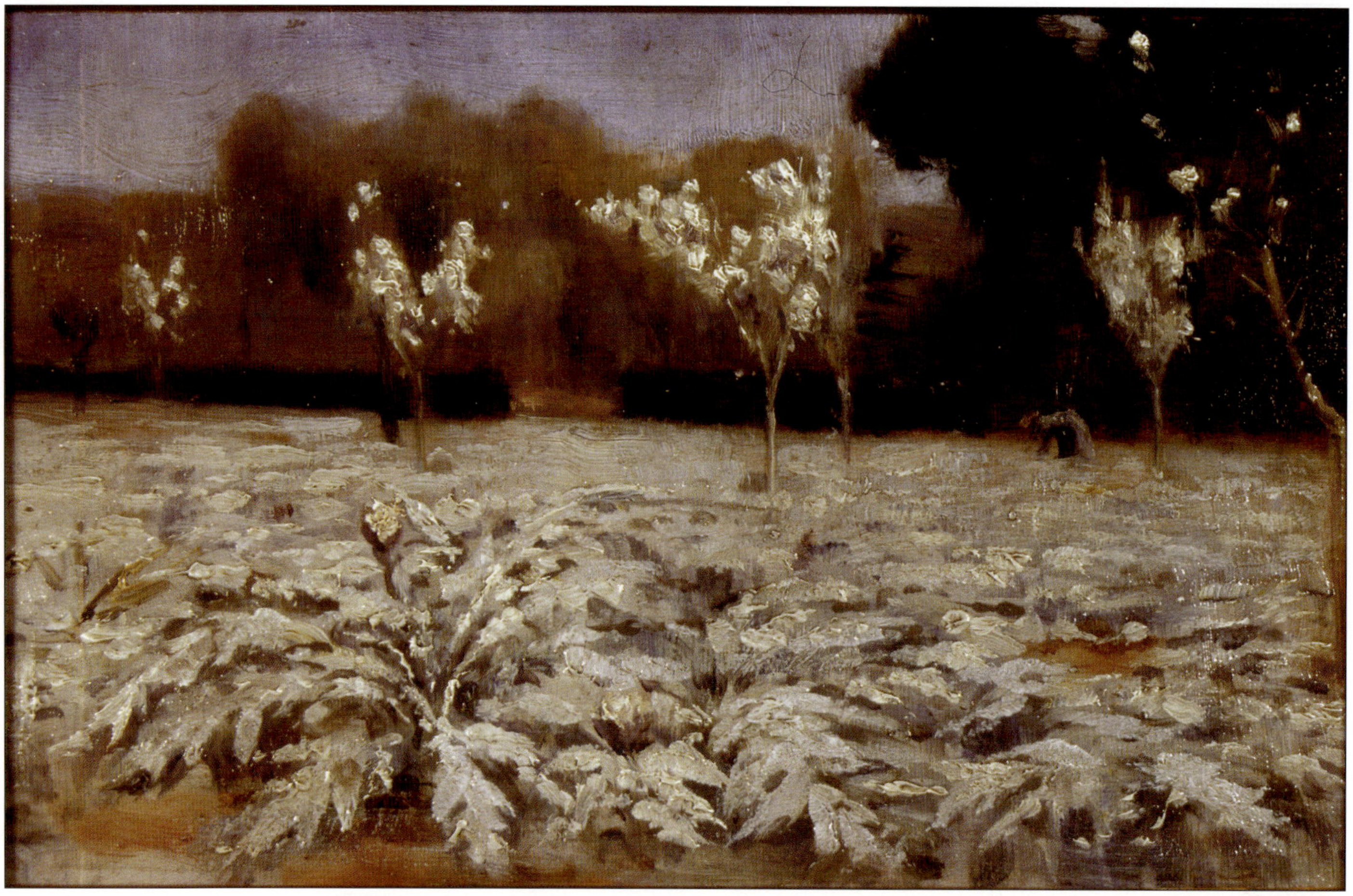

Plate 8 *Artichokes, Hyères,* 1883, oil, 5.5" x 9.25" (Bristol Museum & Art Gallery).

with their limited command of French, would not have known about the movement.[26] However, Garstin obviously did, although it is not clear whether he visited the seventh Impressionist Exhibition of 1882, or saw any of the shows of leading Impressionists during the following year. It would certainly have been very remarkable if Garstin had become an Impressionist at this early period. Steer was the only British artist who, during the eighties, experimented with a highly keyed palette. Even Sickert, who knew Degas well and was acquainted with the work of the Impressionists, went on using dark tones. Impressionism would, even to those who were familiar with it, only have appeared to be one line of advance. Not until much later was it seen as *the* main road, or (wrongly) regarded as a unified movement.

Painting and Exhibiting: Some Success at Last

Another reason why Garstin's period in Paris was so important was that he began to exhibit his pictures. His first known exhibit was at the 1882 Spring Exhibition of the Atkinson Art Gallery, Southport. It was a small oil called *Trophies of the Port* for which he asked only £17. This was followed up by two exhibits at the

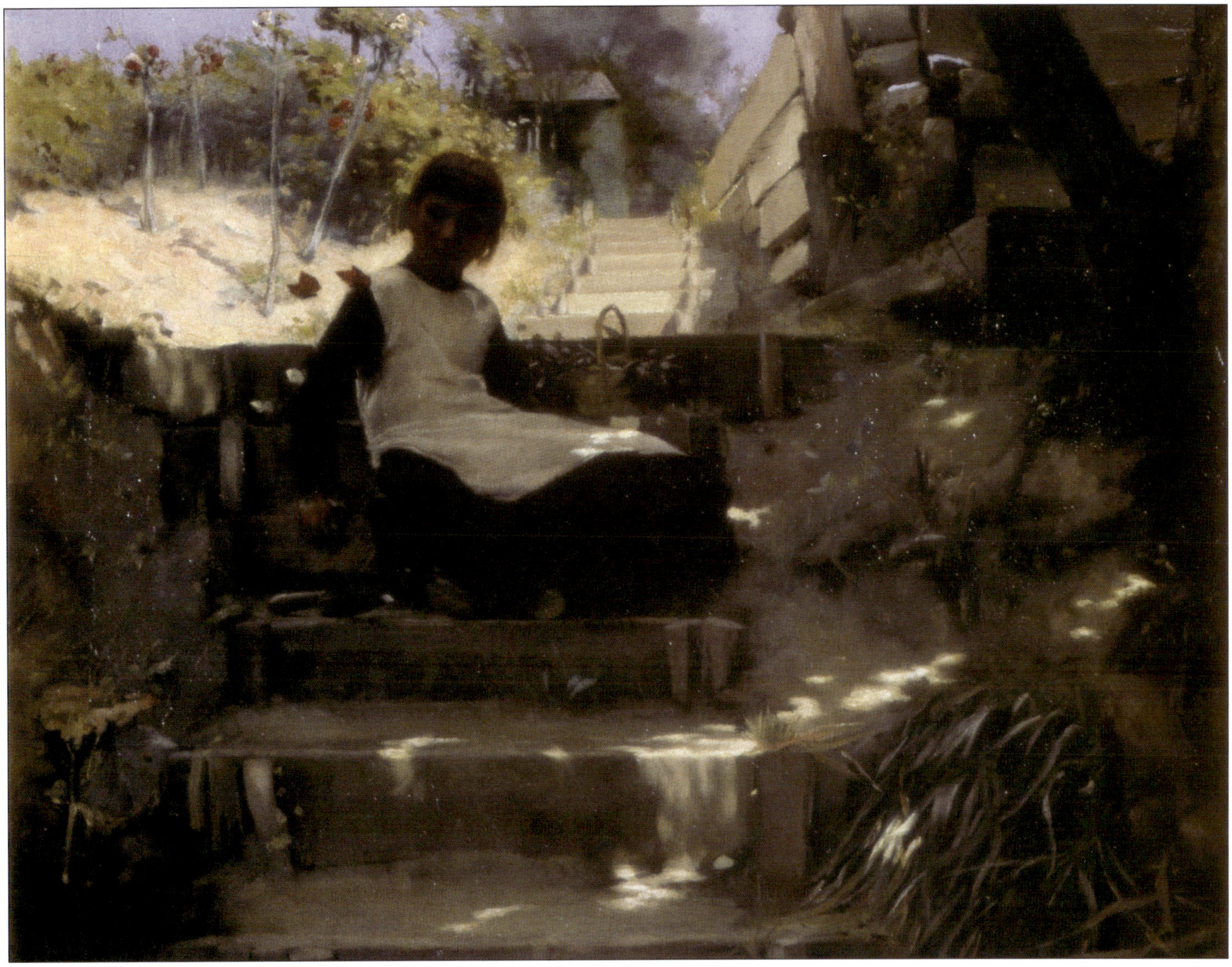

Plate 9 *The Gardener's Daughter,* 1883, oil, 19" x 24" (private collection).

prestigious Autumn show at the Walker Gallery in Liverpool. In the following year *Philomène* was hung at the most celebrated place of all, the Summer Exhibition at the Royal Academy, where it was bought by an RA, though, according to Garstin, it only got in by accident. These pictures, and other exhibits, were in oil (as were all his exhibits until the next century), and they were all small works except for *The Gardener's Daughter*, which was exhibited at the Walker in 1883.

Parisian ateliers were closed during the summer and students were expected and encouraged to leave Paris and paint in the French countryside. Foreign students congregated at small towns on the Brittany coast, and at Grez-sur-Loing or other places in the Forest of Fontainebleau. Instead Garstin went south in 1883, and painted at Hyères, which is close to the Mediterranean and near Toulon. This was where he produced *Artichokes* (Plate 8) and probably where he painted *The Gardener's Daughter* (Plate 9). Both are most pleasing

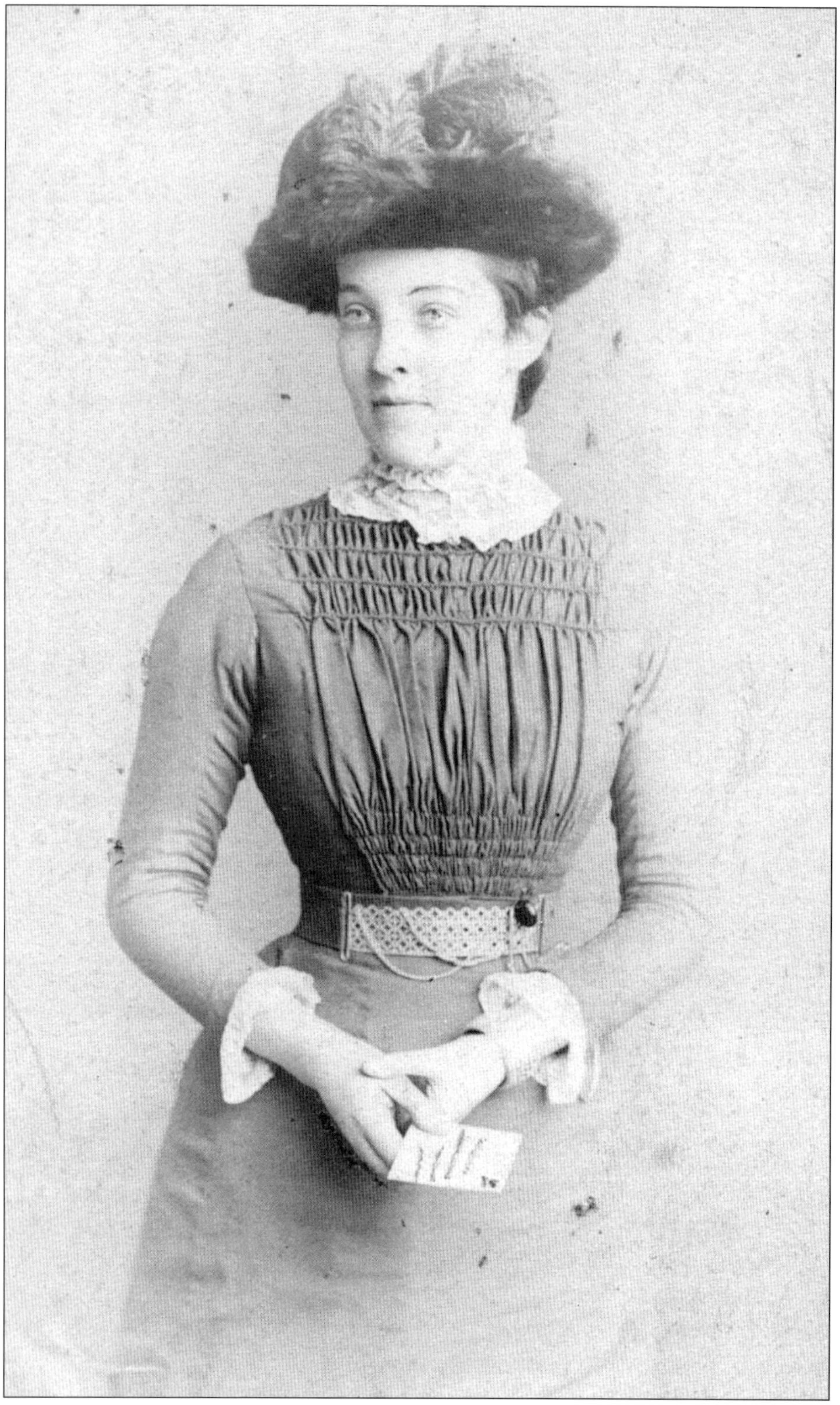

Dochie Jones, the future Mrs Garstin, *c.*1885.

pictures and have great freshness and vitality. *Artichokes* has an impressive sense of depth, produced by the way in which Garstin differentiates the leaves on the nearest artichokes, and his thick dabs in the foreground. As the perspective recedes his use of paint becomes more sparing. The impasto of the foreground differs from Garstin's later style of painting, which was more economical and smoother. There are strong contrasting colours, in particular the silver of the artichokes and the deep brown of the hedge and the trees on the right. The limited range of hues and the carefully controlled and harmonious tones exemplify the teaching of Carolus-Duran. Monet would have achieved the effect of sunlight by using bright colours, but Garstin has done so by producing an almost luminous effect.

The Gardener's Daughter is another picture that, if only because of its boldness, shows the influence of Duran. There is a striking contrast between the dark and almost gloomy lower section, which is in shadow, and the bright sunlit garden above. What is remarkable here is not merely the contrast in colour and tone but, even more, the difference between the way in which the foreground appears to press forwards towards the viewer and the background which, with its strong sense of recession, seems to absorb one into the picture. A lesser painter would have given the young girl a pretty face, and made her features clear. Garstin has placed them in deep shadow because they are being viewed against the light. The dappled sunlight, and contrasting light and shade anticipate many pictures that Garstin was to paint. A subject viewed against the light was also characteristic of some of his later work. This approach is often associated with the Newlyn School, but is here being used some years before Garstin joined the colony.

Although *The Gardener's Daughter* is a bold and striking picture, one of the features of Garstin's works is that they require time and effort in order to become fully intelligible and for their strengths to become apparent. Time and again, when looking at a Garstin picture, one's initial reaction is of slight disappointment; this, one says to one's self, is not a particularly good example of his work. If, however, one concentrates on the picture its true composition becomes evident and its different parts fall into place. The pictures of some artists can perhaps be taken in at a single glance but Garstin's pictures are not of this type: it is necessary to look hard in order to see, and the more you look the more you see.

Engaged to Dochie Jones, 1884

Finally, while Garstin was still a student of Duran, he became engaged to be married. During 1883 Garstin must not only have visited the south of France but also have paid a visit home, as he later exhibited a painting entitled *Ireland*. Then, presumably to make some money, Garstin tried his hand at portrait painting. During the second and third weeks of October he was in London painting Maria, the daughter of Alfred Jones of Bedford.

In this way he met her sister Louisa, or Dochie as she was always known. On his part it seems to have been love at first sight. He made only eight visits, and wrote most affectionately from Marseilles in January 1884. At Easter, or perhaps earlier, he proposed. Dochie dithered, and it was only after some weeks' consideration, and strong prompting by her sister, that she 'at last consented to Mr. Garstin's wish'; to quote her sister.[27] It is not difficult to see why she hesitated. Garstin might be handsome and charming, but he was nearly 37 and was still only an art student with slender private means. Although Dochie was herself 31, having been born in 1852, Garstin was a poor prospect by the standards of bourgeois Bedford. She came of a large and prosperous family. Her brothers included a colonel in the Bengal Infantry and a clergyman.

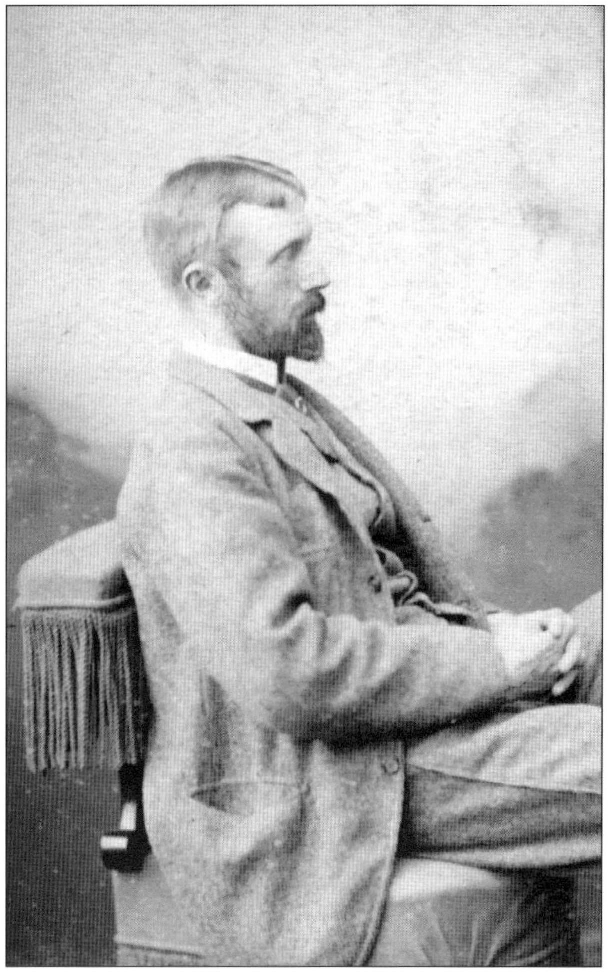

Norman Garstin in 1884, photographed by G. Vianelli, Venice.

The Grand Tour from Venice to Morocco, 1884-6

After nearly three years, Garstin finally left Duran's atelier in the summer of 1884.

He obviously decided that he should, before marrying and settling down, broaden and deepen his artistic experience through travel. Like the Grand Tour of old, it was to be a leisurely progress, in which there was not only time to see historic places, look at pictures and visit artists, but also time to paint.

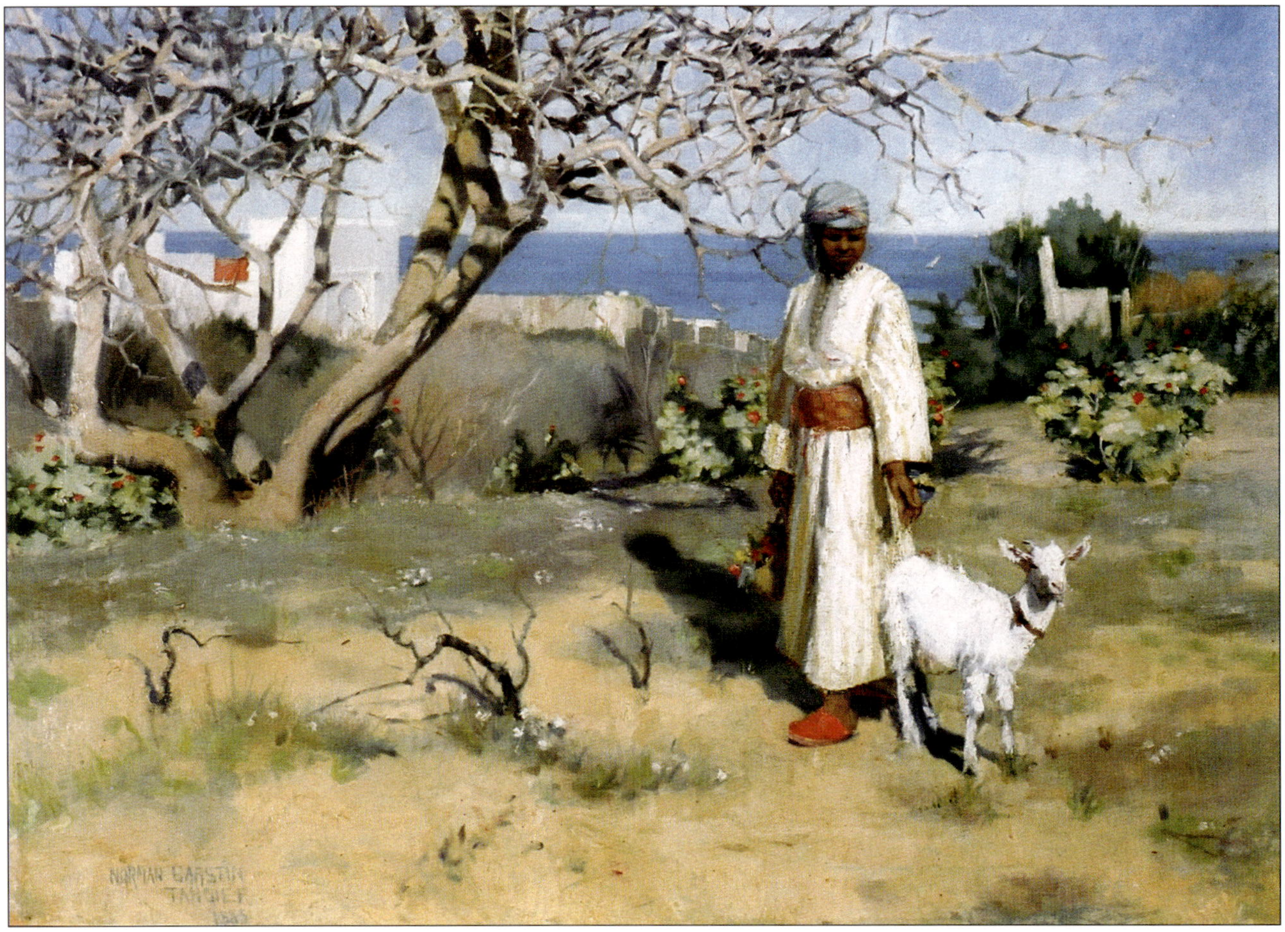

Plate 10 *Summer in Winter/Alienis Mensibus Aestas*, 1886, oil, 23" x 31" (private collection).

He went to Venice, where he appears to have arrived in July 1884. It was, he told Dochie, 'charming, wonderful, rare, peerless among cities'.[28] Within a few days of his arrival friends invited him to share their accommodation. The house

> consisted 'chiefly in artists and American ladies' and each morning he joined a group of the former at a local inexpensive restaurant for breakfast. They all met again at the same place for lunch and after seven for dinner. Coffee was taken at Florians on the piazza, followed by either a stop at a beer garden or a leisurely homeward stroll in which they 'talked despondingly about art generally and our chances in particular and so on *da capo* [repeating ourselves]'.

He was painting, with another artist, 'in a court looking on a small canal with some jolly old houses on the other side'. In September Garstin said that he had found a pretty little model who posed well, and had made a preliminary sketch of her looking into the garden from the balcony. But he did not seem able to finish the flower picture. The two pictures are likely to be *Sunshine and Blossom – Venice* and *Che Belle Fiori*. Both were hung at the RA in 1885 and were large canvasses. The picture that was painted in the court, is likely to be *A Venetian Well*, a small canvas exhibited at the Royal Society of British Artists in its show for 1884-5. It is frustrating that none of these paintings have come to light.

After, or perhaps before, Venice, Garstin went to Genoa, and he then visited Florence, Rome and Naples. Rather surprisingly, Genoa made a stronger impression than Rome, where he arrived during the winter of 1884. While in Rome Garstin visited Mancini, who was an Italian Realist. It must have been too cold to paint, and there are no pictures from this Mediterranean section of the Grand Tour.

In the New Year Garstin appears to have returned to the British Isles, presumably to see Dochie.[29] With her he visited his Irish aunts at Birr in King's County during the spring. Norman was reported to be most devoted to Dochie, to whom he had previously written in the most affectionate of tones from Venice. It seems likely that while he was in England, either then or later, Garstin made an exploratory visit to Newlyn to see whether this would be a good place to live. In the middle of the year he went to Tangier in Morocco, by way of Gibraltar. Here he appears to have stayed until the spring of 1886, perhaps as late as May. After this, or while he was in Tangier, he squeezed in his visit to Spain, before finally returning to England in June.

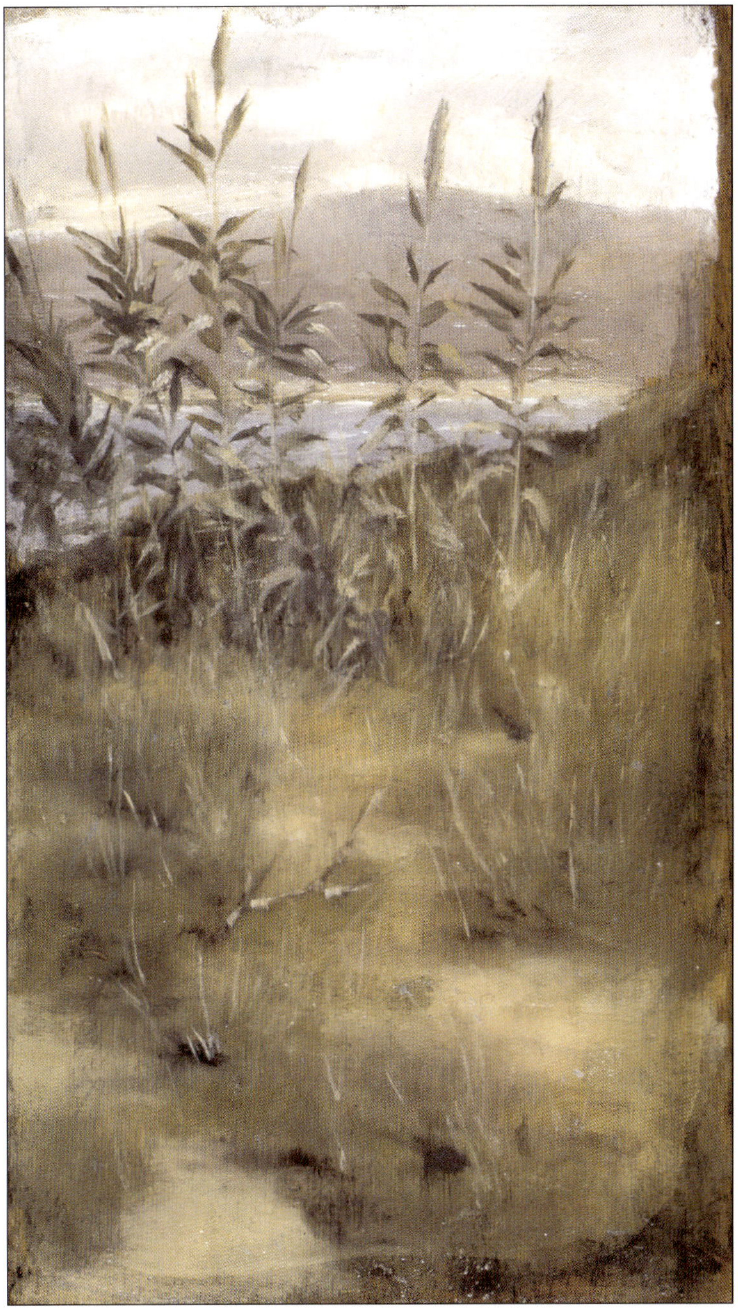

Plate 11 *Glimpse of the Bay, Tangiers*, 1885, oil, 9" x 5.25" (private collection).

In Tangier Garstin stayed with Ion Perdicaris, who was another larger than life character whom he had the good fortune to know, having become friends with him in Paris. Perdicaris was a Greek-American millionaire who, after fleeing South Carolina during the Civil War, travelled around Europe, and settled in Morocco. He called himself a Socialist, knew Karl Marx, was a friend of the Marxist Henry Mayers Hyndman, and championed the Moors against the great powers. Perdicaris had a fine house in Tangier, and occupied another high up in the hills during the summer. (From the latter he was taken prisoner by a brigand chief in 1904, and then ransomed by the Moroccan government, after gunboat diplomacy by Teddy Roosevelt.) Perdicaris cultivated young artists, and there is a photograph showing Garstin and no less than three other British artists – all in local costume – outside one of Perdicaris' houses. Garstin appears to have been a favourite because he figures, as Frank Weston, in a tedious novel that Perdicaris wrote.

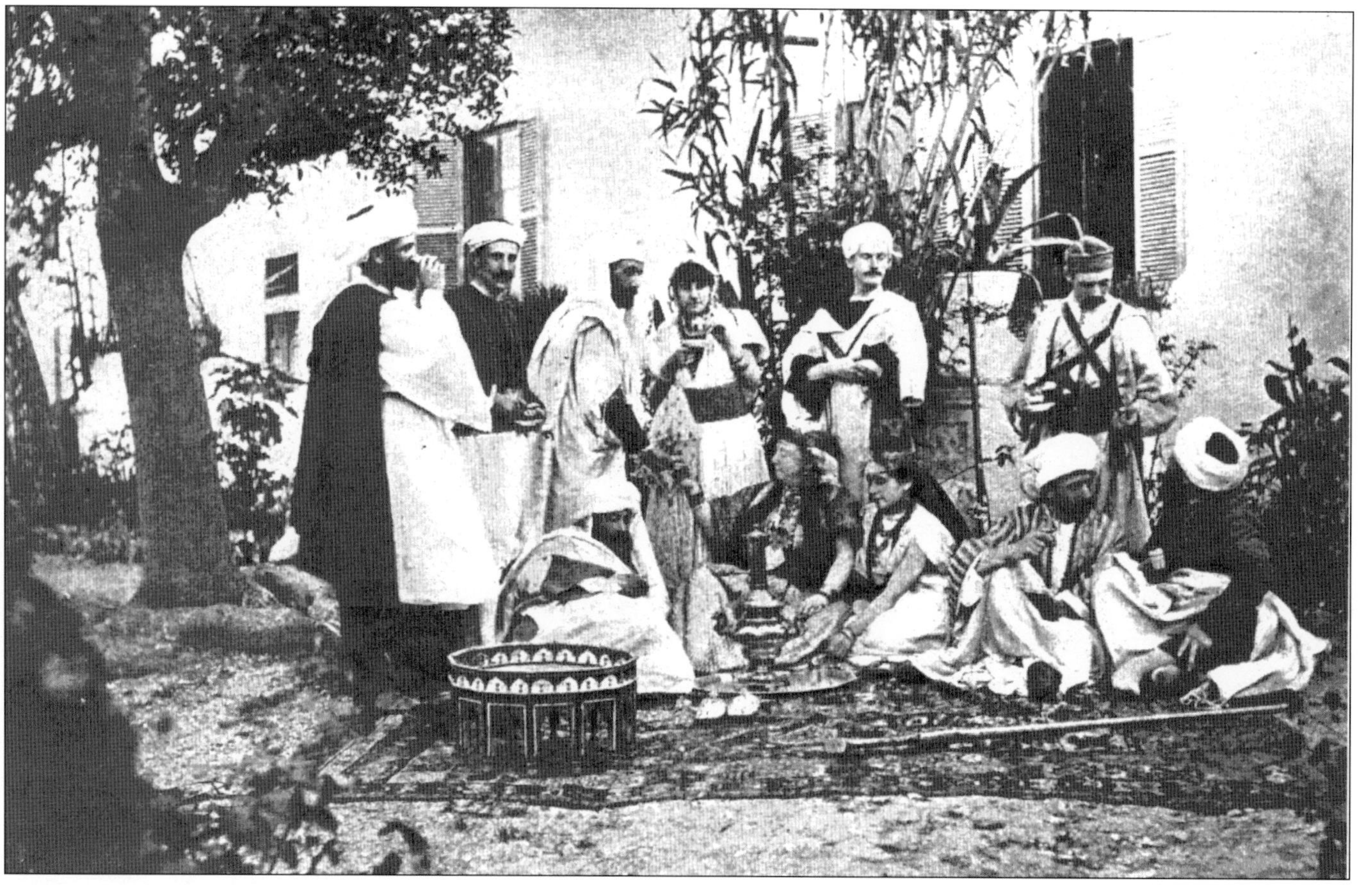

Ion Perdicaris, his wife and Norman Garstin (front row, second from the right) and other artists (Tom Faed, Talbot Kelly, J. Coutts Mitchie back row) at Tangiers.

How a Realist Saw Morocco

The countries of the Middle East and North Africa had by this time become highly popular among artists. Many, perhaps most, of those who went there to paint concentrated on the exotic and/or the erotic. Gérôme is a classic example, as shown by numerous pictures that show beautiful and vulnerable young girls in the nude such as *The Slave Market* and *Moorish Bath*. Garstin deliberately avoided subjects of this type. In his later article 'Tangier as a Sketching Ground' he observed that, when the commonplace painter goes to the East, 'he is apt to mistake the freshness of his surroundings for something fresh and striking in itself, forgetting that it is only fresh to him', and warned against 'the commonplace rendering of harems and bazaars in the gorgeous east of the world'.[30]

Garstin was nonetheless captivated by Morocco. It was to him a place of delight and beauty, which inspired him to paint. Probably in the late autumn of 1885 he wrote to Dochie that,

> It is simply paradise this place. The mere act of living is a pleasure. I was walking in an orange garden this morning … It was like the Garden of the Hesperides with golden fruit thickly clustered in the dark green foliage … I am going to paint this garden I think, but I have so many schemes on hand and the time is so short. I have made

> a rather elaborate sketch of the commission picture ... It represents a lot of Moors squatting about selling oranges, vegetables, etc ... I want to paint a wretched man crouching under the shadow of a leafless fig tree in a waste of sand. The idea touches me and I think I will try it rather big.[31]

This short passage embodies and exemplifies much of what Norman Garstin believed about art. Although he considered that its purpose was to create beauty, he disliked subjects where the beauty was contrived or too evident. An orange grove was a legitimate subject, but he was wary of any hint of excess. In his article he drew favourable attention to the absence, in Morocco, of 'those obtrusively beautiful creations of architecture that are so apt to distract a painter from his true mission of creating beauty out of simple material'.[32] What did fascinate him were those who followed age-old pursuits, or were simply doing nothing. This was why he wanted to paint Moors selling fruit and vegetables, and the crouching man. In a word, Garstin was a Realist, and not, like Gérôme, an academic painter.

The Moroccan and Spanish Pictures

Garstin painted at least 27 pictures while he was in Morocco and during his short trip to Spain. This does not include any of those that are described in the previous letter, because there is (apart from the sketch) no evidence that they were ever painted.

Some of the pictures that can be viewed are small tonal studies with dull hues. This is remarkable, given that Morocco is a land of bright light. In one of them, *On the Sands, Tangier*, Garstin may, as Professor Rezelman observes, be following Whistler's example and painting parallel bands of land, water and sky.[33] Moreover this and other pictures could be described as Whistlerian Symphonies in a restricted and muted range of colours. It is, however, difficult to work up much enthusiasm for most of these works. *Tangier Landscape*, and some of the other Moroccan pictures, are, I think, dull in every sense, but it should be noted that Patrick Heron takes a very different view.[34]

Two of Garstin's small Moroccan pictures, which did sell, are of much superior quality, namely *Israel in Morocco*, and *Glimpse of the Bay, Tangiers*. They are both pleasing harmonies of soft colours and the latter is reproduced in Plate 11. It has some of the mystery and atmosphere which, as we shall see, was to be one of Garstin's distinctive features. *Israel in Morocco* is a street scene with an old Jew in a skull cap. It has some nicely contrasting areas of shadow and brighter light.

In *Summer in Winter*, or *Alienis Mensibus Aestas* (Plate 10) Garstin did attempt to paint a scene in bright sunlight. He used pastel shades,

Let us pass under the archway by the mosque ... In a mysterious gloom of another chamber just beyond, I remember, there was wont to sit another ancient white bearded man, paled and almost transparent with age. He waited there for corpses! It was his business to wash and prepare them for the grave, and so he sat and awaited the doom of mortals. There are people who might not care to choose this for a calling; not lively enough forsooth, and yet there is much to be said for this blanched elder's occupation – it is certain beyond the calculations of an insurance office; it was more tranquil than that of a custodian of a gallery of old masters; he injured no man and importuned no man's custom. Perhaps the soul of him was nourished and uplifted in the grey gloom of his surroundings, when the dispossessed corpse of what was some wealthy man was brought to him for his offices. He was the chamberlain of the great Leveller, the groom-in-waiting upon Death; he saw that all, gentle and simple, who passed into that dim kingdom did so with befitting decency.

Norman Garstin, 'Tangier as a Sketching Ground' in *The Studio* (1897).

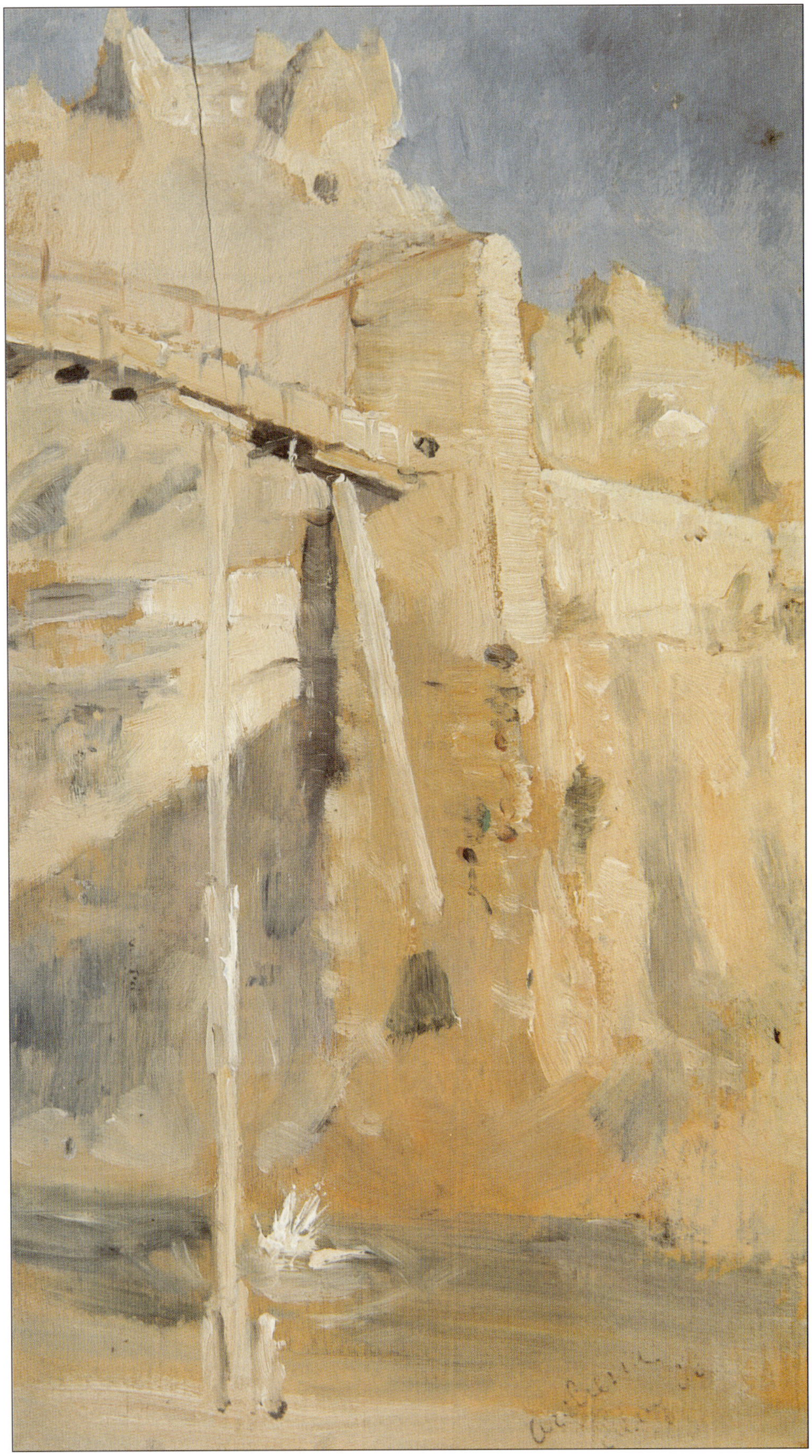

Plate 12 *Ravine and Bridge, Spain*, 1885, oil, 19.4" x 5.4" (Plymouth City Museum & Art Gallery).

but the attempt was not particularly pleasing: the yellow foreground and the blue sea are a slightly bilious combination. Nevertheless, this largish work has excellent features, and the tree with its tangle of branches, which cast shadows on each other, is extremely well done. As might be expected, there is nothing very exotic about the scene. To the right there is a young woman with red sandals and a turban-type headdress, but this must have been quite normal. A touch of sweetness is imparted by the flowers she is holding and by the goat, but the flowers are not emphasized, and her nearness to the goat shows the tranquillity of the scene. Garstin's small *Ravine and Bridge, Spain* (Plate 12) contains both sunlight and shadow. The colours, in contrast to those in the previous picture, are clean and clear. Although, after leaving Spain, Garstin does not appear to have painted many other pictures of this type, it shows that he was able to produce works containing bright and almost impressionistic colours.

The pictures that were painted in Spain and Morocco are varied and not always successful. Even the greatest artists have painted disappointing pictures. But it seems likely there is another reason why these pictures are so uneven: Garstin was experimenting both with colour and with style. Some of these experiments are of interest because of the way in which he was following in the footsteps of other artists, notably Whistler. However, what is perhaps more significant was the way in which he was successfully starting to paint small street scenes and pictures with atmosphere. These were fields that he was to cultivate for the rest of his life.

Garstin's Moroccan and Spanish pictures were exhibited in a number of places. These included Liverpool, where he showed *Tangier Sands Evening*, and Aberdeen where he exhibited *Alienis Mensibus Aesta*s, together with a number of small pictures. *In a Weary Land* was hung at the Academy in 1886. Because of its title and date this sounds like a Moroccan picture, and may have been the wretched man under the leafless fig tree that he mentioned in his letter. Finally, in 1887, he had a small show of Moroccan pictures at Goupil's, the prestigious gallery in New Bond Street. Three pictures were sold but they did not fetch very much, and three small pictures went for a derisory sum at Aberdeen. Many of the Moroccan and Spanish pictures were not disposed of until years later, or were never sold at all. These were ultimately presented to galleries after the death of his daughter Alethea Garstin. Some of these pictures may have been favourites, but many must have been leftovers, sketches and experiments. Hence the selection of pictures on which these generalizations are based may not be entirely representative.

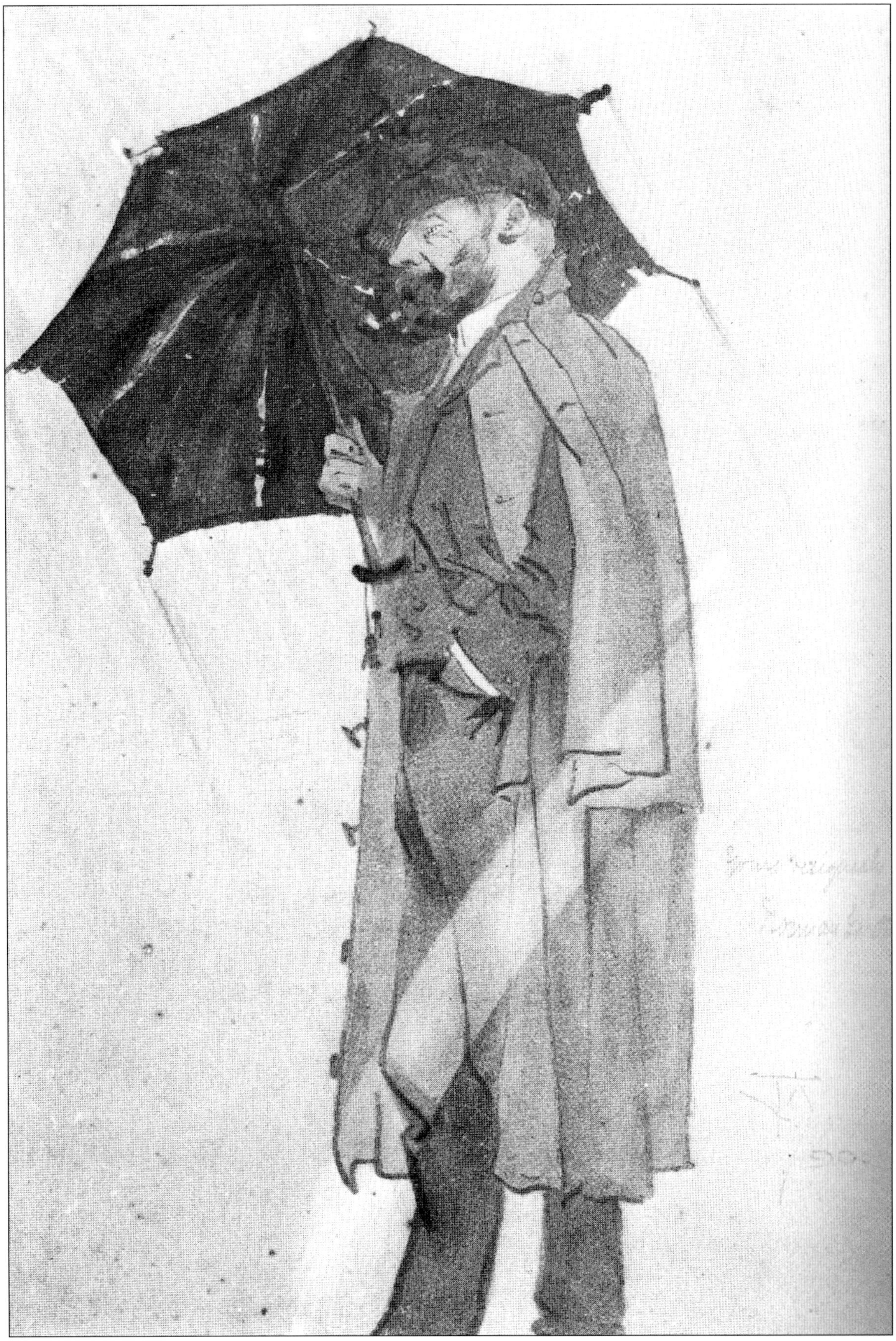

Fred Hall, *Caricature of Norman Garstin*, 1890 (Tate Gallery Archives).

Chapter 3

A Promising Start at Newlyn, 1886-89

The period from Garstin's marriage in mid-1886 until 1889 is short but of great significance. Norman and Dochie settled in Newlyn, where he became a prominent member of its colony of artists. Here Garstin had a substantial output and, even more important, he produced some of his greatest canvasses. However, his work only gained limited recognition, and his pictures either failed to sell, or did not fetch much. To make matter worse he lost his small private income, at a time when his family responsibilities were increasing.

Mount Vernon, where the Garstins lodged soon after arriving in Newlyn.

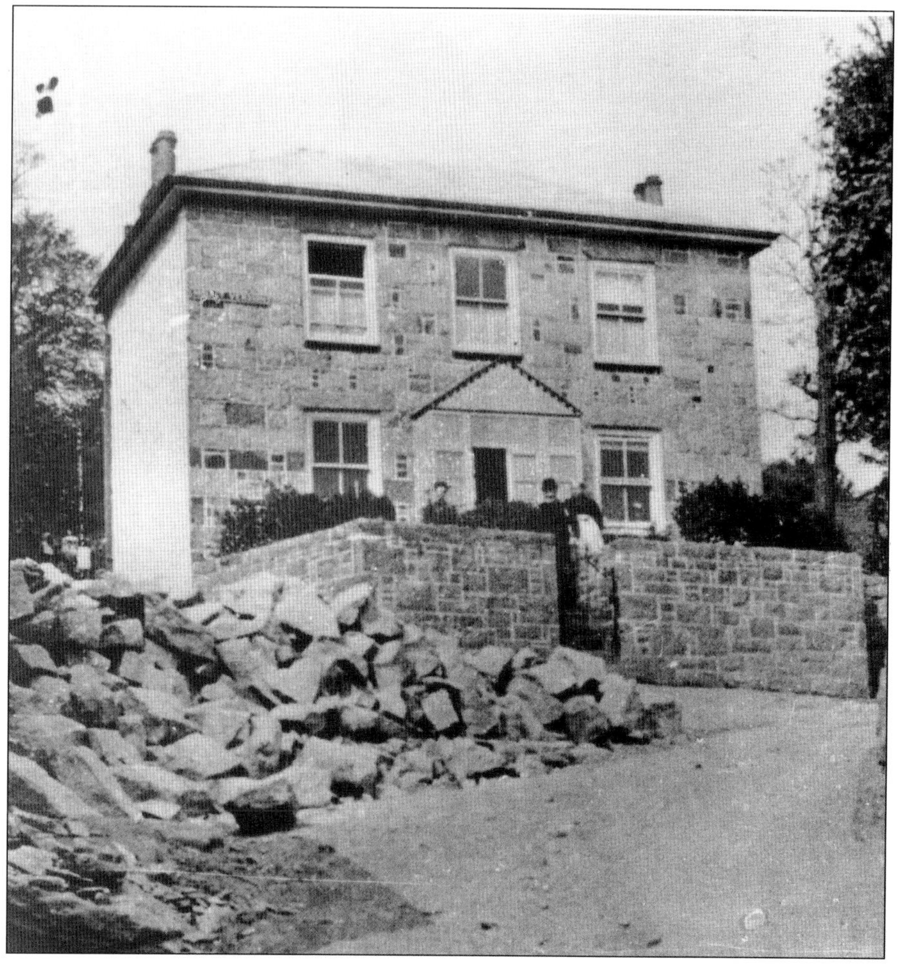

What Manner of Man – and Woman?

By early June 1886 Norman was back in England and re-united with Dochie; her diary for 9 June containing the terse but significant entry, 'Norman came at ten in the morning'.[1] They were married from the house of Dochie's sister Maria, in Hampstead parish church, on 14 July. After a fortnight's honeymoon near Polperro, they arrived at Newlyn, where they took lodgings. They were to live at Newlyn and its sister town, Penzance, for the rest of Garstin's life.

This is a convenient point, before considering the early Newlyn period, at which to pause and look more closely at

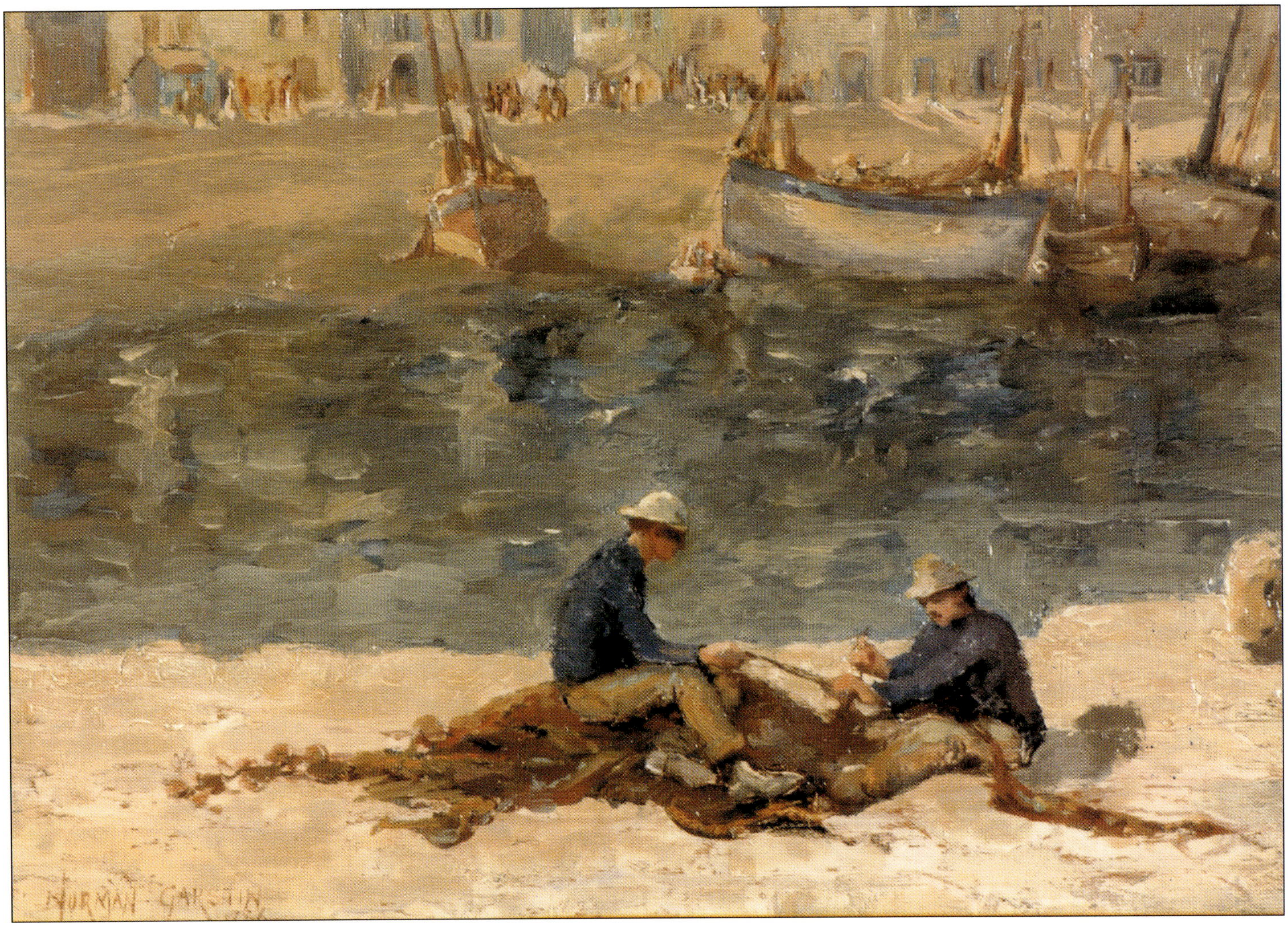

Plate 13 *A Fishing Village in Normandy*, 1886, oil, 10.75" x 15" (private collection).

Opposite:
Plate 14 *The Painter's Wife/A Portrait*, 1887, oil, 28" x 20" (National Gallery of Ireland where it is known as *The Artist's Wife*).

the man Dochie had married, and, more briefly, at the woman who had become Norman's wife.

At the age of 80, Stanhope Forbes clearly recalled the arrival in Newlyn of 'a certain distinguished looking Irishman whose delightful wit and fine artistic insight soon began to charm us'.[2] Garstin owed his distinguished appearance to being tall and slim, and to holding himself so erect that it was quipped, 'If Mr. Garstin held himself any straighter, he would fall over backwards'.[3] Red hair must have made him even more distinctive, especially as he had, since his days in South Africa, a bushy beard. His voice was high and drawling with an Irish accent, which, when he told Irish stories, would become a brogue. He possessed great physical stamina: he could walk and cycle for long distances; and, even in his early sixties, he was proficient on stilts. As Fryn Tennyson Jesse reported, when a young pupil begged him to give an exhibition of his stilt-walking powers, 'These proved to be truly wonderful, and I watched in respectful admiration as the painter descended a flight of steps, and hopped

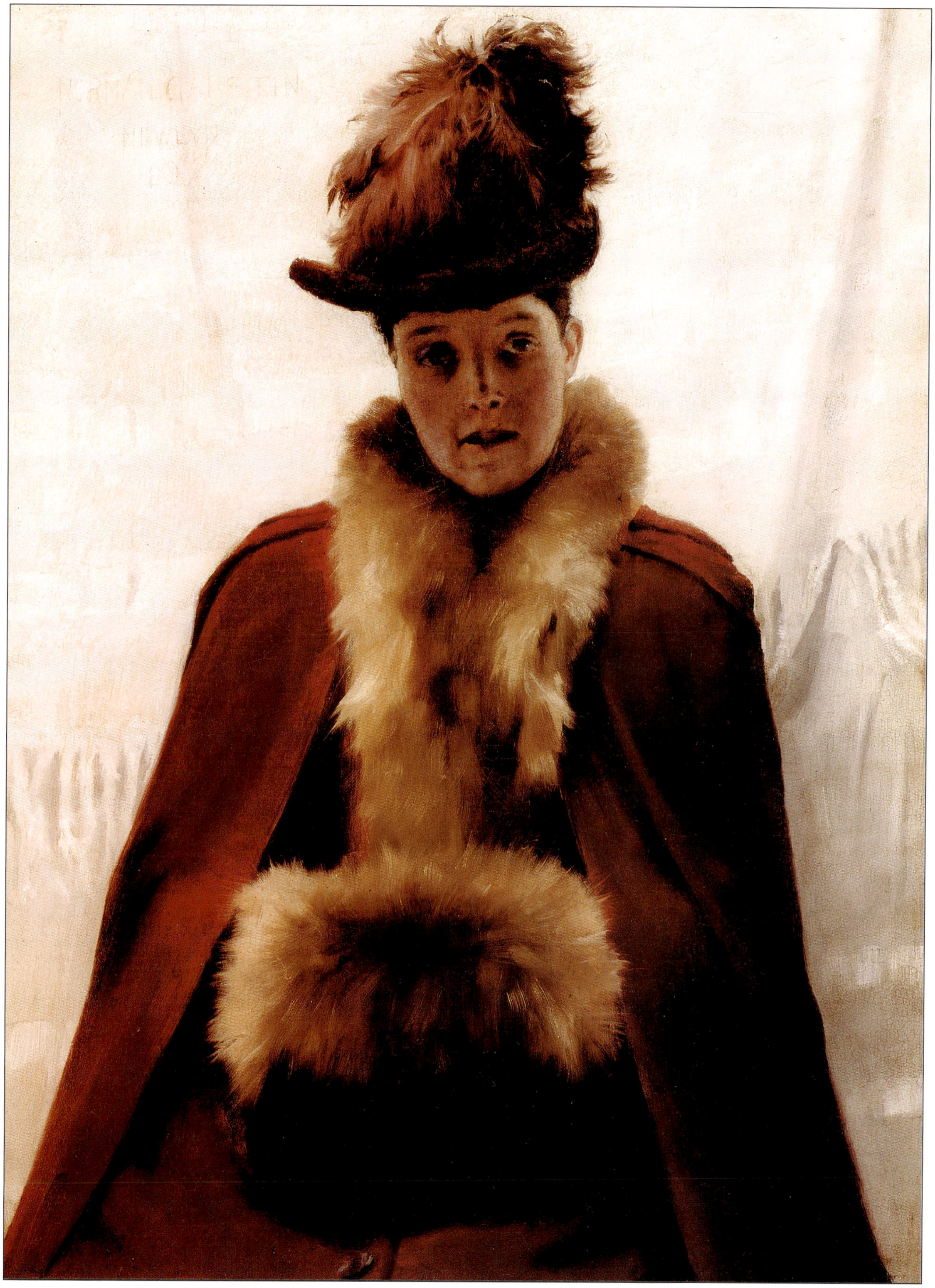

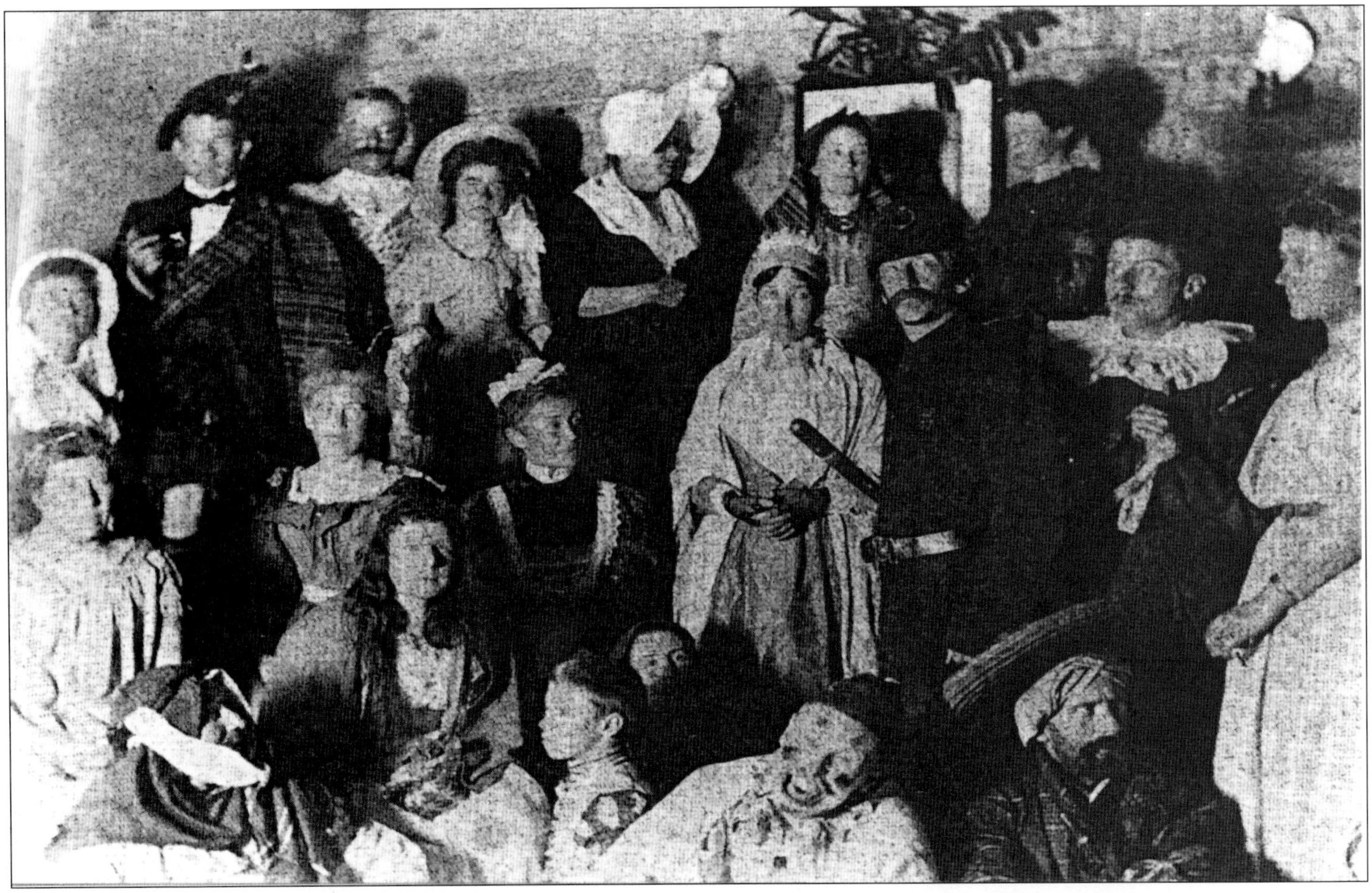

Newlyn Players *c.*1887. Garstin is in the front row at the right-hand end dressed as an Arab. Stanhope Forbes is standing in the centre dressed as a policeman and Dochie is next to him.

along on one stilt … '.[4] Despite occasional attacks of lumbago, he enjoyed good physical health.

Garstin was a man of parts. He was the most effective public speaker among the Newlyn artists, and a talented actor. He became a member of the theatrical group, the Newlyn Society of Artists, which was founded soon after his arrival, and his performances received high praise. The local paper commented on one performance that 'his cool, nonchalant manner, which carries him from start to finish, is simply delightful'.[5] Garstin was a great raconteur and an entertaining conversationalist, both of an informal type and at dinner parties, which he sometimes dominated. He had the gift of repartee. In one farce he was supposed to hide in a shower and emerge wet through. Garstin said that a few drops would suffice, to which it was objected that this would ruin the humour. 'I am sorry,' said Garstin, 'but I prefer a dryer style of humour!' [6] When in his latter years Garstin met Bernard Shaw, it was the former who displayed a Shavian wit.

> Norman Garstin [reported Bernard Walke] opened the conversation in his most courteous manner: 'I am most delighted to meet you, Mr.

> Shaw, for we have several things in common.' 'And what may they be?' said Bernard Shaw, resting a hand on Norman's shoulder and looking quizzically into his face. 'I am an Irishman, Mr. Shaw,' Norman replied, stepping back with both hands clasping the lapels of his coat, 'and I too am an admirer of Bernard Shaw.' [7]

Up went Shaw's beard, and with head back he roared with laughter.

But what, above all, was so notable was Garstin's personality: kind, modest and self-critical. He was kind to Fryn when, as a young art student who had come to interview him, she was 47 minutes late for lunch; and he often, although this was much later, helped the maid to make his bed; he was forever going to the station to meet those who were arriving by train; and he wrote to other artists complimenting them on the success which he never enjoyed. Garstin's generosity to Stanhope Forbes has already been mentioned, and, in his notices on local artists in *The Studio*, Garstin commended paintings that cannot have been much to his taste. On the other hand, he rarely mentioned his own pictures. He was conscious of his own possible imperfections, as shown by a letter to Dochie just before his marriage;

> I wish and hope earnestly to be a good husband and let as little sorrow in upon your life as may be. But, even with all the resolve strong in my heart, I foresee that I shall not be able to shield you, my darling, from the one person who can hurt you most, myself. I am so irritable and then a word darts out, and wounds the one of all others one should shelter.

He also convicted himself of self-indulgence.[8]

Because Garstin was so conscious of his faults, and so determined to be a good husband, he went to some lengths to make his wife happy. 'He confessed to me the other day', Stanhope Forbes reported in 1886, 'that he is dragged to church every Sunday. Poor woman if she knew the effect of this on her husband I do not think she would do it. For he is far from a religious man, has very advanced views, and is of a nervous and irritable temperament ... How he does hate it. I don't think he will continue to go much longer'.[9] Forbes was wrong: Garstin continued to accompany Dochie to church until the First World War.

Dochie was intelligent, energetic, practical, level-headed, and extremely public spirited; but she was not artistic or introspective. She was well educated by the standards of the time, having attended five courses of Cambridge extension lectures at Bedford. The subjects ranged from English literature to geology, and she passed the exams for both with merit or distinction. 'She is a nice woman,' observed

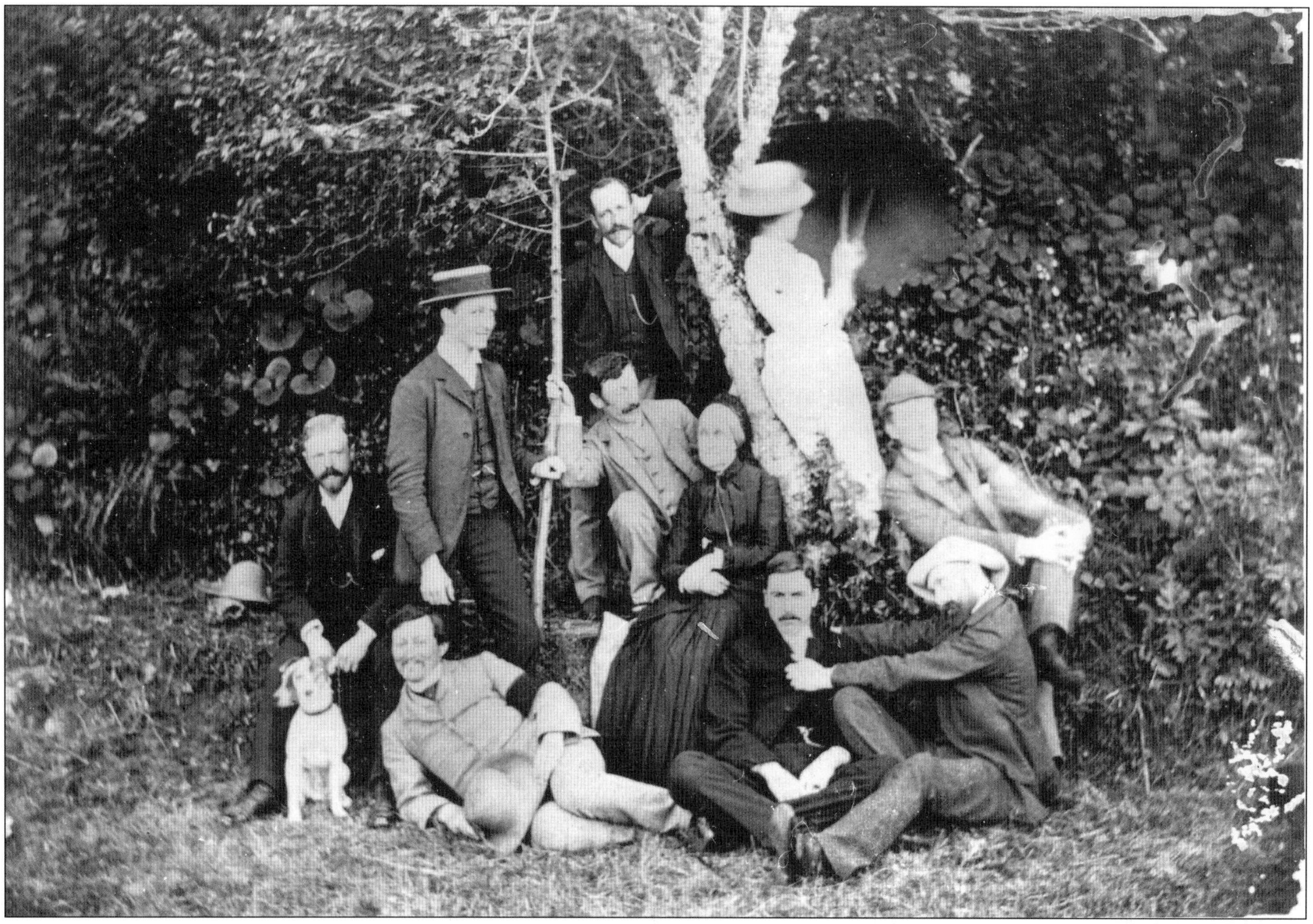

Norman Garstin (front row right) in playful mood with other Newlyn artists. Stanhope Forbes is clasping the tree, Elizabeth Armstrong, Forbes' future wife, is leaning against the big tree and her mother is next to Forbes.

one of Garstin's students, the painter Frances Hodgkins, 'very practical and clever and manages her husbands business for him. She knows nothing at all about painting and never knows her husband's sketches from one of ours'.[10] Although this was written in the early 1900s, when the Garstins had started to take painting parties abroad, Dochie had long been managing their slender resources efficiently. Her good works had a modest beginning when she became secretary of the Newlyn Society of Artists; they continued with her helping, while pregnant, to nurse the dying wife of another artist; and they had their full flowering with help at the local workhouse, and for the Penzance branch of the Charity Organisation Society. She joined its committee in 1888 and, by 1913, was the secretary.

'A very stunning couple' was Forbes' verdict on the Garstins not long after they had arrived at Newlyn.[11] He, and much later Frances Hodgkins, commented on their devotion to each other.

The Newlyn Colony and its Attractions

As Garstin was an Irishman, and never ceased to regard himself as one, it might have been expected that the newly married couple

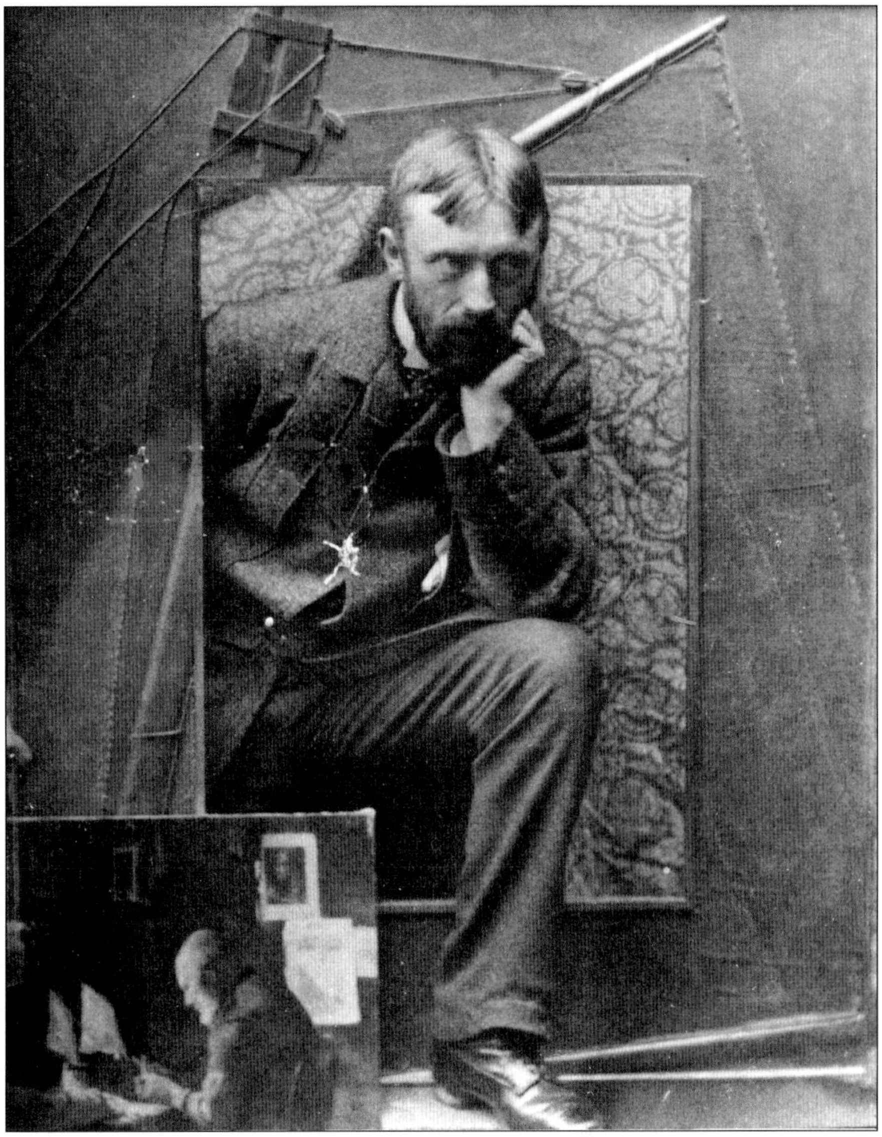

Norman Garstin stepping through a picture frame that he designed, 1886.

would have lived in Ireland. Yet it seems doubtful whether Ireland was given more than a passing thought. That unhappy island was passing through one of its most difficult periods: political assassination, agrarian outrage, boycotts and Coercion Acts were daily news. What was perhaps worse, and more fundamental, the Protestant minority in the south, having ceased to be a garrison, had become a ghetto and a shrinking one at that. John Frend and Ada had already left for Canada, and Elizabeth followed.

Nor was the decision to live in Newlyn difficult to understand. The withdrawal of artists from the urban scene was common at this time. This was the era in which colonies of artists formed at numerous withdrawn spots in Britain, and in other countries from Russia to the United States. Newlyn contained a growing colony of artists. Many of them were Garstin's former colleagues in Antwerp (Frank Bramley, Fred Hall, Fred Millard, Leghe Suthers, and Ralph

Todd). Moreover he appears to have become acquainted with Stanhope Forbes during his preliminary visit to Newlyn. Garstin and the Newlyn artists had a common hostility to academic art, and they shared a commitment to *plein air* painting and Realism. Cornwall seemed an ideal spot in which to paint, combining as it did superb coastal scenery, sheltered inland valleys, and a fishing community that appeared more in tune with nature than were townsfolk. Newlyn also had the great practical advantage that the cost of living was low.

If the Newlyn artists had been a quarrelsome lot, the Garstins might not have stayed. They were, however, a remarkably harmonious group. There was mutual support at times of illness, and a variety of group activities, which ranged from acting to entertaining. The Garstins shared in these to the full, with the exception of the artists' cricket team, Garstin having no interest in the game. The Newlyn artists had a common hostility to the Royal Academy. Garstin criticised the Academy for being 'so constituted as to preclude nearly all growth except perhaps the inalienable right of each member to

Plate 15 *In the Cottage by the Sea*, 1887, oil, 14" x 18" (Penlee House Gallery, Penzance).

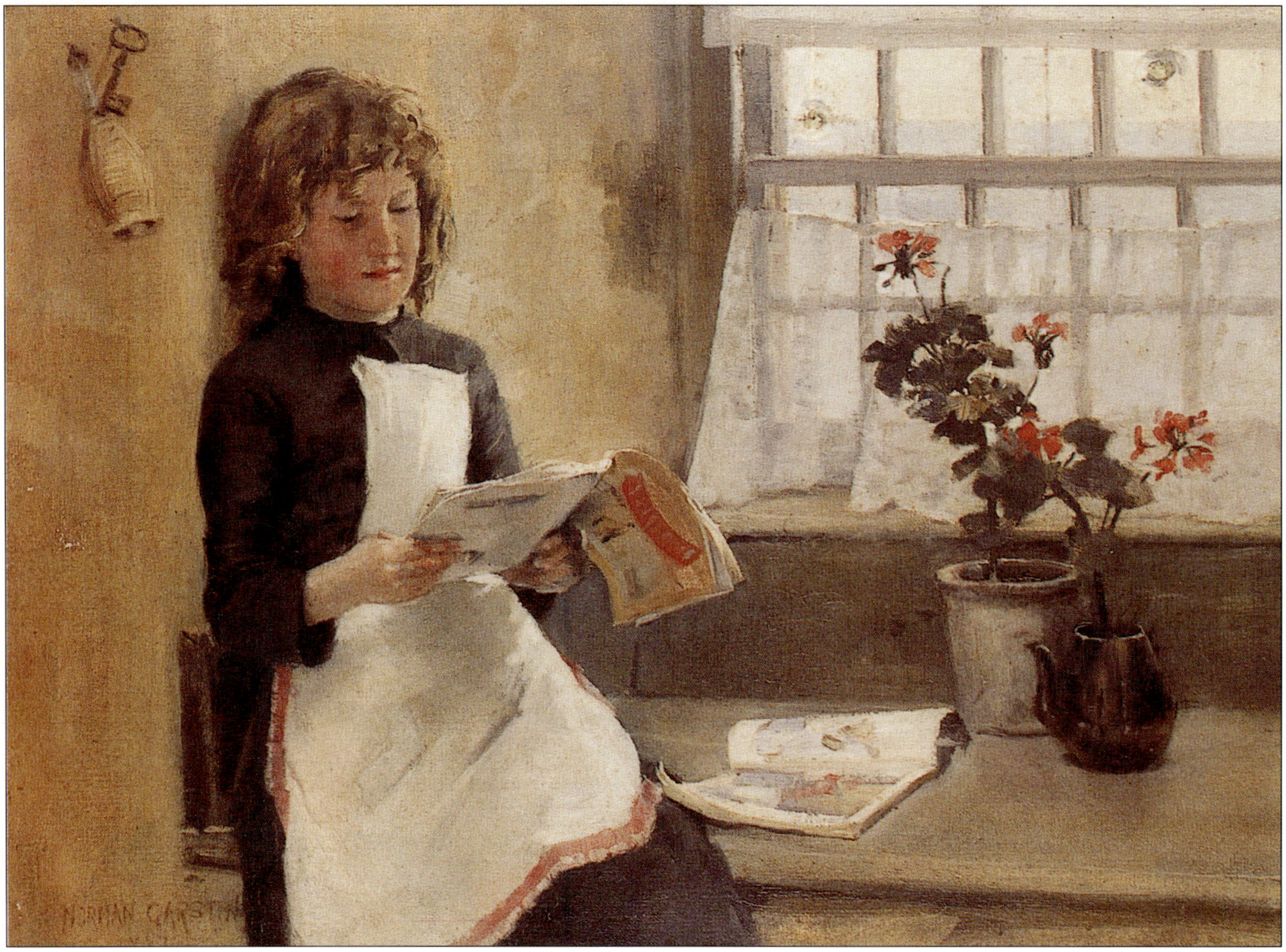

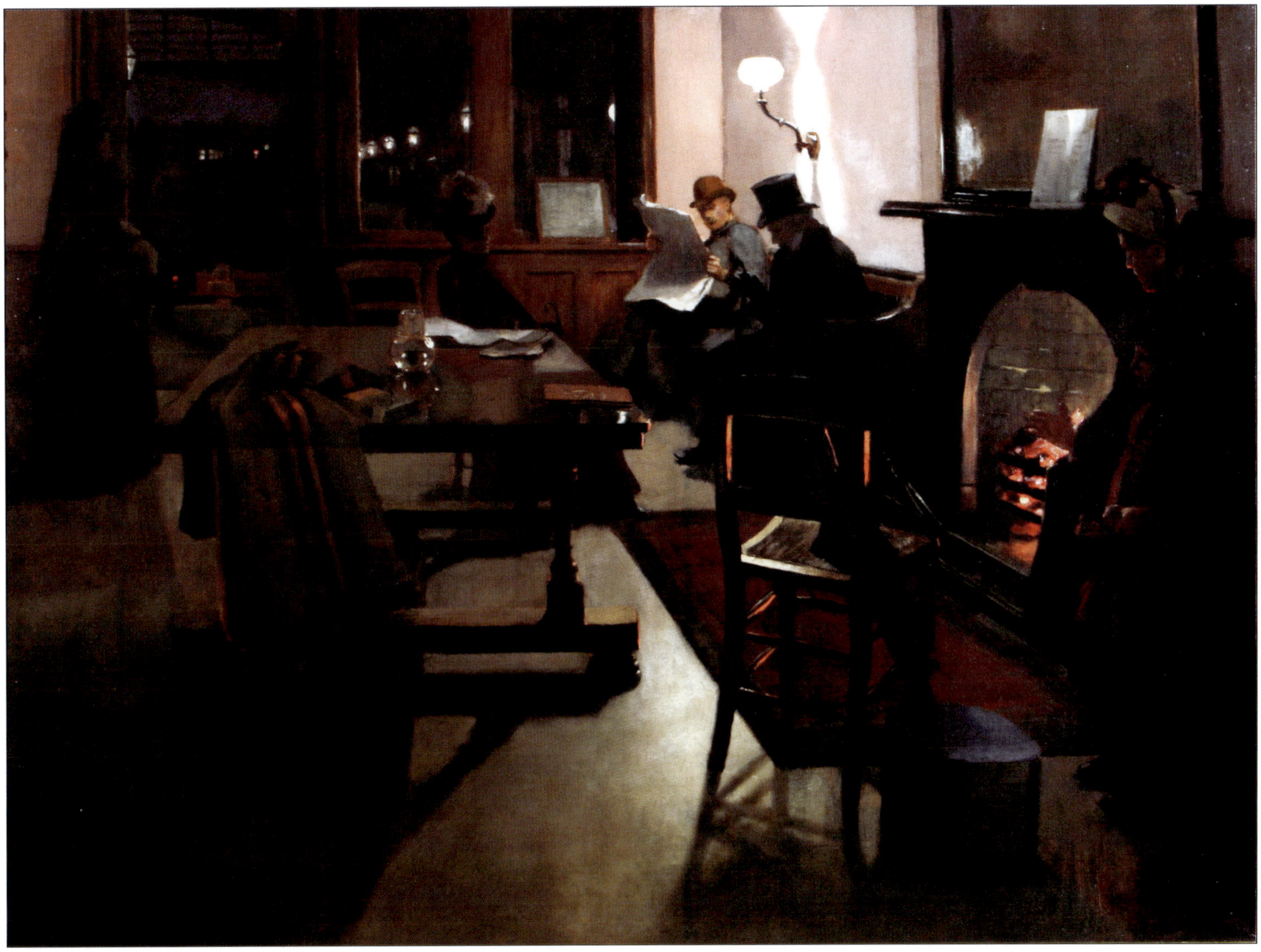

Plate 16 *Overdue* [at Penzance Station], 1889, oil, 26.5" x 35.5" (private collection). The waiting room no longer exists, though its whereabouts can be identified.

grow old ... And so, by sheer dint of longevity, he wields an extravagant power'.[12] Britain should have an annual national exhibition, to be selected by a jury elected by the artists themselves; and there should be a Royal Commission to consider the proposal and examine the RA. At that time, opposition to the Academy was widespread among younger artists who had been trained in France, and this led, in 1886, to the formation of the New English Art Club. Stanhope Forbes and Thomas Gotch, who were involved from the very beginning, brought in Garstin and other Newlyn artists. In November there was a meeting of artists at Forbes' studio, and Garstin drafted a letter to the press. He joined the Club in 1887 and exhibited there, but does not appeared to have played any other part.

Garstin's Distinctive Subject Matter

Garstin's early years at Newlyn were some of the most productive of his working life. During the three years from 1887 to 1889 he

Values prior to the First World War can roughly be converted to 2004 prices by multiplying by 60. Hence an expenditure, or receipt, of £25 in, say, 1900 would be equivalent to about £1,500 after allowing for inflation. Alternatively, allowance can be made for the rise in incomes, due to both inflation and increasing affluence, by multiplying values by around 300. Hence, an expenditure, or receipt, of £25 in, say, 1900 would represent about £7,500 in 2004, after allowing both for inflation and the growth in real incomes.

An Iron Master, 1888, oil, 44" x 35" (whereabouts unknown; from the *Art Journal*, 1889).

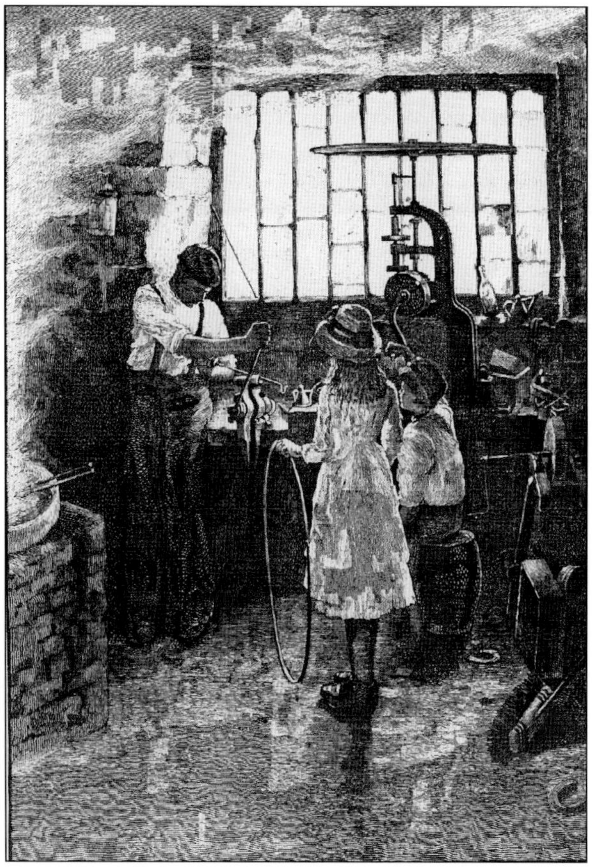

exhibited at least eighteen major works for the first time, or in a few cases, where no place of exhibition is known, *painted* the canvas. (To comply with my definition of a major - i.e. large - work, a picture must be an oil; have at least one side of 20 inches or more; or, what comes to much the same thing, have been priced at £25 or more at its first place of sale.) Garstin also exhibited (or painted) thirteen other works, including one or two where it is impossible to tell whether they are large or small. By the standards of, say, the Impressionists this was a small output. Impressionist pictures could be painted quickly because of their lack of finish and the use of unmixed colours. When a like-with-like comparison is made, Garstin's output appears far more impressive. Stanhope Forbes, who was a dedicated worker, does not, for instance, appears to have been any more productive.

Given that he had joined the Newlyn group, the type of work Garstin now produced might seem predictable. One would expect pictures of everyday life, or genre paintings, such as the other prominent Newlyn artists (Stanhope Forbes, Frank Bramley, Walter Langley and Thomas Gotch) produced, and that he would largely devote himself to painting traditional lifestyles; and, in particular, members of the fishing community. On the other hand, he would seldom paint the modern urban environment, industrial workers, or the middle and upper classes. This was the era in which British painters, unlike their French contemporaries and earlier British artists such as Frith, turned their back on modern life; and these were the years in which the new generation of foreign trained artists devoted themselves to painting peasants, or rather those who, in this country, approximated most closely. Obviously there were exceptions, such as Sickert, but the exception merely tests the rule.

The likelihood that Garstin would conform was all the greater because of his eloquent statement of the aims of the young artists of the day, which were to depict

> not men and women with all their edges smoothed off and bearing a strong family likeness to images carved in Athens 2000 years ago but the men and women of our own day ... ; the poor as well as the rich, indeed the poor even more than the rich, for their battle of life is generally sterner. They live nearer to nature ... It is this oneness with nature, who ... is a great artist, that draws the painter away from the large towns and the artificial life of the rich to study and paint the simple daily round of the poor man's work and pastimes. The fisherman may be a dull man, his mind hopelessly bounded by the price of herrings or pilchards, but his warfare with the great simple powers of nature fills your imagination ... and lifts him up as an heroic figure far above the man who buys his fish or those whose ways lie amongst the complex conditions of what we consider the

more exalted states of life. So too with the husbandman and the shepherd ... We seek to represent not only the man but as it were his very atmosphere ... and it is in making this atmosphere as much part of the picture as the mere actualities that our chief claim to an original view of nature lies.[13]

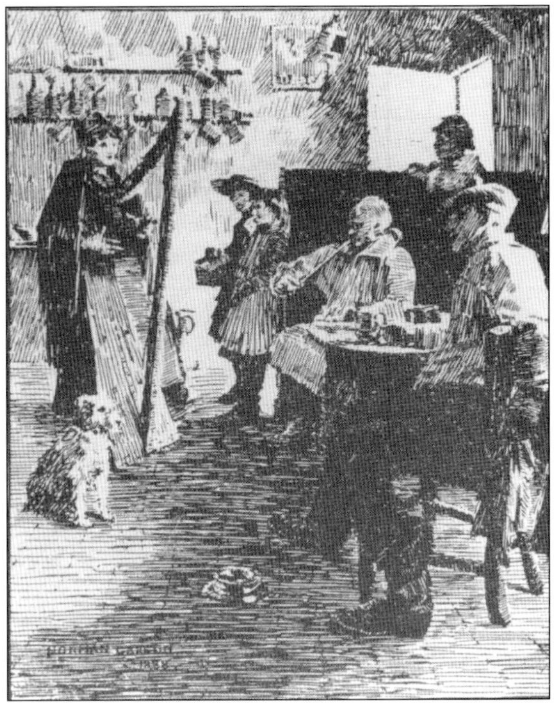

Progress and Poverty, 1888, oil, 44" x 35" (from *Academy Notes*, 1888).

An examination of Garstin's work, however, does not wholly bear out one's expectations about his subject matter. In particular, he does not, during his early years at Newlyn, appear to have painted any pictures of fishermen or their families. Even if we go forward, the one possible exception is *What's News?* (1892), which shows a sailor reading that product of modern civilization, a newspaper. Garstin gave no explanation as to why he painted so few pictures of fisherfolk. Probably, like his friend Bourdillon, he felt that there were already too many local artists producing pictures of this type. Moreover, he was always an individualist.

Garstin did, however, paint a number of pictures which, although they do not include members of the fishing community, depict those engaged in traditional pursuits or belonging to the lower class. Nevertheless only two of these are confined to those engaged in such activities or wearing traditional costume. *Farmer and his Daughter* (1889) shows a girl and an old gaitered husbandman standing outside a barn, and the other picture is of a Breton peasant girl (1887). The latter together with *A Fishing Village in Normandy*, which is dated 1886, indicate that Garstin must have visited France during this period. It is, as can be seen from Plate 13, an unusually bright and impressionistic picture.

Other canvases which depict those from the lower classes are not typical Newlyn pictures. In *Progress and Poverty* (1888), Garstin shows what appears from a sketch to be a middle class lady. She is playing a harp in a public house, with an audience consisting of three yokels and two children. *An Iron Master* (1888) shows a small workshop, with an artisan ironworker, watched by two children. Although this is not a modern factory, Alice Meynell observed, in an early and perceptive article on the Newlyn School, that Garstin 'had some courage in bringing the details of machinery and iron within the glance of Art'. However, as Meynell observed, this picture does employ 'that favourite Newlyn effect of looking against the light, an effect producing in small the characteristic aspect of Penzance and all south-facing places, where turning naturally towards the sea, one turns also towards the sun, and catches the numberless nameless shadows that make the light apparent'.[14] Another picture painted against the light is *In the Cottage by the Sea* (Plate 15).

Finally, *Temptation* (1888), displayed in Plate 2, shows a seamstress with a sewing machine, which was then a fairly recent innovation.

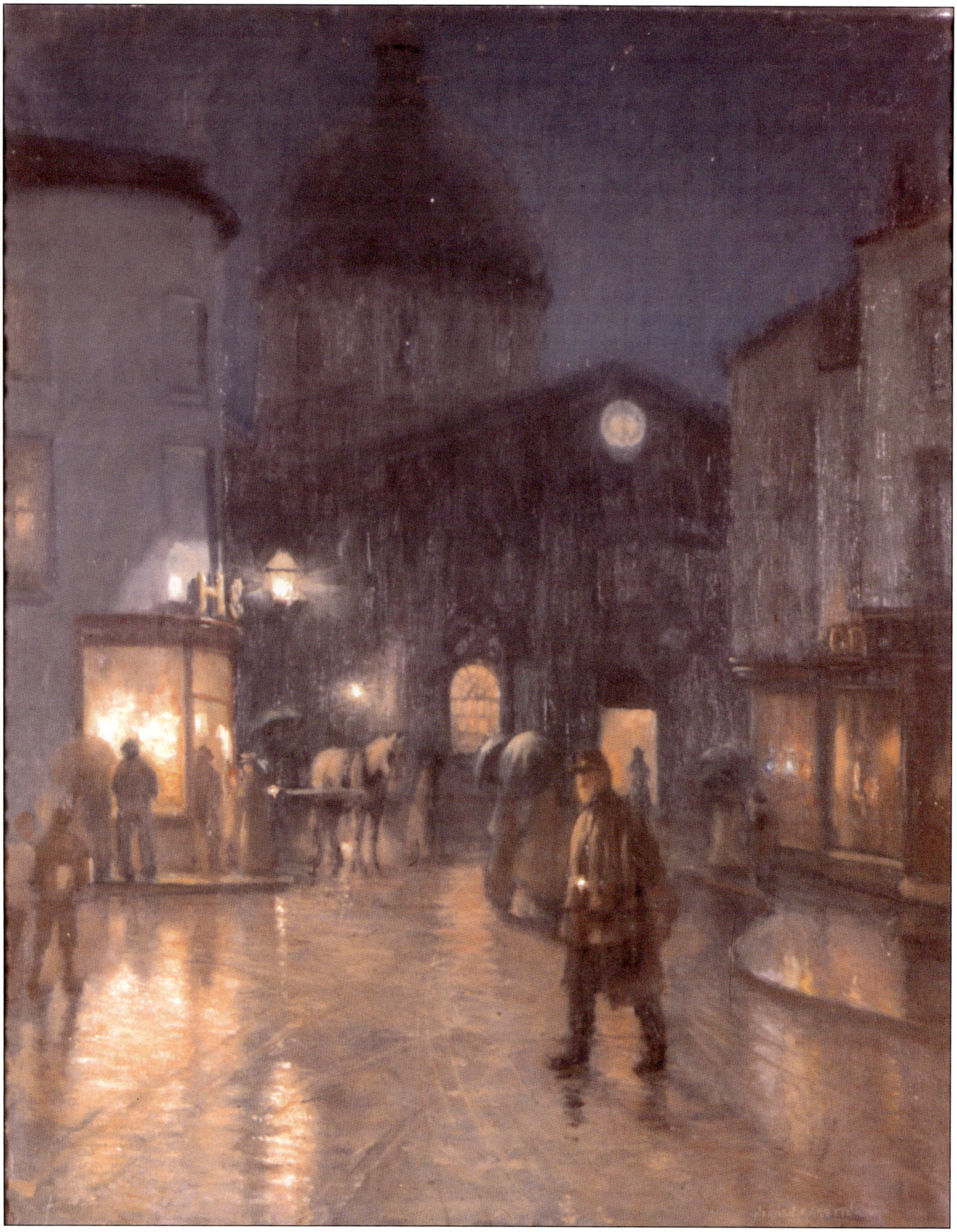

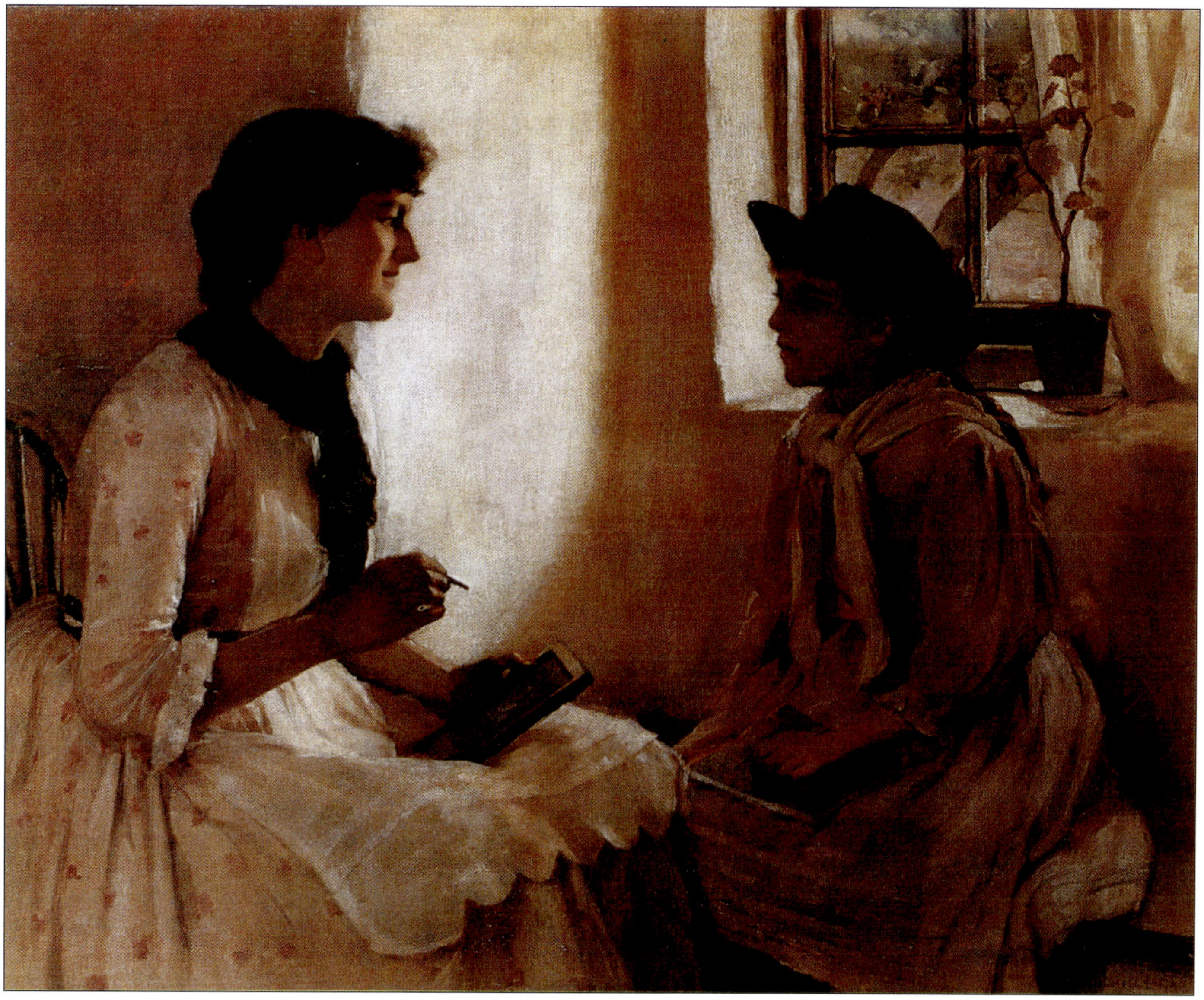

Nevertheless this was in some ways the most typical Newlyn picture that Garstin painted because its beauty and appeal are of a more obvious nature than in his other works. The young woman is very pretty, she is sad looking and the colouring is strikingly harmonious. Yet the picture is not without its subtleties: the woman's sadness is, for instance, brought out by the flatness of her black dress and her apparent deflation.

Three Key Works

Among the eighteen major works of Garstin's early Newlyn period, there are at least three that are outstanding, not merely by the standards of Newlyn, but by those of the greatest artists of the time. One of these was his portrait, *The Painter's Wife* (1887), which is shown in Plate 14. This has a sophisticated colour scheme, including the distinctive deep brown-red of Dochie's cape and what Patrick

Opposite:
Plate 17 *A Steady Drizzle*, 1889, oil, 35.5" x 27.5" (Royal Institution of Cornwall, Truro).

Plate 18 *Two Heads are Better than One*, 1889, oil, 16.5" x 19" (private collection, auctioned as *The Morning Lesson*).

Heron describes as 'the miraculous luminosity of its creamy ground'.[15] This is a shawl, which has with its tassels, folds and banding been made a feature of the picture. It contributes to the picture's originality, with the sitter being viewed against the light, and her face being the darkest part. It is a very human picture: Dochie's lips are slightly parted, as if she is about to speak. The muff with its fur edging is, as Heron observes, 'a miracle of illusionistic figuration'. The use of paint displays that care and economy which was so characteristic of Garstin's pictures of this period. It is, Heron concludes, 'of the highest distinction amongst the portraits of its day', which is a large claim, but one from which it is difficult to dissent.

The Rain it Raineth Every Day and, what is very much a companion picture, *Overdue* (both 1889) appear in Plates 4 and 16. They are Realism *par excellence*. So much so that one almost begins to fancy that Garstin, having read Professor Nochlin on the subject, has decided to provide an ostensive definition of Realism. What, in *The Rain it Raineth*, could be more humdrum than a promenade on a wet day? The picture has not one iota of romance or drama. True, there is a wave breaking over the front, but this does not show the power of nature; the spray is not upstanding, but a spent force. Nobody could imagine that the sea, however long it may assault the promenade, will ever inflict the slightest damage on such a massive structure. The rain may be depressing the spirits of the walkers, but they are well protected with umbrellas and a cape. Above all, urban development has triumphed, and a hotel and houses have been constructed along the margin of the unmighty ocean. The Penzance waiting room, in *Overdue*, may appear more romantic, but this is merely nostalgia. To a contemporary, a group of passengers, mostly without occupation and tired of waiting, would have seemed commonplace.

These pictures are excellent examples of Realism *sensu stricto*, which is Naturalism. They are composed of half tones and harmonious muted colours. Nevertheless there is an interesting contrast between the pale green of the sea, the varying tints of the promenade, and the red-brown of the hotel. In *Overdue* there is also the bright red of the coals, and this highlight is all the more striking because, as in the work of Verstraete, most of the picture is so dark. In both pictures the paint has been applied flatly, 'comme une porte', and with a compelling illusory effect. The wet promenade is an impressive piece of painting, which invites comparison with the wet pavement in Caillebotte's *Paris Street; Rainy Day* (1877). Garstin may have seen pictures by Caillebotte at the Seventh Impressionist Exhibition of 1882, though not this particular work. In the waiting room the contrasting reflections of the fire and of the gas light on the empty chair, and the table, are exquisitely observed. The Newlyn painters were fond of painting pictures in which there were dual sources of light, although this work is distinctive in that both are artificial. As in other paintings by Garstin, the newspaper is convincingly done. The only slipshod touch is the left hand edge of the table, and possibly the travelling rug on the table, where the top, which is rolled forward, seems odd. However, it may have looked like this: reality can sometimes appear unrealistic.

The Rain it Raineth and *Overdue* are masterpieces of Naturalism, but they are more than that. What is so exciting about the former, and to a lesser extent the latter, is the composition of the picture, and the spacing of the figures. In *The Rain it Raineth* the buildings are restricted to the top third of the picture, and the figures in the bottom section are few in number and relatively small in size. Most of the promenade is just empty space. This does not mean that the figures are unimportant; they are crucial. They serve, together with the rain, to emphasise the emptiness and dismal nature of the scene. It is a picture with great atmosphere, but of a disconcerting, and even slightly sinister, type. Caillebotte's picture has a very different feel partly because the principal woman is smiling, but mainly because the surrounding buildings enclose the space in which the figures move. So they do in *A Steady Drizzle* (1889), another Garstin picture of wet pavement, which as Plate 17 indicates is, in consequence, less bleak than *The Rain it Raineth*.

The spacing of, and relationship between, the figures in *The Rain it Raineth* gives the picture a sophisticated asymmetrical balance. This may well owe something to Whistler, and it certainly owes much to Garstin's study of Japanese art. The Japanese concept of composition had, he argued, 'largely helped to form our present feeling in that direction; a certain delicate balance taking the place of our western idea of symmetry in their arrangement of subject. This is vastly more advanced and subtle as an artistic principle'.[16] When Heron compares the way in which Garstin and Whistler control their empty space, he finds the latter inferior. This may be unfair to Whistler, but he is surely right when he compares Garstin with Stanhope Forbes:

> Forbes I would regard as academic by comparison: a sort of photo-realist of the time: indeed the sort of accuracy of representation we find in him suggests at every turn a photographer's obsession rather than a painterly interest. The outlines of figures [and here Heron must be thinking of *A Fish Sale*] define *inwards*; and they present a silhouetted entity of over-solid density, unrelated to the spaces separating each from each. In Garstin, the *space between* the objects represented is already itself *a shape* of equal pictorial value to that of each object itself ... this distinction alone places Garstin above the academic or the second-rate.[17]

Because space has value in Garstin's picture there is a subtle balance between the sea side, which contains only the receding woman with her dogs, and the road side which is more crowded. Whistler was by no means the only contemporary to use space in a daring manner, as pictures by Degas, Tissot, Sargent and Chase show. Throughout his life Garstin did not hesitate to leave large sections of his canvas empty, or almost empty, as Plate 1 indicates, but he was never again to use space with such telling effect.

A Travers du Cadre *(or through the frame)*

There are other reasons why *The Rain it Raineth* and *Overdue* are interesting, and, this time, it is the latter which is the main focus. The waiting room contains six people, but they are not a group. Only the nursemaid and the child are in any way related, and they are not interacting. Not one of the six is even looking at any of the others. One of the men on the bench is absorbed in his paper, the woman by the door is looking onto the platform, and the other four are self absorbed and/or staring into space. This is a study of isolation, of being together yet alone, of the modern urban phenomenon of being lonely in a crowd. What is even more exciting, *Overdue*, and to a lesser extent *The Rain it Raineth*, are atmospheric pictures. If they are looked at for any length of time, one feels slightly hypnotised and drawn into, and absorbed by, the picture. The illusion is created that it might even be possible to step through the frame and into the alternative world beyond. Denis Diderot, the great French Encyclopaedist and pioneering art critic, recognised this effect, which he described as, 'the strongest magic of art'.[18] As no standard term exists, I shall, as a reminder of the concept's French origin, describe the effect as *à travers du cadre*, or *à travers* for short.

Although an *à travers* effect may seem magical, there is, of course, no magic here, save that of the artist and his skill. It is a conjuring trick in the field of art, and like all such tricks can be explained. One necessary characteristic is that a picture should produce a feeling of depth. The viewer's eye must, by the use of perspective or some other technique, be led up and into the picture. Nobody could conceivably manage to enter a world without a third dimension, and there obviously needs to be a strong pulling effect. Second, it also seems to help if the view is bounded both on the sides and in front, either by buildings or by trees. The enclosed space enhances the impression that there is another world inside the picture. There has to be something to detain the eye and prevent it from travelling too far up the work, and, as it were, passing through the picture. Alternatively, there must be some clear point of focus. Third, the work has to appear to be an objective representation of the real world. If, for example, objects have the wrong colours, the illusion of reality will be destroyed. Fourth, any person or creature that is depicted must not appear to be looking out of the picture and aware of the audience but must, on the contrary, be totally self absorbed or preoccupied by whatever is happening. If this requirement, and it is one that was stressed by Diderot, is violated the illusion of an alternative world is destroyed.[19] Fifth, the picture must not be too bright. Bright sunlight is incompatible with magic: there has to be a degree of mystery, as Diderot long ago recognised. Finally, the picture should be fairly tranquil. Not only is action difficult to depict with any degree of realism, but it too is the enemy of mystery. Well known pictures that satisfy these conditions, and produce powerful *à travers* effects, are *The Fighting Teméraire* by Turner, and *The Tempest* by Giorgione, which was probably the first picture of this type.

Overdue and *The Rain it Raineth* also meet the conditions. In the latter there is a strong feeling of depth because, as the distance recedes, the promenade tapers off and the colour is carefully drained out; and, although the picture is not internally framed on the sides, the view is bounded in front by the hotel and the terrace. The viewer's gaze is also led up and into the picture by the figures and the intervening central space. *Overdue* creates an impression both of depth and enclosed space partly by the use of perspective and partly by the walls on one side and at the back; although the drawing effect is enhanced by the receding lights, seen through the window. A large element of magic is contributed by the tranquil mystery of the scene.

Garstin was not the only Naturalist to paint pictures of an *à travers* type, and their painting was not, as Turner and Giorgione show, the prerogative of the Naturalists of the late nineteenth century. James Paterson, who was one of the Glasgow Boys, is another Naturalist who painted *à travers* pictures of the first rank. Nevertheless such pictures are not common, and many great artists painted none. They were, as we shall see, a Garstin speciality. He never referred to his pictures producing this effect, which is not surprising as he said very little about his own work. That he went on achieving this effect suggests, however, that it was no accident, and that he knew what he was doing. These pictures constitute his principal and his legitimate claim to fame.

Gombrich argues that one of the pleasures of mimesis is to share in the creative illusionist adventure of the artist.[20] If so, this pleasure will be at its strongest where we are invited to make the greatest leap of imagination and step into the picture. An even more important source of pleasure is the almost mystical and trancelike reverie to which *à travers* pictures can give rise. This is the *repos délicieux* that was described by Diderot as being characterised by feelings of tranquillity, passivity, the halting of time, and the sweetness of existence.[21]

This is a subject about which it is difficult to speak with much confidence or precision, partly because of the inherent difficulty of trying to describe such mental states, partly because of a general reluctance to even try to describe one's most intimate feelings; and partly because personal taste and temperament are involved. Nor is this the place for an extended discussion of the subject. It can, however, scarcely be denied that ecstatic and visionary states do exist; that they are sometimes experienced through art (as Pater also knew); and that the *à travers* effect, just because it involves consummate skill and is so difficult to achieve, may produce a profound joy, not only in one's own existence, but also at what the human hand and the human spirit are sometimes able to achieve.[22] Even those who have *not yet* had this experience must realise from the existence of different but related feelings of mental transport that great art sometimes produces a *repos délicieux* – unless they are incapable, for instance, of being profoundly moved by music, and have never enjoyed sexual ecstasy. Enough: to matters more mundane.

Little Recognition and Less Income

During the early Newlyn years, Garstin's work was exhibited at the leading galleries in the land. Although *Progress and Poverty* was the only picture to be shown at the Royal Academy in this period, major works were displayed at other London galleries. These included the Royal Society of British Artists (four pictures); the (future) Royal Institute of Oil Painters (one); the New English Art Club (three); and the Grosvenor Gallery (two, including a re-exhibit). To be hung at the latter was particularly flattering because it was by invitation. In the provinces, works were exhibited at Liverpool (eleven, including four re-exhibits); at Manchester (four, including two re-exhibits); and at the Royal Birmingham Society of Artists (three, including two re-exhibits). These pictures received some recognition. A sketch of *Progress and Poverty* appeared in *Academy Notes*, which was an illustrated guide to the Summer Exhibition; *The Globe* mentioned *The Painter's Wife*, when it was exhibited at the New English Art Club; and *The Pall Mall Gazette* contained sketches of two other pictures that were shown there: *An Iron Master* in 1888 and *Overdue* in 1889. However, the omissions were also significant: there was no mention of Garstin's exhibits in *The Times* or, for instance, in the *Liverpool Daily Post*.

At this time Garstin was able to sell most of his large pictures, and all the small ones, without too much difficulty. Of the nineteen major pictures which were first exhibited at a known gallery between his arrival in Newlyn and the end of 1889, and which Garstin was trying to sell, it appears that only two were not disposed of before the end of the period; although the number could be somewhat greater

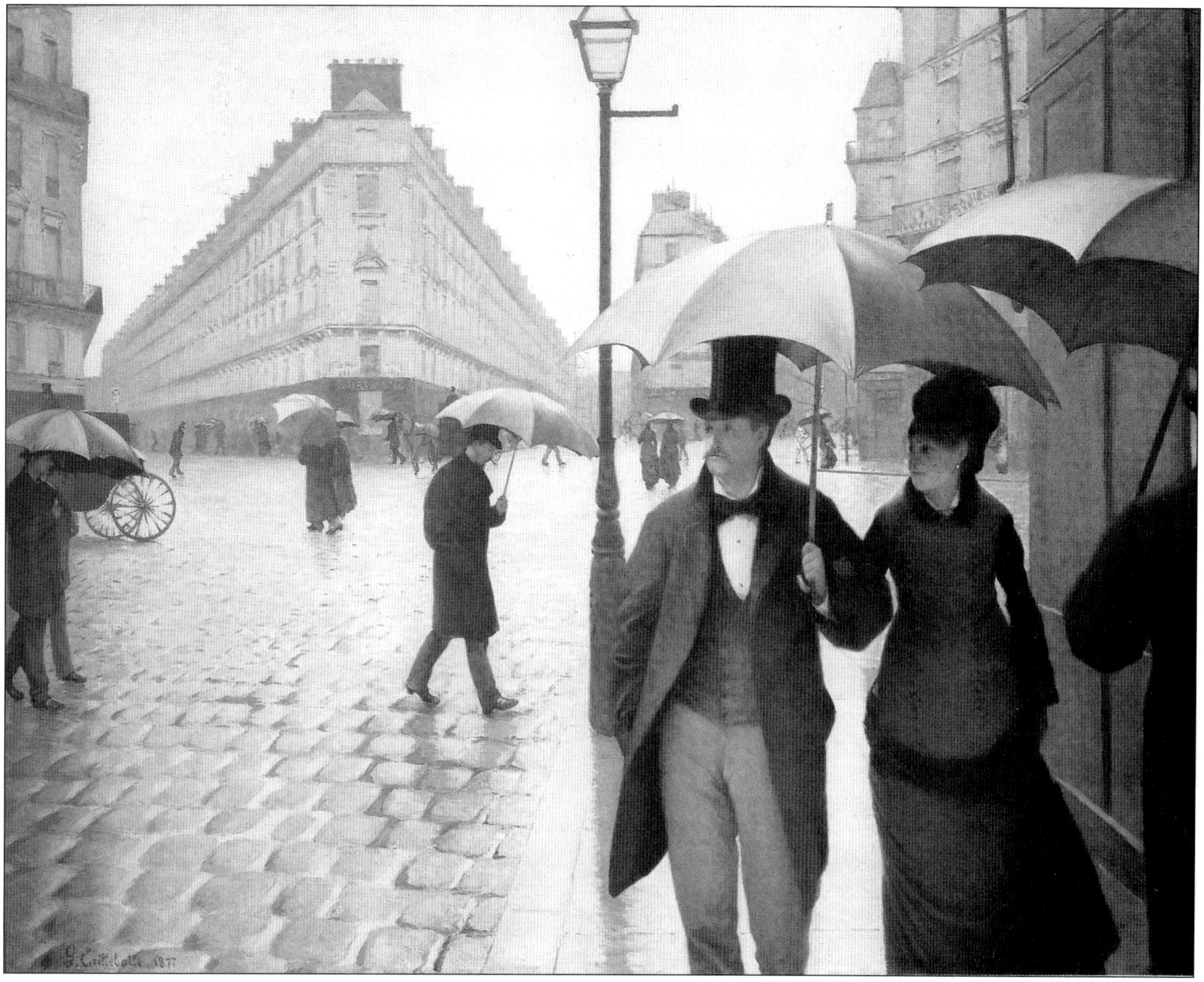

Gustave Caillebotte, *Paris Street; Rainy Day*, 1877, oil (The Art Institute, Chicago).

because, apart from the Royal Academy, there are few details of sales, and it is necessary to rely on information about the last known place of exhibition.

Although Garstin succeeded in disposing of most of his works, his asking prices were low, and he would have received even less. The price which he asked for those major works that were first offered only averaged about £43. Too much significance should not be attached to this figure, because works have been regarded as major even when the price was as low as £25. Nevertheless it is clear that Garstin asked very little. For *The Rain it Raineth*, which was a large picture, at 37 x 64 inches, the initial asking price was £75; for *Overdue*, at 26.5 x 35.5, it was £50; for *Progress and Poverty*, at 44 x 35, it was £42; and for *Towards the Sun Setting* which was, at 20 x 24, on the border for inclusion as a major work, it was only £25. If, as

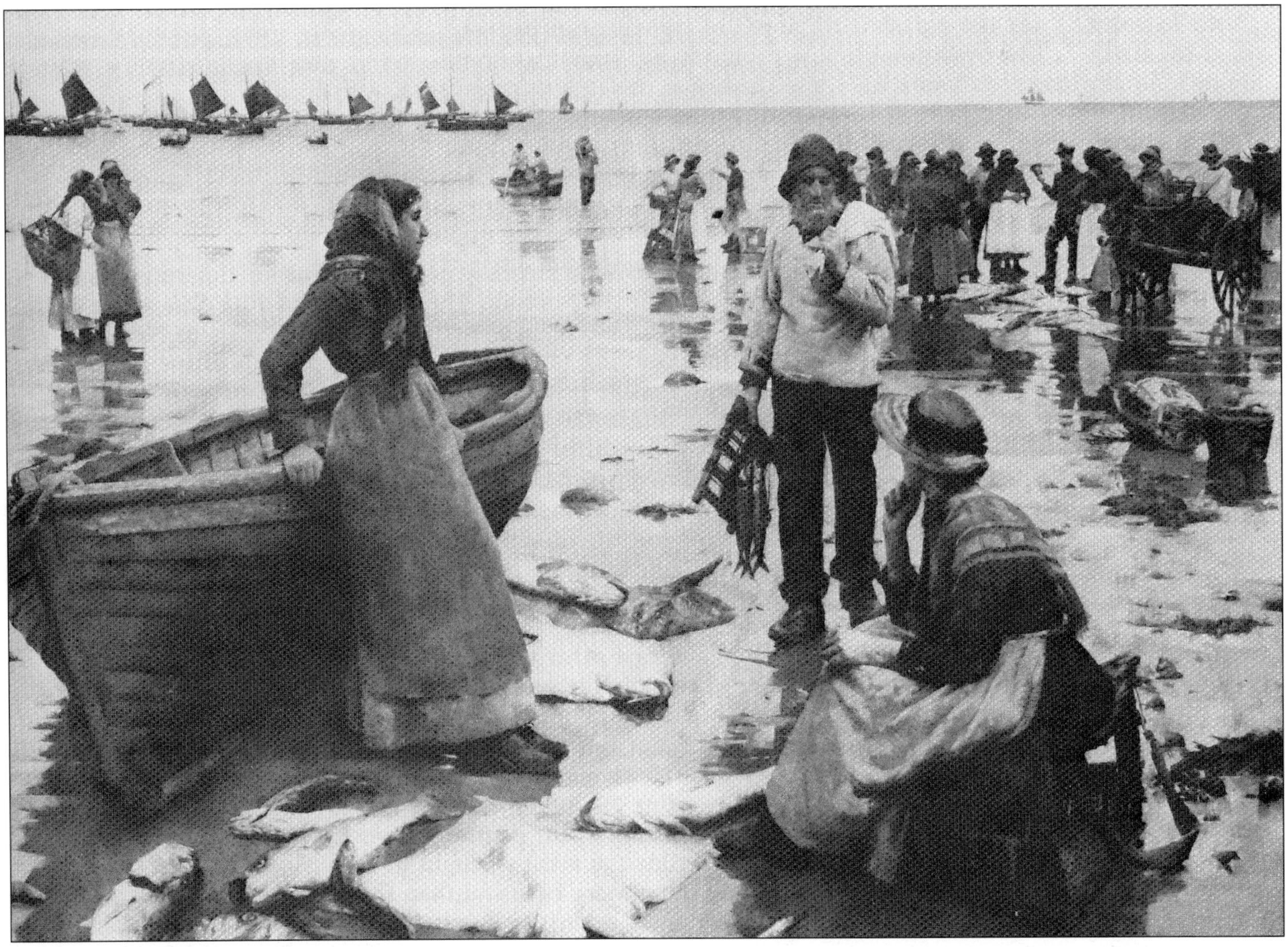

Stanhope Forbes, *A Fish Sale on a Cornish Beach*, 1885, oil (Plymouth City Museum & Art Gallery).

frequently happened, the work did not sell, and had to be re-exhibited, Garstin would usually make a substantial reduction in price; and he, like other artists, would often have cut his price still further to secure a sale. At the Walker Gallery, during the early years of the next century, the average discount was about 40 per cent. Furthermore the cost of making a sale would have been substantial. The Royal Academy did not charge the artist a commission, but at most galleries it was ten per cent of the price received. On top of this, there would have been expenditure on materials, framing and transport.

It can be estimated that between 1887 and 1889 Garstin earned, on average, just over £250 each year from selling pictures. This was the approximate value of his sales at catalogue prices, which, although it does not allow for receipts from undiscovered works, fails to take account of the even greater costs of selling pictures.[23]

Such an income would have been only a fraction of what some of the Newlyn artists were making. Walter Langley's earnings averaged about £730 per annum over the same period, and, though it is not known what Forbes and Bramley were earning during these years it must have been considerable. Forbes sold *Fish Sale* (1885) for £250, *Off to the Fishing Grounds* (1886) for £350, and *The Health of the Bride* (1889) for £600. In 1891, the first year for which his total earnings are known, Forbes made £1434, but his income would not have been as large during previous years.

Lack of Success Explained

Why did Garstin's pictures fetch so little, and why did they receive so little attention? One possible reason is that it takes time for an artist to establish a reputation, and that Garstin had only just embarked on his career as a professional artist. This might account for his relative lack of success in 1887 and 1888, but it cannot account for the failure of *The Rain it Raineth*, which he never managed to sell. Caroline Fox has suggested that, with the exception of this picture, he was not successful at painting large pictures. If only because of the quality of *Overdue*, *Temptation* and, it must be presumed, *An Iron Master*, this cannot be true. Fox was generalising on the basis of insufficient evidence. According to Professor Rezelman, 'It is not difficult to understand why he experienced difficulty finding patrons for works which often appeared to a late Victorian audience no more than preliminary sketches'.[24] This could only have been true of some of his small experimental pictures: his major works did not lack finish.

Frank Bramley, *A Hopeless Dawn*, 1888, oil (Tate Gallery).

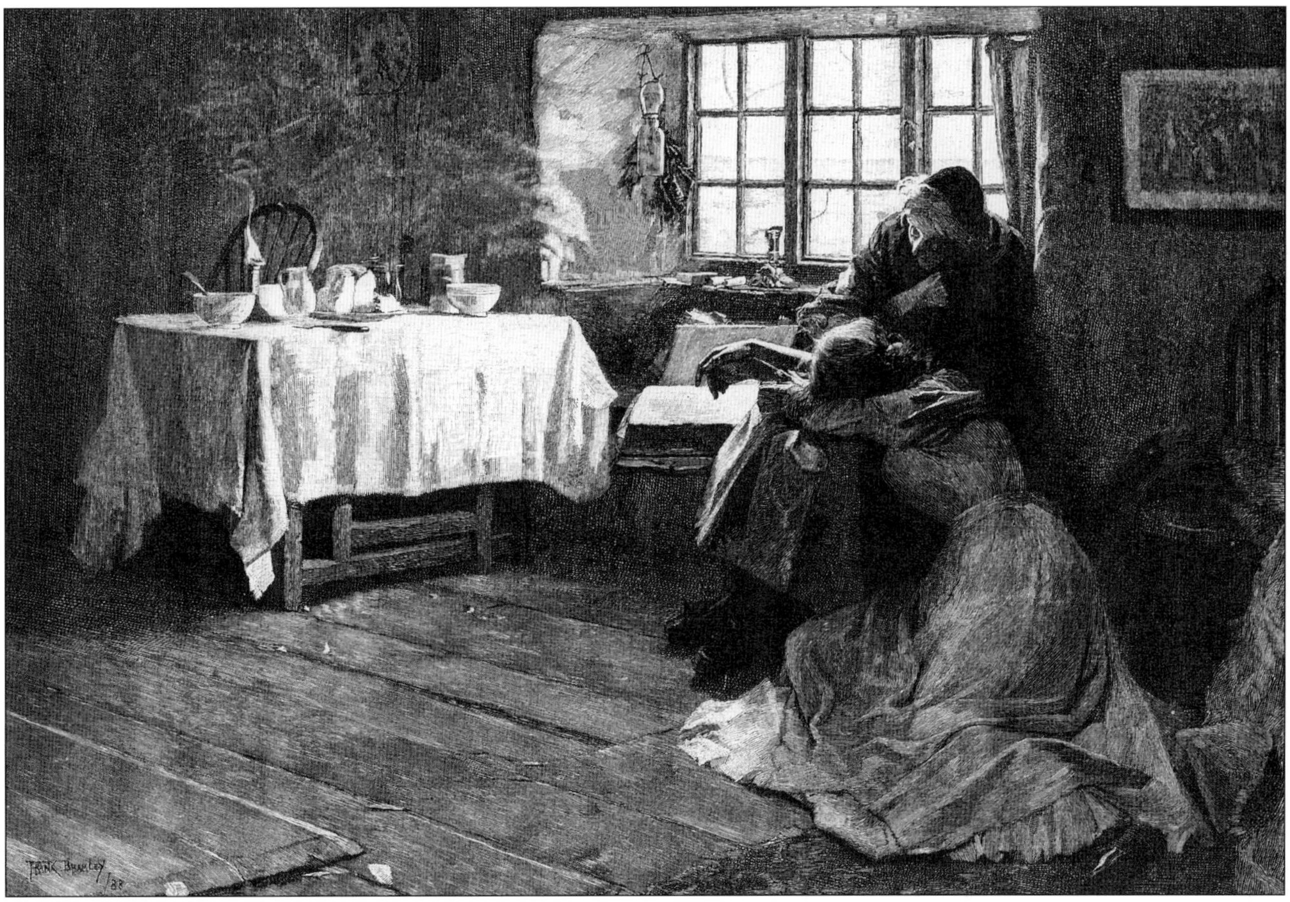

Garstin's relative failure was due not to his style, which was similar to that of other artists who were gaining recognition, such as Clausen, La Thangue and Lavery, but to his subject matter. One important reason for his lack of success was his wide range of subjects. The way in which Leighton, Alma-Tadema, and other leading artists had established themselves was by becoming identified with a particular, and popular, type of subject matter. This was also the way in which Clausen, La Thangue and other Naturalist artists were becoming known; they painted scenes of rural life in which members of the labouring classes were prominently figured. At Newlyn, Stanhope Forbes and Walter Langley were busy making their names by painting those who belonged to the fishing community, or followed other traditional pursuits, subjects that were likely to have a nostalgic appeal to collectors with industrial wealth. When Langley strayed, and wanted to paint those who worked in the factories and forges of the Black Country, his subjects did not find favour, and he quickly returned to his rut.

Garstin's pictures had the distinguishing feature of extreme emotional coolness and the absence of any element of social realism or sentimentality. Bramley with his *Hopeless Dawn* (1888) and Langley with his *Orphan* (1889) painted pictures with an obvious emotional appeal, and Langley's pictures verge on the sentimental. Stanhope Forbes was far more restrained but even his pictures contain an element of social realism and show some interaction between the individuals they depict. Although his *Fish Sale* has a deliberately deadpan tone, there is nonetheless a dash of social realism: there are sellers without buyers and the catch is meagre and of poor quality. However, as Joanna Lace observes, Garstin 'rarely, if ever, chooses close human relationships as subject-matter'.[25] One can indeed go further. A striking feature of his pictures, throughout his career, is that, where they contain more than one person, there is little or no interaction between them. This is well illustrated by *Overdue*, and *The Rain it Raineth*. The only possible exception, during the early Newlyn years, is *Two Heads are Better than One* (1889), which is almost large enough to be a major work (Plate 18). Here a teacher is slightly smiling at her young pupil, who is clearly having difficulty providing the right answer, and is looking into the distance. *The Lesson* (1889) by Edwin Harris is, curiously, almost an exact likeness, but it is notable that in this picture the pupil is looking at the teacher, and her smile is more pronounced.

Some of Garstin's pictures are not only cool but also wet. This is true, during the early Newlyn period, of both *The Rain it Raineth* and *A Steady Drizzle*. The *Cornish Telegraph* commented that the former was 'not the most cheerful of pictures. To look at it is to conjure up thoughts of influenza and its attendant horrors'.[26] It is, as we have seen, a disconcerting work; and it is not surprising that Garstin did not sell either of these pictures.

There may also have been an element of sheer bad luck in Garstin's failure to gain more recognition. *The Rain it Raineth* and *Overdue* were accepted by the Royal Academy, but then crowded out. Had these two great pictures been hung at the Summer Exhibition, it is conceivable that Garstin would have made his name. That they were crowded out shows, however, that the art market was fiercely competitive, and, as we shall see later, it was becoming ever more difficult

Loss of Private Income; Growing Needs

Because it was so hard to make a living by selling pictures, it was a great advantage for an artist to have an independent income, or to be connected to a rich patron. Such benefits were enjoyed by not a few. They included Lord Leighton, who for many years received £240 a year from his father; and, amongst younger artists, Wilson Steer, who was given a £150 allowance by his mother, and Garstin's friend Alexander Mann who received generous support from his father. The Glasgow Boys and O'Meara were helped by the wealthy Gardiner brothers, to whom one of the circle (Guthrie) was related. In default of unearned income or connection, aspiring artists sometimes received a helping hand from dealers. Examples are Wainwright and Tuke, who received numerous commissions from Dowdeswell. The former was a fellow student of Garstin's at the Antwerp Academy, and while he was there, and later in Paris, he sold pictures to Birmingham dealers, one of whom even visited him!

Garstin seems never to have formed a lasting relationship with a dealer, but, when Garstin and Dochie went to Newlyn, they did have the advantage of possessing independent income of reasonable size. Forbes told his mother, 'They have £80 a year each [on] which between them they manage somehow. It must be a tight squeeze'.[27] In the autumn of 1887 Garstin's £80 disastrously vanished. Garstin did not manage the underlying investments, which were held by a trust that appears to have been set up by Matthew Moore, when his daughter married. On the advice of a distant relation, Margaret FitzGerald, who was in turn advised by someone who was little better than a thief, the trust fund was mis-invested. Margaret had a talent for losing money, and her family still have a large bundle of beautiful, but worthless, share certificates. According to one of Garstin's relations, Norman and Dochie were in London when they were told that, 'his half years interest would not be cashed as there was cablegram to say all was smashed up ... it was a fearful shock to dear Norman'.[28]

The concern must have been all the greater because their first

Norman, Dochie and Crosbie *c.*1887.

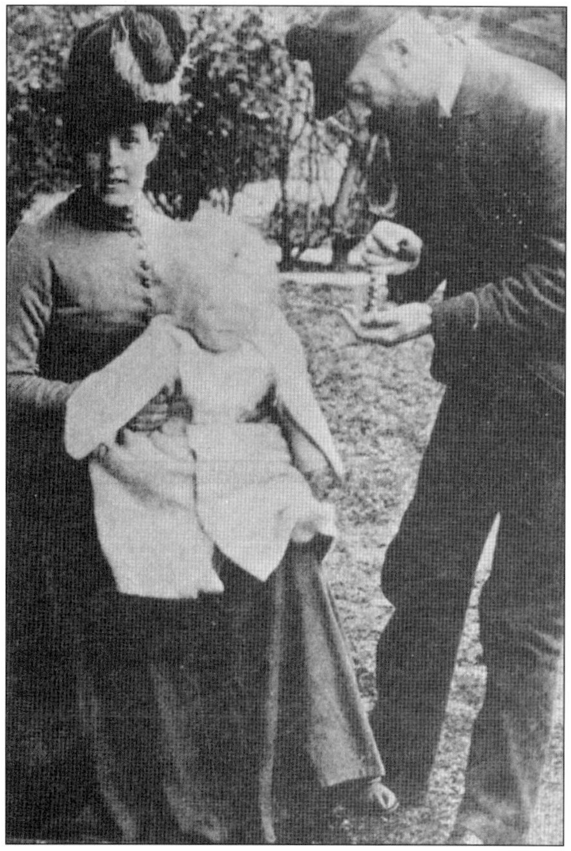

child, Crosbie, had just been born; and in the summer of 1890 Dochie had another son, Denis (christened Denys), which led to the Garstins moving from Newlyn to Penzance, though Norman retained a studio at Newlyn. Confronted, as he was, with mounting family responsibilities, and then a decline in income, it is scarcely surprising that Garstin must have found his lack of success at the Academy hard to bear. 'Poor old Garstin. I am so sorry he takes it so to heart', wrote Forbes in 1887, when Garstin's three entries were rejected but many of the other Newlyn artists were hung on the (eye) line, or just above, and were not skied.[29] The blow, in 1889, of having pictures first accepted but then rejected, must have been particularly hard to bear. 'We are all sorry for the Garstins', reported Frank Wright Bourdillon, 'who can ill afford to lose any chance of selling'.[30] Bourdillon and the others would not have been so sorry if Garstin had not been sorry for himself.

Garstin also had the blow that *The Suitors of Aprille* did not find a publisher. This was an adult fairy story, which he appears to have begun in Morocco and to have finished at the end of 1888. The plot is complicated but is a variation on the old theme of the prince in love with a girl of unknown parentage, who turns out to be a princess, and also his cousin. It is a rich brew of mythological figures, magic potions, sinister old hags, murderous villains, sea raiders, ruined and lonely windmills, and blasted heaths. The writing is vigorous and vivid, and, although the style is archaic, it is in no way annoying. There is no moral. This may seem a curious story for a Realist to write, but the book forms part of a well established tradition. It is reminiscent of *The Princess and Curdie* (1883) by George MacDonald, who was influenced by the folklore of the Scottish countryside where he grew up, while Garstin probably drew on tales he heard as a boy in Limerick.

Lack of success as an artist and an author, and middle class penury, had a number of consequences, but they open a new chapter. This is another of the turning points in Garstin's life. He had, since his arrival in Newlyn, painted a substantial number of pictures, and they included at least three or four works of outstanding merit. In particular, he had succeeded in painting pictures in which there was a subtle use of space and a sophisticated asymmetrical balance; pictures that, above all, had a seemingly magic power to draw the viewer into the alternative world that the artist had created. But although Garstin had succeeded as a painter, he had not enjoyed the success he deserved, and he had failed as a breadwinner.

Chapter 4

The Lean Years at Penzance, 1890-99

The period of artistic achievement at Newlyn was followed by ten lean years at Penzance. During this period, Garstin painted relatively few pictures and, with some notable exceptions, those he

Plate 19 *A Stranger*, 1890, oil, 53" x 83" (Hugh Lane Gallery, Dublin).

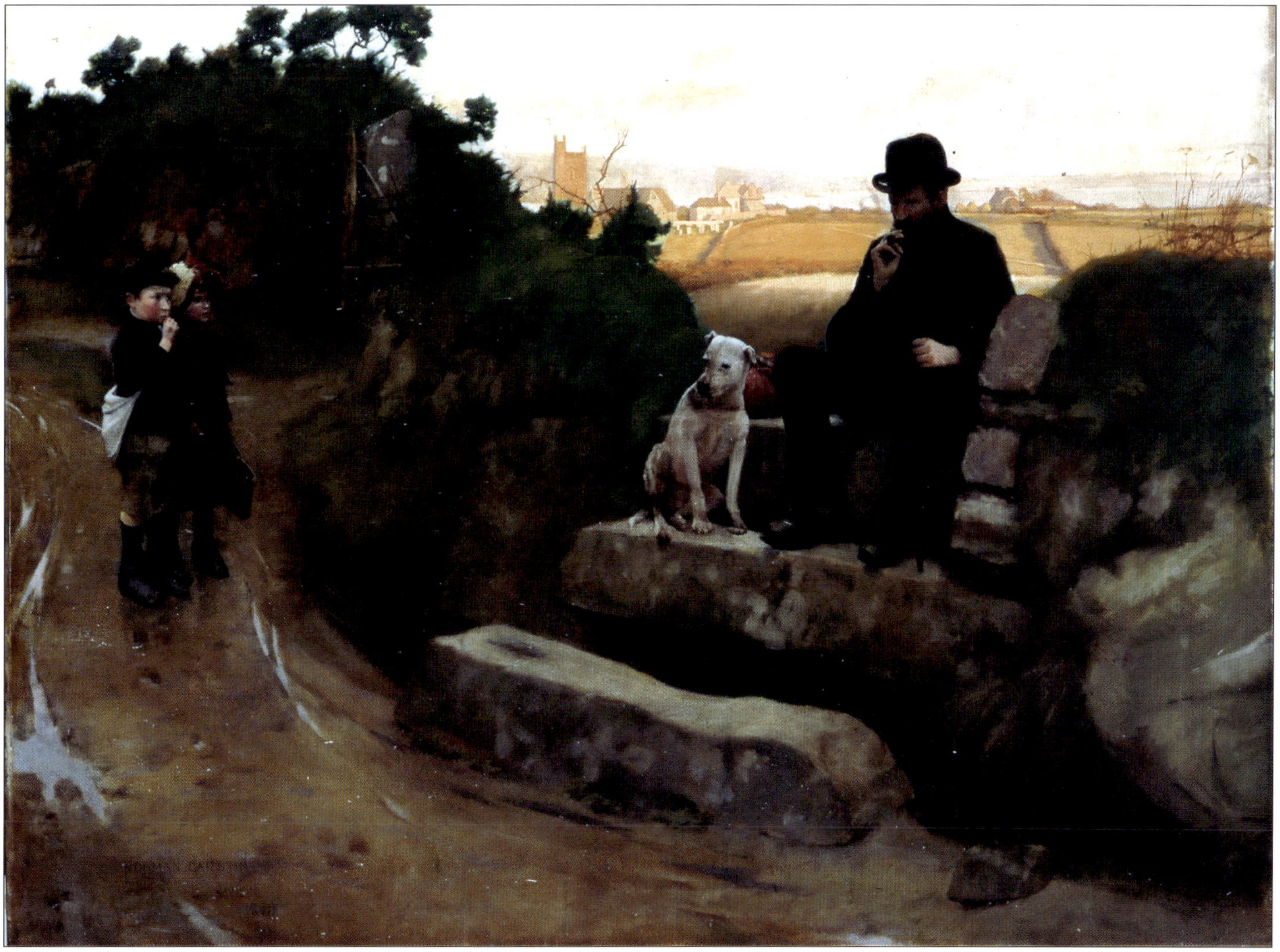

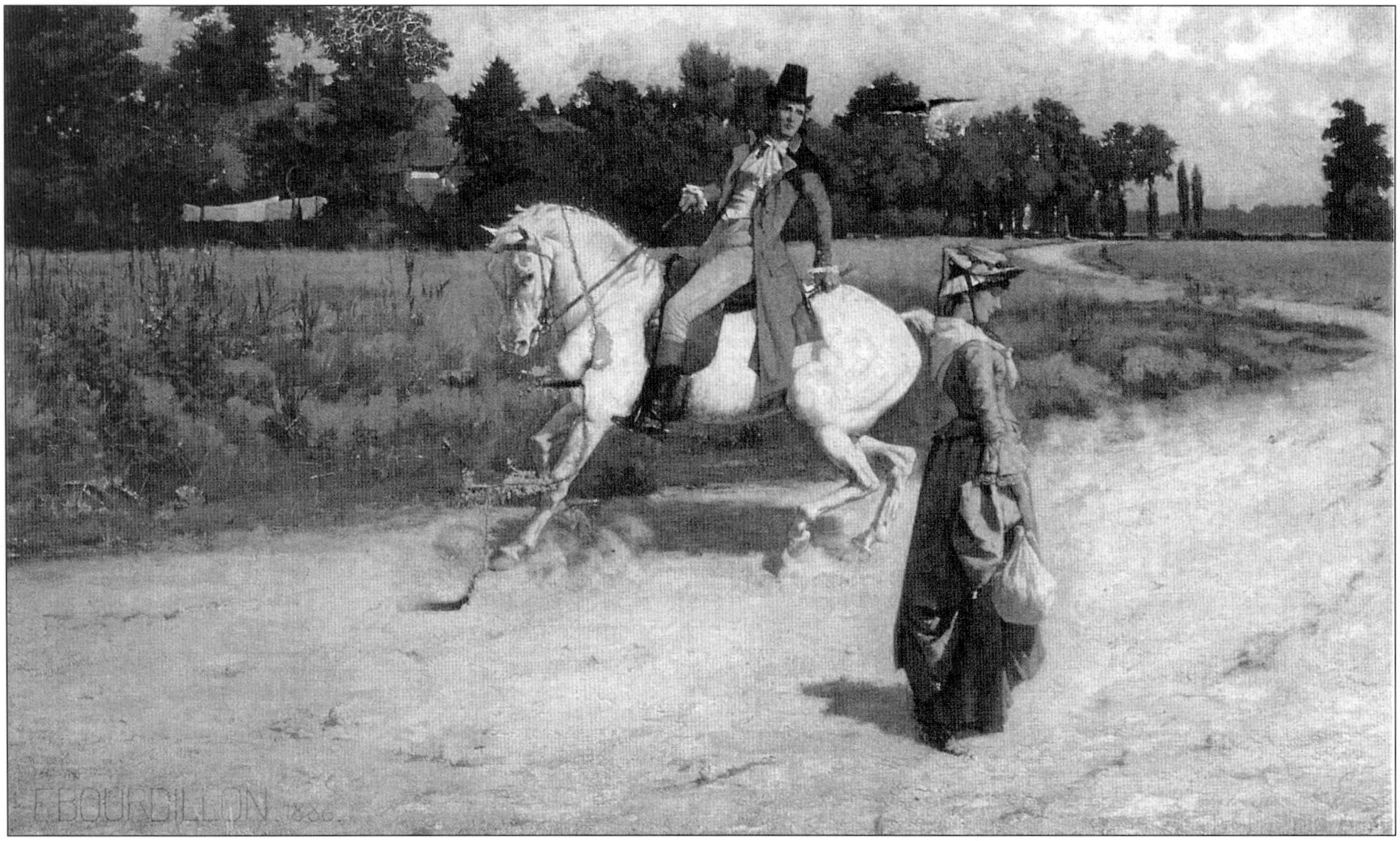

Frank Wright Bourdillon, *The Bailiff's Daughter of Islington*, 1886, oil (private collection).

did paint were somewhat academic or violated his own principles: they told a story badly or were costume works. Although his pictures received greater attention, Garstin was working in a crowded and deteriorating market and his income was meagre. Even worse, he appears to have become seriously depressed, and a trip to Canada, though artistically productive, was no cure.

The Attempt to Paint More Saleable Pictures

The rejection of *The Rain it Raineth* and *Overdue* by the Royal Academy, and other setbacks, were to have momentous consequences. Garstin appears to have drawn the conclusion that he must find new and more popular subjects.

The example of Bourdillon may well have encouraged Garstin to try to paint more saleable pictures. Bourdillon, with whom Garstin was, during 1890, to share one of the glass studios that were being built, complained that, although it might be good for one's development, 'this insatiable need and failure to produce saleable work ... goes near to engendering despair'.[1] It was, in fact, bad for his development: he was, as he said, driven to paint costume pictures instead of concentrating on the fine tonal studies at which he was so adept. Bourdillon's costume paintings began with *The Bailiff's Daughter of Islington* (1886) and, after moving to Newlyn, he followed this up with a picture of an Elizabethan duel, entitled *On Bideford Sands* (1889). Both of these pictures were exhibited at the Royal Academy, at which he was notably successful during the late eighties.

What the Moon Saw and *A Stranger* were the first fruits of Garstin's new phase, which coincided with the move to Penzance. The latter, at 4 ft by 7 ft, was much the largest and most ambitious picture Garstin ever painted. It is reproduced in Plate 19, and shows a somewhat sinister tramp sitting on a stile, oblivious of the two small children, who want to cross but are puzzled as to what to do. The most striking aspect of the picture is the lack of mutual interaction between the tramp and the children; although they are reacting to him he is totally self-absorbed. His emotional isolation is given pictorial expression in the massive stile, which is like an impregnable throne, and by the distance between the tramp, situated at the golden mean, and the children who are pushed to one side by the intervening steps and bank. The sense of isolation is heightened by the contrast between the tramp and the sunlit background against which he is darkly posed. It includes the village (Mousehole) from which the children are being shut out.

A Stranger has been viewed in widely different ways. On the one hand, it has been seen by Fox and Greenacre as 'an example of the intrusion of anecdotal content which Garstin earlier despised', and, by its owner, the Hugh Lane Gallery, as reflecting 'the growing tendency towards sentimental narrative which would dominate Garstin's work for the next ten years'.[2] On the other hand, Joanna Lace denies that there are 'any overtones of gratuitous sentimentality'.[3] It is all too easy to brand pictures as anecdotal and sentimental, without defining these terms or justifying the claim. Lace is surely right: the picture is not sentimental because it is not extravagantly emotional. The children do not even enlist our sympathy and, although the picture is mysterious, it is emotionally cool. Nor is the picture anecdotal in the sense of dealing with a trivial subject.

Nevertheless the picture is much less impressive than the great pictures that Garstin had previously painted. The distance between the children and the tramp is large and is filled by a jutting and obtrusive wall. As a result, one's attention keeps shifting uneasily back and forth between the tramp and the children. Moreover, the spatial relationships are disturbing. The children have been placed so far back that is questionable whether they would be able to see the tramp properly. One has the feeling that Garstin was trying too hard to paint a large and successful picture. It is, like so many Victorian paintings, a somewhat laboured piece of work. Paint is used more heavily and in a less interesting manner than in previous works, with a large area of matt green in the middle of the picture. *What the Moon*

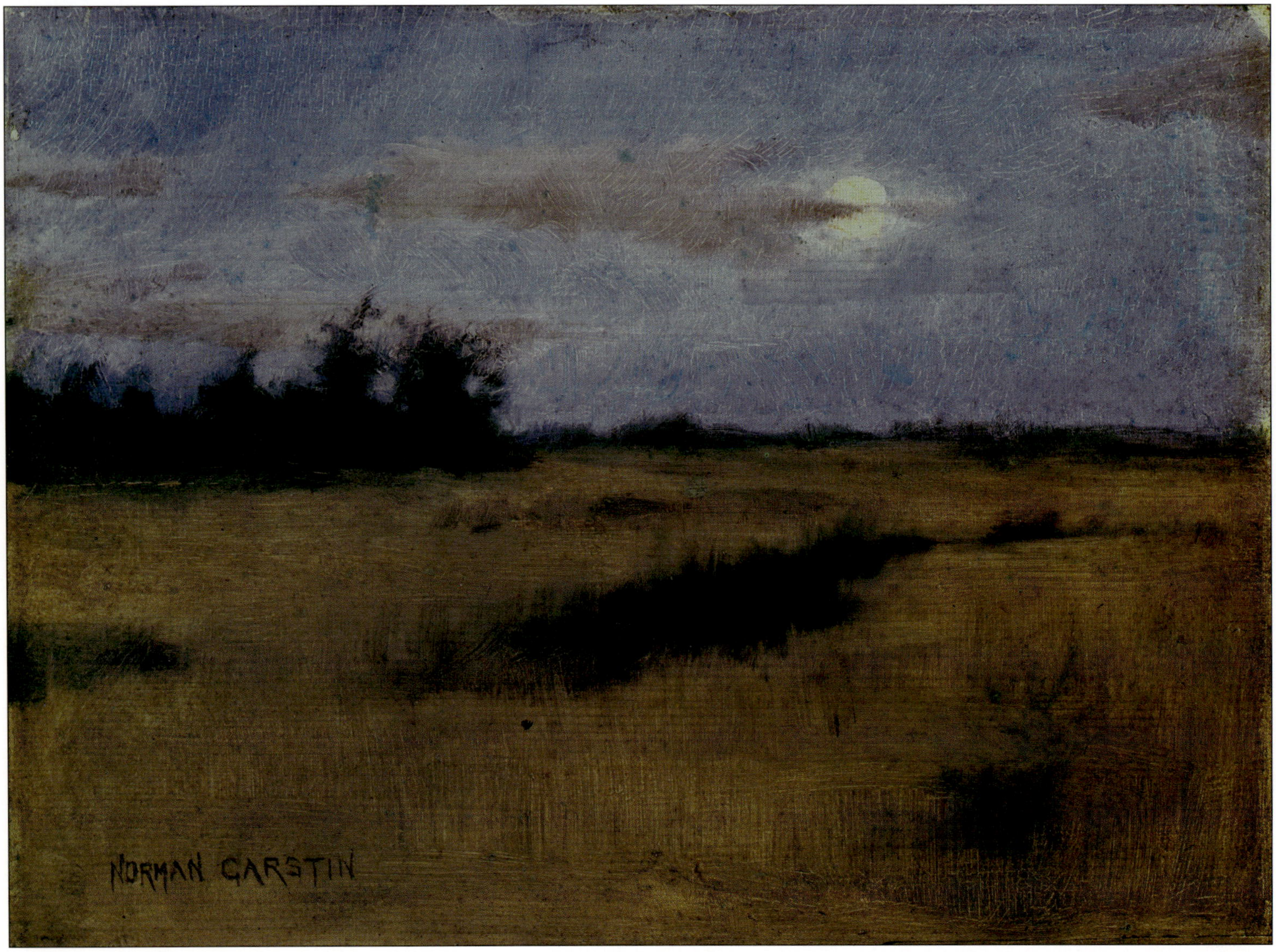

Plate 20 *Canadian Landscape with Rising Moon*, 1891, oil, 7.75" x 10.5" (York City Art Gallery).

Opposite:
Plate 21 *Xmas 99 My 3*, 1899, stencil, 14" x 10.5" (private collection).

Saw may well be open to the same or stronger criticisms. It depicted 'An orchard in the twilight, with the crescent moon over the sea beyond. A little girl [is] endeavouring to reach her doll, which some boys, who are making off, have placed in a tree out of her reach'.[4]

During the summer of 1890, *What the Moon Saw* was exhibited at the Grosvenor and *A Stranger* was hung at Academy. The latter received some attention. There were illustrations in *Academy Notes* and by the *Magazine of Art* and the *Pall Mall Gazette*. There was also a reproduction in the catalogue of the Walker Gallery, where it was exhibited in the autumn. In 1893 it was awarded a gold medal at Calcutta. However, there do not appear to have been any references in the press, and, despite repeated exhibition, it failed to sell. In 1891 Garstin submitted *The Cotillon* to the Academy but it was rejected (though it was accepted in the following year).

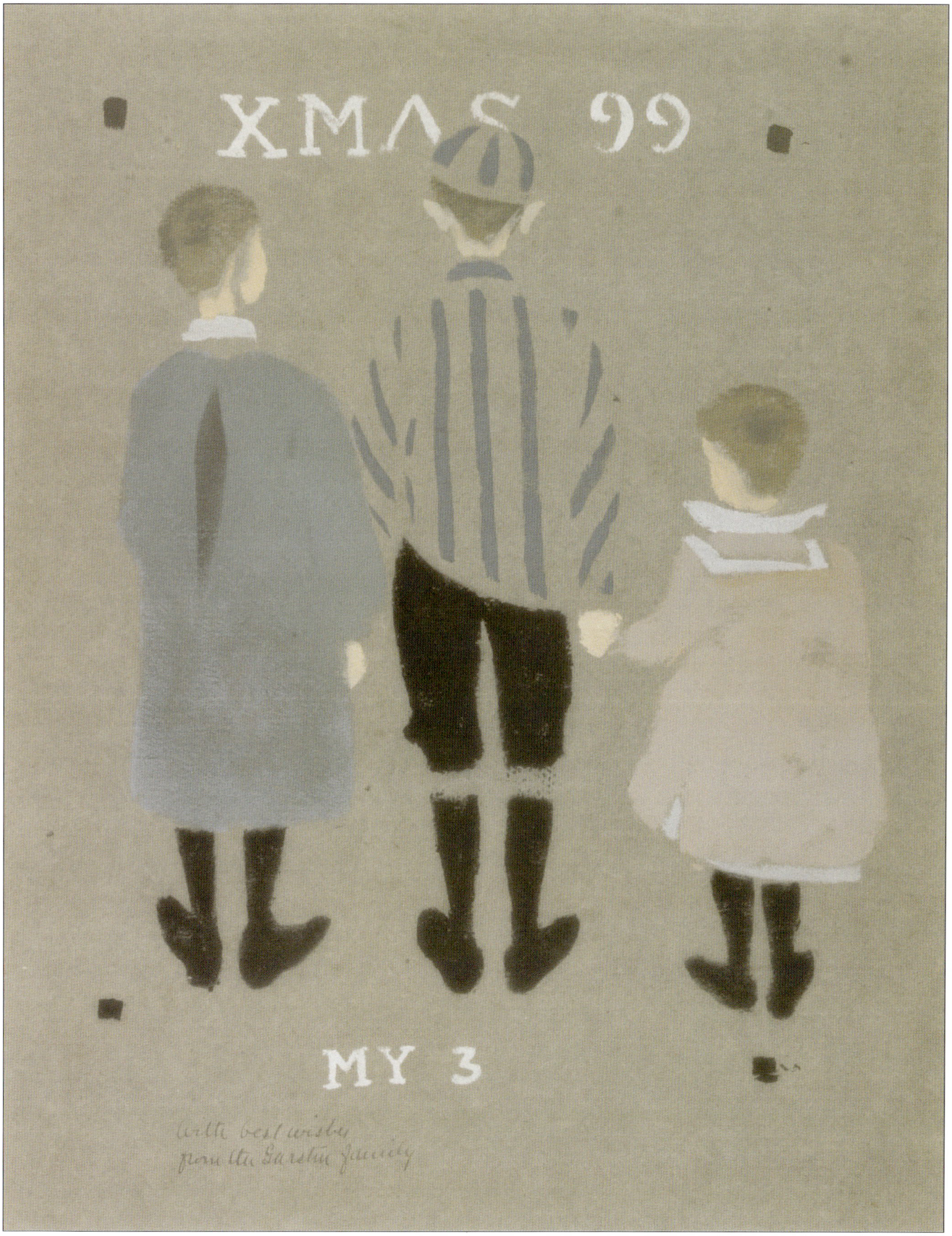
XMAS 99
MY 3
With best wishes
from the Garstin family

Garstin's Breakdown and Trip to Canada, 1891

Although Garstin did not know that *A Stranger* would never sell, he must have been disappointed by its lack of early success. He would have been gratified by its reproduction, but what he needed was money. Garstin appears to have sold only two pictures in 1890, and his net income from pictures must have been tiny. Some money would have been earned by teaching and possibly lecturing. In 1888 he had started the Newlyn and Penzance Art Students' Society, charging £1. 7s. 6d. (£1.38) a month for a term of eight months. Nothing is known about the number of students, but it seems unlikely that there were very many.

Since he had been at Newlyn, Garstin had been painting hard; he had begun to teach; he had written an unsuccessful novel; he had had only moderate success as an artist; his earnings had been small, and appeared to be declining; he had lost his private income; and all this at a time when his family responsibilities were growing. Such a combination of adverse circumstances would be more than sufficient to produce depression, or other mental illness, in a person of robust temperament; but Garstin may well have inherited a tendency towards melancholia from his father, while his early life suggests that, although he was capable of sustained work, it went against the grain.

The evidence is incomplete but it seems clear that Norman Garstin did become mentally ill. In May 1891 Mag Fulton wrote to Ada in Saskatchewan telling her that, 'Poor Norman's picture [*The Cotillon*] has not been hung – sad disappointment. Doctor Myles [at Birr, where Mag lived] says three months [travel] next best thing. So Georgie [another cousin] has given him £30 to go out and see you all'.[5] By this she meant travelling to see Ada and his other relations at Grenfell, Saskatchewan. The Victorians believed that travel was a sovereign cure for depression and other forms of mental distress, and Garstin would scarcely have embarked on an arduous journey to Canada if he had been physically ill.

Garstin left in the middle of May, and arrived at New York. He then visited Niagara where he was at first disappointed: 'I think I had expected more water but after a time one realises the persistence and irresistibleness of it'.[6] After going to Toronto, he proceeded to Grenfell, where he stayed and painted for some weeks. From there he wrote to the Canadian Pacific Railway asking for a free pass, and saying he was travelling 'partly for my health'.[7] After the pass had been granted, he left for the West, going through 'the most wonderful country that ever a train has traversed'.[8]

From Vancouver Norman wrote to Dochie telling her they possessed in their hearts, 'this priceless thing [Love] and we must treat it as a sacred trust and not risk its safety. I will try my dear love to keep my horrid sulky temper in control, to fight it down … I kiss this paper which will be in your hands'. It seems clear from this letter that Garstin's mental distress had led to marital difficulties. While he was at Vancouver, and in the Rockies on the way back, Garstin painted further pictures. After another visit to Grenfell, he moved back east, ending up at Quebec, 'with her glittering roofs one above another flashing in the sun like some decayed noble lady wearing her old diamonds on a threadbare dress'.[9] Towards the end of September he sailed for home.

As so often, travel was not a full cure. In June 1892, after Garstin's return, Ada received a letter saying that 'He and Dochie [are] on a visit to Dr Ross at Manchester for a fortnight'.[10] This can only have been Professor James Ross, the famous neurologist and author of the standard *Treatise on the Diseases of the Nervous System*. It contains a chapter on neurasthenia, which was what we should now call a nervous breakdown or ME: a condition of marked fatigue, depression and sleeplessness. According to Ross neurasthenia was virtually confined to 'the brain-workers of the community' and was particularly common in those who were subjected to a double source of strain. He gave the example of a 'man that has made great efforts for many years to gain intellectual or social success, and yet has hitherto been disappointed in obtaining distinction or promotion'.[11] One can almost hear the local doctor telling Garstin, 'the man you need to see is James Ross'. It seems clear, however, that there was no consultation with Ross, who had died of cancer at the end of February 1892. Possibly the Garstins visited one of his colleagues.

There is no direct evidence about the course of Garstin's illness, but the fact that his output was so small, during the rest of the decade, suggests that he did not recover quickly. However, before looking at this period, we must consider his Canadian pictures.

The Canadian Pictures and Articles

The North American trip was an oasis of output. At least seventeen pictures were painted, though they seem to have been small. Their quality appears to have been high, but it is difficult to be certain, because most are only available as reproductions. Among those that can be viewed, the previously mentioned portrait of Elizabeth Frend is a fine piece of work, and the *Canadian Landscape with Rising Moon* is outstanding. It is reproduced in Plate 20. There is a nice contrast between the straight hedge on the left and the grass, or bush, in the centre, which is at a slight angle. These horizontals, and near horizontals, in turn, contrast with the upright brush strokes in the foreground, which indicate grass. It is a work of subtle and dusky half tones, and produces a powerful *à travers* effect; it is a nocturne of Whistlerian stature. No wonder Heron reported, it 'has haunted me ever since I first set eyes on it'.[12]

After his return, Garstin wrote two articles for the *Art Journal*

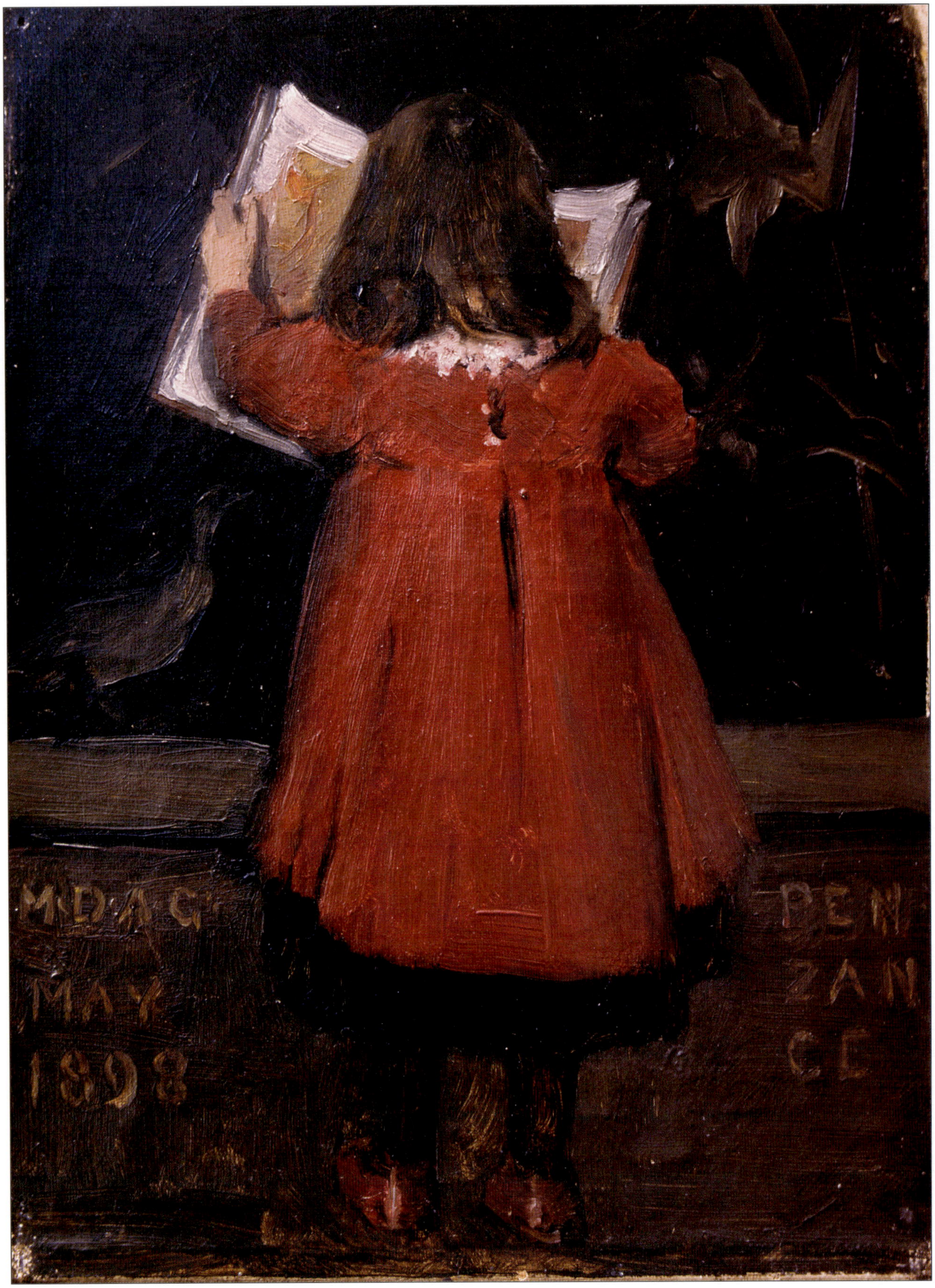
M·D.A.G
MAY
1898
PEN
ZAN
CE

describing the scenery and the inhabitants. They are elegantly written, containing purple passages, humour and acute observation. There is, for instance, a memorable description of a lonely shack on the prairies of

> indescribable desolation and dreariness; it is a one-roomed cottage of lumber, bleached by the weather to a silver grey; there is a little rick of hay near by, a rough sod stable, a wooden house for storing the grain; there are some agricultural implements lying where they were last used, a square patch of green wheat glistening in the sun, an insulating circle of fire guard, and that is all.
>
> A tall, loose-limbed, bronzed man, wearing a torn shirt and trousers, and a pipe, but no coat, and walking as men do who habitually carry heavy boots over a ploughed land, came towards us; he is 'batching it,' this stalwart young gentleman. Now 'batch' is a North-West verb, meaning to live the life of a bachelor; and a grim verb it is. Inside there is a stove, the white wood ashes heaped high underneath; there is a kettle boiling, by far the most cheerful object in the room; there is a bed with the blankets showing exactly the form they took when the master crept out at daybreak to turn the prairie sod.
>
> There is a photograph on the wall yellow and fly-spotted in the fashion of five years before, and I see the photographer's address is

Plate 22 Mary Dochie Alethea Garstin, 1898, oil, 10.25" x 8" (Bristol Museum & Art Gallery, where it is known as *The Artist's Daughter, Alethea Garstin*).

Plate 23 *What's News?*, 1892, oil, 14" x 20" (private collection).

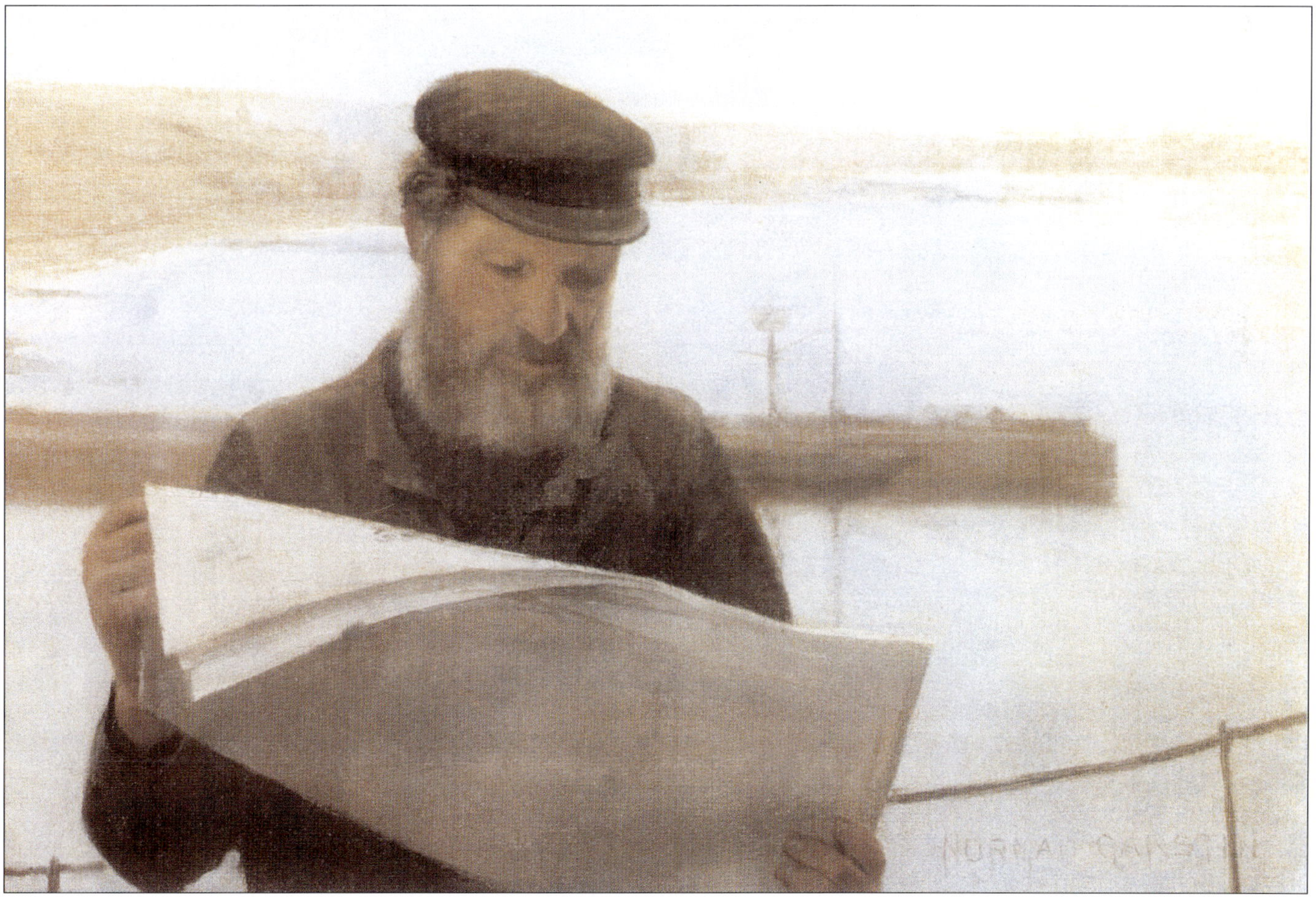

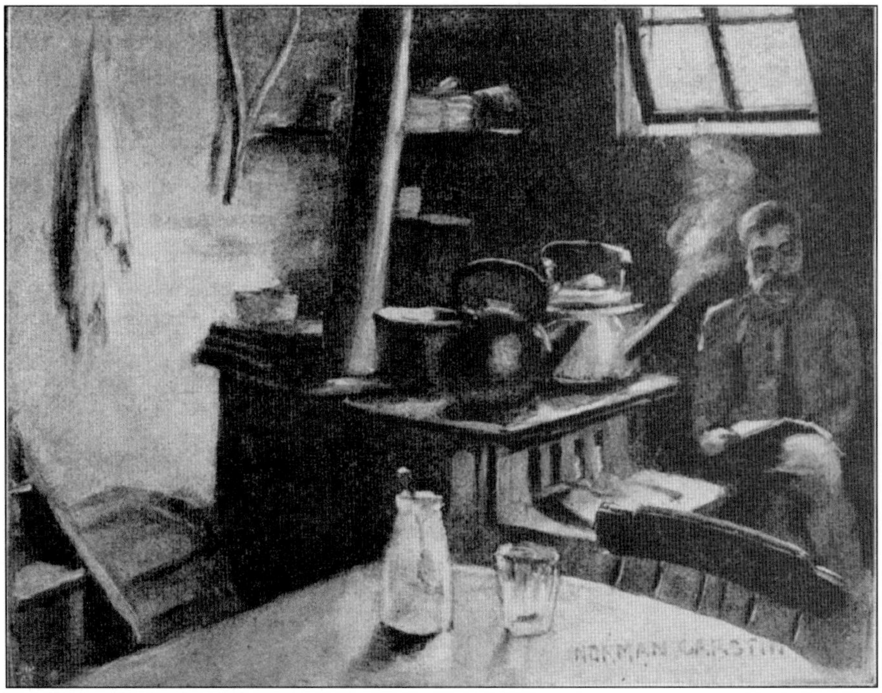

A Settler's Shack, 1891, oil (from the *Art Journal*, 1892).

> Cheltenham; one hopes the girl will never come out here – she might mitigate the severity of the 'batching,' but at what a cost![13]

Garstin painted a picture of this room which is, if nothing else, a fine piece of composition, with the farmer isolated on the margin of the work.

Garstin Paints Fewer Pictures, 1892-99

Between 1890 and 1899 Garstin exhibited only eighteen major works, which was the same number as those shown or painted during the preceding three years. The dearth of large works was not explained by a plethora of small paintings. There were, on the contrary, very few of these, disregarding those painted during the Canadian trip. It could be true that Garstin painted other works that have not been identified because they were not exhibited at the galleries for which there are catalogues. But this seems unlikely because, among the numerous pictures that have now come up for auction, there are very few unknown works that appear to date from this period.

Depression, or other mental illness, is one likely reason why Garstin's output was so small. Another probable explanation is that he was trying to paint subjects for which he had no real enthusiasm, and which he was producing merely because he believed that they would have a ready sale. If this were the case, as seems likely, we have further reasons for depression: Garstin was painting subjects he did not favour and was, in consequence, not making much progress. Before looking at his subject matter, it is desirable to examine Garstin's view

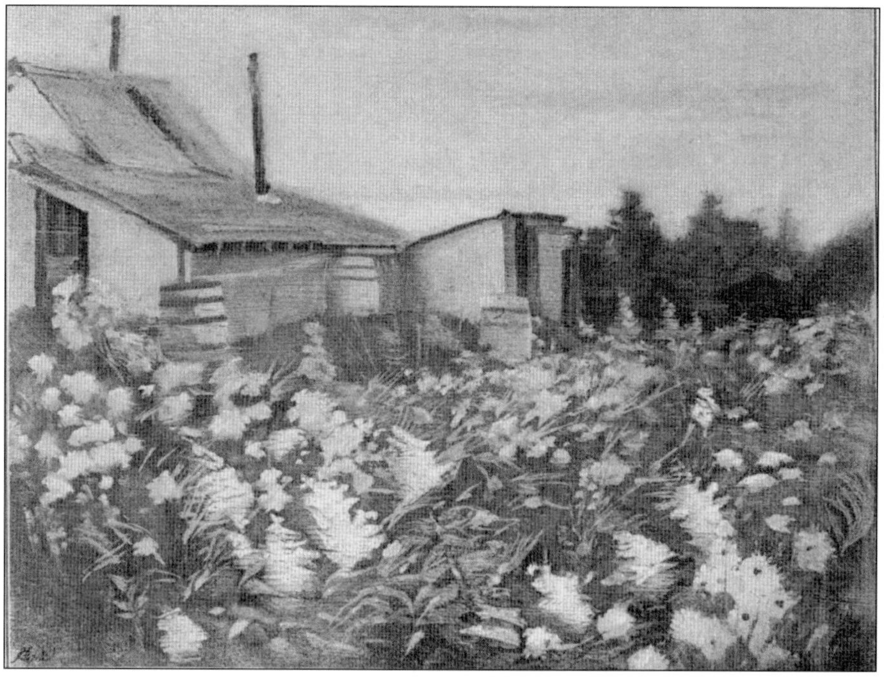

A Home in the North-West (from the *Art Journal*, 1892).

of the purpose of Art, and necessary to discover the type of picture to which he was opposed.

Art: Why it is Important and How it is Betrayed

In his lecture 'Painters and Painting', and elsewhere, Garstin argued that all means perfectly adapted to their end were beautiful. He contrasted the charming and useful cottage kitchen with the ugly and unused parlour. Even if it were true that useful things were not always beautiful, it would not follow that beautiful things were not useful. How then does art provide utility? Garstin began by observing that it was not a newborn luxury but an ancient and universal necessity. This was evident not only from the pictures in the Louvre but also from the cave paintings of the primitive bushmen of South Africa. Art arose because of man's need to overcome his sense of isolation:

> every one of us is condemned to solitary confinement in himself for the term of his natural life … each one looking out of his windows is only conscious of how he himself responds to what he sees and hears without, he does not know how it all seems to others, nor is he absolutely certain that his own sensations have any reality outside his own being. The arts serve to tell him that as other men see, hear and feel the same as he does, then it is impossible that his sensations are mere illusions … This sense of companionship in sensation is the chief satisfaction of Art; it is the means by which we look into one another's souls and minds …[14]

This is open to the objection that companionship in sensation is

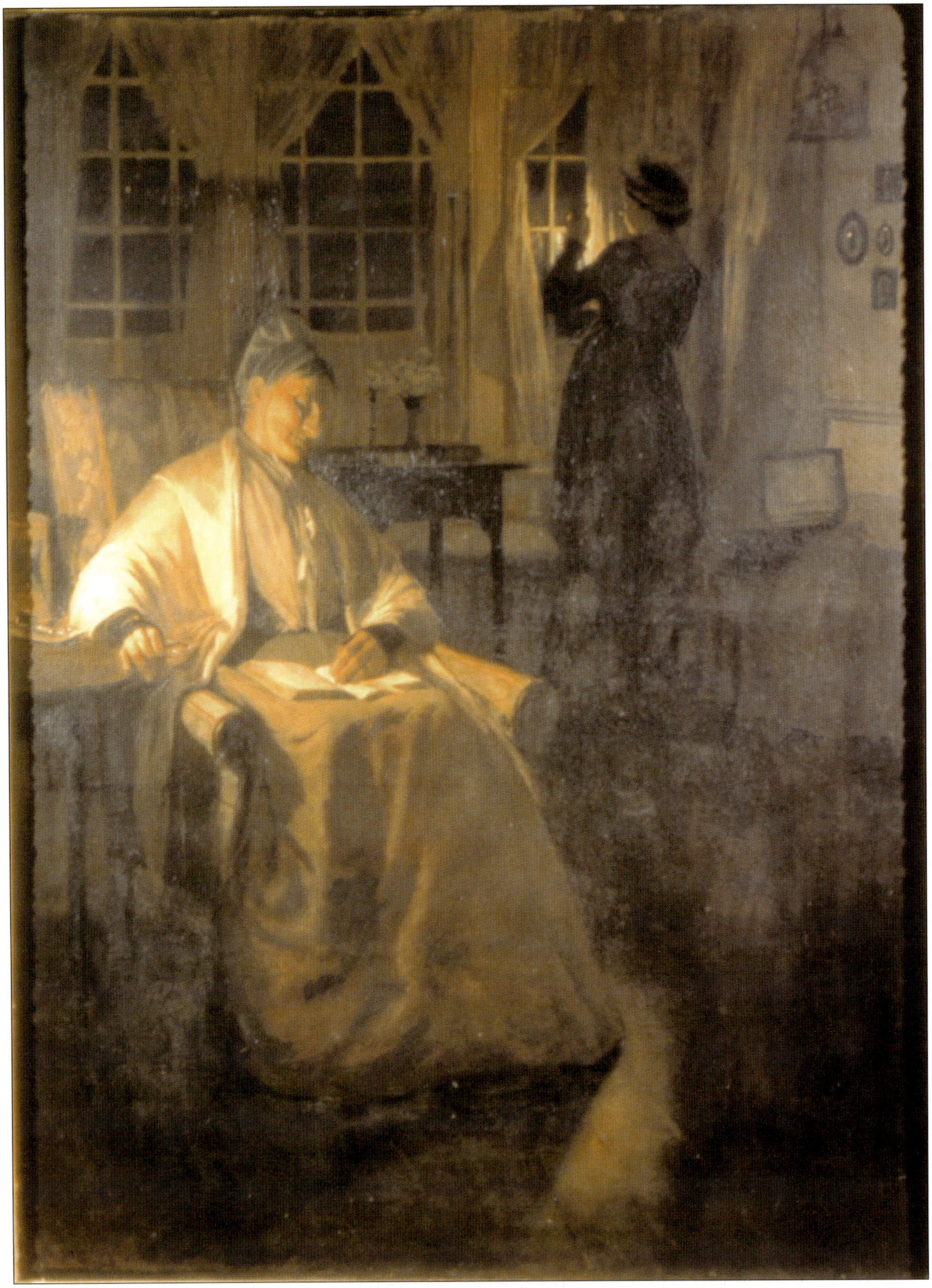

obtained in many other ways, e.g. by going to watch a football match or by making love, but it seems clear that what Garstin was referring to were sensations and emotions of a high order and, in particular, those concerned with beauty. Garstin declared that the whole life of the artist was given up to the search for beauty, but he did not fully clarify what he meant by beauty or say why its communication was of such outstanding importance. He strongly believed that 'what is fittest is fairest' but, frustratingly, it is not clear from his writings whether he was anticipating the Bauhaus or, what seems more likely, was mainly looking backwards to an era of craftsmanship *à la* William Morris.[15] It is certainly important to remember that Garstin belonged to a generation that believed in art for art's sake, and that what this meant was, in Pater's words, 'the desire of beauty'.[16]Although Garstin repudiated the aesthetes' belief that to be beautiful an object must be useless, it seems clear that he shared their belief that Art and Beauty are one and the same thing.

What is abundantly evident is that Garstin believed that Art was profoundly important, and was highly critical of shallow work. In particular he took exception to pictures which need to be accompanied by quotations, those in which the artist

> manages to make his public think they are admiring his work when really they are absorbed in their catalogue, their minds occupied with the scene painted for them by Herodotus, Shakespeare or Walter Scott. Without the catalogue such pictures might attract a puzzled attention but they could not charm or satisfy. Mr Whistler ... speaks of people viewing such a picture as looking through the picture and not at it, a most happy phrase ... my objection is not the telling of a tale, but, on the contrary, to the non-telling of it; to the necessity for elucidating the painted story by the written one... [17]

Garstin was opposed not only to poor story telling but also to artists who pandered to those with conventional and crude tastes

> Now it is for such people that the standard of art is perpetually being lowered. It is for such people that the baby and the kitten, the cheap sentiment, and the pretty girl with big eyes and red lips are eternally being manufactured by artists who both ought to and often do know better – but – and they shrug their shoulders and speak of their wives and families and the big house that has to be kept up – and so the pug dog and the little girl in the Kate Greenaway dress help to nourish the family of the artist, but art is starved ... And so our most famous painter [Millais] gives us a pretty little boy in his best clothes blowing soap bubbles. Bubbles, bubbles they are most of them blowing them, and their reputations will live as long ...[18]

Opposite:
Plate 24 *Her Signal*, 1892, oil, 61.5" x 44.25" (Royal Institution of Cornwall, Truro).

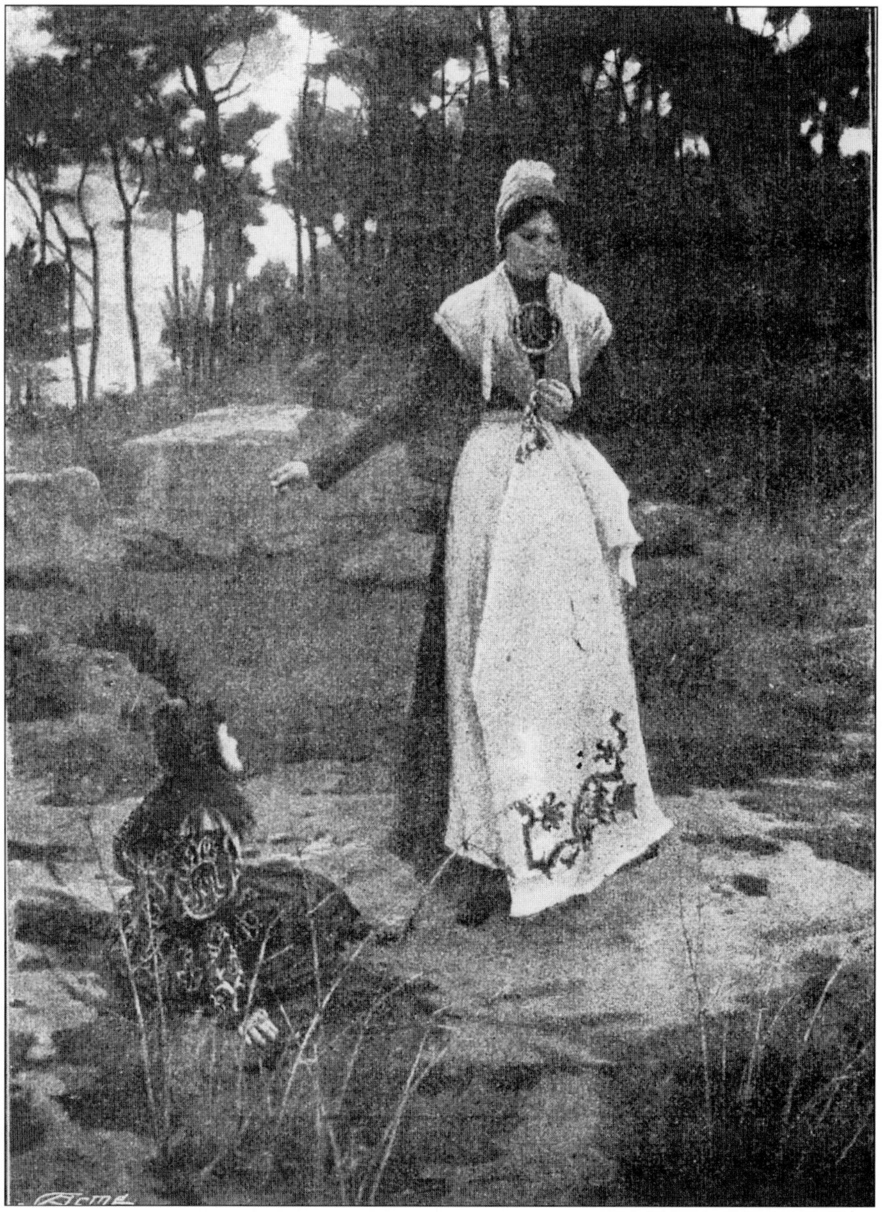
The Scarlet Letter, 1896, oil, 60" x 42" (from the *Black and White Handbook to the Royal Academy*, 1896).

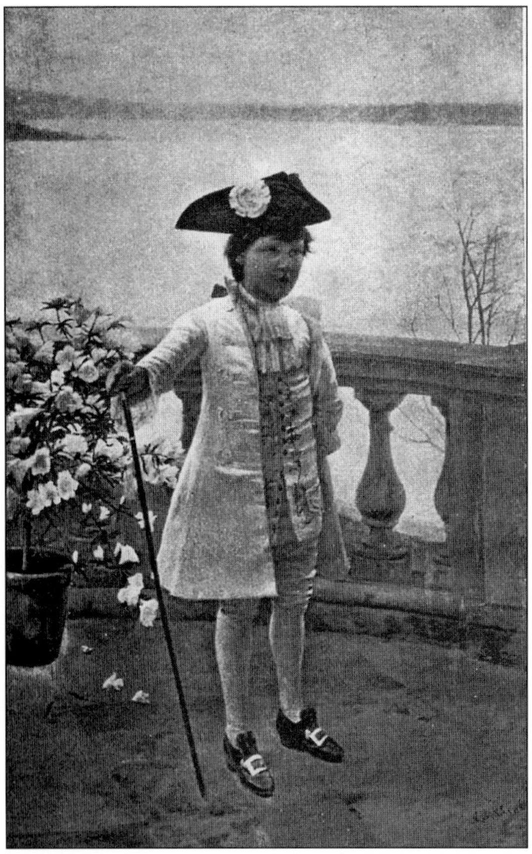
Portrait of a Boy, 1893, oil, 60" x 37" (from the *Pall Mall Gazette, Pictures of 1893*).

Did Garstin himself end up by painting pictures of this type, albeit with the excuse that he was only trying to keep up a small house? The answer is that, during the nineties, some of his major canvasses were at variance with his principles, and that other works, although they were not a betrayal, were somewhat academic.

Pretty Pictures

The most obvious betrayal of Realism was his historical costume pictures. These began with *Portrait of a Boy* (1893), which depicts his eldest son, looking very sweet, and dressed as an eighteenth-century swell. It is a work with few redeeming features, except that it was said to be beautifully soft in tone. *The Scarlet Letter* (1896) was even worse: it shows a scene from Hawthorne's eponymous novel, and is not intelligible without a detailed knowledge of the text. It was, however, described as having some of the weird and haunting power of the story. Next came *Danger* (1898), which shows a timid young Quaker maiden and her young admirer in Georgian dress. This at least has the merit of intelligibility, and apparently of being cleverly painted, because of the moonlight effects and the large amount of white. The final paintings of the costume variety were *A Look of Beauty* (1901) and *A Wolf in the Fold* (1902). In the former a girl is reading and an officer, in eighteenth-century costume, is reading a look of beauty in her face; in the latter a scarlet coated soldier is flirting with a girl, who is bending over some fancy-work, while an elderly and unseen lady listens to what is being said. A critic noted that the attitudes of the figures were fairly well caught.[19]

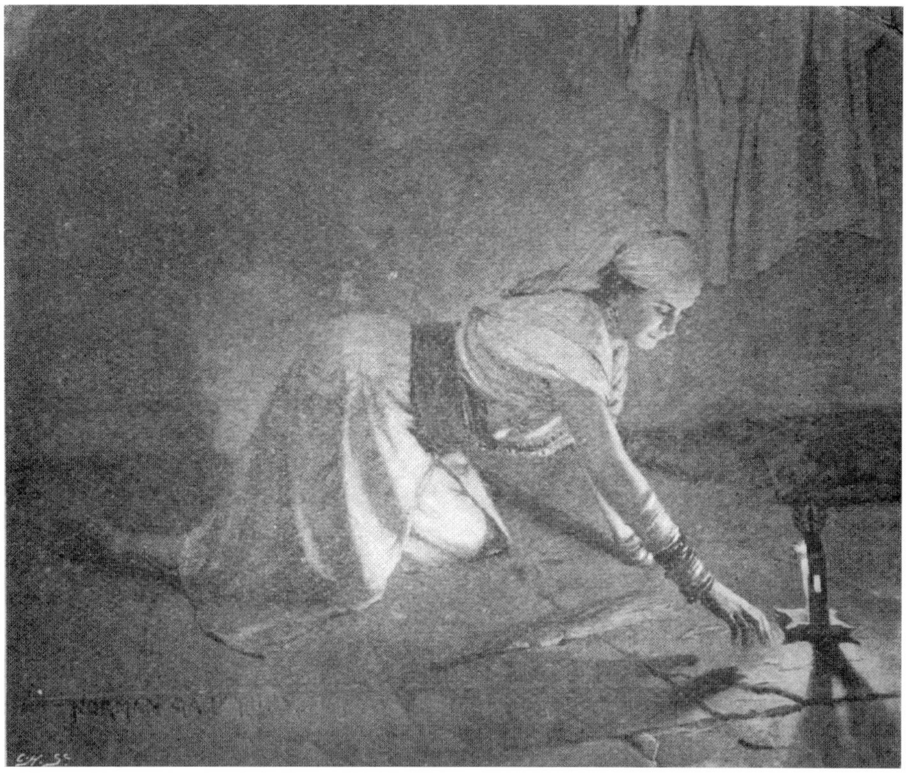

The Piece of Silver that was Lost, 1897. oil. 41" x 47" (from *Academy Notes,* 1898).

There were also two works that, while superior to costume painting and displaying interesting features, are nonetheless contrived and academic; although (as previously) it is necessary to judge from black and white reproductions and/or press comments. *The Piece of Silver that was Lost* (1897) shows a pretty young woman in eastern dress on her knees stretching out for a dropped coin; and in *The Rose and the Ring* (1900) a young woman is kneeling on the edge of a pond into which her reflected sweetheart has thrown a rose. These works are rescued from banality by interesting light effects – respectively candlelight and reflections on ripples – and by the way in which the young woman is seen from behind. This was a device which Garstin frequently employed to avoid sentimentality; in particular in *The Cotillon* (1891), the small picture of his young daughter (1898), and in his 'Xmas 1899' stencil, which shows all three of his children (1899). The two latter pictures are reproduced in Plates 22 and 21.

Prettiness has its place in the world and, though a danger to art, it is not necessarily inartistic. But to those of you who are not artists I would give you this piece of advice, if a picture strikes you as pretty ... distrust it: it may be all right but the chances are too much against it.

Norman Garstin, lecture that begins 'What is our art?'

Story Pictures

During the period 1890-98, Garstin also painted three or four big pictures, which although they may not be among his greatest works and are somewhat academic, do not violate his own principles. They tell stories, but they tell them well and are self-explanatory: no writing either by the artist or by an author is necessary. It may be felt that pictures that involve stories are Victorian and second-rate. Or,

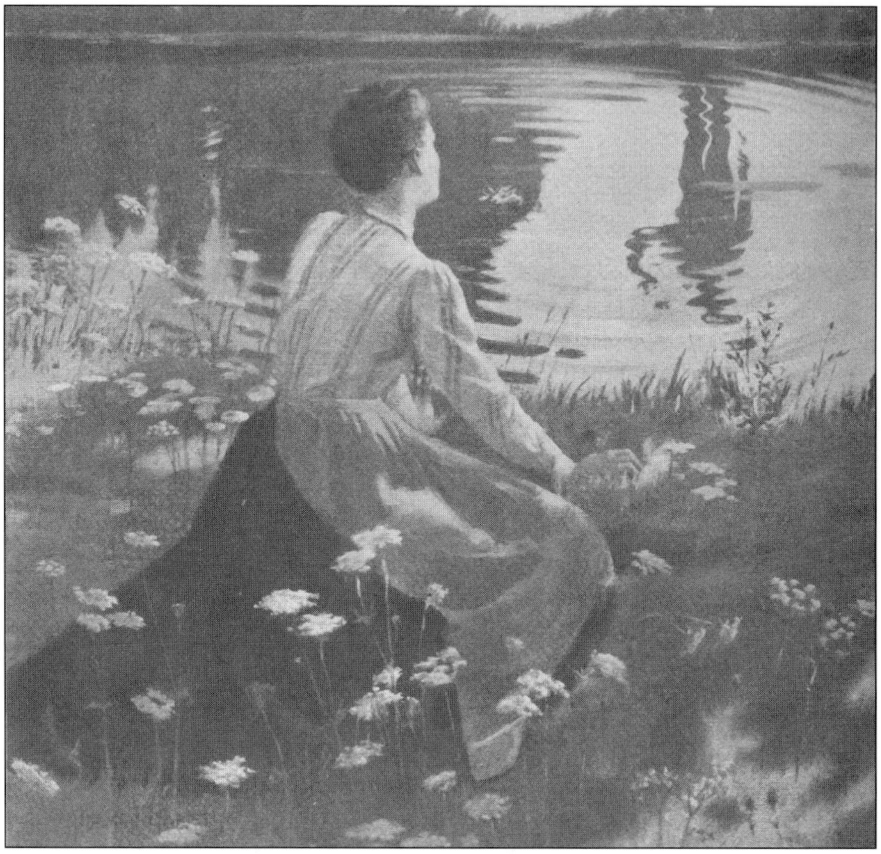

The Rose and the Ring, 1900, oil (from the *Black and White Handbook to the Royal Academy*, 1900).

now that things Victorian have come back into fashion, they may be described as narrative works, which is a fashionable perjorative term. As we shall see, by no means all story pictures can properly be described as narrative works. Moreover many of the most celebrated pictures ever painted are story pictures, including, to choose two almost at random, the *Death of Marat* by David, and Géricault's *Raft of the Medusa*. Furthermore, as Roger Fry, the great scourge of Victorian academic painting, argued so forcefully, pictures – which appear to the casual observer and the ideologue to be merely narrative works – can have painterly qualities of the highest order. Here is what he says in his essay on Giotto:

> It is customary to dismiss all that concerns the dramatic presentation of the subject as literature or illustration, which is to be sharply distinguished from the qualities of the design. But can this clear distinction be drawn in fact? The imaginings of a playwright, a dramatic poet and a dramatic painter have much in common, but they are never at any point identical. Let us suppose a story to be treated by all three: to each, as he dwells on the legend, the imagination will present a succession of images, but those images, even at their first formation, will be quite different in each case, they will be conditioned and coloured by the art which the creator practices ... The painter, like Giotto, therefore, actually imagines in terms of figures capable of pictorial presentment, he does not merely

> translate a poetically dramatic vision into pictorial terms ... To be able, then, to conceive just the appropriate pose of a hand to express the right idea of character and emotion in a picture, is surely as much a matter of a painter's vision as to appreciate the relative 'values' of a tree and cloud so as to convey the mood proper to a particular landscape.[20]

One of the big Garstin pictures that did not violate his own principles was *Her Signal*, which is reproduced in Plate 24. A middle-aged woman is dozing over a book while her young attendant signals from the window to somebody outside, presumably a young man. It is an interesting work because of its subtle tones and multiple sources of light, with the yellow of candlelight contrasting with the cold moonlight. The paint work is deft and economical. The emotional temperature is low. There is no interaction between the two women, and the face of the young one can only just be seen. Hence it cannot fairly be described as sentimental.

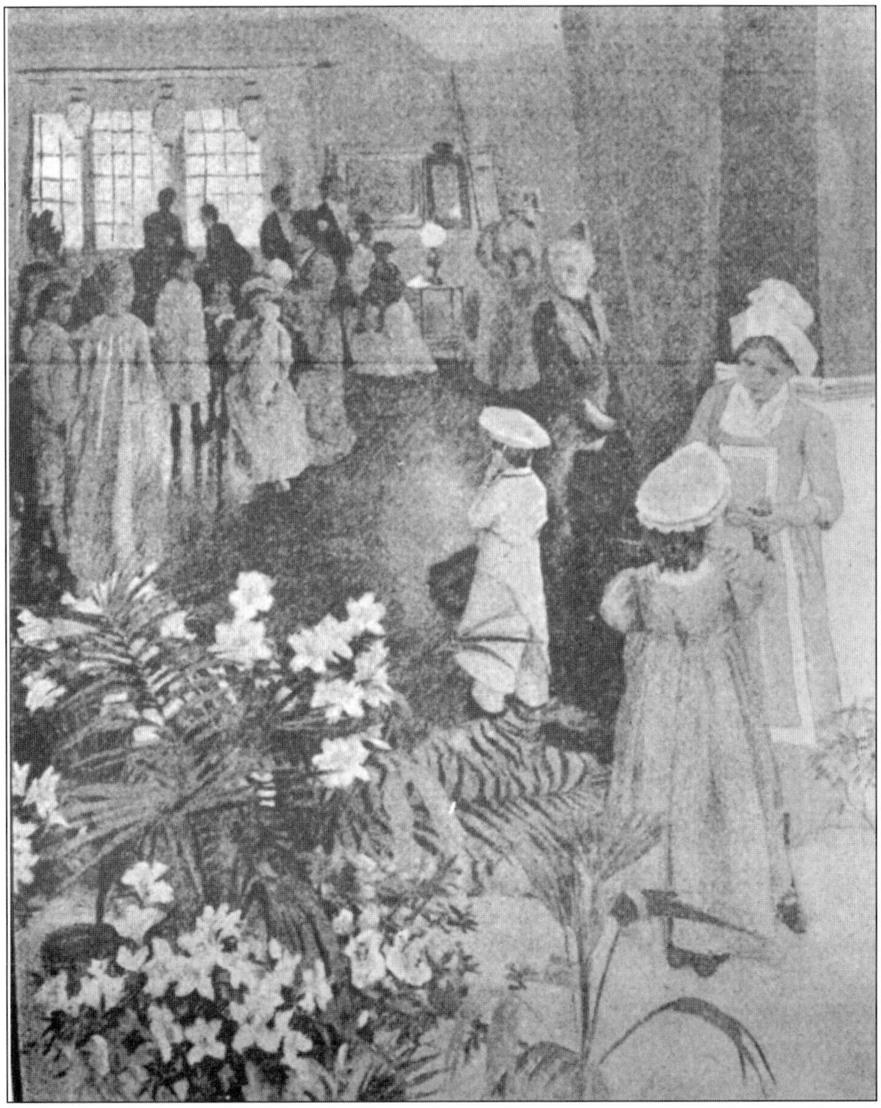

The Cotillon, 1891, oil, 49" x 38" (from *Academy Notes*, 1892).

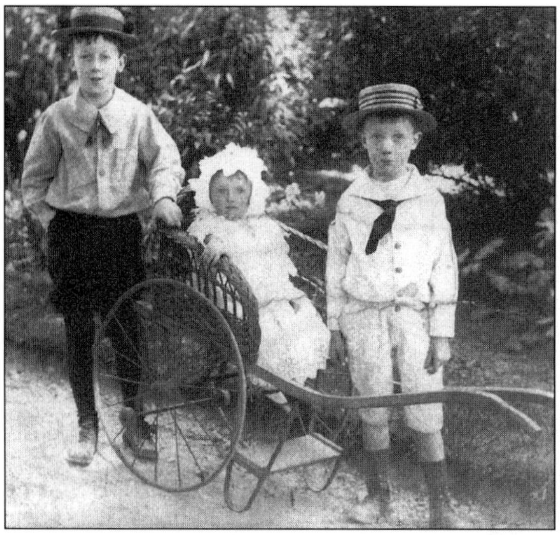

Crosbie, Alethea and Denis Garstin *c.*1896.

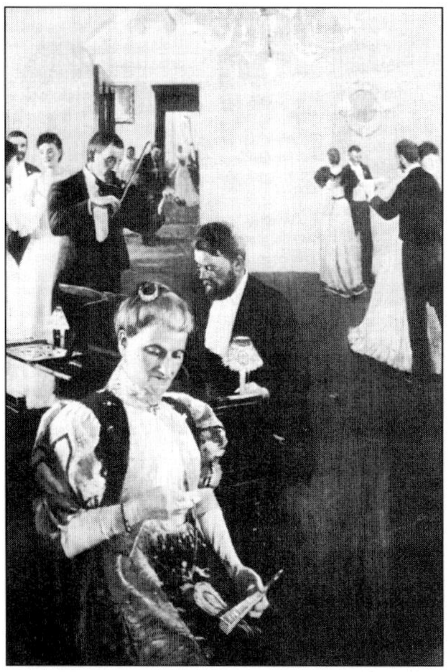

Above:
The Last Dance, 1894, oil, 53" x 35" *Illustrated Catalogue of the Walker Art Gallery*, 1895).

Opposite:
Elizabeth Stanhope Forbes, *A Dream Princess,* 1897, oil (Royal Institution of Cornwall, Truro).

Nevertheless *Her Signal* does not have the originality of *The Rain it Raineth* or *Overdue* and it is less strict in its Realism. One of the characteristics of Realist paintings is that they depict a seemingly random instant in time and do not indicate, within the picture itself, what has happened or what will happen. They may well be a snapshot incident in an ongoing story, which is either self-evident or of which the viewer is likely to be aware, but they will not be narrative works, in the sense that different parts of the same story are, in one way or another, being depicted in a particular picture. This can be done by giving pictorial clues about what has happened or will happen, as in so many Pre-Raphaelite works.

Her Signal, in contrast to *Overdue*, contains such clues. There is a bird cage near the young woman and an hour glass close to the elbow of the older woman, who is a widow, as her ring shows. As the hour glass is only half way through its course, and the widow's hair is not yet grey, she is not very old; nor does her face suggest illness. The book she has fallen asleep over is not the Bible, as shown by the pink bookmark and the absence of double columns. This, together with the warm green of her chair, makes the scene less gloomy. It is, so far as the older woman is concerned, a picture of repose, and even boredom, rather than of suffering. The bookmark and the green chair are painterly touches, and the clues have to be sought out. This means that, unless one has an ideological objection to narrative pictures, some pleasure is to be had in discovering them and reading the picture. Nevertheless their presence does mean that *Her Signal* is more conventional than Garstin's earlier pictures.

Other story pictures that deserve a mention are *The Cotillon* and *The Last Dance* (1894). In the former a young girl in Kate Greenaway dress, with high bodice and puffed sleeves, is shown entering a fancy dress party. It appears from a contemporary report, and a black and white illustration, that this was well painted, with interesting multiple sources of light. In *The Last Dance* a resigned matron consults her watch while dancing continues, though the sun has risen. This is a picture with contending lights, and in which the strong face of the matron is well executed. Because of its humour and the fashionable scene, it is reminiscent of Tissot, although unfortunately only a black and white reproduction is available.

Quality Sustained

That Garstin had not, even for the time being, lost his genius is shown by his major work *What's News?* (1892) and his small picture, *Mount's Bay in June* (1897), which is reproduced in Plate 5. The latter picture is emphatically divided into bands, with the harbour cutting the sea in two. In earlier paintings Garstin had, following Whistler, experimented with parallel bands of land, water and sky. This picture

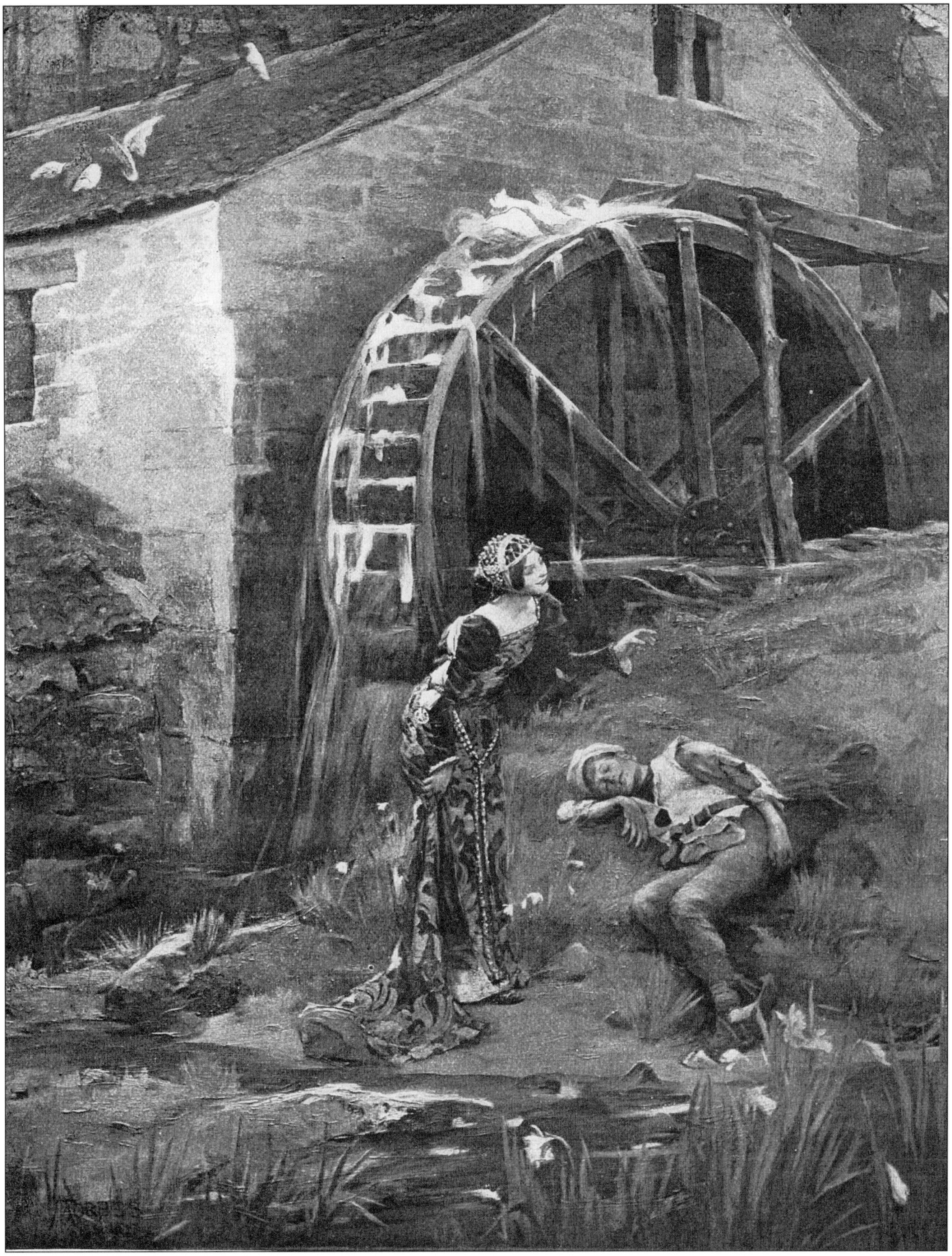

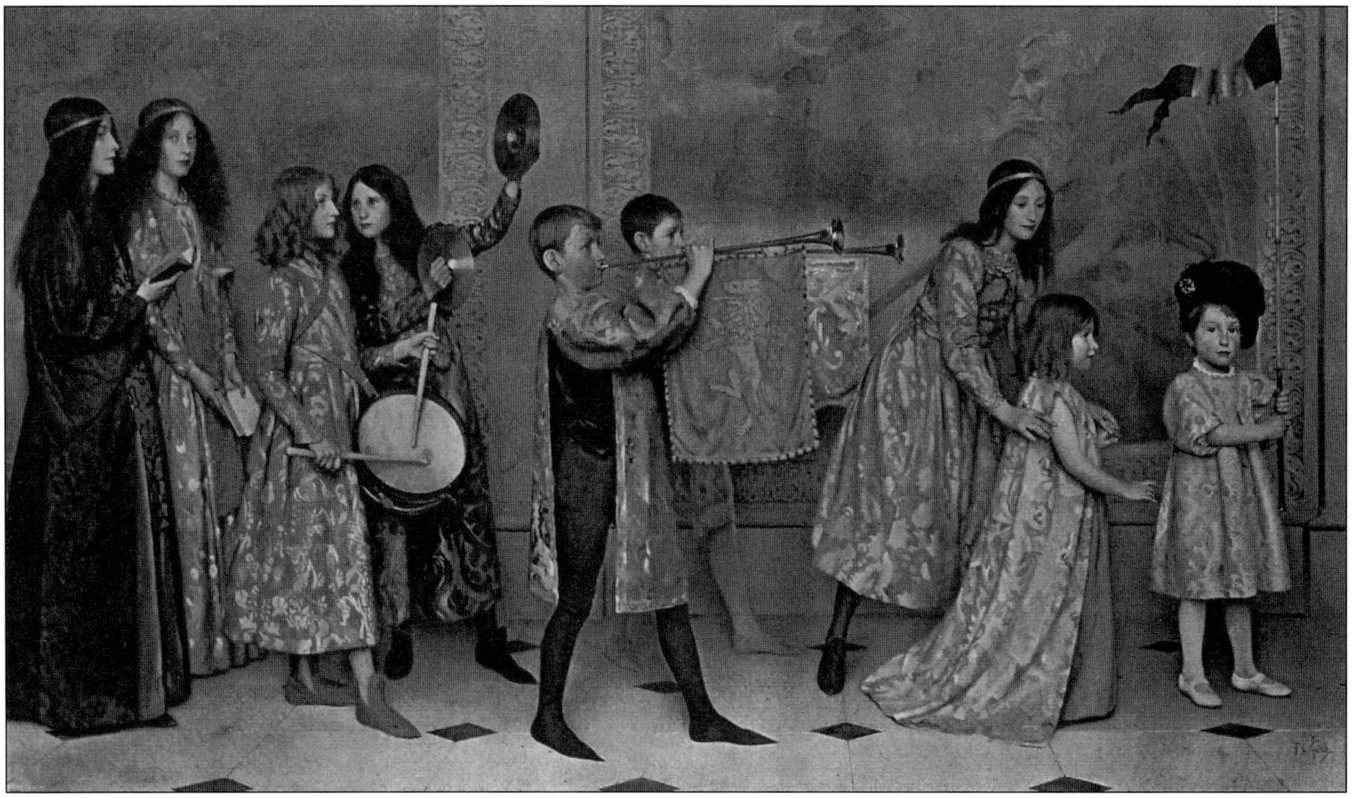

Thomas Cooper Gotch, *A Pageant of Childhood*, 1899, oil (Walker Art Gallery, Liverpool).

is fruition: the relationship between the upper and lower bands of sea is appropriate because of its asymmetrical balance. The colours become darker as the distance recedes, and there is an interesting contrast between the upper and lower sections of sea and between the harbour wall and the distant coastline. The horizontal effect is relieved by the diagonal positioning of the ship and St Michael's Mount and the parallel diagonal formed by the small boats. The colours are gentle and harmonious, and warmth is imparted by the orange sail, its reflection, the small boat, and the harbour rail. It is a work of great beauty and tranquillity, and has a strong *à travers* effect. The small boats draw one into the picture, and the pier and the coastline have an arresting effect: they create bounded space.

Though perhaps less outstanding than *Mount's Bay*, *What's News?*, which is shown in Plate 23, is nonetheless a fine piece of painting. The fisherman's newspaper is especially convincing, and the curves in the paper have an interesting analogue in the curve of the rail. Other creditable works that Garstin painted during the 1890s include *The Tryst* (1893), *Mount's Bay and Tolcarne* (1898), and *Autumn*. The date of the latter picture is not known, but its style and colours strongly suggest the nineties. *Mount's Bay and Tolcarne*, which Heron greatly admired, is reproduced as Plate 25.

A Better Reception but no Improvement in Prices or Sales

Garstin's attempt to paint pictures with greater popular appeal met with some success. There were no more exhibits at the Grosvenor, which closed at the end of 1890, or the New English Art Club, from which all the Newlyn painters resigned in the autumn of the same year, after a series of stinging attacks on their work by Sickert. However, between 1892 and 1900, nine of his pictures were exhibited at the Academy, and pictures were accepted every year except 1894 and 1897, though they were not always hung on the line. His *Portrait of a Boy* (1893) was, for instance, placed high up. Apart from the Academy, his pictures were exhibited in other prestigious galleries, such as Liverpool and Manchester.

Garstin's major works now received greater attention, either in the form of reproductions, or, more rarely, references in reviews. *Her Signal* was reproduced in four places, and there was a short but complimentary mention in the *Liverpool Daily Post*; though *The*

Walter Langley, *Motherless*, 1895, oil (private collection).

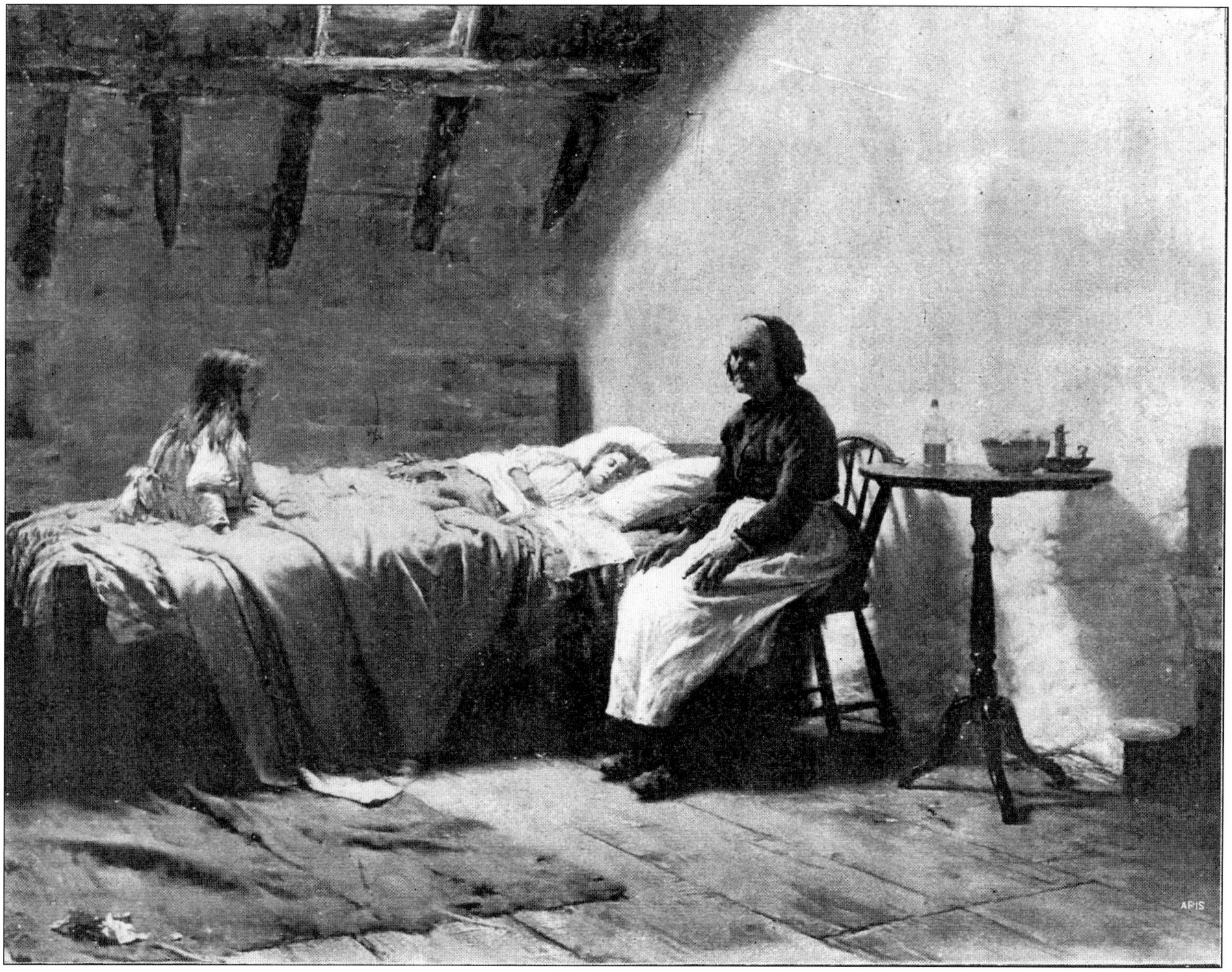

Athenaeum was a little less enthusiastic. *Portrait of a Boy, The Last Dance* and *The Scarlet Letter*, each had three reproductions; *The Rose and the Ring* had two; and *The Cotillon*, *Danger*, and *The Piece of Silver* each had one.[21] *The Athenaeum* described the latter's firelight and shadow as clever. A short biography of Garstin appeared in the Black and White *Handbook to the Royal Academy* for 1893, and he was also mentioned in 1894. An even more exhaustive and exhausting search would probably reveal additional publicity. Another of his pictures, *To Cheat Surprise and Prying Eyes*, was, for instance, mentioned in *The Southport Visitor*. Nevertheless there were significant lacunae. None of the pictures he exhibited at the RA were mentioned in *The Times*.

Although they received slightly more notice, Garstin's pictures did not sell any better or command high prices. One hundred and fifty pounds was the most that he asked for a painting between 1892 and 1900, and £105 was the largest amount he received. This was the sum that T. B. Bolitho, who was the local MP, paid for *Her Signal*. It was a derisory sum compared with the amounts received by other comparable artists. During this period, Stanhope Forbes sold four

Frank Bramley, *After Fifty Years*, 1893, oil (whereabouts unknown).

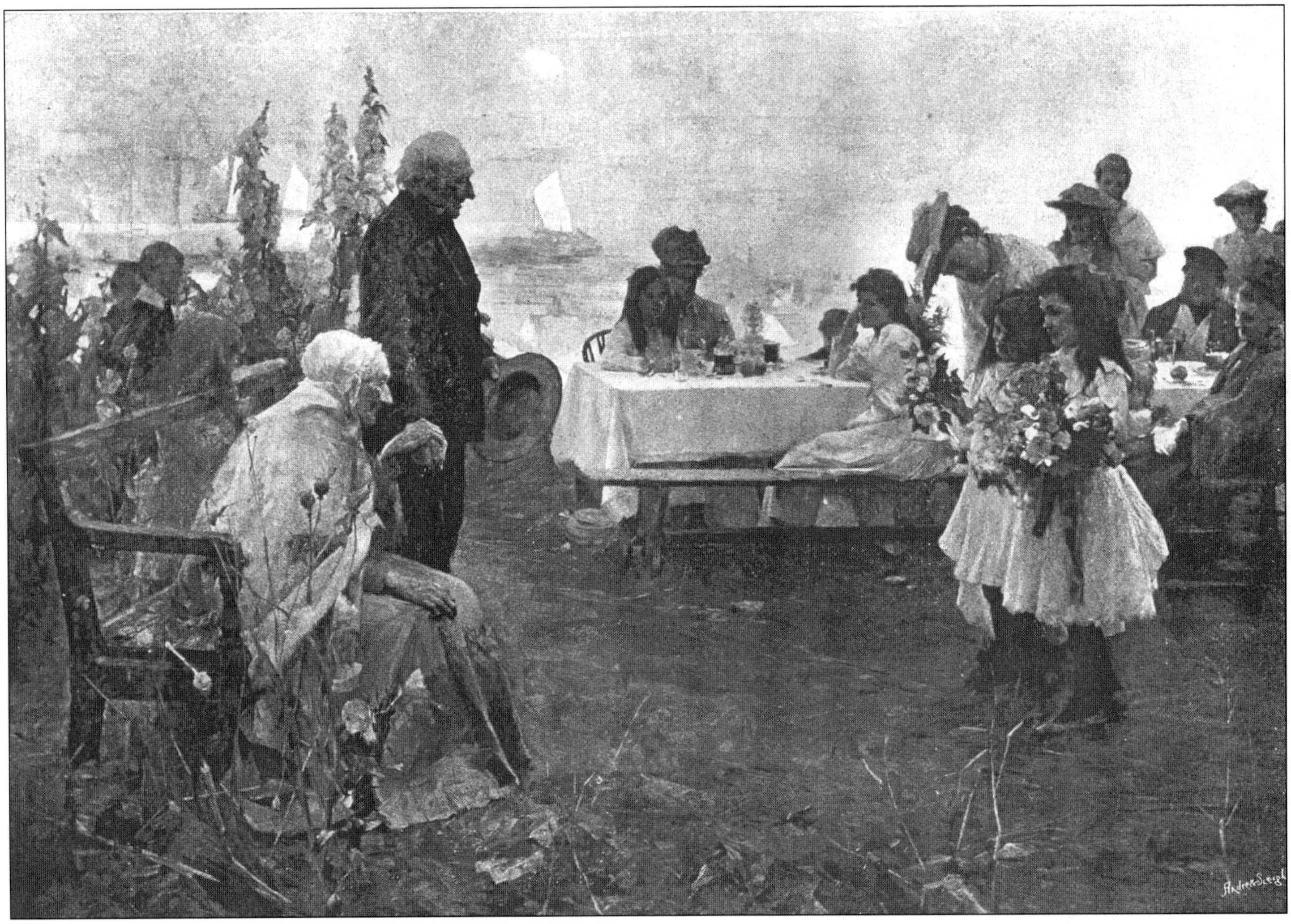

pictures each for £900 or more. Some of Garstin's big pictures were left on his hands, and did not sell until well into the next century. This was true of *The Cotillon*, *The Last Dance* and *The Scarlet Letter*. Garstin's average annual income from selling pictures was only £120 between 1890 and 1899, at catalogue prices.

Attractive and Unattractive Pictures

Why, now that he was painting more appealing works, did Garstin's canvases not sell better? That they had greater appeal is evident not only from the attention they received but also from Jope-Slade's declaration that Garstin, and the other Newlyn artists, were no longer painting dismal pictures. When the demand for pictures of fishing village life appeared to be waning, the Newlyn painters mostly gave up painting genre of this type. Thomas Gotch with his *Child Enthroned* (1894), and Elizabeth Forbes, began painting decorative pictures, often featuring children in pseudo-medieval dress which, especially in the case of Forbes, had a strong mythical content.[22] From *A Summer Dinner Party* (1893) and *Gentlemen the Queen* (1894) onward, Chevallier Tayler mainly painted scenes of upper class life; though he also painted historical and religious works. Frank Bramley continued to paint humble folk for longer, but many of his pictures were of the chocolate box variety, featuring sweet young animals, pretty young girls, or touching old people; and he too ended by abandoning such genre. The only Newlyn painters, either present or previous, who did not seriously deviate from the original path were Forbes and Langley, though the latter had always verged on the sentimental.

Although Garstin painted more popular pictures they were not, faced with competition of this type, sufficiently appealing. He continued to paint pictures where there is little or no interaction between the principal figures, and to range widely in his choice of subjects. He was himself well aware that, to be successful, it was desirable to paint a narrow range of subjects. Indeed, he thought that the English were particularly wary of versatility, remarking later that it was 'apt to stand in the way of popular success, for the world likes to be able to label a man – "Oh, that is the fellow who paints cats or mountains, etc, who does those beautiful gardens, etc."'[23] However, he also saw the danger of becoming stale through painting a worn-out theme: 'the artist who wanders in many fields keeps young and gets more joy out of his visions than does the specialist'.

Success in a Deteriorating Market

Another reason for Garstin's lack of success, even though he was now painting more popular works, was that he was working in a crowded and deteriorating market. It may well be that, during the

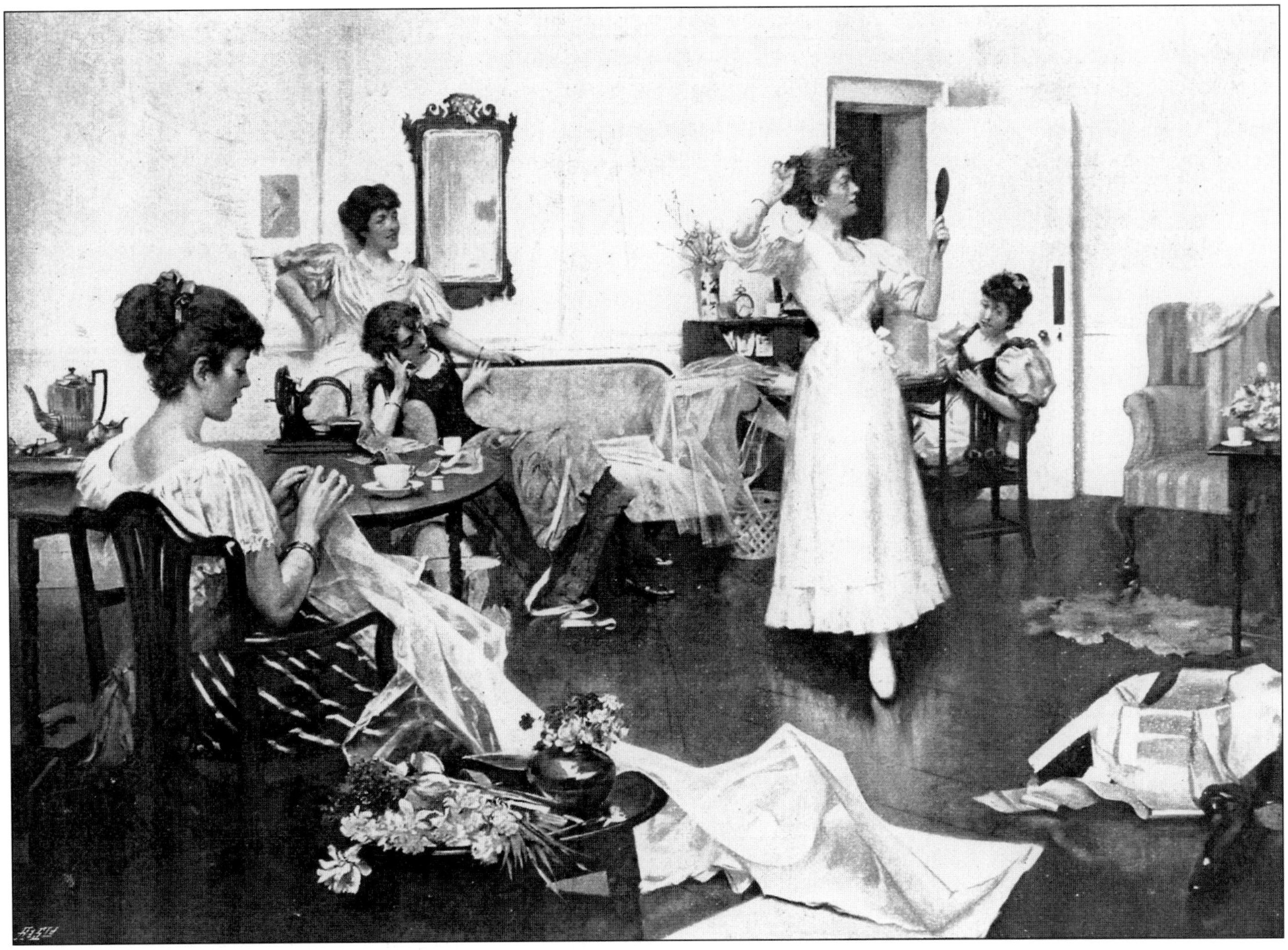

Chevallier Tayler, *Vanities*, 1896, oil (whereabouts unknown).

nineties the number of talented artists was exceptionally great: they included Whistler, Burne-Jones and Leighton among the older generation, and Sargent, Sickert, Steer, Clausen, Lavery and La Thangue among younger artists. It was a period of rich diversity because of the conflict and melding between home grown and foreign styles. Although it would be difficult to prove conclusively that the production of first rate pictures was particularly great, what can certainly be established is that supply exceeded demand.

The third quarter of the nineteenth century had been a boom period for artists. Before that the main demand was for old masters, and, as the home market was unable to cope, this led both to the importation of dubious pictures and the production of fakes. This, together with the emergence of new patrons, and new dealers who met their needs, led to a growing demand for modern British pictures. These patrons wanted genuine pictures for which a living artist could vouch, and paintings which they found interesting. They had made money through trade and industry, like James Leathart (who bought Pre-Raphaelites), Frederick Leyland (the patron of

Rossetti and Whistler), and the Gardiner brothers (who supported the Glasgow Boys); or they had inherited an industrial fortune, like Abraham Mitchell (who was La Thangue's patron). However, after about 1885 or even earlier, the art market turned sour.[24]

According to my estimates, the average price for works sold at the autumn exhibition of the Walker Gallery in Liverpool rose from just under £27 in 1871-4 to just under £32.50 in 1880-4. After this there was a steady decline, and by 1895-9 the average price had fallen to just under £25, which was a decline of approaching a quarter. This was followed by a slight recovery, during 1900-04 to about £27.50. (The decline in the total value of works sold was even more spectacular. Between 1880-4 and 1900-04 the figure fell by half, with all of the reduction taking place by 1890-4. But no great significance should be attached to this, because of the substantial increase in the number of municipal galleries holding annual exhibitions at which artists could offer their pictures for sale.)

The *Magazine of Art* attributed the low prices being received, during the mid-1890s, partly to the death of some of the old patrons, but mainly to adverse economic conditions. There was less demand by the affluent (especially for new and more speculative paintings) at the very time when there was an enhanced supply of old pictures, because existing collections were being broken up. These pictures included many eigtheenth-century paintings, which were increasingly favoured. During the 1880s a nostalgic eigtheenth-century revival gained momentum. Lord Leverhulme, a huge collector, began by purchasing many contemporary pictures, but then largely turned to English pictures from the eigtheenth century. During the latter part of the century, there were too few collectors like George McCulloch, who made it a rule not to buy any picture which had not been painted during his lifetime, and who, incidentally, acquired a canvas by Garstin. The Aesthetic Movement also helped to restrict the demand for contemporary works. It became unfashionable to cover walls with pictures of indifferent quality, and fashionable to value other types of decoration.

Not only was there a reduction in the average amount received for new pictures, but it also seems probable that the incomes of artists became more unequal. During the first half of the nineteenth century even the best-known artists often lived in modest houses. In the 1860s, '70s and '80s they moved into palatial studio houses in Chelsea, Kensington, St John's Wood, Hampstead, and, above all, Holland Park, where Leighton, Watts, Fildes, Val Prinsep, Marcus Stone, Colin Hunter, and Shannon all settled. Herkomer built a house at Bushey, and Watts and Holl in the Surrey countryside. These houses were not infrequently designed by fashionable and innovative architects, such as Norman Shaw (Holl, Fildes and Goodall) and the

American Henry Hobson Richardson (Herkomer). Big houses in London were not only a sign, but also a cause, of success. Artists held Show Sundays at their houses in Holland Park prior to the opening of exhibitions at the Royal Academy and Grosvenor Gallery, and Fildes had his house specially designed for this purpose. In this way they further enhanced their sales.

This was but one aspect of the circle of success, which Garstin never entered. Another was to become an ARA and then an RA. Holman Hunt recalled that, 'a new associate of the Academy immediately received an accession of demand for his works'.[25] Moreover Royal Academicians were entitled to show eight works and their pictures were hung in the most advantageous positions. If the Academy was the great prize, membership of other bodies was also helpful. Mann reported that 'Lavery is in luck just now. This week he has had estimates to give for two portraits and to-day he has got a commission for a third. He says this comes of being an ARSA! [Associate of the Royal Society of Artists]'.[26]

Portraits were the way to make money, even during the difficult economic circumstances in the latter part of the century. Throughout his life, Watts painted portraits to pay the bills, and both the Glasgow Boys and the social realists tuned to portraiture. Herkomer and Holl both became portrait painters in 1881, and Luke Fildes followed their example six years later. With the exception of *The Doctor,* Fildes completely abandoned Social Realism.

How the Effort to Earn Led to Fewer Works

Garstin tried to increase his earnings by painting portraits. His sugary *Portrait of a Boy*, which was exhibited at the Academy in 1893, must have been an attempt to become better known as a portrait painter. Between 1893 and 1899 he is known to have painted six other portraits, and there may well have been others that have not yet come to light. It is, however, unlikely that portraits were a major source of income. There would not have been much scope for portraiture in Cornwall, because of the dearth of wealthy families. The Bolithos were an exception, but Stanhope Forbes had become their portrait painter. Another way in which artists could increase their incomes was through book illustration. Garstin had, back in the mid-1880s, provided an illustration for a novel. It was, however, a wooden piece of work, which is not surprising as his cool style was unsuited to the depiction of dramatic scenes.

Garstin did try to make money through journalism, especially in the newly founded journal, *The Studio*, for which he wrote twelve notes on current painting in Cornwall between 1895 and 1899, together with articles in 1893, 1896 and 1897. Articles and stories were also published in *Black and White*, the *Daily Graphic* and *Temple Bar*. Furthermore, as we have seen, Garstin taught and lectured.

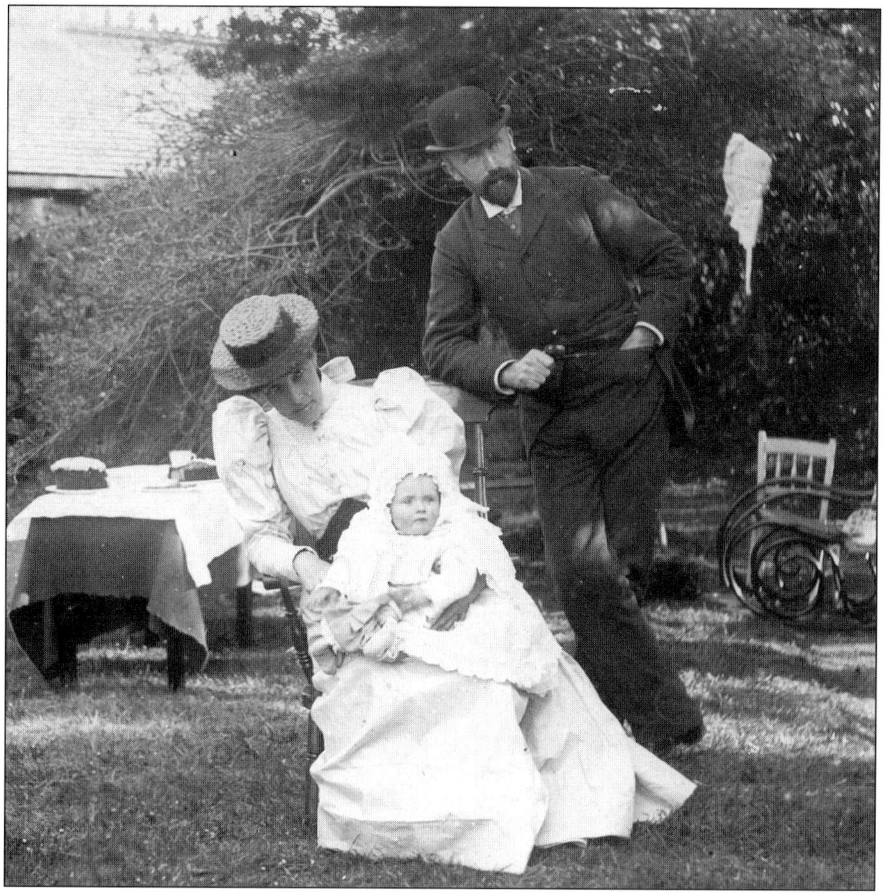

Norman, Alethea and Dochie, 1 June 1895.

All this activity helps to explain why, after his return from Canada, Garstin painted so few pictures, and how, despite this, the family managed to survive. Even so, the strictest economy was necessary. In 1894 the Garstins' third and last child, Alethea, was born. By then they had moved to 4 Wellington Terrace, Penzance, which was to remain their home. This was a substantial and attractive Regency house, but the rent (£22 a year), must have absorbed a significant part of the slender family income. The three children would have entailed substantial expenditure, especially when Crosbie went to prep school, at Brandon House, Cheltenham. The Garstins were so poor that, when Norman had a picture at the Academy, Dochie, who managed the finances, gave him his train fare and half a crown for pocket money! Nevertheless they had two resident servants – a cook and housemaid – in 1901, which was before there can have been any improvement in their financial position.

Even taking a narrow financial view, Garstin almost certainly made the wrong choice when he let his standards slip, and tried to paint more popular pictures. There was too much competition both from those painting fine pictures and those producing kitsch. That it was possible for Naturalists to succeed was shown by Forbes, Clausen and La Thangue. Garstin should have stuck to his last, while developing a speciality. *Overdue*, *Her Signal* and probably *The Cotillon*, show that he had a talent for interiors, and all three had a ready sale. Garstin had taken the wrong path, and become caught in a slough but, as we shall now see, he found a way to escape.

Opposite:
Plate 25 *Mount's Bay and Tolcarne from Trewiddon Farm Footpath with Alethea and her Mother*, 1898, oil, 8" x 10" (Tate Gallery).

Chapter 5

A Summer School Renaissance, 1900-13

One of the many exceptional features of Garstin's life was that he had a second birth. Some artists improve as they get older, many deteriorate, but very few, having entered a period of decline, enjoy a renaissance. Garstin was an exception. His new period of excellence began when he started to take summer painting parties abroad. This had a beneficial effect on his work, and, ultimately, his

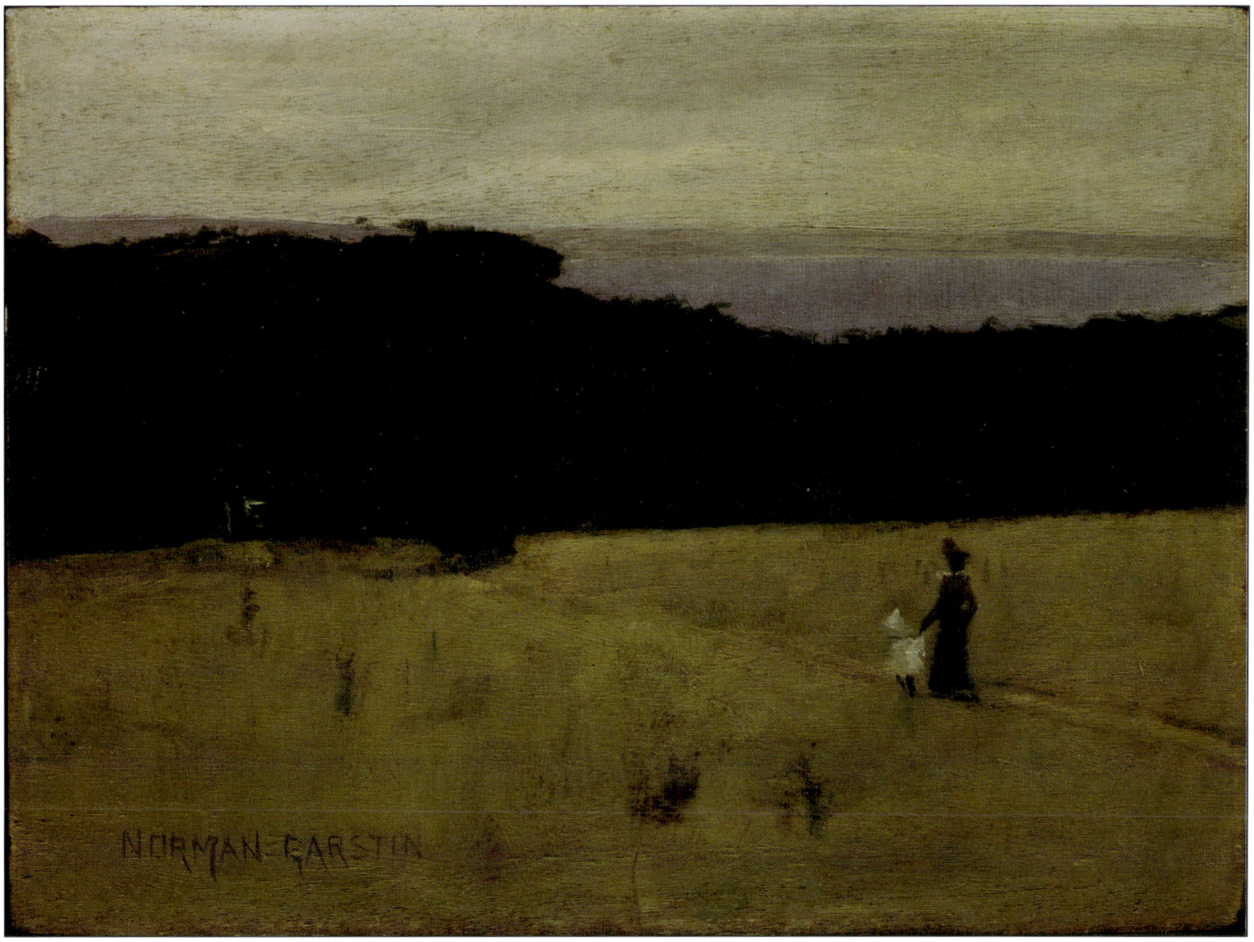

Norman Garstin, *c.*1900, outside 4 Wellington Terrace, Penzance.

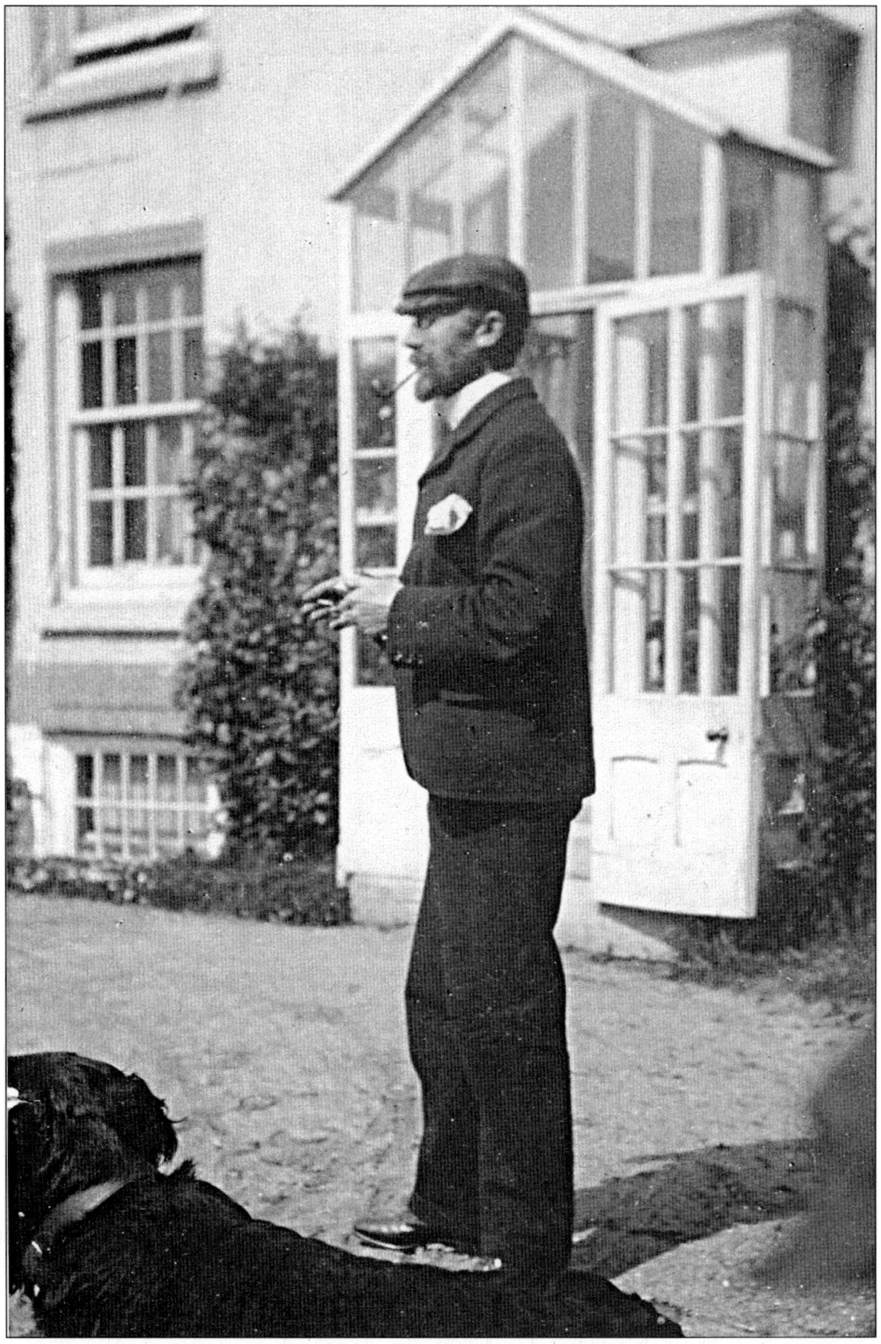

finances. It also led to a partial switch to watercolour. That Garstin's output recovered both in quantity and quality has not been sufficiently recognized, and the impression has been conveyed that, during the nineties, he went into terminal decline. Although Garstin's best work during his renaissance period may not surpass his earlier masterpieces, it is of matching quality.

Painting Parties in France and the Low Countries

While he was not the first, Garstin was among the earliest to take painting parties abroad. (The first advertisement in *The Studio* for a

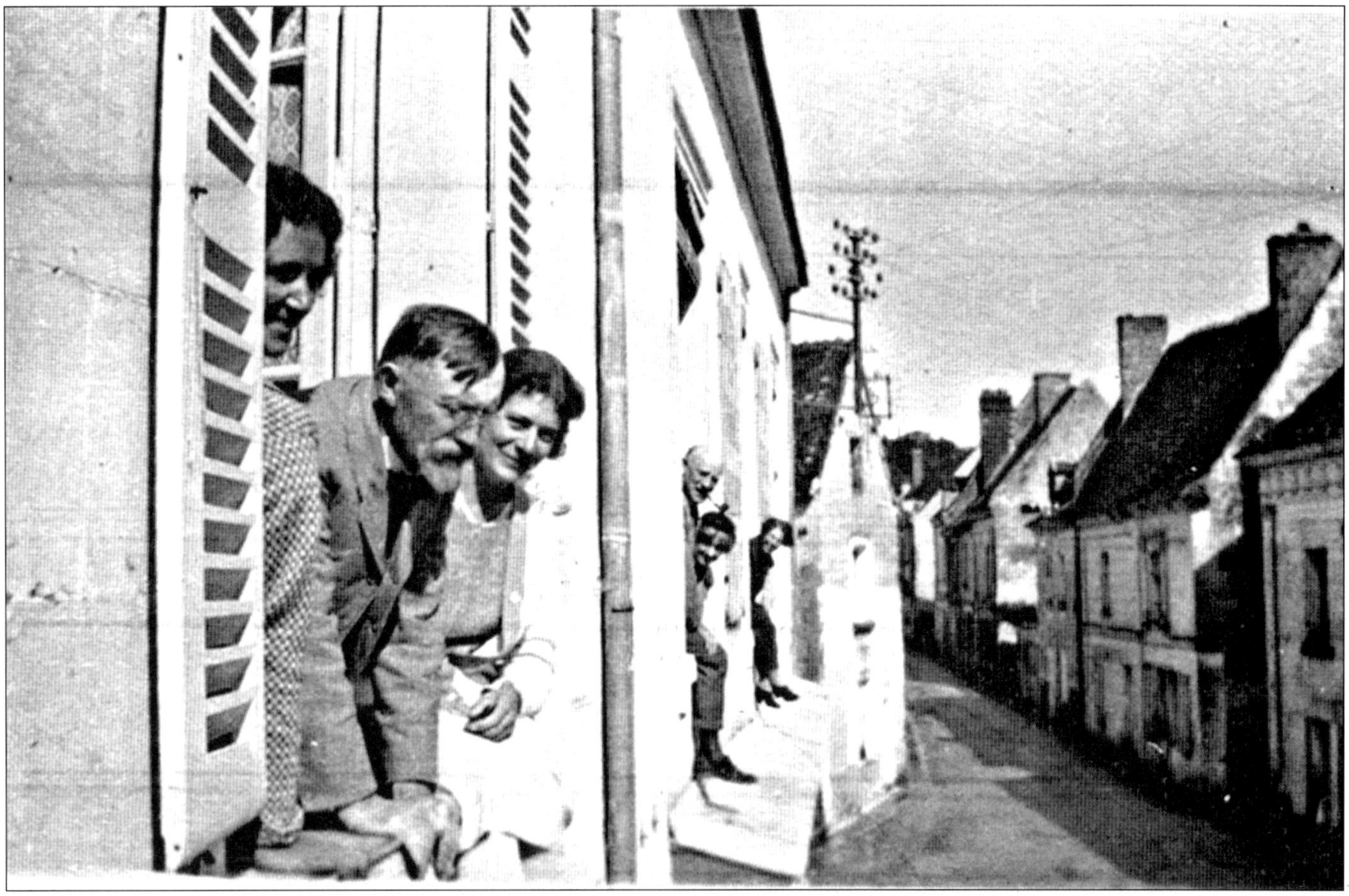

Garstin with pupils on a Continental summer school, probably at Wissent, near Calais, in 1921.

continental sketching class appeared in 1897, placed by The Grosvenor Studio, which had run a summer sketching class as early as 1895.) Garstin held his first foreign summer school in 1899 at Caudebec-en-Caux, a little town near the mouth of the Seine and he was away from mid-July until the last week in September. In August, there appear to have been as many as 27 students, since Dochie, who organized the social side, recorded a picnic party of this size. Alethea's earliest memory was of hearing shouts of 'A bas les Anglais – Vive les Boers!', when perched on the handlebars of her father's bicycle.[1] This was ironic as Garstin was almost certainly a pro-Boer, like the local MP Leonard Courtney, whom he knew well.

Up to the First World War the Garstins organized painting parties abroad, every summer. They had a common pattern, although the place and the weather varied, with many a long Edwardian summer afternoon being wet and windy. All the classes took place in north west France and the Low Countries, with Brittany (1900, 1902, 1904, 1911-14) and Flanders (1903, 1906-08) being the favourite areas. Sometimes the school would begin in one place and then transfer elsewhere, as in 1903, when they moved from Bruges in Belgium to a little place near Dordrecht in Holland. Garstin tried to find picturesque little towns, where he and his students could find interesting subjects, and stay in inexpensive hotels, although they

Over:
Plate 26 *Saturday* [Josselin], 1912, oil, 9" x 6" (private collection, auctioned as *Continental Street Corner*).

Plate 27 *The Beganier Garden, Josselin*, 1912, oil, 10.5" x 8" (private collection).

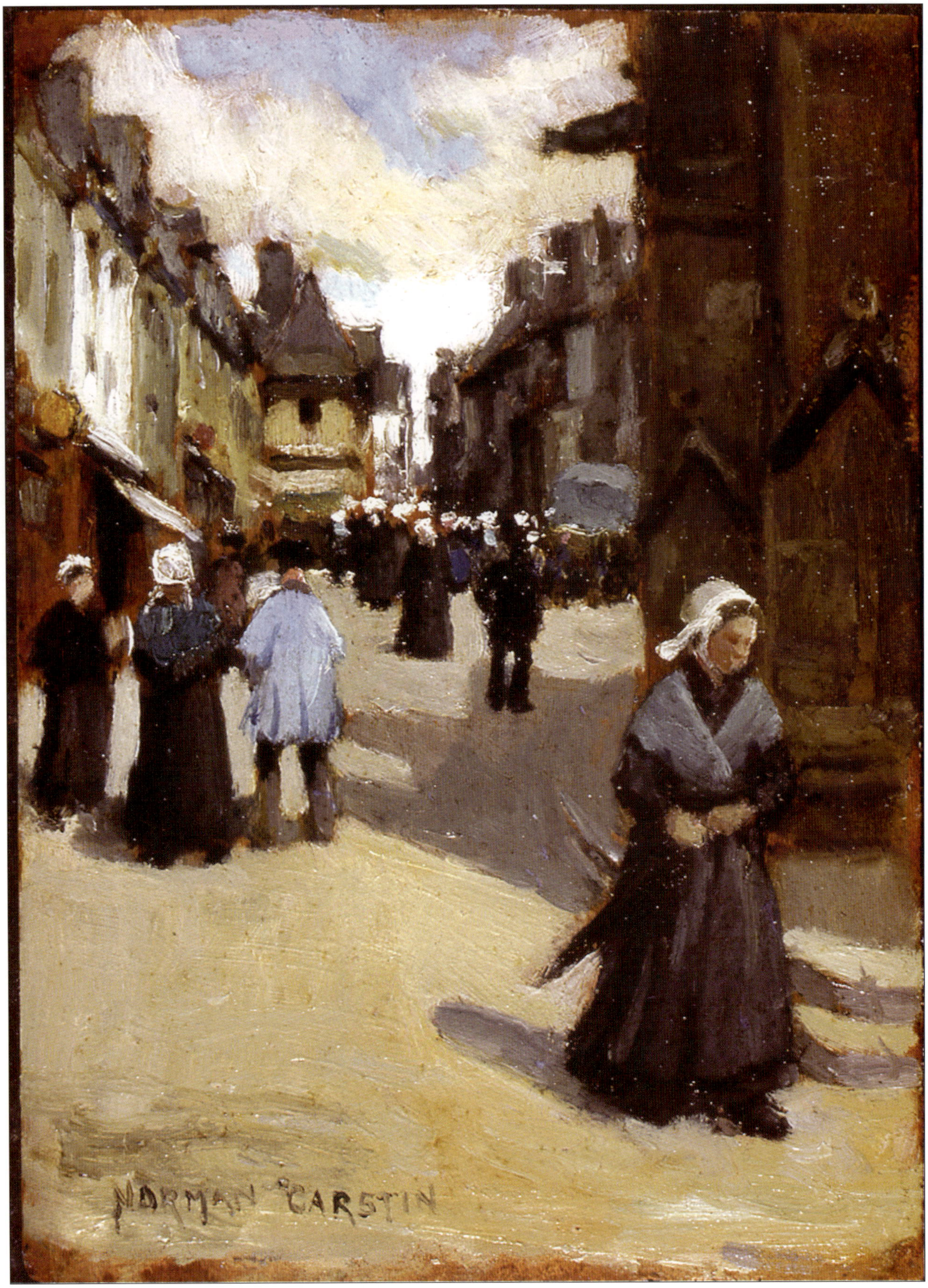
NORMAN CARSTIN

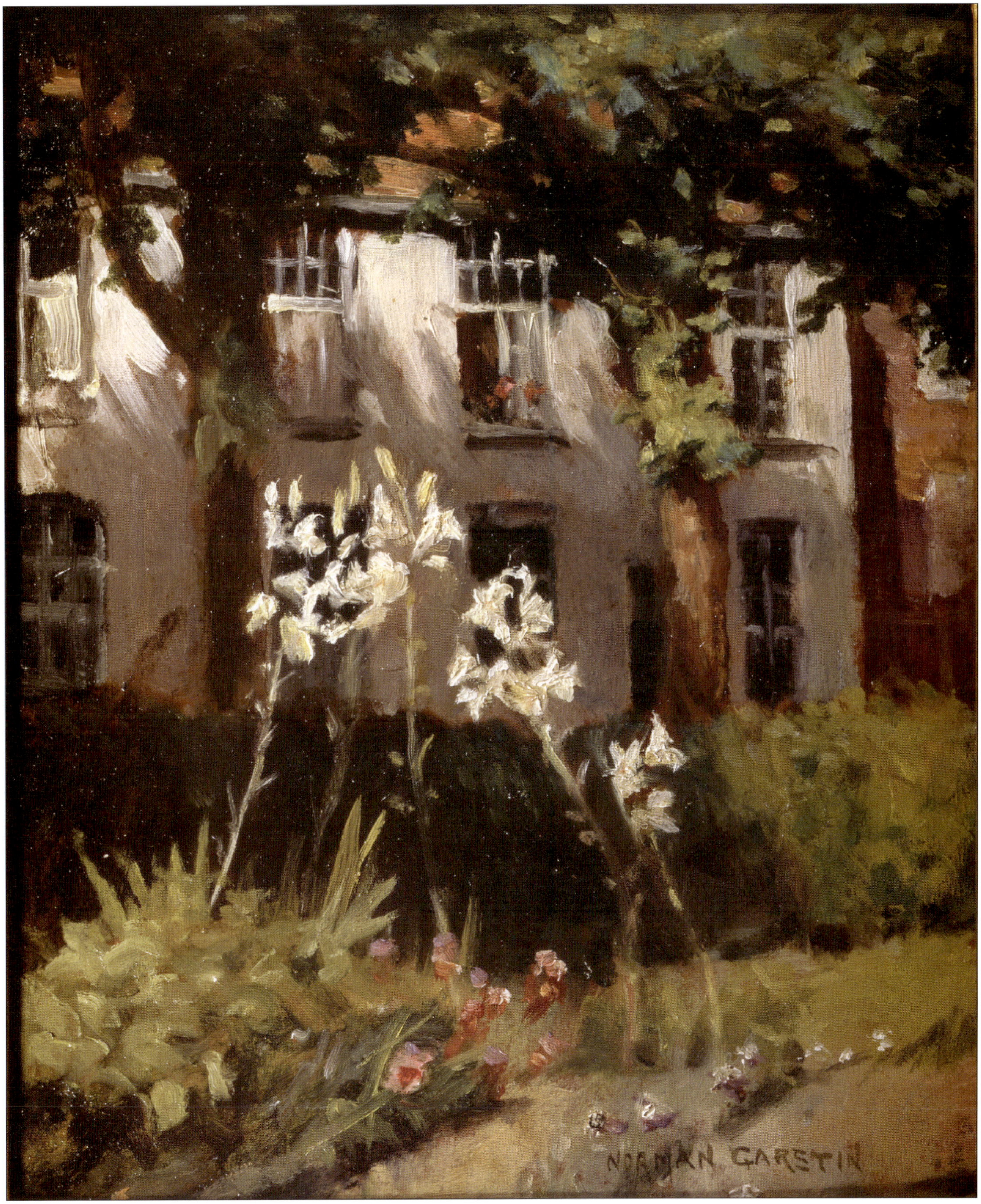
NORMAN GARSTIN

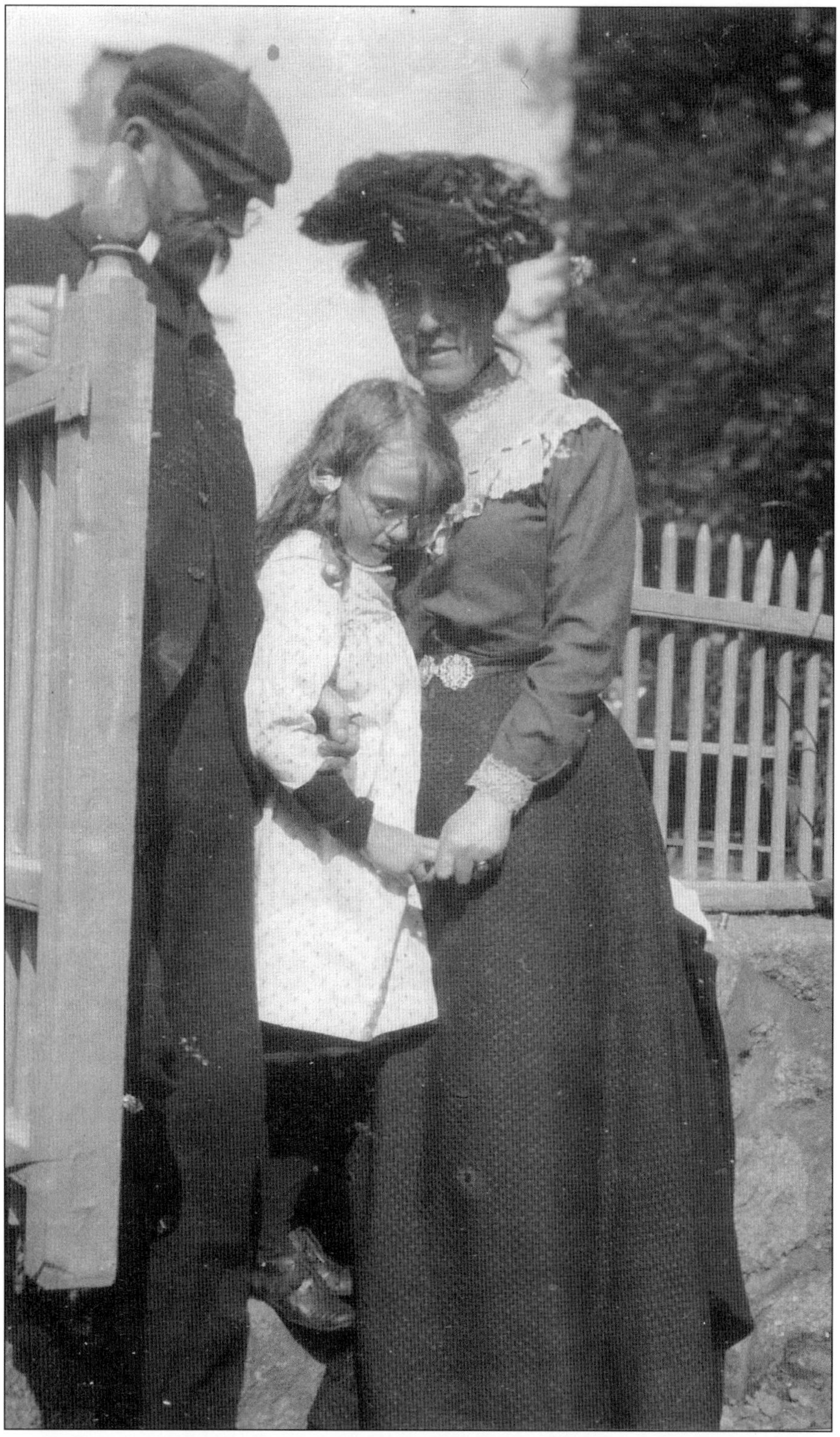
Norman, Alethea and Dochie, *c.*1901.

were not always comfortable. Sometimes they were so small that extra accommodation had to be found elsewhere.

The classes started in June or July, with perhaps a dozen students; the number would rise to as many as 40 in August, but by the middle of September there would be only a handful. The students mainly consisted of single women, with a sprinkling of couples. There were also a few emerging artists. These included Dorothy Richmond (1901-03) and the more famous Frances Hodgkins (1901-03 and 1906), both of whom were from New Zealand. The latter observed that, 'With the exception of Miss Richmond and a very few others I have never met anyone who is really serious about their work – most of the girls who come to a class like this come to amuse themselves and pass the time, but very few work earnestly'.[2]

The students made an early start, with breakfast at 7.30, assuming that an early Dutch class was not atypical. They worked during the morning and Garstin walked or cycled from student to student, offering advice and criticism. Then, according to Hodgkins who is describing Brittany, they returned for *déjeuner*:

> a comprehensive meal consisting of many courses mostly vegetables and very under done meat, puddings never, and copious libations of cider ... After déjeuner we rest till 3, when we all meet in a large room and have afternoon tea and criticise each other's work, then out again for evening effects and at 8.30 we have another huge meal which lasts till 10 o'clock and we end the evening with a stroll ...[3]

After tea, when the students were free to work or play, Garstin would himself paint.

Hodgkins reported that, 'Mrs Garstin's soul loveth a picnic and she never misses a chance of getting one up'.[4] Although Hodgkins complained that they absorbed valuable time, they provided incident and fun, with the New Zealanders boiling water over a fire and, when it smoked, being chaffed for making kippered tea. Occasionally there were other diversions, such as religious ceremonies and the boat race against American artists in 1903. When Hodgkins remarked that she was related to those who had captained boats, Mr Garstin immediately lifted a loud voice and said

> 'Miss Hodgkins says her brother-in-law is Admiral of the Australian Squadron and if anyone should know how to row she should' and thereupon I was unanimously elected [cox].[5]

The boat ran onto a mud bank, the improvised rudder got fouled with weeds, an oar was lost, and one lady rower ended up in the bottom of the boat. When Hodgkins was called out to practice late in the evening by the irrepressible Crosbie, she hurled a tin of insect powder and a stick at him, and 'told him to clear but with the pertinacity of the household flea he kept up his ground and finally to get rid of him I went with him'.[6]

The summer schools owed their success to the characters and abilities of Norman and Dochie. 'Miss Richmond and I', Hodgkins wrote, 'are never tired of congratulating ourselves on our good luck

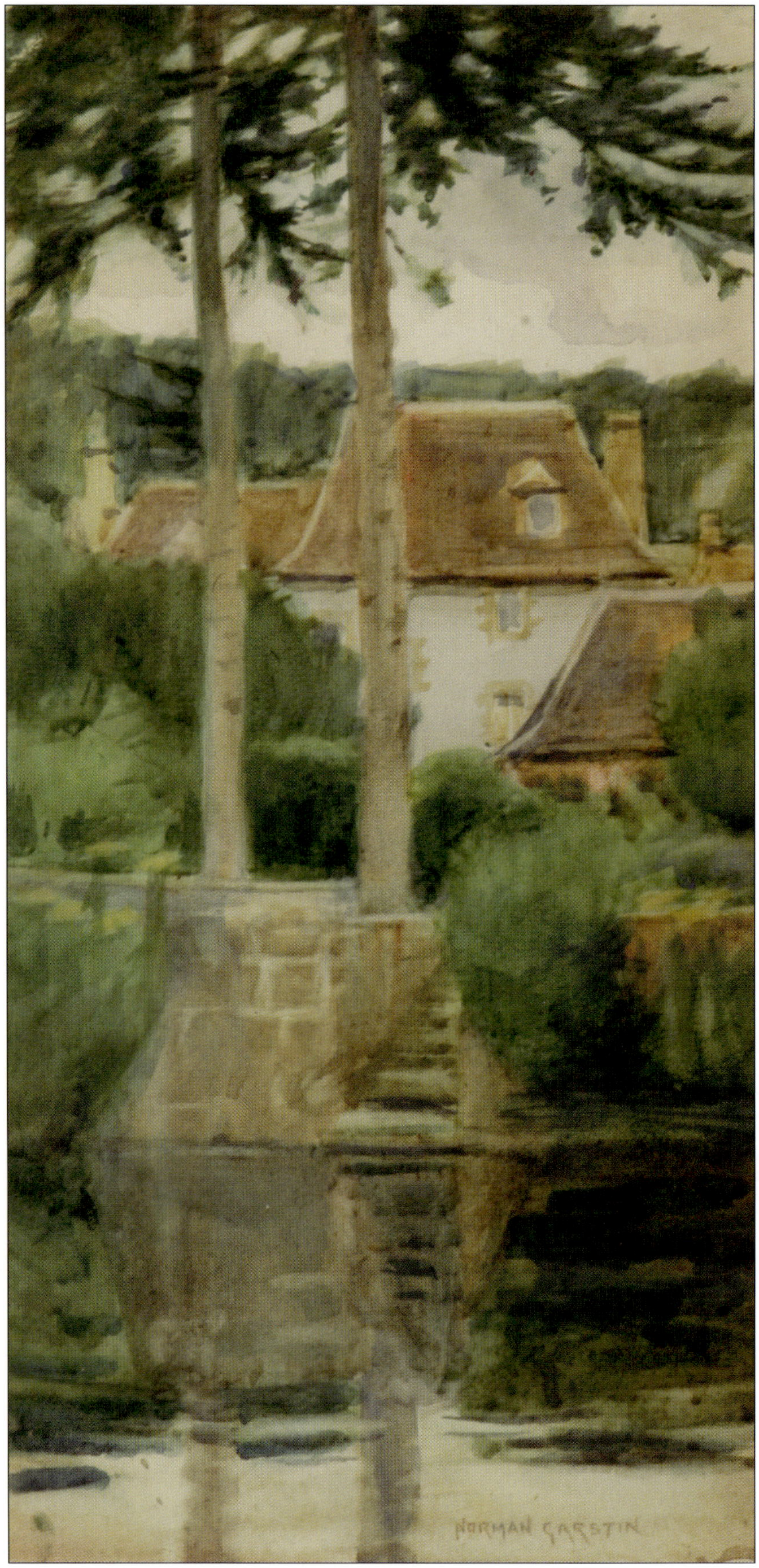

Plate 28 *A Château by the River* [Ellé], *Quimperlé*, 1904, watercolour, 14.25" x 10.5" (private collection).

Right:
Plate 29 *Madonna Lilies*, 1912, oil, 10.6" x 8.25" (private collection).

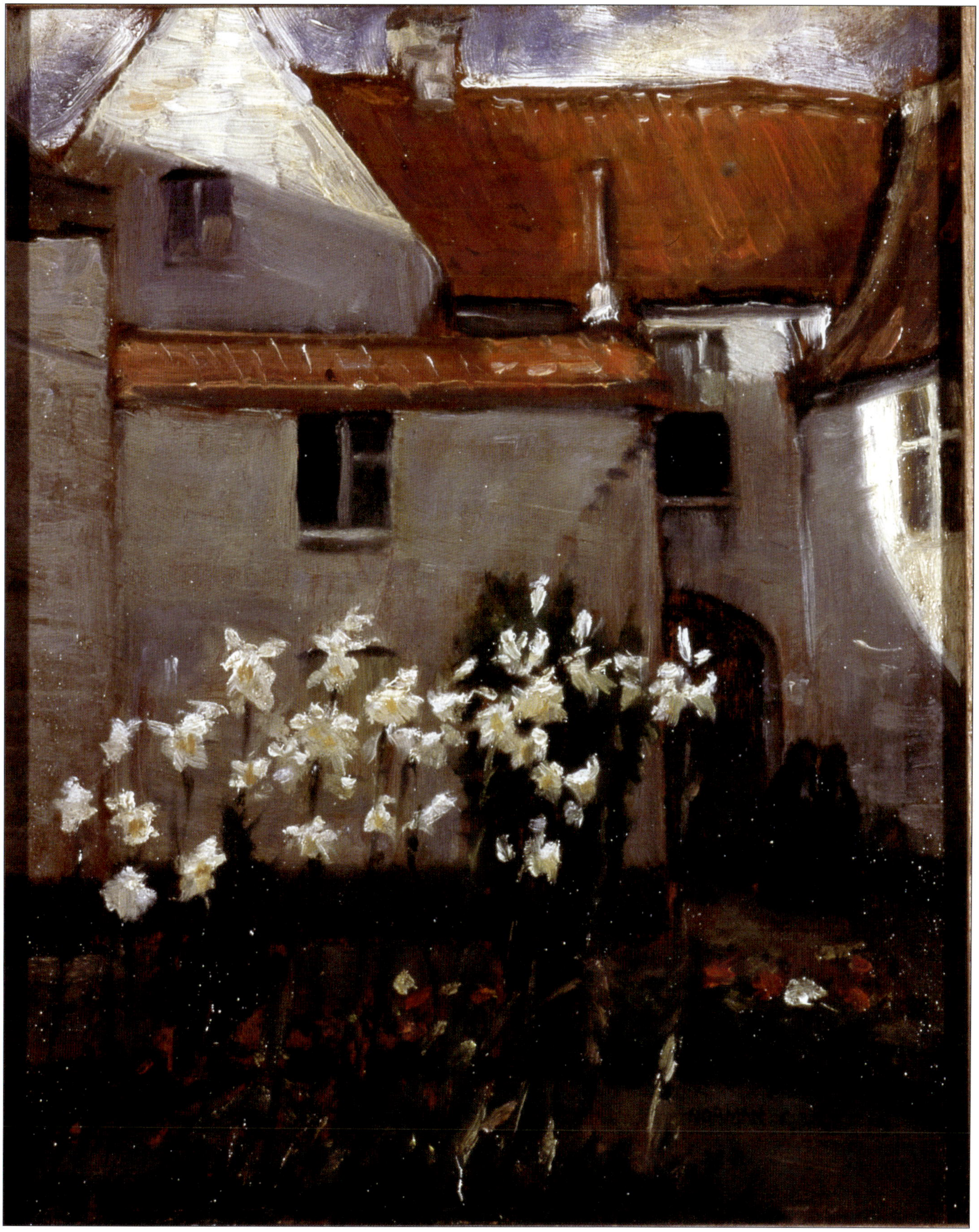

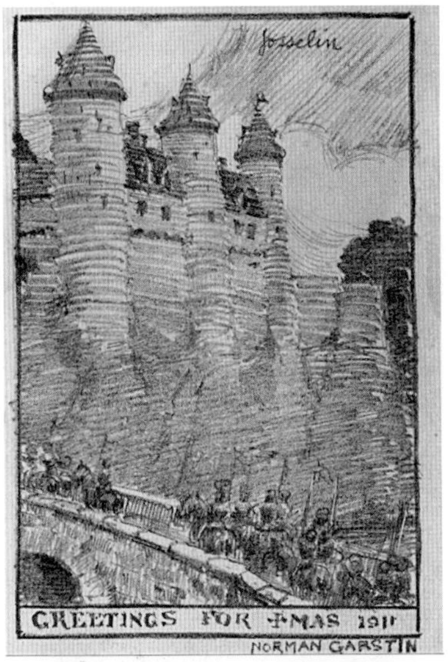

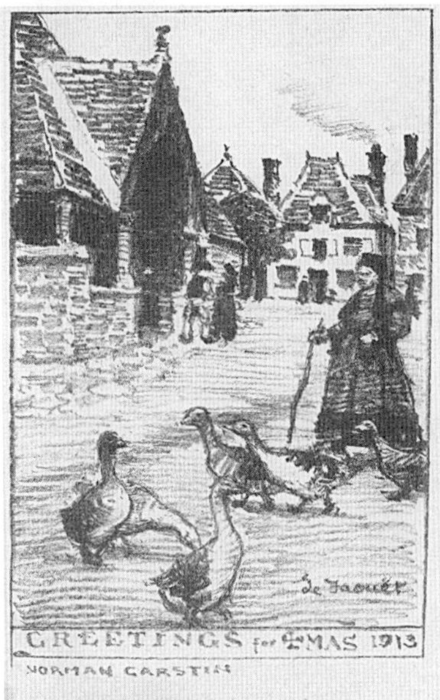

Top:
Greetings for Xmas 1911, Josselin, lithograph, 8.25" x 5.5" (private collection).

Bottom:
Greetings for Xmas 1913, Le Faouët, lithograph, 8" x 5" (private collection).

coming abroad with such delightful people as the Garstins'.[7] She was capable and friendly; while 'the Prof' was gay, amusing, and, even in 1902 when he was not well, generally resilient and cheerful in the face of difficulties. Above all, he was kind and generous, providing Hodgkins with helpful advice, useful letters of introduction, and refusing to accept any payment for her tuition, despite his own lack of funds.

Garstin was a dedicated and accomplished teacher, as students from both the 1890s and the 1900s testified. Hodgkins greatly valued his advice and example, and the Irish watercolour painter Mildred Anne Butler, who studied under Garstin at Penzance during the summers of 1894 and 1895, referred to his 'capital criticism'.[8] He came almost every day to inspect her work, and it appears that of May Guinness, another Irish artist, who was with her, at least in 1895. Garstin had a considerable influence on his students. Both in subject matter and technique, Hodgkins' pictures were for a time remarkably similar to those of Garstin, and he had a continuing effect on Butler's work. (Other artists who studied with Garstin at Penzance included the New Zealander Margaret Stoddart in 1902 and Clare Marsh from Ireland in 1897.)

Garstin's advice to his summer school students was frank, although his manner was disarming. Many years later one of them recalled his criticism that a sketch was,

> 'Dirty, and sad, and uninteresting. It wouldn't matter being dirty and sad, if it had been interesting.' He gave me good advice. The first time he came up to me when we were sketching ... I was scared stiff with fright. He said 'are you frightened of me'. 'Yes' I said. 'Well say to yourself before you start painting, I don't care a damn what he thinks'.[9]

Frances Hodgkins deserves the last word: 'Miss Richmond and myself are quite hopelessly in love with [Garstin] ... and agree that we have met our ideal artist and man at last ... It has been a great privilege to have had his friendship. I think of Spenser's "very gentle perfect knight". He was so courteous and kindly to everyone and so witty and charming'.[10]

The Benefits of Teaching

How much did Garstin earn from his teaching, both in Cornwall and abroad? Cornwall is unlikely to have been very remunerative. There would have been too much competition, including that from Stanhope Forbes' school of art after 1899. Even before it was set up, Garstin had only charged Butler and Guinness a total of £1 a week when he supervised them. His fee for summer school teaching was

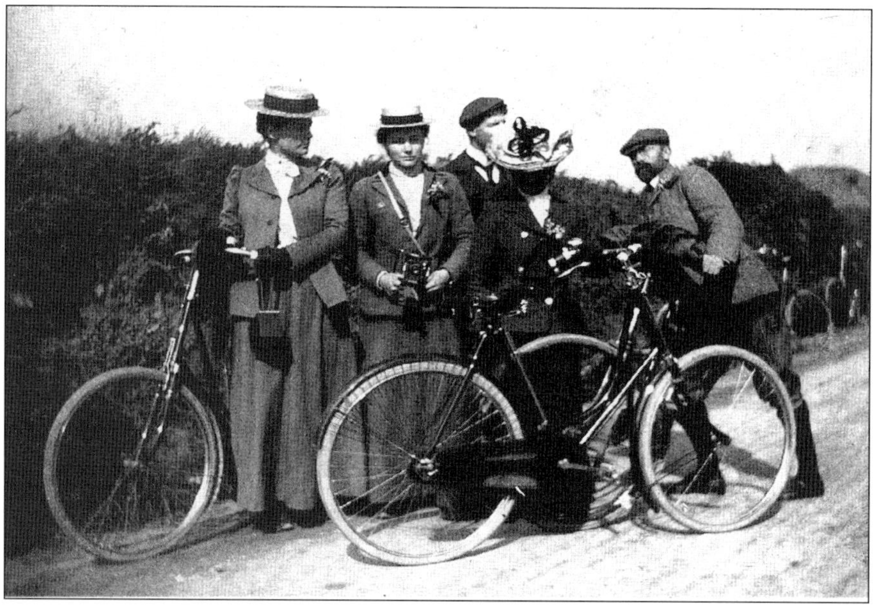

Garstin and pupils returning from Helston's Furry Dance, May 1902. Maud Nickalls is second from the left.

three guineas for a period of four weeks, although students could, at a proportionate rate, come for however long they liked. Students paid for their accommodation, and, presumably, met their travel costs. Nevertheless there was a loss of almost £50 on the first school, and of £25-30 in the following two years. Not until 1903, when there was a profit of £37, did the schools start to make money. The financial picture may have been brighter than these figures suggest, partly because the Garstins sometimes, but not always, re-let Wellington Terrace, and partly because expenditure on housekeeping would have been avoided. Had it not been for these benefits, it is difficult to believe that the Garstins would have persevered with the painting parties.

Apart from providing some much-needed income, the schools had other advantages. They provided Garstin with constant company and with friendship. Some students attended for as many as ten years, and some of those whom he had taught at Penzance later went on the painting trips, and vice versa. In this way Garstin became familiar with many of his students, and some of them became lifelong friends. Frances Hodgkins is one example, and the amateur artist Maud Nickalls, who had originally been a student in Penzance in 1897, is another. In 1911 the students showed their regard in the most tangible manner by presenting Garstin and his wife with £77 on the occasion of their Silver Wedding. The companionship and friendship that he enjoyed must, together with the extra income, have helped him to avoid depression. It may well be true, as Canney says, that Garstin was irked by having to devote so much time to his students, but his letters scarcely ever betray any personal

Dochie in middle age.

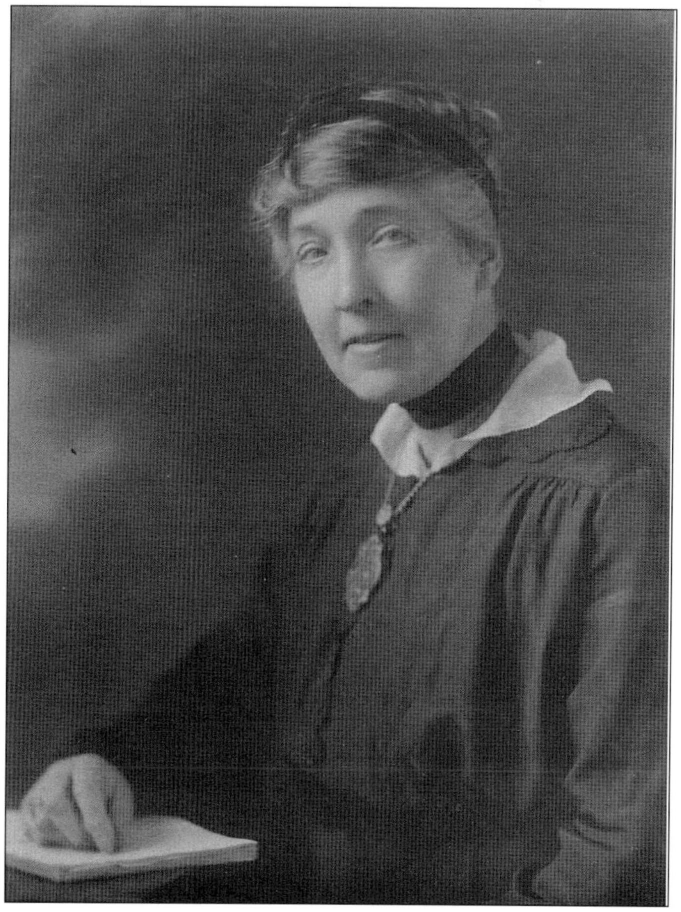

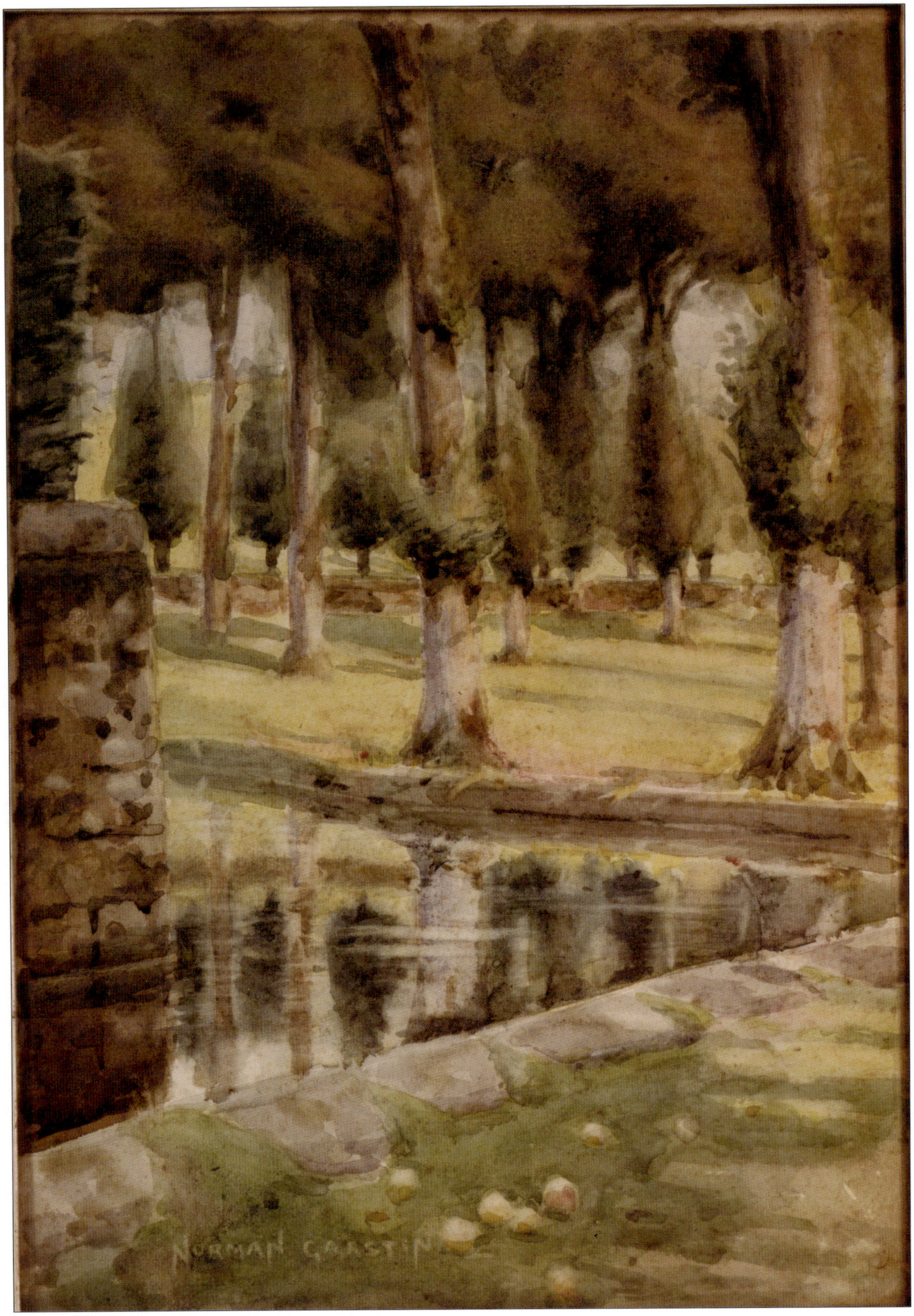
NORMAN GARSTIN

irritation with his students. On the contrary, they show that he liked them and was concerned for their welfare.

Another non-monetary benefit of the summer schools was that they enabled Garstin to paint abroad, where he enjoyed working more than in England. When the school of 1905 was almost over Norman wrote to Dochie saying that, 'if the weather only keeps up I will not hurry back yet awhile. I seem to find so much more to do and feel so much more keen and excited over my work here than in PZ'.[11] His delight at being abroad, and enthusiasm for foreign subjects, is confirmed by other letters:

> I am writing this in the little cafe [at Nogent-le-Roi] which hangs over the river. This river goes in amongst the houses in the most intimate manner I have ever seen, and the houses are the most picturesque I have almost ever seen, with all sorts of delicate colours. The tiles are very subdued and fine ...[12]

Garstin was particularly captivated by the Pardons that were a

Opposite:
Plate 30 *The Water Garden*, 1912, watercolour, 13.25" x 9" (private collection, auctioned as *Garden Arbour and Pool*).

Plate 31 *Antwerp Street Scene* [auction title], *c.*1910, oil, 8" x 10" (private collection).

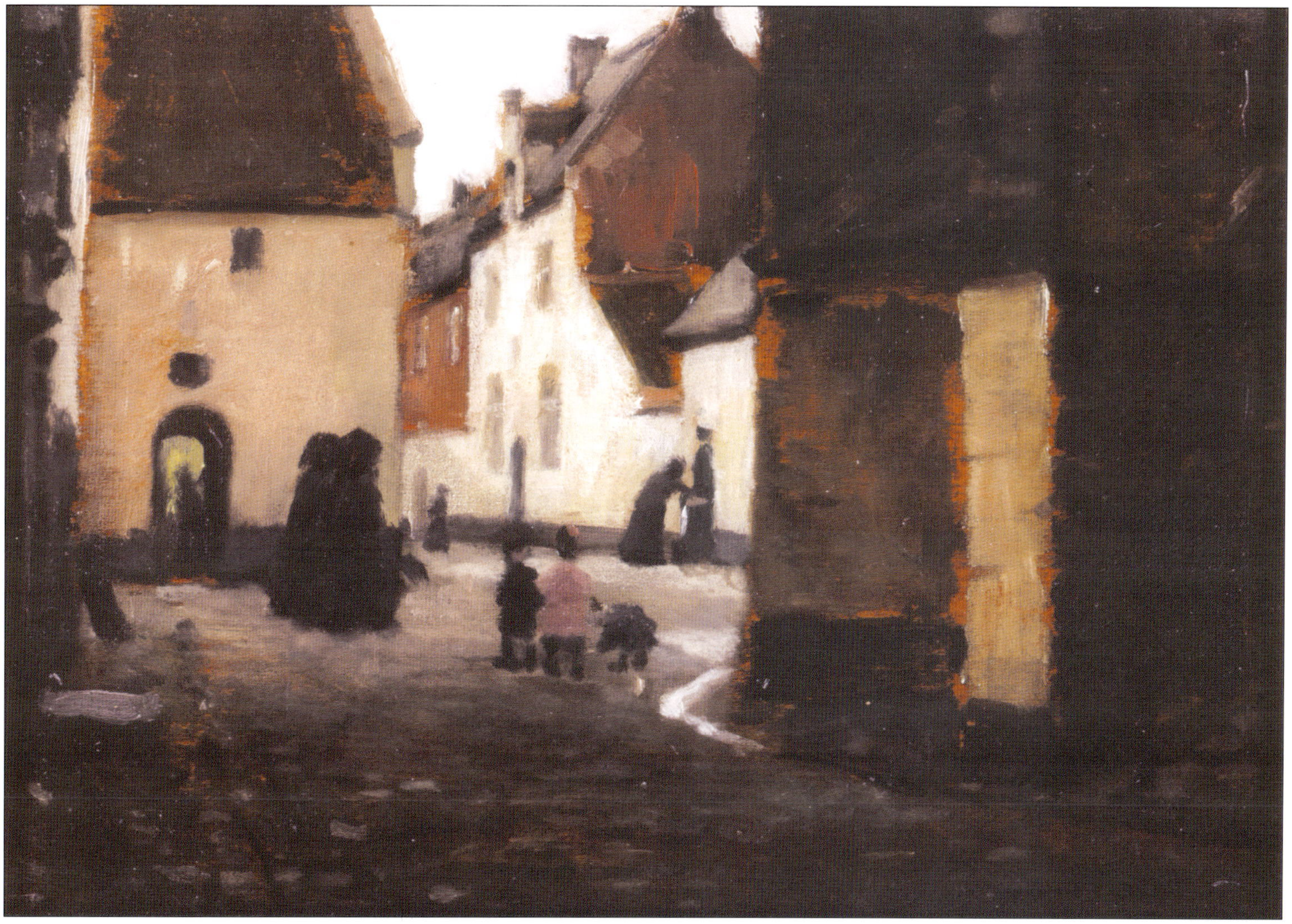

feature of Breton life. Here is his description of one near Guémené, in 1912:

> we ... suddenly came upon a tiny church by a couple of farmhouses, very primitive and simple. Just as we arrived the procession started, all peasants, some men and women carrying banners, and a few little red acolytes attending a priest in a yellow gold cape. The peasants were all in costume coifs and lovely aprons, and, as they wound about amongst the farm buildings, and thro' the defiles of a little wood flecked with sun, they made lots of delightful pictures. Then out into a meadow with apple trees where they sang and played on terrible trumpets, but it was all wonderfully pictorial. Then they filed back again singing their ora pro nobis and came to the back of the church, where there was a great pile of brush wood. The people stood in a circle and the yellow robed priest set fire to the great pile ... I stood on a cart and made a scribble ... but I cannot help thinking it might be a jolly subject for a fairly large picture.[13]

It is significant that Garstin wanted to paint a big picture, because of the oft-repeated canard that he was only happy with small ones. A large picture called *A Breton Pardon* did result, and was exhibited at the Academy in 1913, though only the preliminary sketch has come to light.

Politics, Painting and the Picturesque

There was a connection between Garstin's love of the picturesque and his left wing political views and skepticism about the benefits of economic development. He hated the way in which quaint old towns were being torn down and, in the pursuit of illusory progress, the good life they provided was being destroyed. Here, for instance, is his lament for an old French town:

> Alas, alas for the narrow street! ... the narrow shadowed street, with its friendly gossip across from door to door ... the Sanitary sense, and the requirements of an expanding traffic, have combined against you, and you must go. Go to make room for wide, arid thoroughfares, with tram-lines, and water-carts, and automobiles and omnibuses, drains and gas pipes, and telephone wires, and all the many conveniences of our exigent civilization. No, we must make the most of you, dear little intimate, garrulous, picturesque lanes of ancient cities, for the eye of the improver is upon you ... It is in the air already that the demolisher is at hand, coming to make straight the way for the jerrybuilder.[14]

Even where the old and picturesque survived, Garstin thought that it was being steadily spoilt by the tourist.

Although there was a link between Garstin's political views and his subject matter, it would be wrong to make too much of this.

Garstin painting on the Continent.

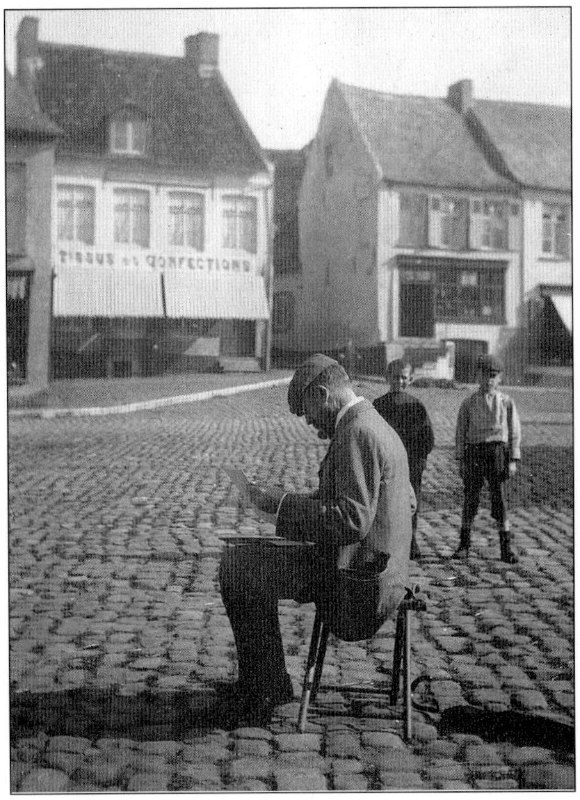

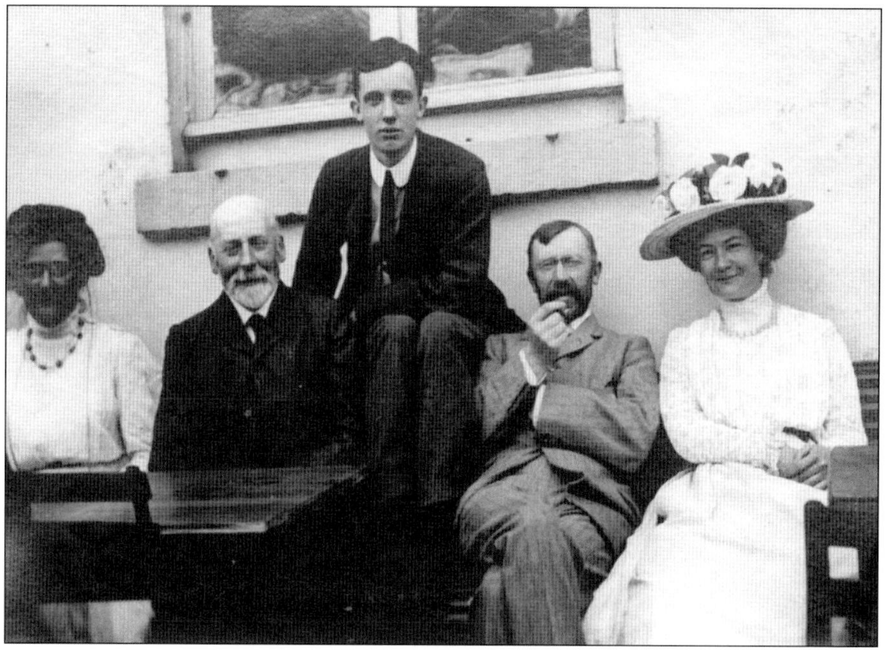

Norman (second from right) and Denis (centre), at the summer school in Diest, 1909.

Opposition to modern urban development was widespread among artists at the time, and his hostility was shared by his friends Stanhope Forbes and Alexander Mann, who were not socialists. There was also a potential contradiction not only between his socialism and his hostility to modernization and the crowd, but also between his love of the picturesque and his Realist principles. The Realist should, if he is to be true to his faith, find his subject matter in the contemporary world and everyday life. Those who seek out those few places in which the past is preserved are moving away from Realism.

The extent of the movement was, however, smaller than might be imagined. Garstin did not stress the picturesque aspect of the town scenes he painted. Figures do not appear to be posed but to be going about their normal daily business. Nor is there any stress on the more quaint and curious features of old buildings, which do not seem to be posing themselves and inviting the viewer to gaze. Garstin's pictures have a snapshot quality in which people, and also buildings, seem to have been caught unaware, as shown, for instance, by *Saturday* and *The Beganier Garden* (Plates 26 and 27).

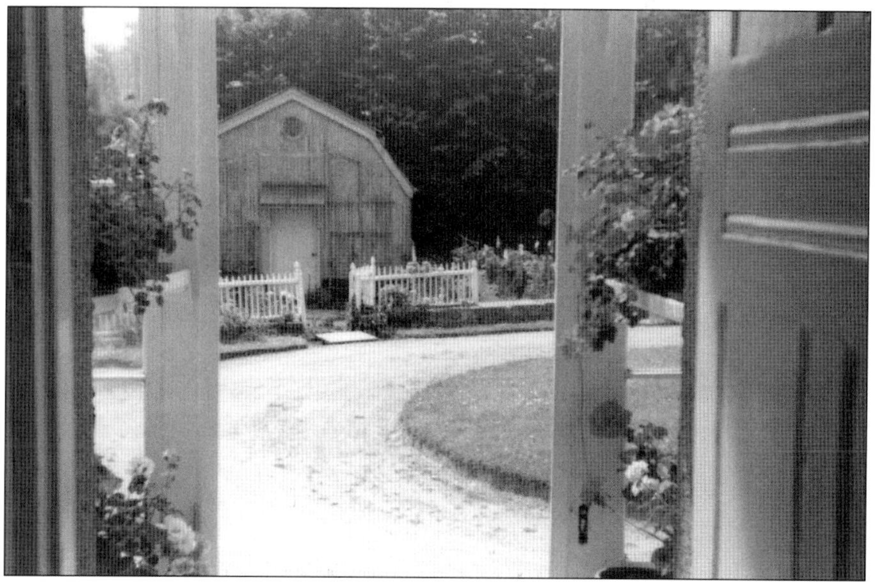

Garstin's studio at Wellington Terrace, built in 1903.

Did the Summer Schools Mean Fewer Paintings?

The drawback of the summer schools was that, because so much time was occupied in supervising students and socialising with them, Garstin had relatively little time to devote to his own work. During the summer months he

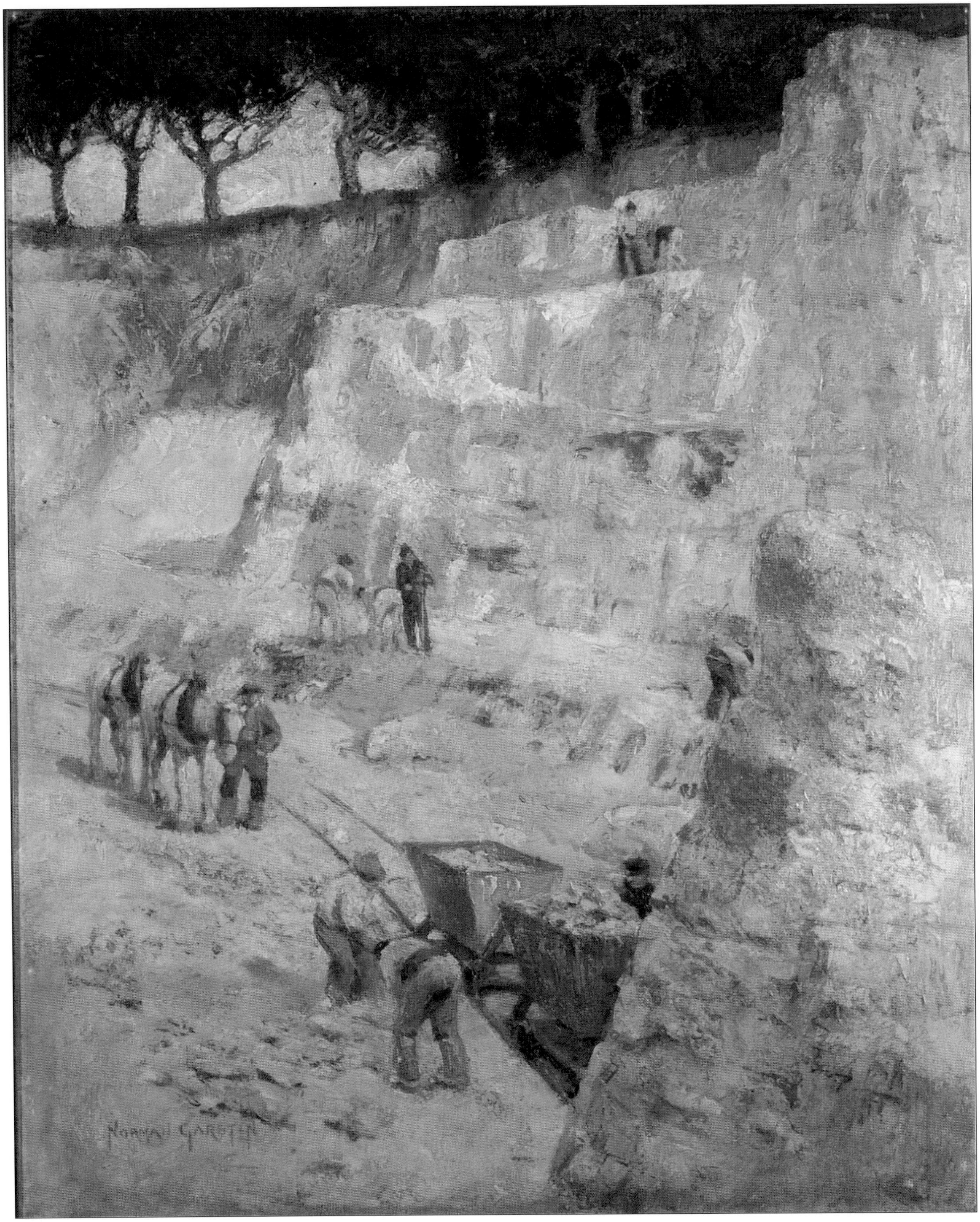
NORMAN GARSTIN

could only paint between tea and dinner, which would have been about four hours a day. The time available for work would have been further restricted by the weather; and by picnics and other activities in the afternoon, although these were probably mainly confined to weekends. It was not until the painting parties were over, or almost over, that Garstin was able to work during the mornings. If the weather was fine, he would stay on and paint, sometimes almost until the end of October. During 1905, in the middle of that month, he reported to Dochie that he would leave before long, because, although it was fine and sunny, it was exceedingly cold, and 'hardly possible to do anything out of doors, except in the sun. I was nearly frozen solid yesterday'.[15]

Nevertheless it would be wrong to jump to the conclusion that, because the summer schools absorbed so much of his time, they restricted his output. No doubt it would have been greater if he had enjoyed a comfortable private income that enabled him to paint abroad without it being necessary to teach; but, in the absence of such an income, the summer schools almost certainly boosted his

Opposite:
Plate 32 *The Chalk Quarry*, 1908, oil, 36" x 28" (private collection).

Below:
Plate 33 *Kermesse. Diest*, 1912, watercolour, 9.1" x 11.5" (V&A, London).

Over page:
Plate 34 *The Evening Fête. Diest*, 1912, oil, 21.75" x 18.25" (private collection, auctioned as *Circus Performers by Torchlight*).

Plate 35 *Bright October, Delft*, 1904, watercolour, 21" x 15" (private collection).

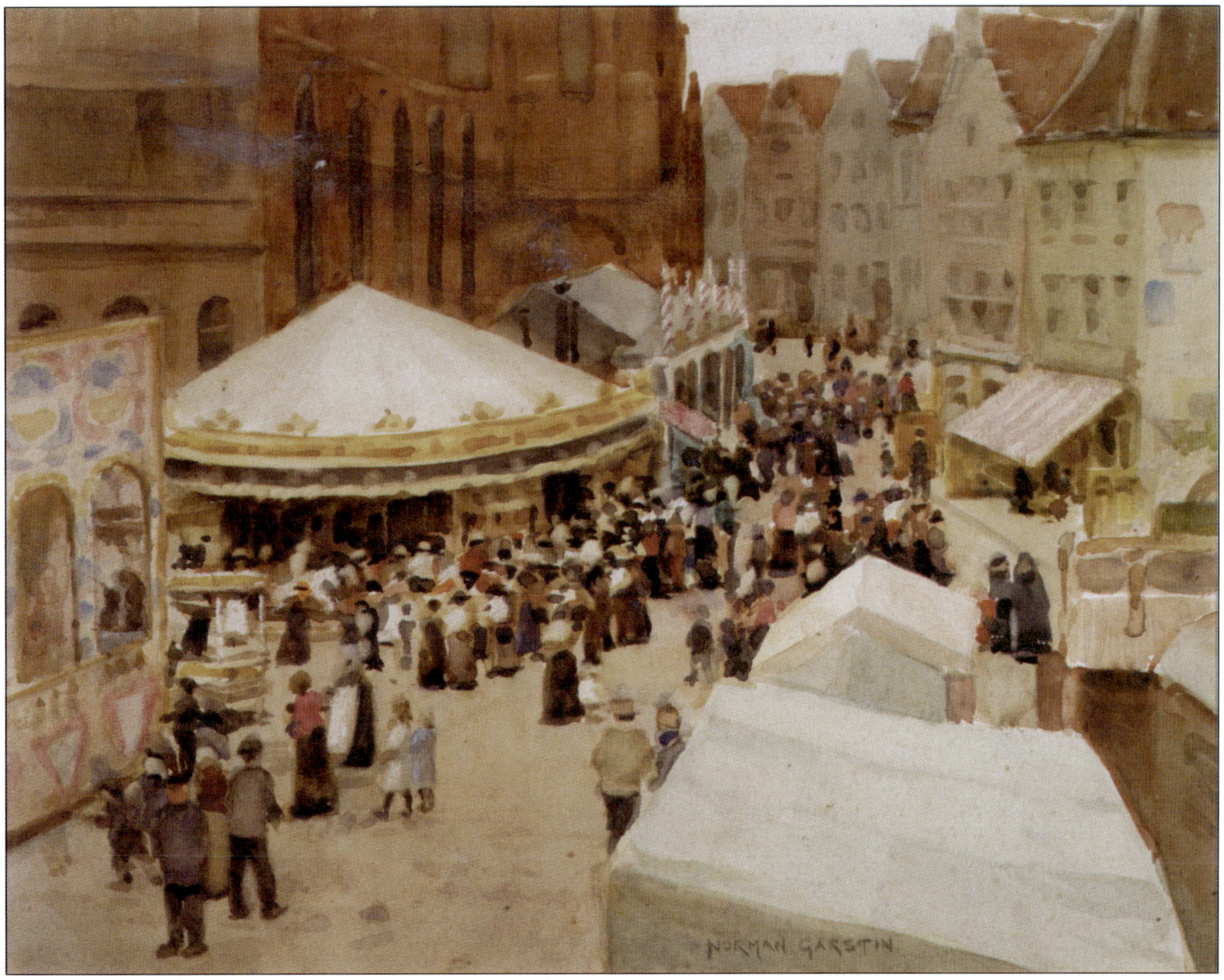

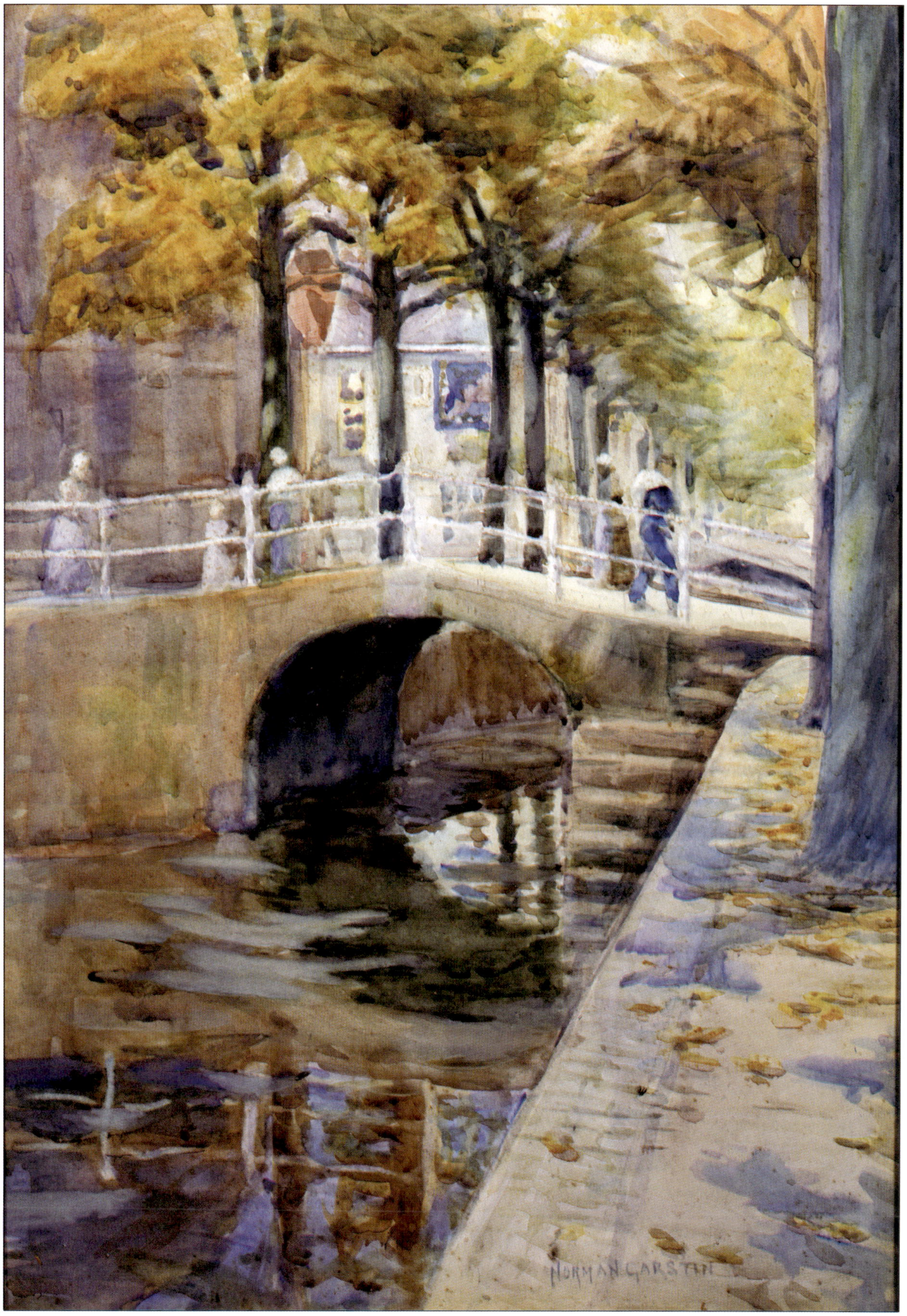
NORMAN GARSTIN

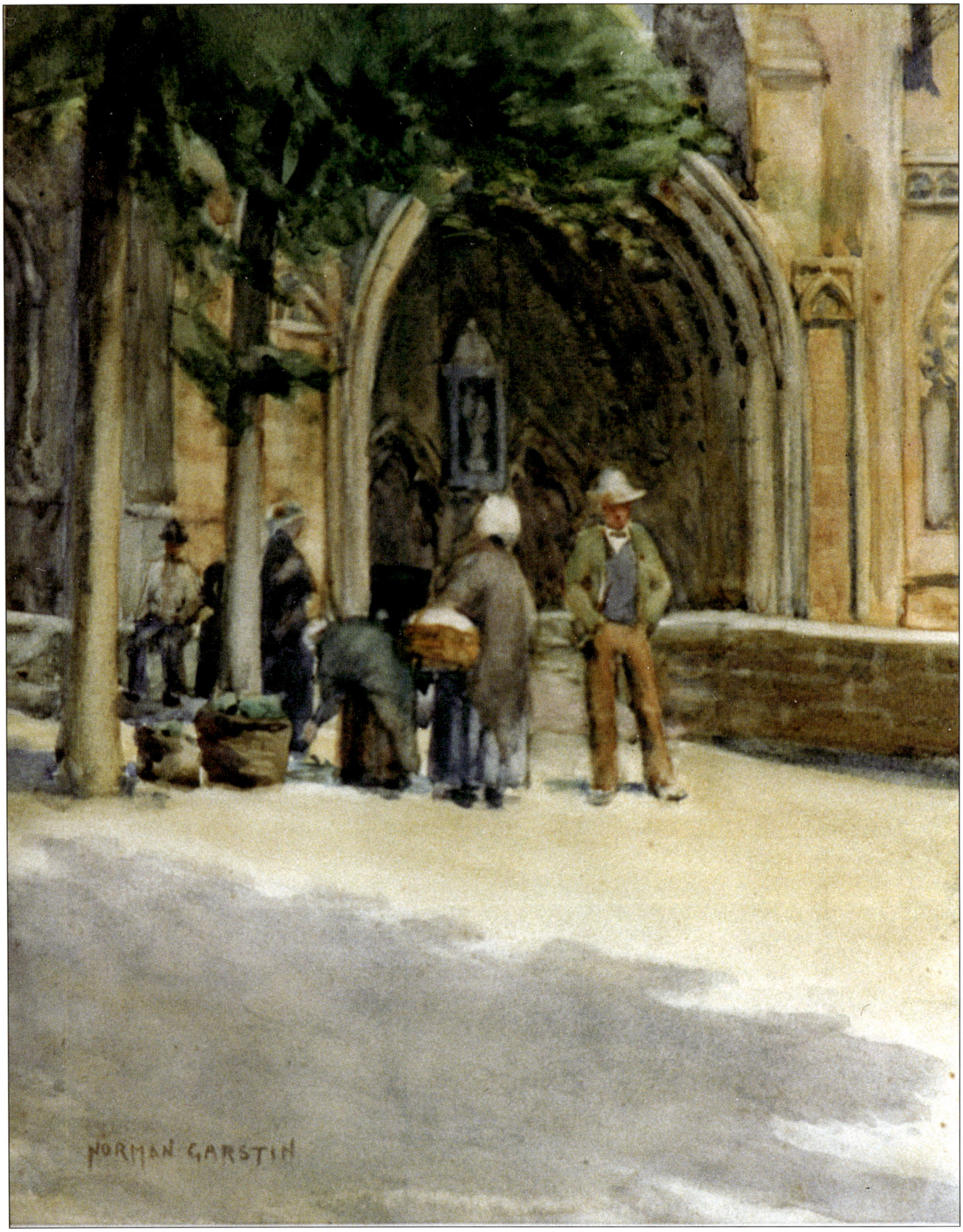
NORMAN GARSTIN

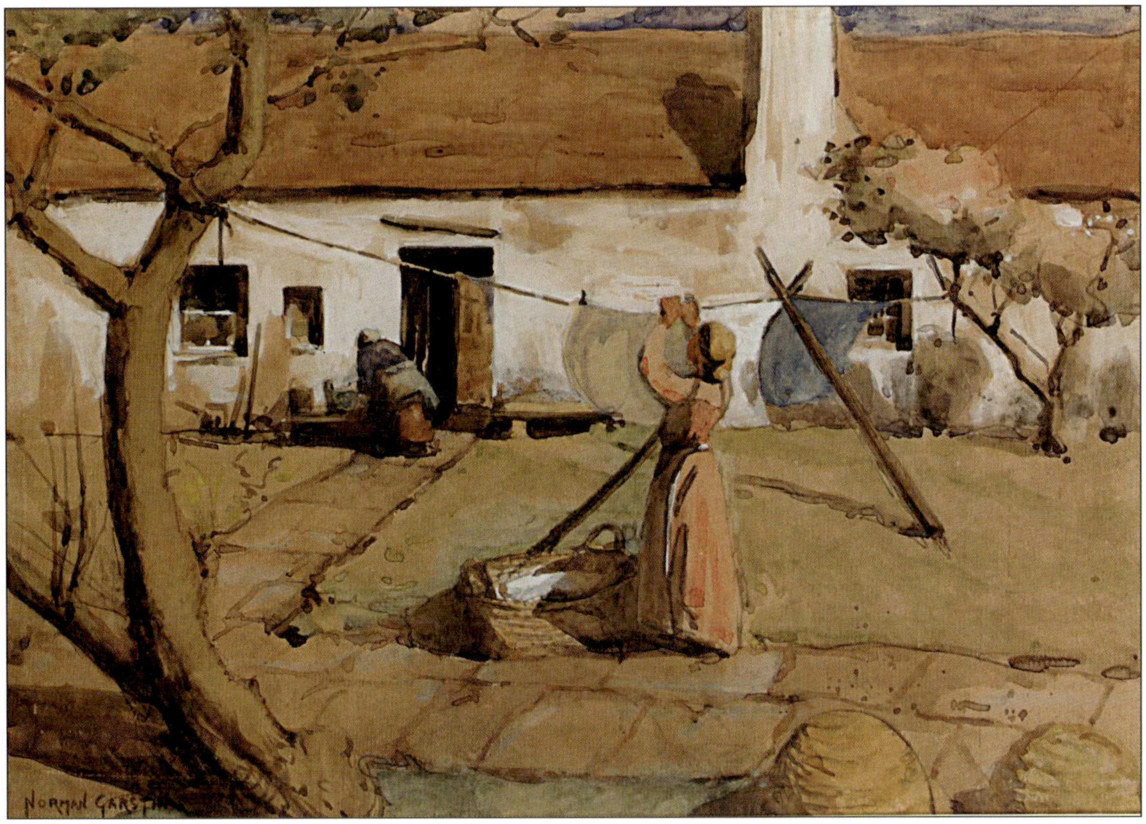

Opposite:
Plate 36 *The Cathedral Door, Trèguier*, 1909, watercolour, 12" x 9.5" (private collection).

Above:
Plate 37 *Hanging out the Washing* (auction title), about 1907, watercolour, 10" x 15" (private collection).

output. He was now able to paint on the Continent, which he found highly stimulating, and, as we have seen, they provided him with companionship and made a welcome contribution to his finances. All this must not only have helped to keep depression at bay, and so prevented it from restricting his output, but also have had a favourable effect by reducing the need to produce work, which he hoped would sell, but for which he had little enthusiasm, and on which he made slow progress.

Between 1900 and 1914, Garstin exhibited (or painted) at least 41 major works and no less than 273 other pictures. Over the somewhat shorter period 1890-9 he had only exhibited eighteen major and 68 other works. That his output was so much greater than previously, even for large works, confirms that the summer schools had a favourable impact.

Painting Parties' Effect on Media

Many of his pictures were now watercolours, or sketches in oil. Watercolour has the obvious advantage of being quick, and Garstin must have turned to this medium because of the pressure on his time. His first known watercolour – *Garden Gates* – was painted in 1895, and it is significant that the picture was a gift. It was not until 1900 that he exhibited any watercolours. Shown at the Passmore Edwards Gallery, Newlyn, they included pictures of Caudebec that would

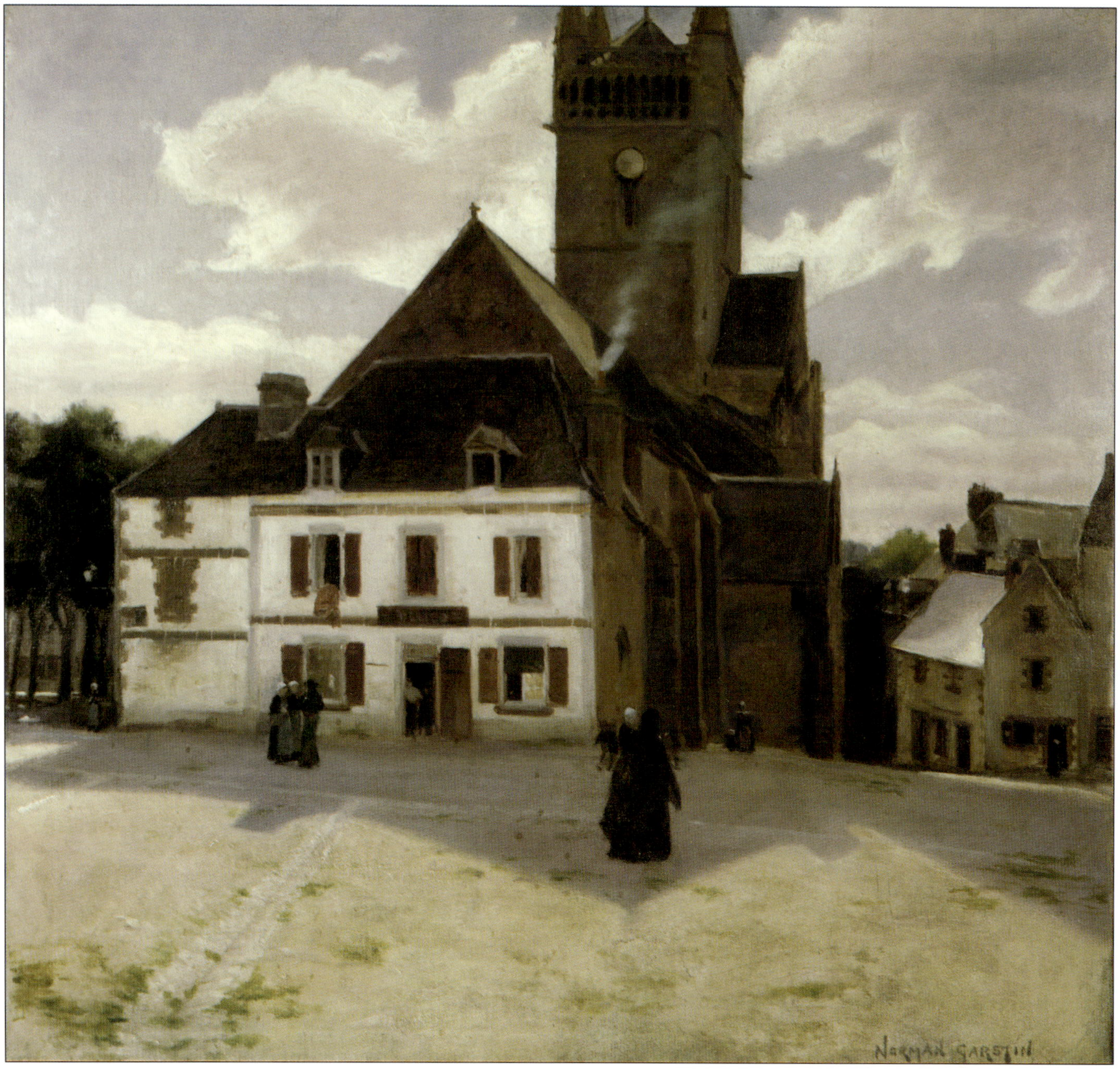

Plate 38 *Place St Michel, Quimperlé*, 1901, oil, 35.25" x 35.25" (Plymouth City Museum & Art Gallery).

have been painted during his first summer school. They were probably small experimental works because they were disposed of cheaply. It was not until the spring of 1901 that Garstin showed his first watercolour at an important galley: *The Mill of Les Gouls, Quimperlé* at the Royal Birmingham Society of Artists, for which he asked twelve guineas. This had obviously been painted at the summer school in the preceding year.

For some years thereafter, he exhibited very few watercolours. In July 1902 Frances Hodgkins reported that, 'Mr Garstin has been working three summers and has not yet got enough to fill a small room – he is not a slow worker either, but you can never count on

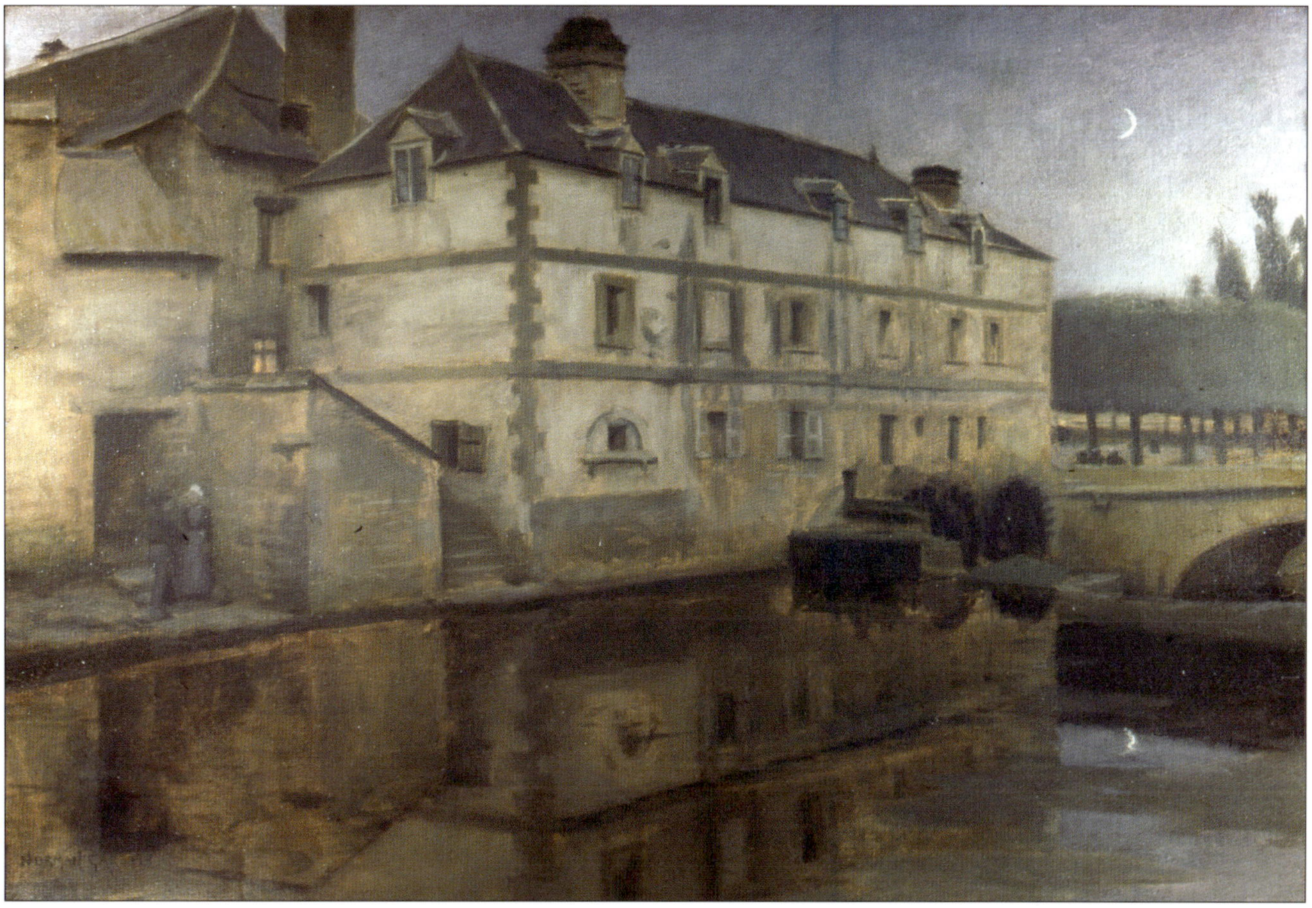

Plate 39 *Le Moulin de la Ville, Quimperlé,* 1901, oil, 26.5 X 36" (Brighton Museum & Art Gallery).

doing tip top work straight on end'.[16] He was now holding his pictures back for the major exhibition, *In Border Lands*, that ultimately took place at The Fine Art Society of New Bond Street in January 1904. It contained 91 watercolours painted during the summer schools at Quimperlé (1900), Caudebec and Les Andelys in Normandy (1901), Dinan (1902), and Bruges and then Holland (1903). *Château by the River* (Plate 28) was, to judge from the price, a representative work. A further large exhibition, *Chiefly in France*, was held at Walker's Gallery, New Bond Street, in April 1909. It comprised works painted at the schools in Brittany (1904), Montreuil-sur-Mer (1905), St-Valéry-sur-Somme (1906), Furnes (1907), and Cassel (1908). Excluding the few known oils, there were 65 paintings.

Garstin concentrated on small oils during the following years, presumably because he had tired of watercolour, and did not return to this medium until the summer of 1914. In April-May 1912 he exhibited 51 oils at Walker's, together with a few watercolours. These were produced at the painting parties at Diest (1909), at or near Oudenaarde (1910?), and at Josselin (1911). If *Madonna Lilies*, and *The Water Garden* (Plates 29 and 30) are typical, it was an impressive show. How the oil sketches from the schools in 1912 and 1913 at

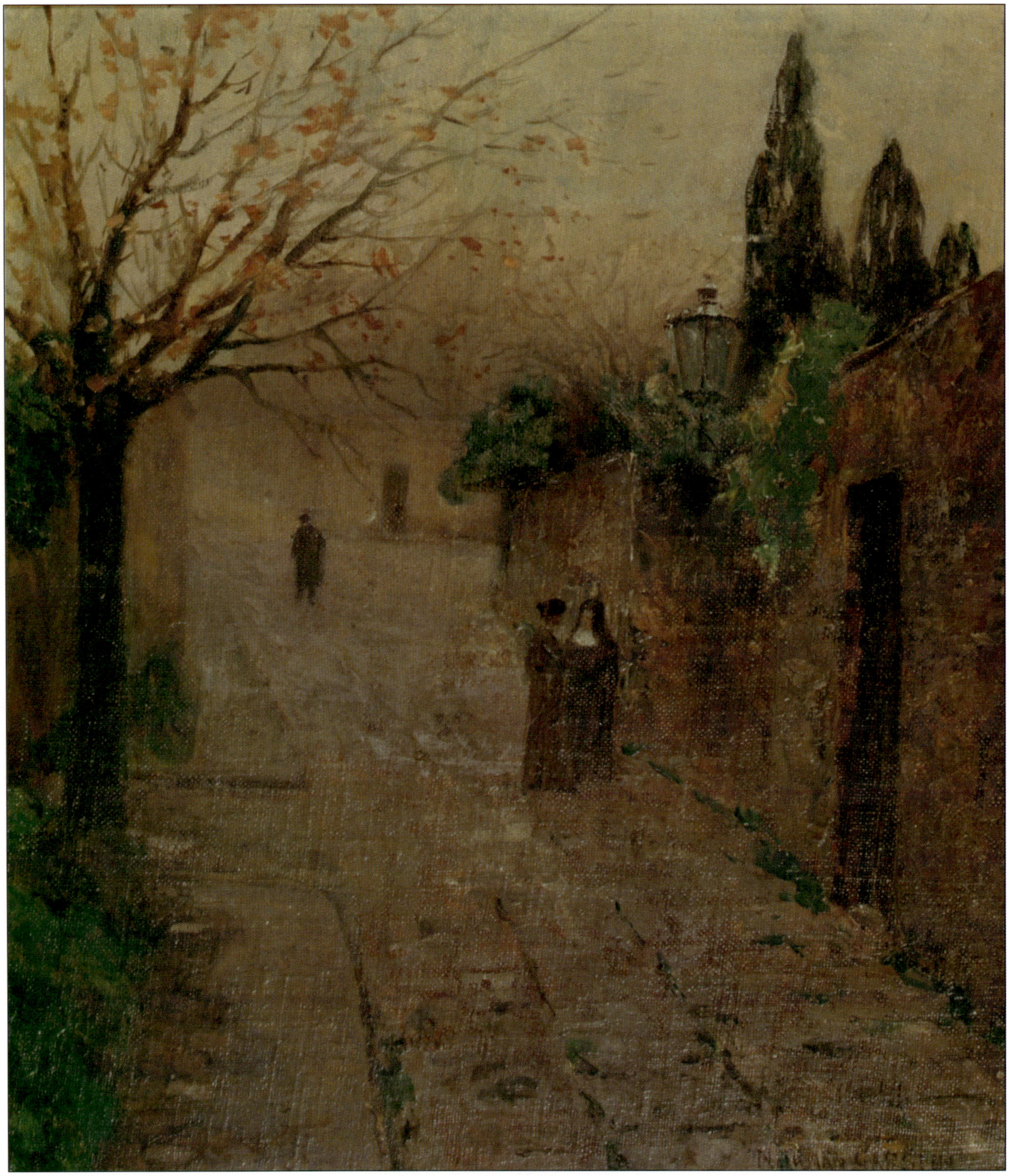

Plate 40 *The Convent Gate. Evening*, 1912, oil, 18" x 15.5" (private collection, auctioned as *Convent Gossipers*).

Guémené-sur-Scorff were disposed of is not known. Presumably, they were taken by dealers.

Although he might already have made preliminary sketches, it was not until the summer schools had wound down that Garstin was able

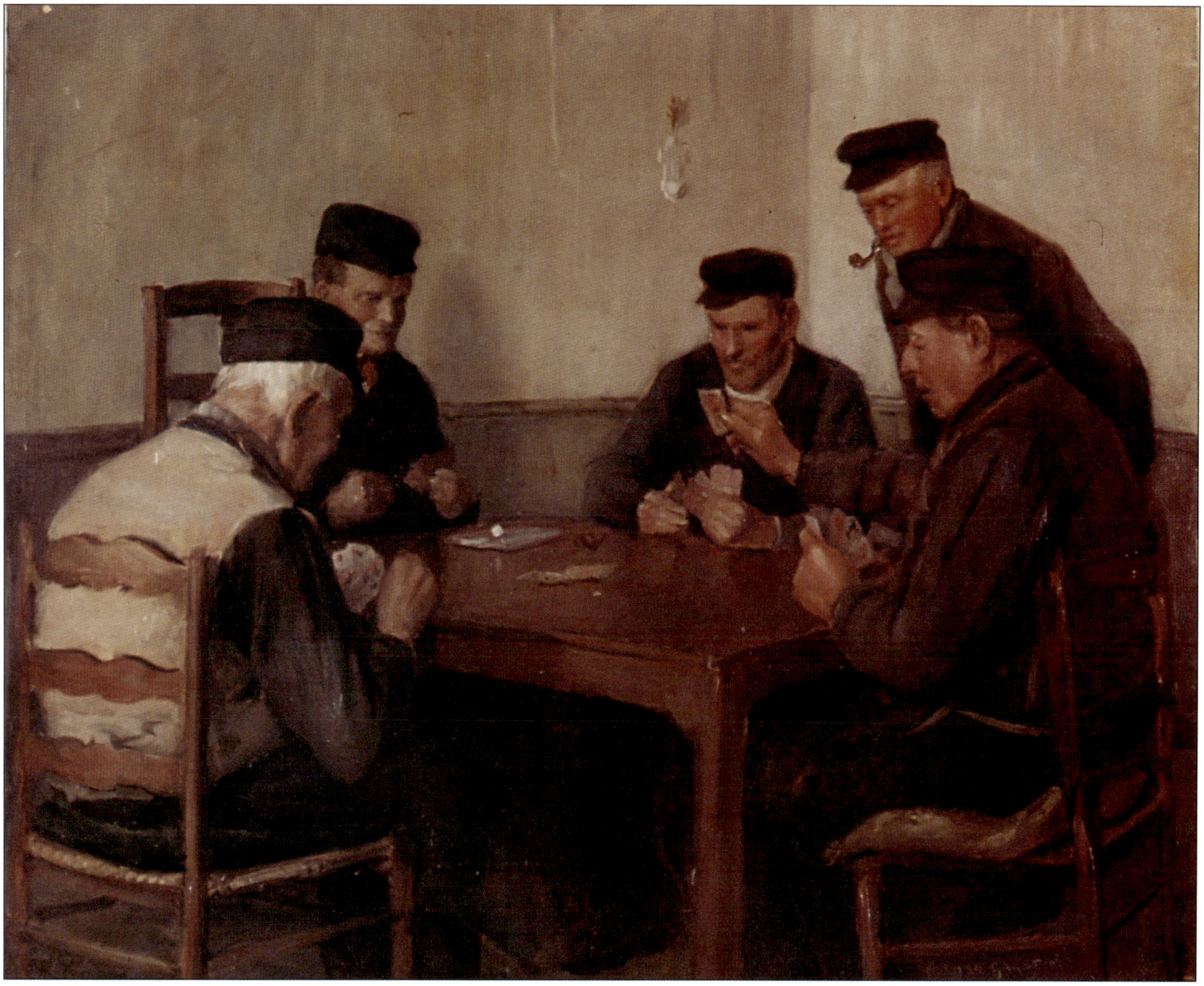

Plate 41 *The Card Players/In a Flemish Hospice*, 1909, oil, 30.5" x 36.25" (Manchester Art Gallery).

to begin serious work on a major picture. Sometimes it would be finished on the spot, but on other occasions it would be completed at Penzance during the winter. In some cases photographs must have been used, because there are snaps from which he must have painted *A Watch Tower in the Low Countries* (1907) and *The Chalk Quarry* (1908), which appears in Plate 32. His large pictures were, in most cases, submitted to the Academy for the summer exhibition. The months at Penzance would also be taken up with a little portrait painting, some teaching, journalism, and the production of the stencils and engravings that Garstin sent out at Christmas.

The latter were given to friends and contacts, such as the editor of *The Studio*, but they may also have been a way of reminding past summer school students about the next trip. The first Christmas greeting appears to have been produced in 1899 shortly after the first

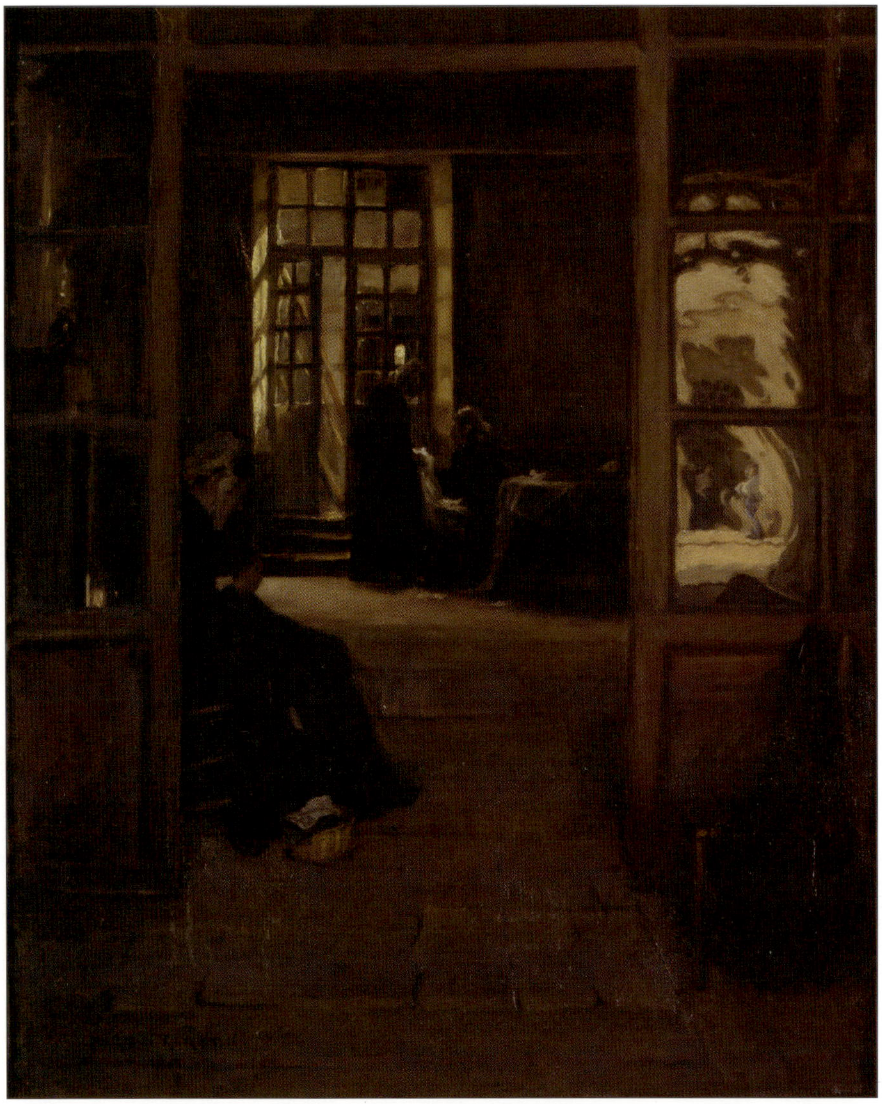

Plate 42 *Breton Needlewomen*, 1912, oil, 36" x 30" (private collection, auctioned as *An Interior, Brittany*).

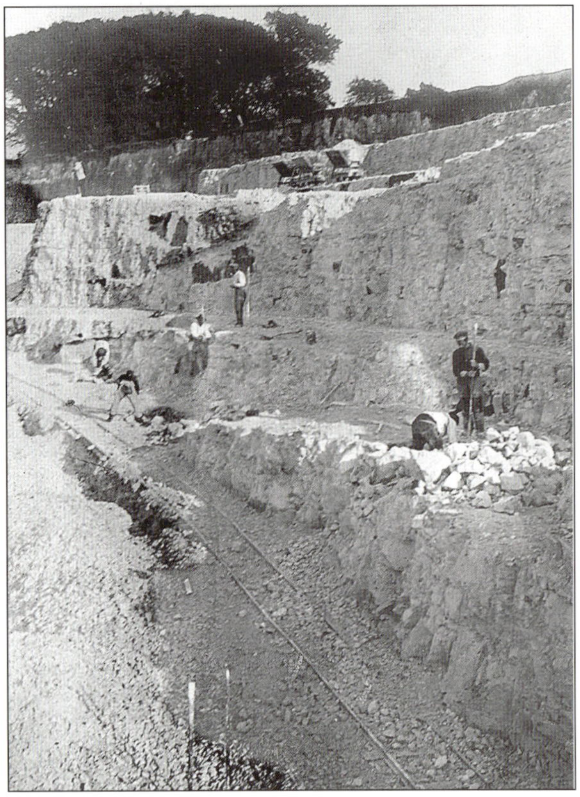

Photograph of a chalk quarry from the Garstin family album.

painting party; and many of the subjects were places where the last summer school had been held, or where the next would take place. It therefore seems probable that the painting parties provided Garstin with the opportunity to become proficient at stencilling, and to employ his skills as an engraver. Garstin's earliest known engravings date from his period with Carolus-Duran, when he presented a fine lithograph to Alexander Mann. After this he appears to have made little use of his talent, apart from an engraving of a Breton girl reproduced in *The Studio* in 1896 (which provokes the question of whether Garstin visited France – and possibly even Morocco – at about that time).

Summer Schools and Subject Matter

The summer painting parties led not only to a diversification of the media Garstin employed but also to a shift in subject matter. Hitherto he had ranged widely, but now he concentrated on a much narrower band of topics, apart from the three costume and story pictures mentioned in the previous chapter, that were exhibited between 1900 and 1902 but probably begun before 1900. Urban scenes with figures became by far the most common type of picture. Something like 100 of these were painted between 1900 and 1914, though this is only a rough figure because titles are sometimes a poor guide to subject matter.

The small oil now known as *Antwerp Street Scene* (Plate 31) is a good example of the type of subject that Garstin favoured. That it was a quick sketch is evident from the broad brush, and almost crude, manner in which the building on the right has been painted. This does not matter as attention is focused on the brighter and more distant houses, in front of which some of the figures are silhouetted. All the important details have been included. It has been raining, as indicated by the full gutter. The way in which this is glinting provides the picture with interest, as do the subtle contrasts between the different shades of white and brown. It is a work with both depth and atmosphere. Another typical townscape is Garstin's watercolour *The*

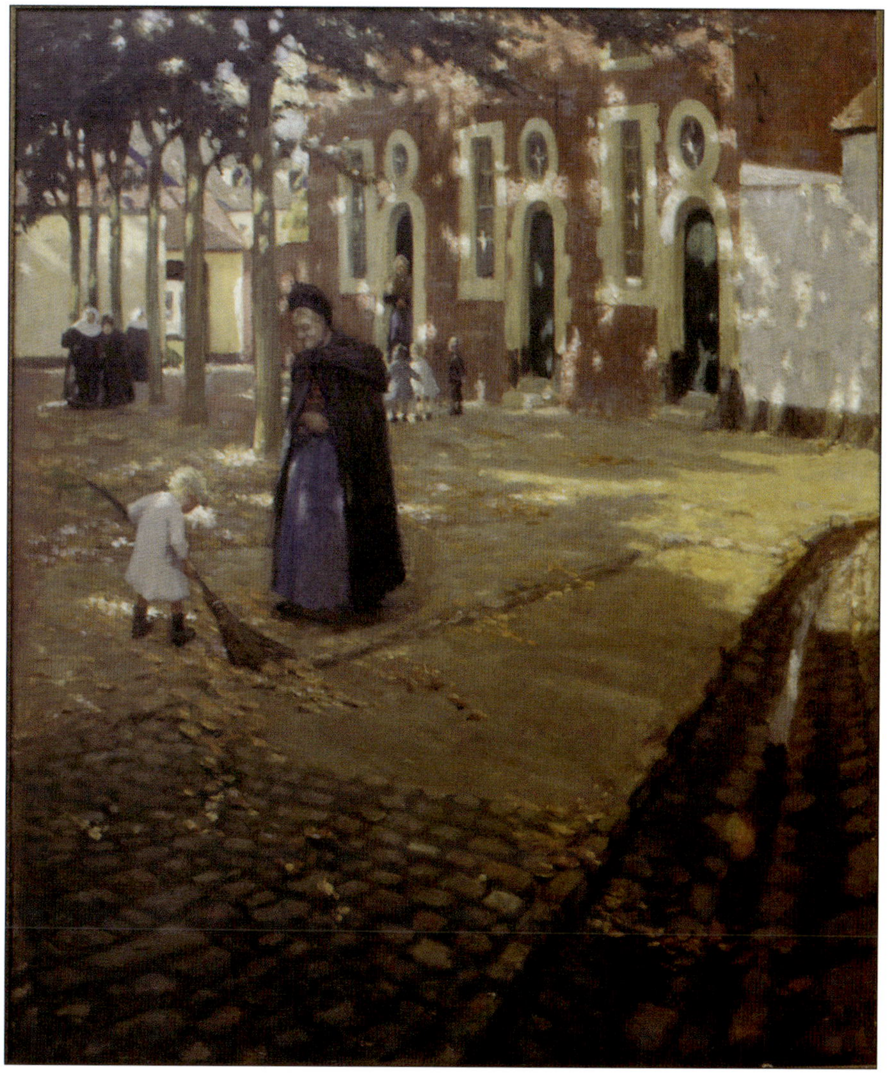

Plate 43 *Sunshine in the Beguinage/Le Beguinag*, 1910, oil, 35.75" x 29.75" (Crawford Art Gallery, Cork).

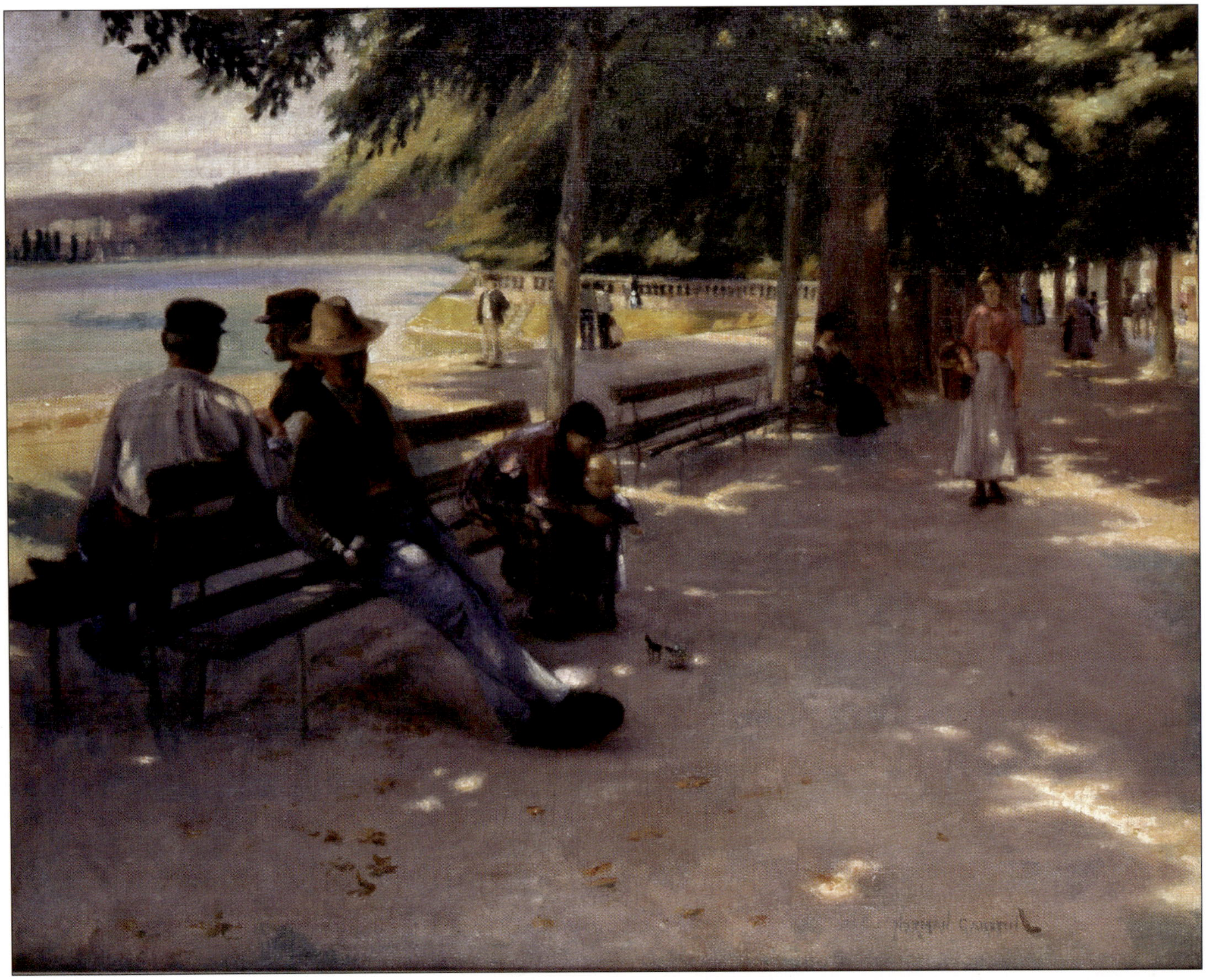

Above:
Plate 44 *In the Heat of the Day* [Caudebec-en-Caux], 1904, oil, 31.75" x 39.5" (private collection, auctioned as *In the Shade*).

Opposite:
Plate 45 *Among the Pots*, 1911, oil, 50" x 40" (Plymouth City Museum & Art Gallery).

Cathedral Door, Trèguier (1909), shown in Plate 36. Its harmonious colours, large area of blank space, snapshot effect, and undramatic nature are all characteristic of his work. The picture also displays Garstin's humour: the man and woman in the centre are not looking at each other and must be having an argument. The picture is inscribed 'Different Opinions'.

Within the overall group of urban scenes with figures there is a wide variety of subjects and a number of sub-categories. There are, for instance, several pictures of fairs. A good example is the watercolour *Kermesse. Diest* (1912), which is reproduced in Plate 33. Once again, it shows the way in which Garstin concentrated on what was important, and omitted the inessential. Although it is only a small work, the crowd has been painted in some detail, and certain individuals have been painted with especial care. In contrast, the buildings have been barely outlined and the roof of the carousel is

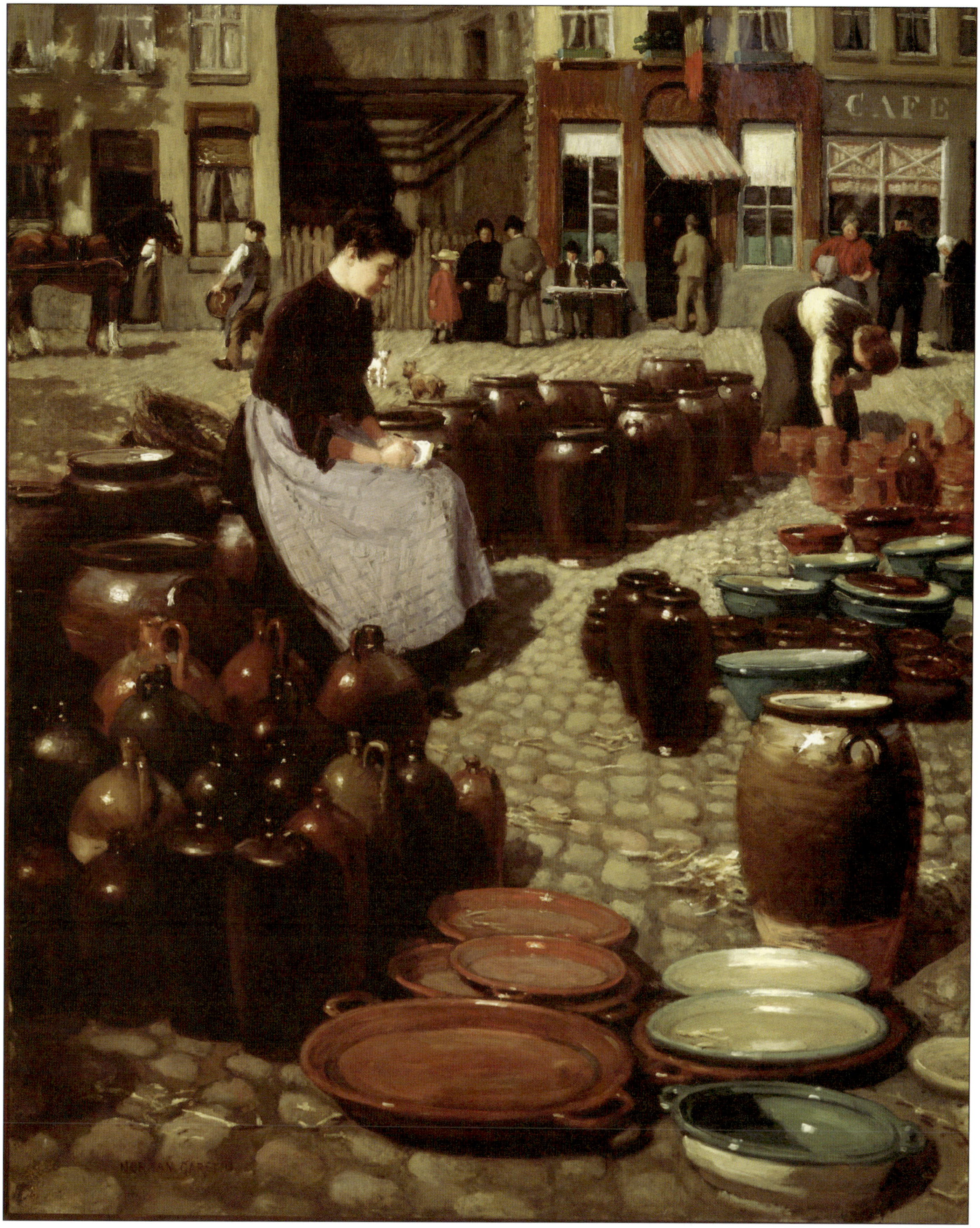
CAFE

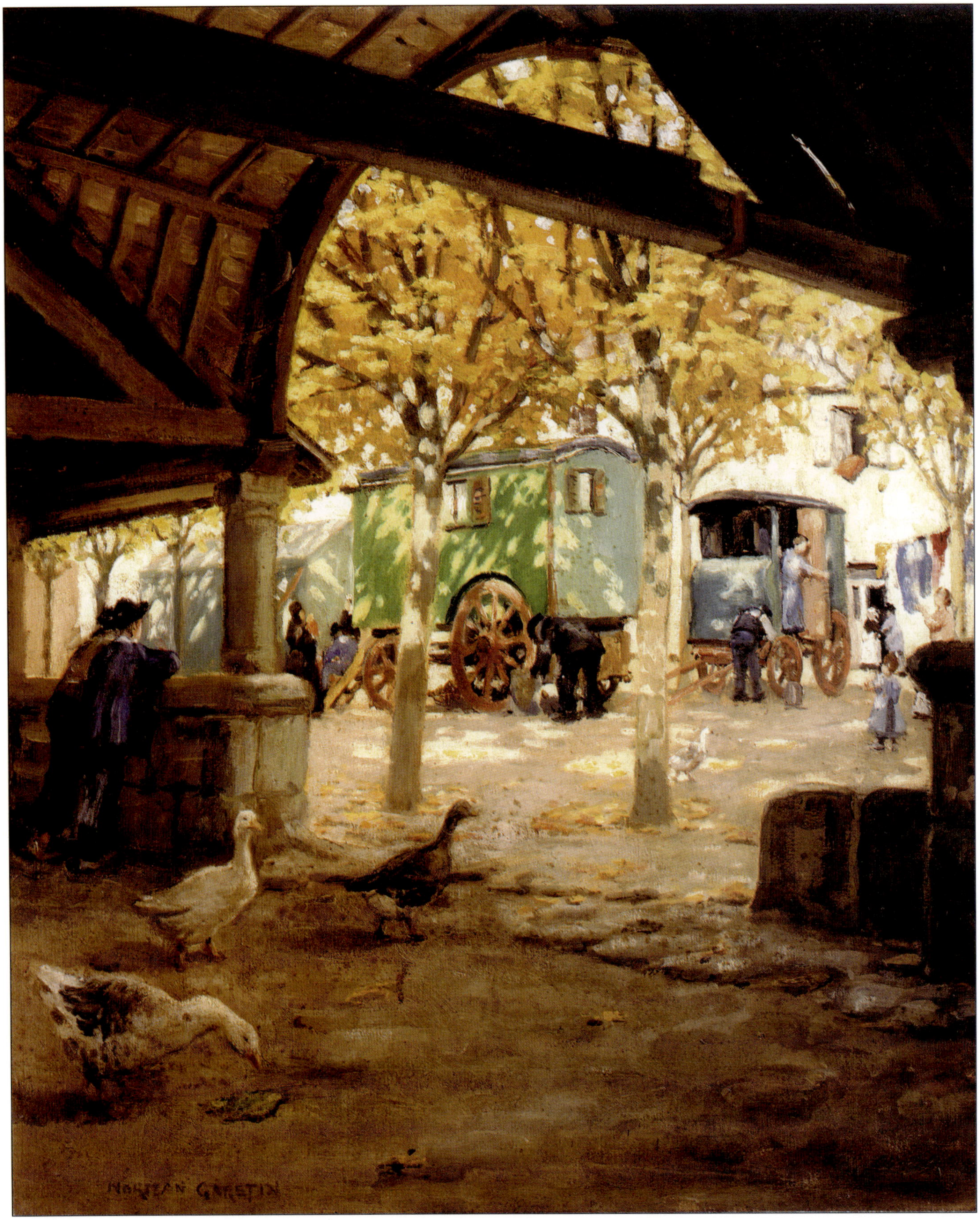
NORMAN GARSTIN

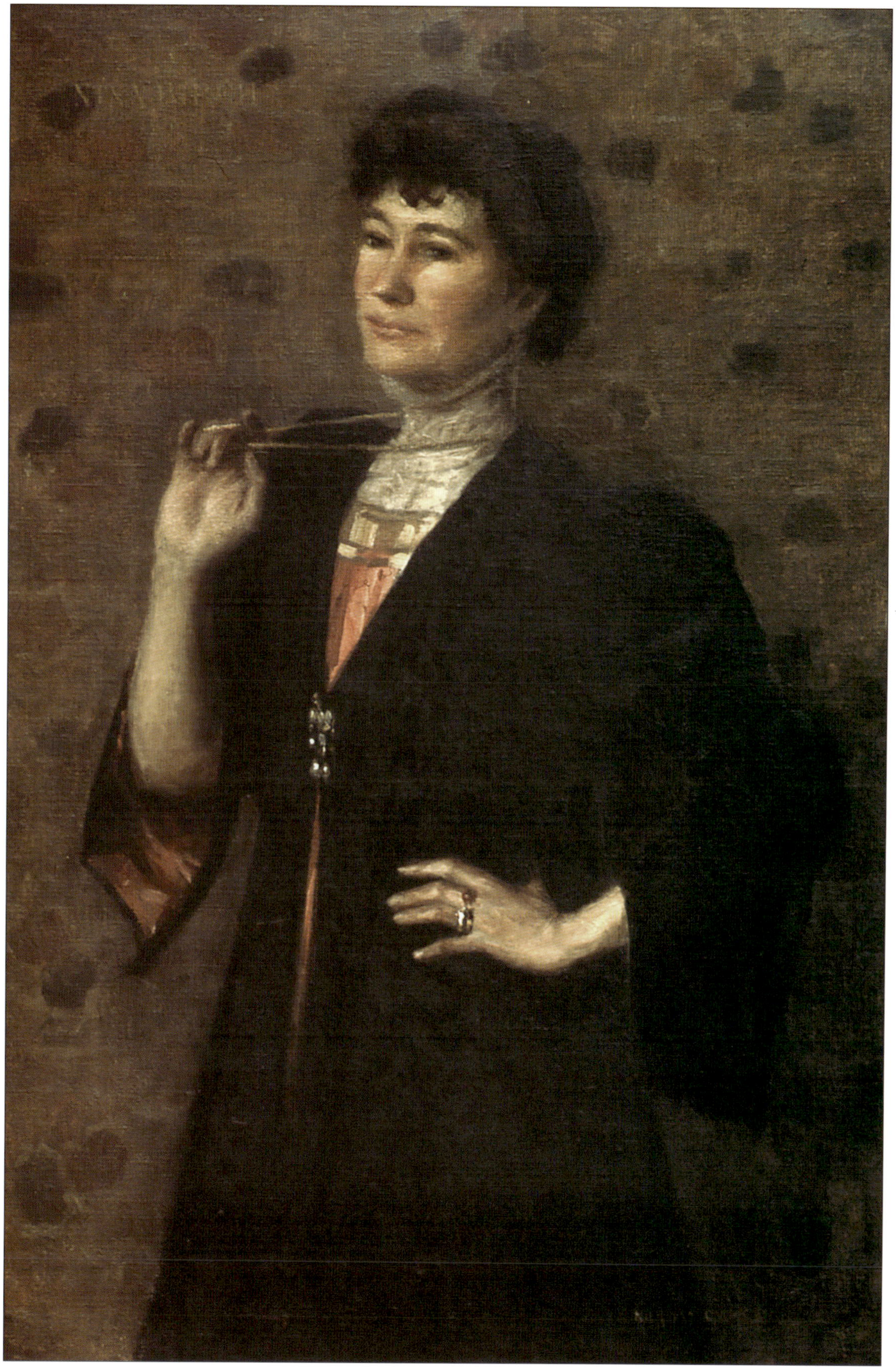

Opposite:
Plate 46 *The Last of the Fair*, 1914, oil, 30" x 25.5" (National Gallery of Ireland, Dublin).

Right:
Plate 47 *Nina Birch*, 1909, oil, 29.5" x 19.25" (private collection).

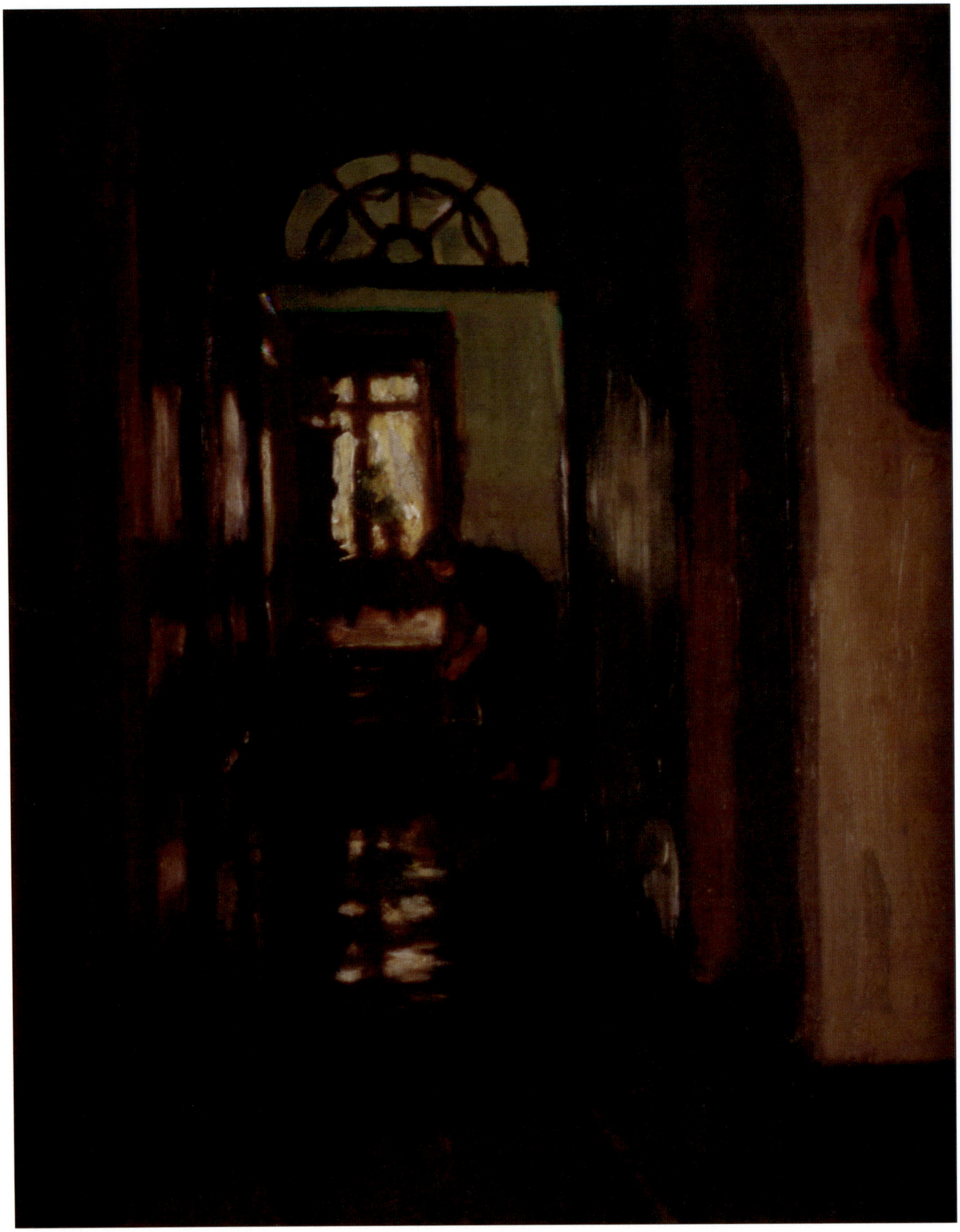

almost stark. Garstin has managed to impart a feeling of life and movement to the crowd, and the eye is led up the street by its members. This is an accomplished piece of painting, and even the small blurred area turns out, on close inspection, to be the smoke from the carousel. *The Evening Fête* (1912), which appears in Plate 34, is another striking picture of a fair.

Canal pictures are another type of town scene with figures. The watercolour *Bright October, Delft* (1904), which is a particularly fine example, appears in Plate 35. Although it is easier to produce a bad oil than a bad watercolour, it is more difficult to achieve high standards in the latter medium. Here Garstin has certainly succeeded. At first glance, the picture, which is very much a tonal work, may seem a little dull but it turns out to be crowded with life and interest. The figures on the bridge are not static. Interest is imparted by the red roof and, less obviously, by the man in blue and the way in which the two windows differ in size. Above all, there is the underside of the bridge, which is splendidly painted. What is special is the way in which the blue becomes darker as the top of the arch is approached. The reflection of the bridge and, in particular, the reflection of the arch is well painted, and there is a pleasing contrast between the blue underside and the brighter wall beyond. The bottom right corner is, however, slightly surprising. The level of detail is less, although it is the nearest part of the scene. Presumably Garstin did not want to divert attention from the crucial central section of the picture. The more one looks at the picture the greater the sense of depth becomes. It is notable that it is a picture that produces some *à travers* effect, because this is more difficult to achieve in watercolour.

Although the summer schools were mostly held at small places in the country, rural scenes are much less common than urban subjects, and they almost always contain buildings and figures. A good example is the watercolour now known as *Hanging Out the Washing*, which is shown in Plate 37. This is a gentle tonal picture, although it contains pleasing blue and light green washing. It is a happy picture: the wind is blowing the washing, the central woman's hands are uplifted, and she is wearing a warm coloured dress. Attention is focused on the two women, the washing and the door; and inessential detail has been omitted. There is an interesting inconsistency between the shadows cast by the prop and by the chimney. The sun shifted but Garstin was too busy to notice.

There were not many pure landscapes, although there are a few empty gardens. Garstin liked painting urban scenes because he found them picturesque, but the relative absence of rural pictures may seem surprising. It was partly explained by the places in which the summer schools were held, and by Garstin's lack of time. Although he does not always seem to have been successful, he tried to find places where there would be plenty for his students to paint within easy walking

Opposite:
Plate 48 *The Wet Passage* (small version), 1910, oil, 10.6" x 8.5" (Penlee House Gallery, Penzance, where it is known as *Saturday, an Interior View of Garstin's Home*).

distance, and he himself did not have sufficient time to go far afield. There was another and more fundamental reason why he painted so few landscapes. 'During the summer', as he explained when asked about his painting parties, 'pure landscape is apt to be very green, the grass and the trees are chiefly viridian so we try to find subjects [in old fashioned towns] with a rather wider range of colour both for myself and my pupils'.[17] Not until the coming of autumn did the heavy greens become less obtrusive. Even so, his exhibition of 1909 was criticized in *The Times* for 'the peculiarly ugly green which crops up over and over again'.[18]

Renaissance by Painting Party

The end result of the summer schools was a marked recovery in the standard of Garstin's work. It was renaissance by painting party. Despite the excellence of Garstin's tuition, the chief beneficiary of his efforts seems to have been the Prof himself! That his work during the pre-war period was often of a high order is evident from the quality of the small pictures that have been shown in the Plates, and also from other works that have not reproduced. However, the clearest evidence of recovery is provided by his major works, to which we shall now turn.

Place St Michel, Quimperlé and *Moulin de la Ville, Quimperlé*, which are reproduced in Plates 38 and 39, were first exhibited in 1901, but originate from the summer school of the previous summer. They show the immediate impact which the painting parties had both on Garstin's subject matter and on the standard of his work. They are large townscapes containing figures, and are both strong and confident piece of work. There is nothing laboured about their painting or their contents, as in so many of the pictures of the nineties. One has the feeling that they were pictures that Garstin wanted to paint. The use of paint is economical and deft, and, although the technique is perhaps a little more impressionistic than previously, the difference is not great. They are well-executed pieces of work: in both pictures the complicated roofs have, in particular, been well handled, with convincing perspective. In the *Place* Garstin has succeeded in making the figures seem natural, and there are stimulating contrasts between the various browns on the front of the hotel. In the *Moulin* the small, lighted window gives the picture interest, and so does the couple on the left side. These features both relieve and emphasise the gloom of the main building and the canal. There is a nice relationship between the blue of the early evening sky and the dark reflections of the mill onto the canal. It is a picture with considerable atmosphere. Both the inclination of the building and the reflection of its string course draw the viewer in. They are both *à travers* pictures.

In the following years Garstin was to paint at least two twilight scenes, which is not surprising given his opportunity to paint during the early evening, and as the days were drawing in towards the end of the summer schools. It is a great misfortune that neither of these pictures can be seen, but, insofar as it is possible to judge from a black and white reproduction and a detailed description, they were impressive works. *A Watch Tower in the Low Countries* shows a town square with figures and, in the top half of the picture, a massive Gothic tower. This dominates the scene and makes the houses below seem puny and ineffectual. Once again the gloom is both relieved and emphasized, although, this time, by the glowing shop windows. *A Late Load* (1909) shows,

> a Flemish scene, leaden-hued clouds rolling up behind a windmill, the sails of which stand out gauntly. In the pale, weird light the road looks like a broadened splash of silver, and in the foreground, almost under the shadow of the mill, two horses come along the way … Everything seems strangely subdued, and the effect is heightened by several wraith-like trees which, with the old mill, are the sole watchers, over the deserted countryside.[19]

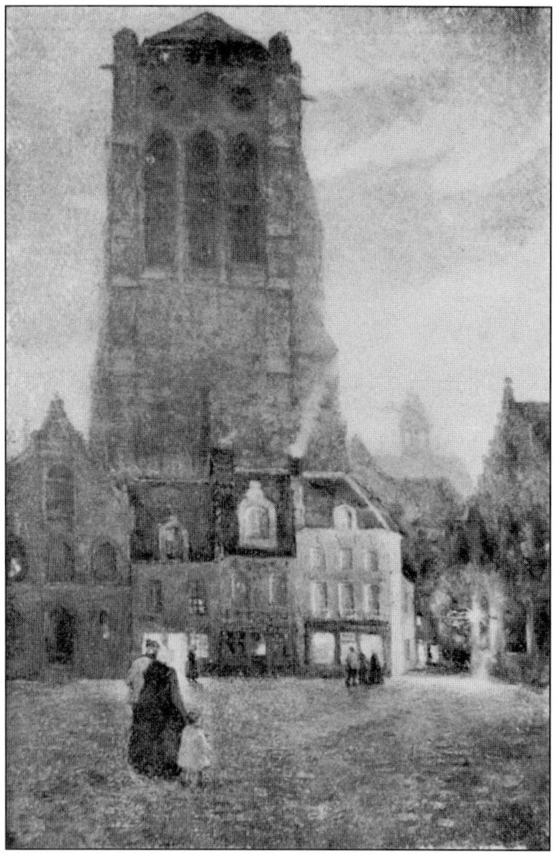

A Watch Tower in the Low Countries, 1907, oil (from *Academy Notes*, 1907). This is La Grande Place, Furnes.

There are at least two other pictures that share the melancholy, or even the sinister nature, of these works. One is *The Last Furrow* (Plate 51), though it belongs to the last phase of Garstin's life; while the other is a smallish work inscribed *Convent Gossipers*, but probably exhibited as *The Convent Gate. Evening* (1912). Once again, as Plate 40 indicates, this employs the device of figures that both enhance and relieve the sadness of the scene; but here there are two women, engaged in comfortable conversation, together with a distant and lonely man, who is walking into the distance.

In a Flemish Hospice (1909), later known as *The Card Players*, is a work of muted tones and Garstin has used a restricted palette. It is nevertheless a happy work, as can be seen from Plate 41. The old men, who are playing cards or watching, are at a church hostel, as indicated by the cross, just visible on the wall. The way in which Garstin has caught a moment in time, when one of the men is about to play a card, is reminiscent of *Overdue*. What is impressive about the picture is that Garstin has painted a group scene in which the figures are not stilted. It sounds simple but is not easy to achieve, as a visit to any art gallery will show. The relationship between the men is notable. Although the seated ones are absorbed in their own thoughts, they are companions, as emphasised by the standing figure who is bending over his colleague. This was as near as Garstin was to come to a picture of intimacy. The chalk with which the score is being recorded seems like a flash of light, and gives the picture a

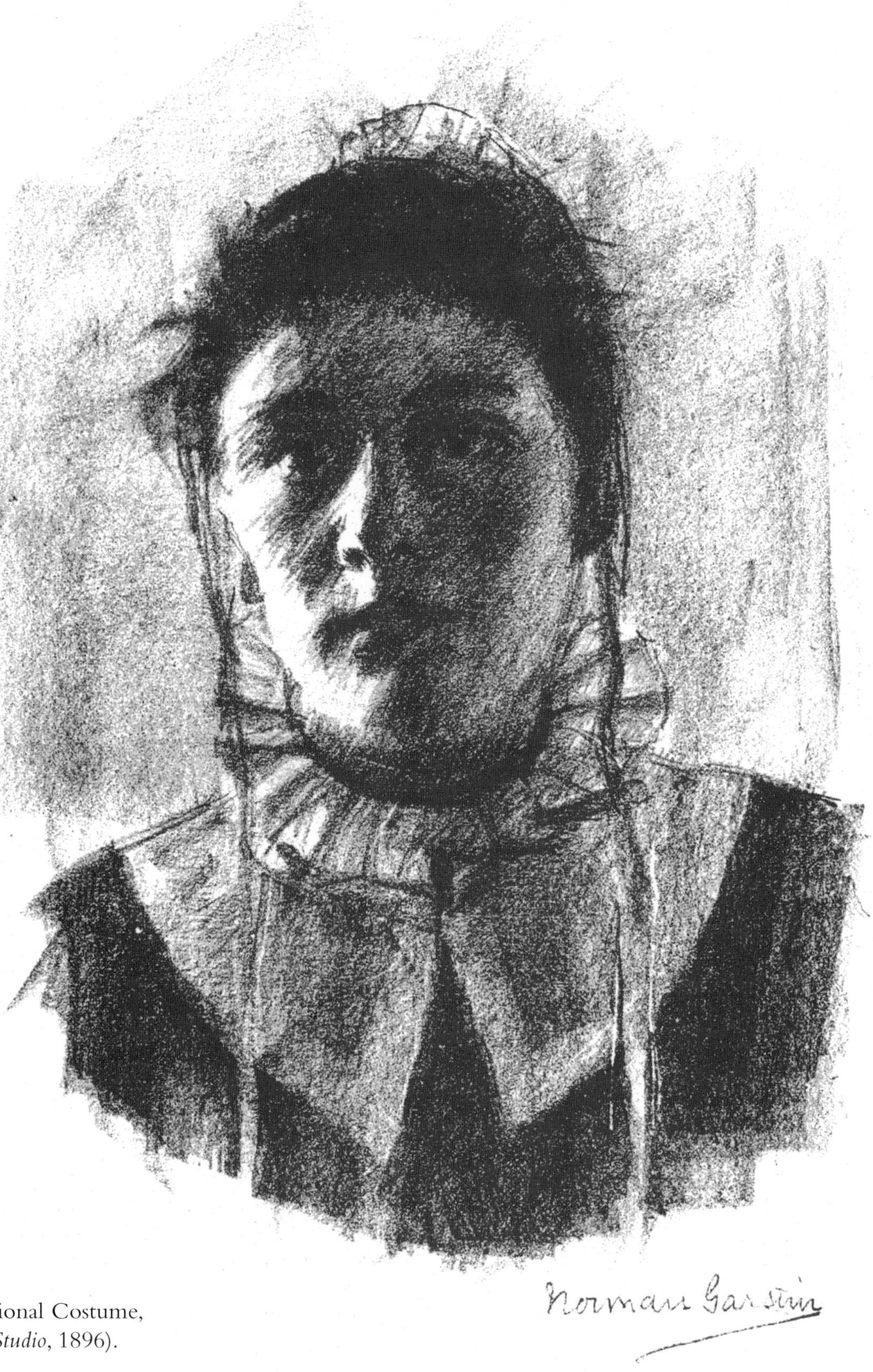

Woman in Traditional Costume,
lithograph (*The Studio*, 1896).

heightened interest. As shown by the chair back to the left, the painting is somewhat freer than in earlier works. *Breton Needlewomen*, reproduced in Plate 42, is in some ways a companion picture, showing as it does a group of old women.

Garstin was particularly fond of religious institutions for the elderly, and *Le Beguinage* (1908) is another treatment of the subject. This work, later known as *Sunshine in the Beguinage*, is another happy picture, but, as Plate 43 indicates, it is an exterior and the colours are much brighter and more varied than those of the previous work. The way in which the light breaks through the trees and produces pools of brightness, on both ground and the walls, together with the dark shadows, is slightly reminiscent of some Impressionist paintings (as also is the effect created *In the Heat of the Day*, which is reproduced as Plate 44). Nevertheless the contrast between the colours is much less extreme, and it remains a work of harmonious tones. The small patches of blue sky do not appear any more distant than the surrounding foliage and buildings. Here there is a similarity with Brangwyn, whom Garstin knew and admired. Except for the sky it is a picture with great depth, imparted, for instance, by the way in which the path tapers off. It is one of the most Diderotian, *à travers* pictures that Garstin ever painted. The brick wall of the beguinage in front; the yellow wall to the left; and the gutter on the right produce a strong feeling of enclosed space. The picture, with its old lady and the young child, shows youth and age, but there is no hint of sentimentality because the child is seen from behind and is not interacting with the woman. Nevertheless it is interesting to observe that the old woman and child do not appear in *The Red Houses* (1912), which must be a preliminary version. Here, as can be seen from a frontispiece, there is a nun and child, but they are further back and less prominent. They are also less posed, and hence the preliminary picture produces a greater feeling of tranquillity.

Among the Pots (1911) and *The Last of the Fair* (1914) are the last major works of the pre-war period that will be considered in detail. Reproductions appear in Plates 45 and 46. Although they are very different, they are both new initiatives.

Among the Pots is an interesting attempt to paint a large picture where the principal interest is still life. Garstin does not seem to have been particularly interested in still life in its pure form, and the only known picture which contains this and nothing else is a study for this big work. Nevertheless he was obviously fascinated by the pottery market depicted here, and took the trouble to paint a number of preliminary studies. 'Among the Pots is as good as anything in the Academy;' commented *The Observer*, 'the rendering of the textures and glazes of the pottery testifies to the artist's delight in producing this *tromp l'oeil*'.[20] The jars, plates and bowls are indeed painted in a masterly manner, and the pots and cobble stones display a marvelous range of browns. There are also some differing greens, including a turquoise that was for Garstin an unusual colour.

The Observer complained, however, that Garstin had destroyed the unity of the picture by introducing some unrelated figures, while *The Times* said he was more interested in his pots than his people, and had painted them better.[21] To say that there is no unity is too harsh, although there is certainly a contrast, which provides interest, between the static bottom section and the band of bustle above. The bright diagonal pathway between the pots leads the eye up and into the work and thereby provides a linkage between the top and bottom. Nor does the impressionistic treatment of the small figures detract from the picture. On the contrary, it helps to provide a feeling of depth. Nevertheless the picture does have faults. Part of the pot seller's dress is poorly painted, and as this is in the middle ground it is a little jarring. As with *Her Signal*, one has the feeling that Garstin was trying too hard to produce a masterpiece, though he gave up before he had perfected the woman. There is a certain lack of spontaneity, and the small figures seem contrived. *Earthenware* (1912), which is a small picture of pots on display in the same place, is more spontaneous, as can be seen from Plate 3. The brushwork is somewhat looser and Garstin does not seem to have been over-concerned with the pots. A notable feature of the picture is the way in which the nearest pots seem to advance out of the frame: here there is an *au dehors* effect.

The Last of the Fair is a striking combination of a bright central sector surrounded, or almost surrounded, by grisaille; though the centre is itself a contrast of dappled light and shade. Another interesting contrast is provided by the emerald green of the central caravan and the bright orange of its wheel. There is indeed much to look at, including, for instance, the woman and child by the left hand pillar. The picture is not however in any way cluttered. One of the great strengths of Garstin's works is that they provide sufficient detail to be interesting, without slipping into excess. In both the use of grisaille and the painting of a barn-like roof the picture is reminiscent of Alexander Mann's *Sheep-Shearing in Berkshire*: a picture that Garstin knew well, having included a reproduction in his memorial article.

Garstin's work developed in a number of ways during the period before the First World War, and this was probably when he painted a few pictures that can legitimately be described as Impressionist. One example is the major work now known as *Morning in the Creek*. It is a great misfortune that only a poor colour photograph is available. Although Garstin was principally engaged on town scenes and landscapes, he continued to paint portraits, of which *Nina Birch* is a notable example. Here, as can be seen from Plate 47, we have an elegant and sensitive woman, as shown by her tasteful clothes and jewelry, her refined features, and her neck, which is extremely slender. The way in which she is playing with her necklace, and leaning slightly backwards, convey an initial impression of tenseness, but this is not borne out by her relaxed hand-on-hip stance, and by her distant, and perhaps wistful, gaze. The construction of the picture is also of interest: it has a bright focal colour – her blouse – and an outer triangle of brightness consisting of her face, forearm and hand on hip.

Garstin Gains Recognition

Between 1900 and 1914 Garstin's work received greater recognition than ever before, though much less than it deserved. Fifteen pictures were hung at the Academy. With one or two exceptions, all were major works, and from 1904 one or more pictures were hung every year. At least two were placed on the line, including *Sunshine in the Beguinage* in 1910, although his other two exhibits of that year were badly placed; and in 1907 *A Watch Tower in the Low Countries* had been skied. Other prestigious galleries at which big canvases were exhibited included the Royal Society of British Artists, the Royal Institute of Oil Painters, the New English Art Club, the Royal Birmingham Society of Artists, and the Walker at Liverpool.

Not many of these pictures were reproduced in catalogues and exhibition guides. *A Watch Tower in the Low Countries* appeared in *Academy Notes*, and *Among the Pots* and *Prentices* were in the illustrated catalogue for the Walker. On the other hand, there was rather more press comment about his RA pictures than there had been previously. As we have seen, there was at long last a mention in *The Times*, albeit a slightly carping one, together with a more balanced judgment of the same picture – *Among the Pots* – in *The Observer*. The play of sunlight in *Sunshine in the Beguinage* was described as 'extraordinarily successful' by the *Evening Standard* and *St James's Gazette*; and the *Black and White Guide to the Academy* for 1912 had a brief but favourable mention of *Breton Needlewomen*.[22]

What, however, tips the balance, and leads to the conclusion that Garstin received more notice, were his three solo exhibitions at leading galleries. *The Studio* had a short but favourable notice about the display at The Fine Art Society in 1904, and there was a longer, and even more laudatory, review of the exhibition at Walker's in New Bond Street, in 1909. There was also a shortish, but largely favourable, notice about the latter in *The Times*. The 1912 exhibition at Walker's also had enthusiastic but brief mentions. That Garstin was at long last gaining some prestige was shown by his election to the Royal Institute of Oil Painters, in 1909. This he declined, *à la*

Groucho Marx, with the comment that, if they wanted him, they must be having problems.

An Increased but Inadequate Income

During the pre-war period, Garstin earned more from painting than ever before, largely as a result of his substantial output of small oils and watercolours. They did not fetch much, but they sold relatively well. A third of the watercolours exhibited at The Fine Art Society were disposed of on the spot; and the first exhibition at Walker's must have been fairly successful, or there would not have been a second. The latter was described by Garstin as a bad show. It is not clear what he did with the works that remained unsold. Only a few were re-exhibited or offered to galleries after Garstin's death, and nothing from this period was bequeathed by Alethea. Hence it seems likely those watercolours and small oils that remained on Garstin's hands were sold off to dealers. His success at disposing of his major works continued to be very mixed. Two works were sold at the Academy, *The Wet Passage* in 1911 for £50 and *The Cabaret* in the following year for £80. To judge from the preliminary version of *The Wet Passage,* which is shown in Plate 48, it deserved to sell. On the other hand, six works, despite repeated re-exhibition, never sold at all.

It can be estimated that between 1900 and 1914 Garstin made, on average, £315 each year from selling pictures, though this was at catalogue prices which gives an exaggerated impression. Now that the Garstins also had the profits from the summer schools, their income would have been substantially greater than during the 1890s, but they had heavy family commitments. Until 1904 they were maintaining two children at boarding school, Crosbie at Bedford County School and Denis at a prep school. After this, there was only one lot of fees to find because Denis had a house scholarship at Blundell's, followed by an Exhibition at Sidney Sussex, while Alethea would not have gone off to her boarding school until about the time that Crosbie left his (1906). It is clear that the Garstins were seriously short of money. 'They are', observed Frances Hodgkins, 'such dear delightful people but I do wish they had a little more of this world's goods – living on pictures is a dog's life … Mr Garstin says despondently you must be dead before you can make a living at Art'.[23]

Nevertheless it would be wrong to end this Chapter on the pre-war era on this sour note. What is even more memorable is Hodgkins' description of the time she and Garstin visited galleries, in drenching rain, to try find pictures for the New Zealand Academy of Fine Arts:

> We went to 5 galleries that day [at the end of April 1907] … we lunched at an Italian restaurant in Leicester square and pretended we were on the Continent. At 6.30 we dragged ourselves out of the last gallery and staggered to a bus – poor Mr Garstin very dead tired and jaded. We had a dinner that night too at Mr Farquharson's [who was a colleague at Duran's] … no doubt meat, wine, wit and women would work wonders – and indeed it did for when I called for him the next morning he was in great form … we went on [after visiting the studio of Edward Stott] to see Mr Fred Hall … He is an old friend of Mr Garstin [from Newlyn] and was glad to see us and insisted on sharing a beef bone and some wine and biscuits with us … It was great fun and they told long yarns about themselves and brother brushes and old times … I left them to their cigars.[24]

This is by no means the only account of Garstin happy with his friends.

Chapter 6

War Without Peace, 1914-26

Garstin's period of happiness and high output, which had begun with the foreign painting parties, was torn apart by the First World War. His productive trips abroad ceased and did not recommence until 1921. Although there were summer schools in England they were, with the possible exception of 1920, no substitute but pale occasions. What was worse, his peace of mind and concentration were sapped by a War that was the antithesis of the rationalism in which he believed, and which led, in 1918, to personal tragedy. Garstin did not cease to paint pictures of great merit, but his output was sparse. It was not until the twenties that there was, despite his underlying gloom, to be a final burst of creativity. Then dust to dust, ashes to ashes.

The War Begins

The outbreak of First World War found the Garstins in France, where he was happily conducting a class at La Faouët in Brittany. He painted the view from his hotel bedroom and it is shown in Plate 49. Garstin was enthusiastic about his students, who were painting better than usual, and was himself determined to do some splendid work that summer. Vain hope. France entered the war at the beginning of August, and the Garstins, after bureaucratic delay, left on the tenth. Frances Hodgkins, who at Garstin's suggestion had just joined the party, reported that, 'he and Mrs and the 17 virgins, all very young and frightened poor dears, went off in a great hurry, I assisting to poke things into bags and tie on labels'.[1] A passport photograph from this time shows Garstin standing nonchalantly and with a look of stoic, and even slightly amused, calm.

Garstin went to London and saw his son Denis on 14 August and, what was more significant, met his old friend Leonard Courtney, who had become a Lord and a Liberal Nestor. 'When ... I came back

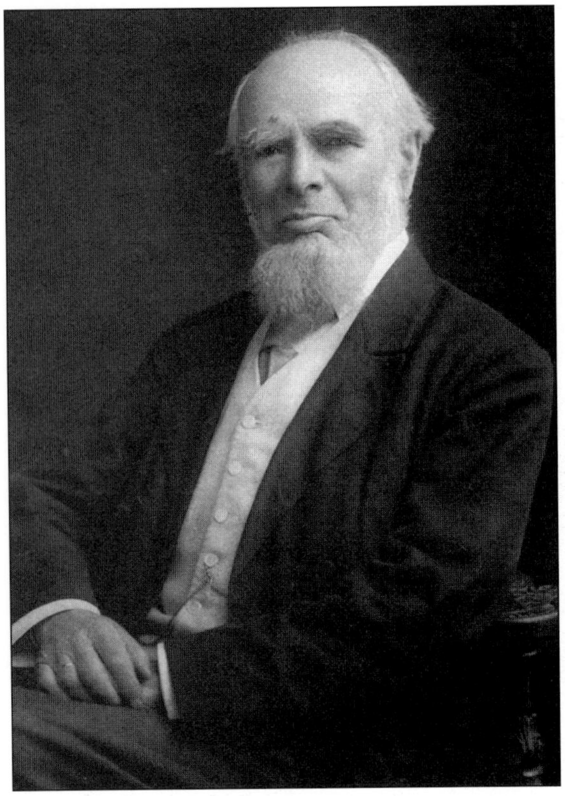

Lord Courtney of Penwith.

from France', Garstin later wrote to Lady Courtney, 'it was to your house I came feeling that there at least I will learn what men of principle and fair dealing were thinking ... You and your husband gave me a sense of the real situation and I was able to get into touch with sanity once more'.[2] What did sanity mean? After Germany had attacked Belgium on 4 August, Courtney, who had hitherto been a neutralist, backed the declaration of war. He was, however, strongly critical of Grey, the Foreign Secretary, for not having responded to a final peace initiative from the German ambassador. Courtney believed that, by drifting into a secret understanding with France, and so with Russia, the Government had sacrificed its liberty of action and ability to mediate.[3] Opposition to secret diplomacy, secret agreements, and malign forces that operated behind the scenes, became the credo of the group of militant doves with whom Garstin was to ally himself. The immediate consequence of the outbreak of war, and the return from France was more humdrum: the painting party re-assembled at Wareham in Dorset.

Summer schools in England, and semi-pacifist opposition to the war, became, from 1914, the dominant features of Garstin's life, and were to have a crucial impact on his painting.

Radical Politics and Militant Pacifism

The war made it impossible for Garstin to take painting parties abroad, and, during its early and middle years the schools were located in the Cotswolds: at Burford in 1915 and 1916, and at Chipping Camden in 1917. In the final year of the war, Ludlow was the venue, in 1919 it was Wells, and in 1920 Pin Mill on the Orwell in Suffolk. Not until 1921 was there to be another foreign trip.

War also changed the course of Garstin's life by radicalising his politics. He had long held political views of a most advanced type. In what were probably lecture notes, dating back to the late nineties, he argued that part of the population was condemned to poverty and degradation by heredity, environment and old age; that, even if all were hardworking and sober, the consequent increase in labour supply would drive down wages; that the criminal class was steadily growing with the rise in population density; that there were pronounced class differences in height and health; and, he implied, that inequality was growing as big capital crushed out competition and those unprotected by unions were forced to live on the lowest possible wages.

Such a critique of capitalism would, at that time, have been shared by collectivists of many different shades. What, however, made Garstin so original was that he went further and attacked the whole notion of economic progress. Civilization, he wrote

> has made many things less lengthy but it has not given us time. In spite of steam and electricity we have less time than our fathers had, we are more hurried ... conveniences become necessary to us, in great part because of other conveniences, but it is a grave question whether any of them make us happier. A watch is a convenience to a man who wants to catch a train but if the train does not make him happier what's the good in the watch.[4]

Garstin anticipated Galbraith's argument that wants were themselves created by the process of production, and that the growth of output did not necessarily involve a rise in welfare. Garstin concluded that 'civilization has gone on the wrong track, that whereas savages practice mutual aid we practice competition, that whereas they are communists we are individualists, and so in spite of their ignorance and simplicity they are nearer happiness than we are.'

The war led to a profound change in Garstin's political ethos. Hitherto his views had been of a philosophic, and utopian socialist, nature. The system was inherently faulty and it, rather than any particular group, was to blame. Henceforth responsibility was specific, not general: there were villains at work. These were the 'Big wigs and autocratic forces ... soldiers and Kings and big financiers are always the same, they want the same things while the centuries go by'.[5] What they, or rather some of them, wanted, was domination, gain and empire. Imperialism and opposition to imperialism led, in turn, to frequent warfare and the disintegration of one empire after another. Before the war our politicians had entered into secret engagements, denied their existence and drifted on, hoping that they would never be called upon to honour their commitments. During the war politicians, with the help of the press, denied the public the vital facts. What was wanted was a negotiated peace where there were no victors, and hence no losers to one day avenge their defeat. Garstin ended up believing force was always futile, and should not be used even by the League of Nations.

Holding these views, Garstin must have felt obliged to become more actively engaged in politics. He followed up his meeting with Lord Courtney by writing some lectures on Disarmament and the Prospect of Peace. On New Year's Day, 1915, while he was engaged on these lectures, Garstin visited Frances Hodgkins in St Ives, and she reports that he 'talked very fervidly of the War and its horrors'.[6] The lectures seem to have involved a lot of work and to have only been completed in June. In November Garstin wrote to Lady Courtney about her husband's speech in the Lords, which he described as courageous and temperate. Courtney concluded that the war had resulted in a deadlock of force, and called, in effect, for a negotiated peace.

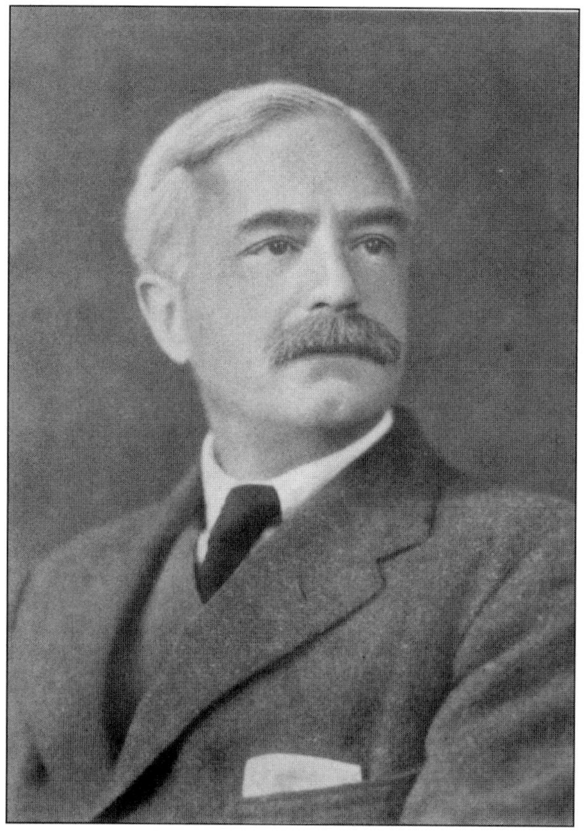

E. D. Morel.

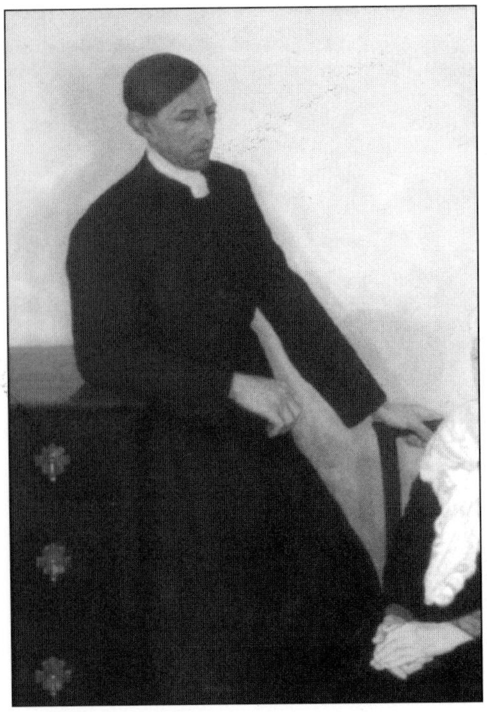

The Rev. Bernard Walke (detail from an oil painting by Annie Walker at the Royal Institution of Cornwall, Truro).

It was probably during 1915 that Garstin joined the Independent Labour Party, which opposed British participation in the war. The ILP co-operated with The Union of Democratic Control, which was the leading quasi-pacifist organization. The Union began with opposition to secret diplomacy and the military-industrial complex, but soon started to press for a negotiated peace. Its organizing genius was E. D. Morel, who had previously campaigned against the atrocities in the Congo. By the beginning of 1917 Garstin had, after what he called a *démarche*, made contact with Morel and a little later he wrote two short articles for the Union's magazine. In August, he became President of the West Cornwall Peace Society, in which the leading spirit was his friend the Rev. Bernard Walke, the high church vicar of St Hilary.[7] It had one rowdy meeting that Garstin, who was away at summer school, cannot have attended, but then appears to have fizzled out.

Garstin's views and activities must have aroused considerable hostility. One of his obituary notices refers darkly to him being, 'a man of intensely individual impulses and opinions, and [having] incurred unpopularity at times through his views on war and other topics'.[8] Pacifist views of whatever variety were rare even among the Cornish artists. The only exceptions were Harold Knight, a conscientious objector, and Ernest Procter, who was a Quaker. Some at Newlyn went so far as to cut Knight in the street. It is not known how much hostility the Garstins encountered, but it may be significant that, during the war, they absented themselves from Penzance for considerable periods. After the summer school in 1915, they went to stay with relations in Ireland, including two months, as paying guests, with May Routledge – Mag Fulton's daughter – at Castleconnel, Co. Limerick. The Garstins did not return to Penzance before the end of March 1916. Moreover they stayed on in Chipping Camden after the painting party of 1917.

Both Denis and Crosbie signed up and Garstin's pacifist opinions led to a rift with Crosbie. 'It is extraordinary, it is unthinkable', he commented, 'that the ideas I hold should prove a barrier in the family'.[9] But so it was, and only by rigid silence was any form of relationship preserved. Garstin must also have found Denis's opinions hard to bear. In June 1917, Denis sent his father an emotional but reasoned plea to reconsider his position. The Allies had, he argued, now proposed the very same peace terms that Garstin had said the Germans would accept. In response, Germany, which thought it was winning, had 'burst out into the wildest bombast'. Denis felt that his father was indulging in vague talk of evil powers, that he wrongly believed in 'the infallibility of the minority', and that, even supposing he was right, he might well be fouling his own cause by cheap abuse.[10] How Garstin reacted to this letter is not known, but it can scarcely have contributed to his peace of mind.

In 1918 the Garstins received the long-dreaded news that one of their sons had been killed. It was Denis, who had died at Archangel, during the abortive intervention to help the anti-Bolshevik forces. That Garstin was strongly opposed to the adventure can only have intensified his grief; and Denis had always been his favourite boy.

The Artistic Consequences of the War

The Great War harmed Garstin's painting because it greatly depressed his output. One obvious reason was the cessation of the foreign painting trips that he had found so stimulating. Garstin was for the most part unenthusiastic about painting in England. His letters during the war years contain several references to lack of stimulation and the difficulty of getting down to work. It might have been thought that he would have liked Wells, a picturesque old town, but instead he complained, 'I am not very taken with Wells … it is fine in certain aspects but I don't very much warm to Cathedrals and ecclesiastical buildings. Generally and beyond that there is absolutely nothing to do that I can find in the town'.[11] Although he described Burford as a lovely little town, it seems significant that he only painted a few pictures there, or at the other places at which schools were held.

The other reason for Garstin's low productivity was his preoccupation with the war. His anti-war activities must have absorbed a substantial amount of time and energy, and, perhaps even more important, the war made painting seem a trivial and pointless activity. In 1916, having just sent off a picture (probably *Breton Needlewomen*) to the RA, he commented bitterly, 'It seems strange that one should go on with this futile thing which no one wants, instead of turning our energies to some homicidal industry, some method of destroying life or maiming human beings'.[12]

Garstin's mood was one of bleak despair, and this cannot have been conducive to painting. 'Things', he commented to Lady Courtney in 1915, 'seem to be moving more and more into the shadow'; and in the following year he lamented to Ada that, 'all that is fine and noble on earth is being destroyed'.[13] Garstin was a super-affectionate father, and his differences with Crosbie and, far more important, the death of a beloved son, left him drained and depressed. After a visit for tea in early 1920, at which Garstin showed his pictures, Lily Collier was haunted by 'the memory of the sad old faces of my host and hostess'.[14]

There were a number of reasons why the wounds of war might have been slow to heal. The War Office and its crass inefficiency helped to keep the memory of Denis raw. It was not until the late summer of 1922, after a protracted correspondence, that the Garstins

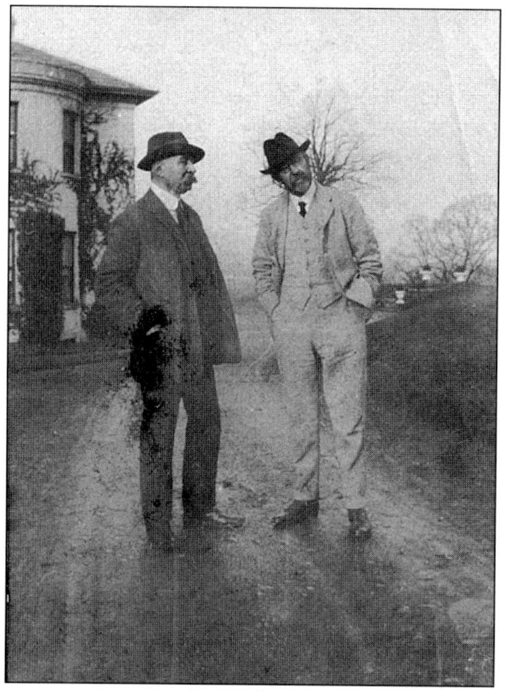

Garstin and Bob Twiss with whom the Garstins stayed in January 1916 during their visit to Ireland. In a letter to Ada FitzGerald he wrote that 'Twiss begins with a tankard of ale for breakfast and he declares that he drinks a bottle of whiskey a day ... He is anxious to give the worst impression of his vices ... I think he is extraordinarily amiable ... He is generous and gentle with far better brains than either he or anyone else gives him credit for. Had he fallen young into another environment, I cannot help thinking things would have been different, but the army and general Irish outlook of the country gentleman sent him along a decline that has seriously undermined his nature.' (Letter to Ada FitzGerald, 26 March 1916).

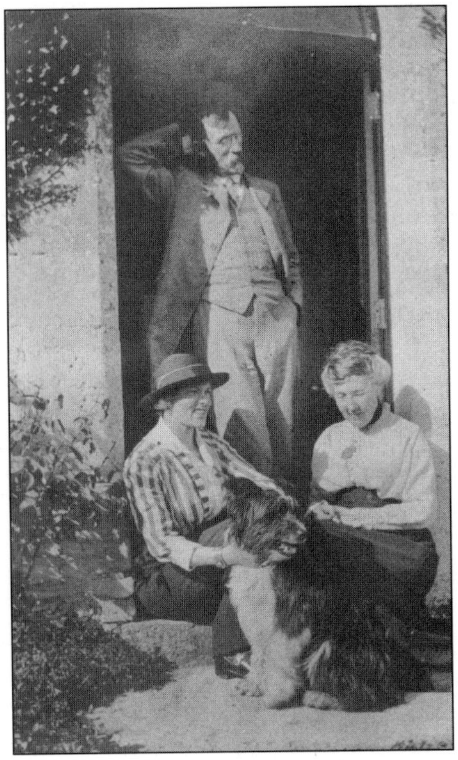
Norman, Alethea and Dochie, 1918.

were finally sent his MC and DSO, though they should have been presented to them, in person, years earlier. Even then, the War Office would not acknowledge that Denis had been awarded two Russian orders, about which Dochie was still writing in the summer of 1923. War and its consequences continued to be very much at the front of Garstin's mind. In the spring of 1920, he helped Bernard Walke organize a public meeting about hunger in Austria, and he was distressed by events in Ireland. He was strongly critical of the execution of 'those poor fellows' – the leaders of the 1916 Dublin rising – and believed that 'a policy of coercion and force was always the plan in Ireland'.[15]

Few in Number but of High Quality

Between 1915 and his death in 1926, Garstin exhibited sixteen major works for the first time. All but four of these pictures were shown during the war and the immediate post-war years. Twelve large pictures during the seven years 1915-21 may not seem an exceptionally low output. Why then has so much emphasis been placed on the war's adverse effect on his production? The reason is that he painted very few small works. Between 1915 and 1921 he only produced 22 minor works, or just over three a year. This compares with 272 between 1900 and 1914, an average of eighteen. Only during the final phase of his life, after the foreign painting parties had recommenced, did Garstin, once again, have a high output of small pictures.

It is, however, possible that his *oeuvre* was much greater than it appears. Norman may have participated with Alethea in a show at the Alpine Gallery in January 1921, but, even if he did, it seems unlikely that many of his pictures would have been shown. He may also have exhibited new works that he painted on his English summer schools at local galleries, as he did in 1920. It can be estimated that Garstin painted a substantial number of pictures that have not yet come to light (175); and some known works cannot be dated (41 excluding studio pictures).[16] A few of these pictures must have been painted between 1914 and 1921, but only one painting that can be firmly attributed to this period, and was otherwise unknown, has come up for auction. It therefore seems unlikely that the inclusion of undiscovered works would alter the conclusion that Garstin painted relatively little during the war and the following years.

The reduction in painting between 1915 and 1921 led to a sharp fall in Garstin's income from the sale of pictures, and this at a time of rapidly increasing prices. Over this period he earned, on average, less than £115 each year, at catalogue prices. How the Garstins survived is a mystery, but it appears that he lectured for the WEA.

Although the war led to a decline in output, it did not impair the quality of his work. This is demonstrated, for example, by *The Workshop* (1917), later exhibited as *The Sculptor* (1921). It can be seen from the reproduction, in Plate 50, that this is an interior painted against the light, and therefore reminiscent of many Newlyn pictures of the years around 1890, including Garstin's own work *An Iron Master*. The window is a pleasing and harmonious glow of light, and there are patches of even brighter colour above the sculptor's hat, to the right of his hand, and on the far right. Nevertheless it is, in general, a work of muted tones with some notable contrasts between the brighter parts of the picture and those parts of the workshop that are in shadow. The contrast between the brick red of the chimney and the sculptor's dark beret is particularly striking. There are more subtle contrasts within the darker part of the picture, in particular the distinction between the field grey of the sculptor's smock and the surrounding browns. Another type of contrast is provided by the stillness of the room and the animation of the sculptor. Life, and even movement, is imparted by the way in which he is placing his weight on his left leg.

Though much of the work is rather impressionistic, the picture is, where necessary, painted with all of Garstin's old clarity. This is true of the window and the reflections to the right, together with the dark shadow of the small bust. Garstin's power of observation is shown by the bluish tint in two of the small panes of glass. This is a beautiful and atmospheric picture but, in contrast to many Garstin pictures, there is no great *à travers* effect. Although the view through the window draws one into the picture, the nearness of the bench has a repelling effect, and the sculptor is not sufficiently far back for the picture to have any great depth.

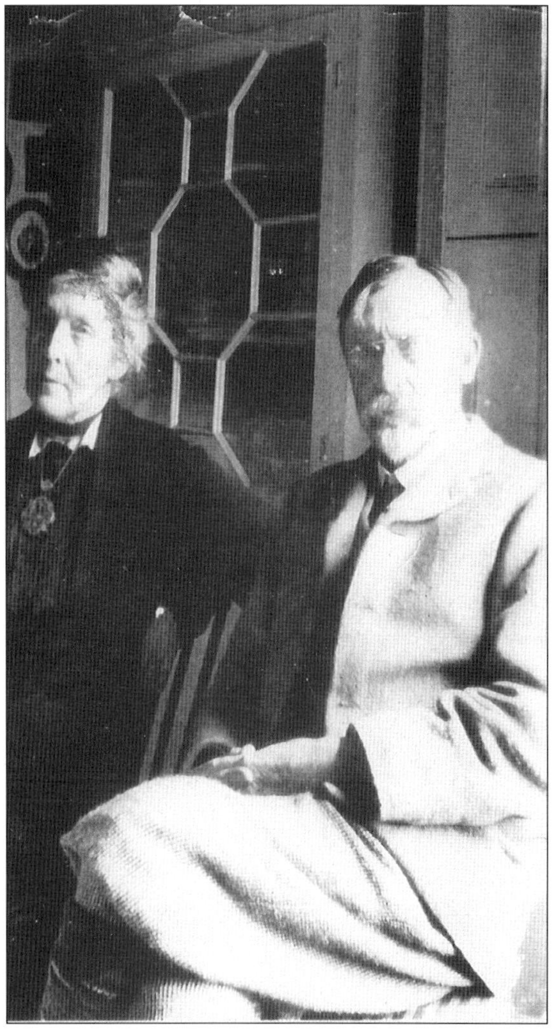

Norman and Dochie, old and sad.

At first sight, this is a picture without a hint of story. It was, however, completed in 1917, when Garstin was in despair over the war. This provokes the question of whether the sculptor, or perhaps monumental mason, could be fashioning a figure for a memorial, possibly for a soldier. This seems unlikely partly because it does not appear to be an angel, and partly because it appears that the workshop is in France or Belgium, *vide* the crucifix on the wall and the sculptor's beret and clogs. If so, Garstin would have had to make his preliminary sketches on a summer school before the war. Nevertheless it is possible that Garstin turned back to earlier sketches, because the subject now had a greater appeal.

The Last Furrow, a picture that which does appear to be connected with the war, is shown in Plate 51. The work is dominated by the engine and its oblique plume of black smoke. There is an absence of perspective at the bottom of the picture that brings the engine forward and makes it look heavy. The way in which Garstin has focused on essentials also concentrates the viewer's attention. It is, for

Plate 49 *From my Window* [Hôtel Croix d'Or, Le Faouët], 1914, oil, 21" x 16" (private collection, auctioned as *The Window View*).

Opposite:
Plate 50 *The Sculptor/The Workshop*, 1917, oil, 28" x 23" (private collection).

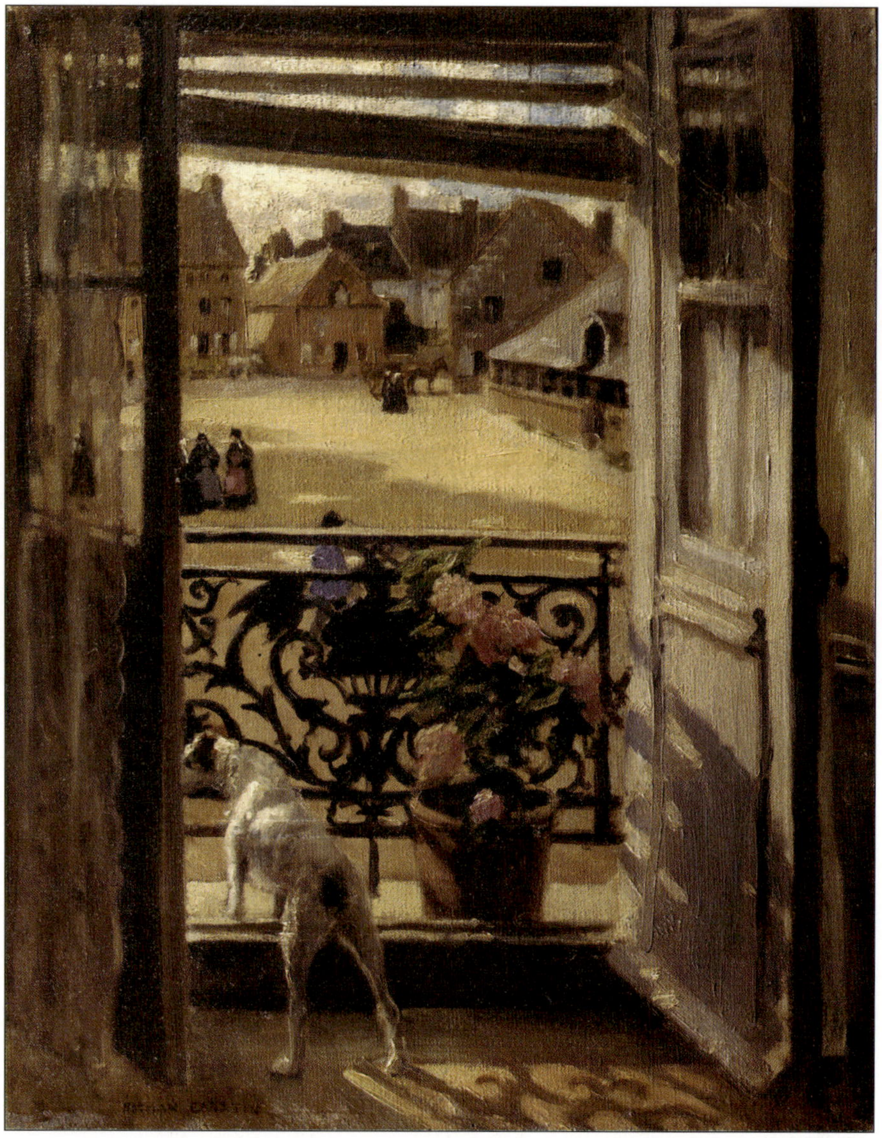

instance, only just possible to identify the furrow and the machinery at the other side of the field. Drama is imparted not only by the engine, and its pall of smoke, but also by the low horizon and overcast sky; though there is one small patch of blue for the purpose of contrast. A strong feeling of menace is produced by the intrusive engine and the deep red glint of the sunset.

Garstin seems to be contrasting the old and natural world of the countryside with modern industry; and this point is emphasized by the horse and plough, representing the old ways, that are just visible to the left of the engine. The horse must be ploughing its last furrow before being replaced by the engine on the morrow. Although not exhibited until 1918, it is dated 1915, a time when Garstin's mood was exceptionally dark. The picture is reminiscent of a Whistlerian nocturne, but Garstin has painted an elegy or allegory.

It may simply be an elegy for the triumph of machinery over the

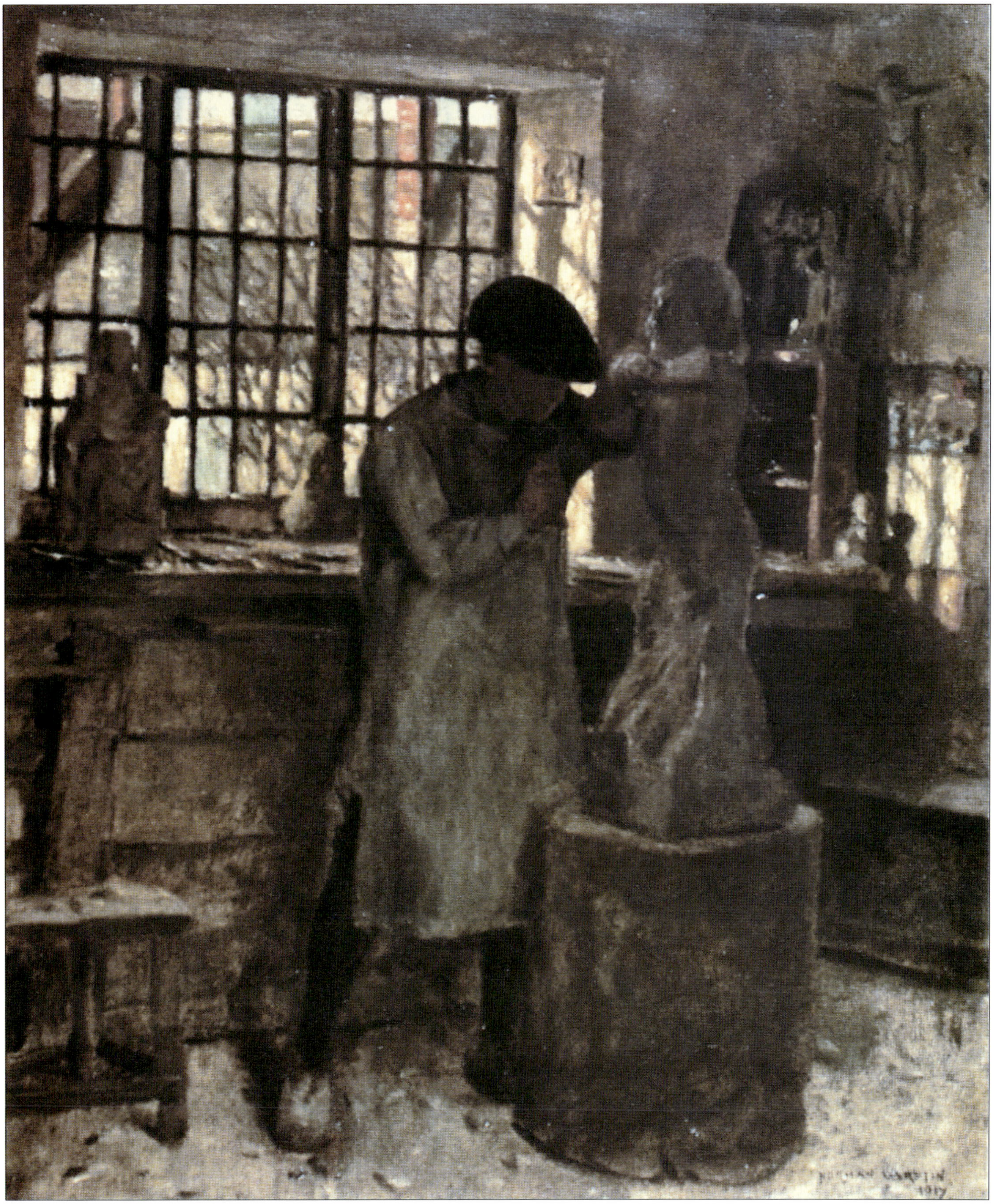

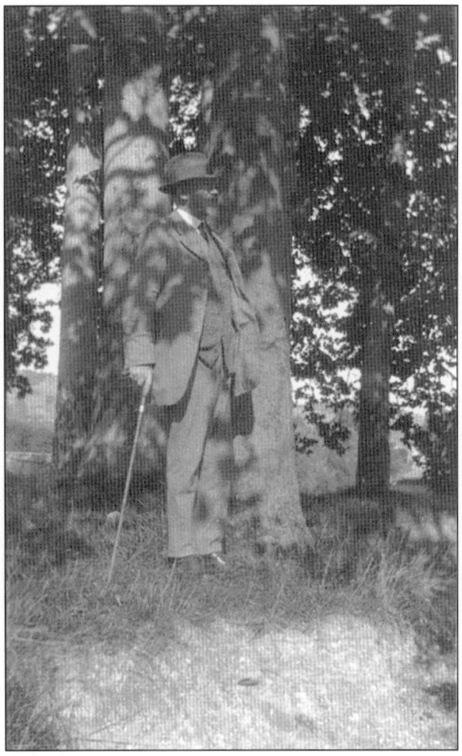
Garstin in the early 1920s.

horse, and immemorial methods of cultivation, but it could also symbolize the smoky field of battle. It is surely significant that La Thangue's well known picture with the same title (RA 1895) shows a ploughman who has collapsed and appears to be dead. Whether Garstin's picture was an elegy or an allegory it is impossible to tell, and the distinction may not be a sharp one. There was, at that time, a widespread hostility to urbanisation and concern about the ruin of the countryside. Man's power over nature seemed to have outstripped his moral and mental development, hence the engines of destruction unleashed by the First World War.

The London Pictures

Although Garstin seems to have painted comparatively few small pictures between 1915 and 1921 he did paint at least ten in London, probably in the early winter of 1920. One of the finest of these, *Battersea Bridge*, is shown in Plate 52. This picture is, once again, reminiscent of Whistler, with interesting contrasts between the cloud grays and the yellowish orange of the sky at sunset. The clouds are nicely reflected in the water, which has a very glassy effect. Both here and in another picture - *Across the River, St Paul's* (Plate 53) - a strong sense of depth is produced by the use of bolder colours in the foreground, while in yet another London townscape - *St Mary-le-Strand* (Plate 54) - this has been achieved by placing the monument close to the picture plane and cropping its top. In the view of St Paul's, there is an interesting contrast between the gloomy warehouses, relieved only by the red sail, and the soaring white and grey cathedral; in *St Mary-le-Strand* the spire and monument give the viewer a sense of uplift. In both works Garstin has employed tone and colour to achieve a pleasing harmony. These three London townscapes may be tiny, but their quality is of the first order.

It is slightly puzzling that Garstin, who did not like large towns, painted these London scenes. The explanation may be that he was dissatisfied with his picture of Wells and was trying to find a subject for another large picture. There is certainly a big version of one of his small London pictures. It is entitled *Wren's Monument* and, at 40" x 50", it is one of his largest pictures. Because it is a big canvas, and because the façade and dome of St Paul's occupy so much space within the picture, the great church has a striking and dominating effect, as can be seen from Plate 55.

It does not appear to be a particularly beautiful, or even triumphant piece of architecture, but merely to loom over the scene in an almost sinister fashion. The feeling of oppression is intensified partly by the suppression of detail and hence the blankness of the facade, and partly by the way in which the street is reduced to a cavern by the buildings on either side. Those to the left are leaning

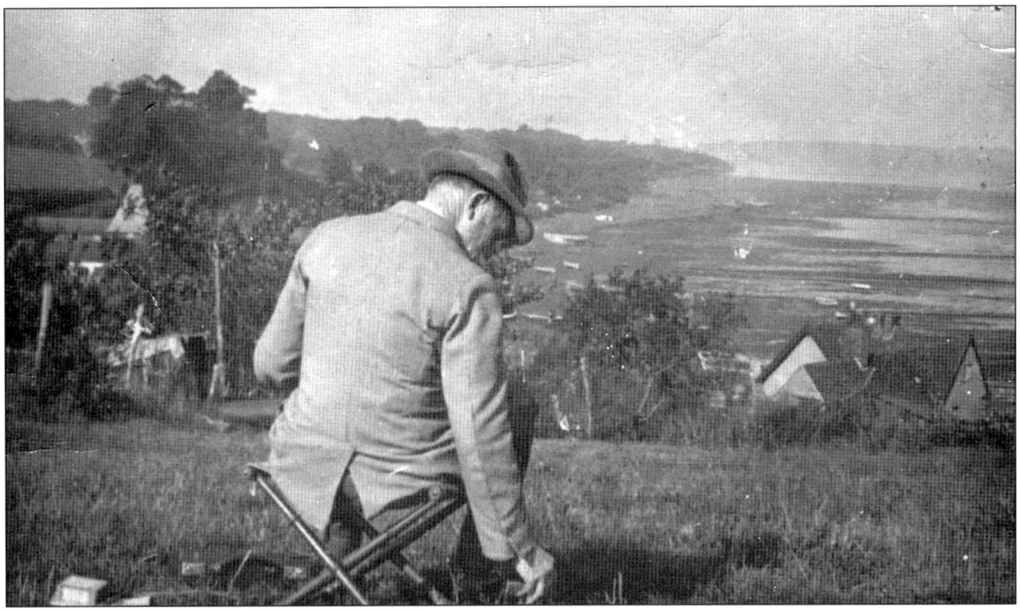

Garstin at Pin Mill, Suffolk, 1920.

slightly over the street, and this, again, contributes to a feeling of unease. Menace would be too strong a word; this is a subtle picture with an emotional impact that is insidious, and because of this, and the absence of any manifest danger, all the more worrying.

The figures in the street display no awareness of the great and overshadowing cathedral. Nobody is bothering to look up: everyone is too busy and too absorbed in their own affairs. Nevertheless, although the pigmy humans do not know it, the city buildings command the scene. Even the birds have not managed to rise very far from the pavement. Naturally, since the buildings shut out so much of the light, dull tones predominate, but some welcome relief is afforded, on the right side, by the red chimney, the red sign, and the woman in purple, and by the relatively bright sky and tower on the left. Last but not least, there is a powerful *à travers* effect.

Although the picture has its faults – the boy who is crossing the road looks somewhat posed – this is a masterly work, and its merit was recognised at the time. *Wren's Monument* was purchased by public subscription and the city trust for the Mappin Art Gallery, Sheffield, and it was to be the only one of Garstin's works bought by a public gallery during his lifetime.

The Last Furrow and *Wren's Monument*, together with earlier works such as *A Late Load*, provoke, once again, the question of whether Garstin was any longer a Realist of a strict type. The Realists were, as we have seen, concerned with ordinary people and the poor; with the impartial and unemotional depiction of a particular moment in time. To search out times, places or viewpoints in which persons or scenes appeared heroic, grand or mysterious, is to move beyond Realism. Monet's pictures of sunlit countryside are examples of realist art, but Whistler's nocturnes are not. Reality is not a fit subject for the Realist when it becomes ghostly, strange or enigmatic. Nor should the Realist seek out subjects that have a symbolic aspect, where the viewer is being invited to look through the painting and to see something else. On both grounds, Garstin has in *The Last Furrow* and *Wren's Monument* passed beyond Realism. This is not intended as a criticism, if only because it means that Garstin's work was still developing. It therefore contrasts with that of Stanhope Forbes, who never moved away from strict Realism.

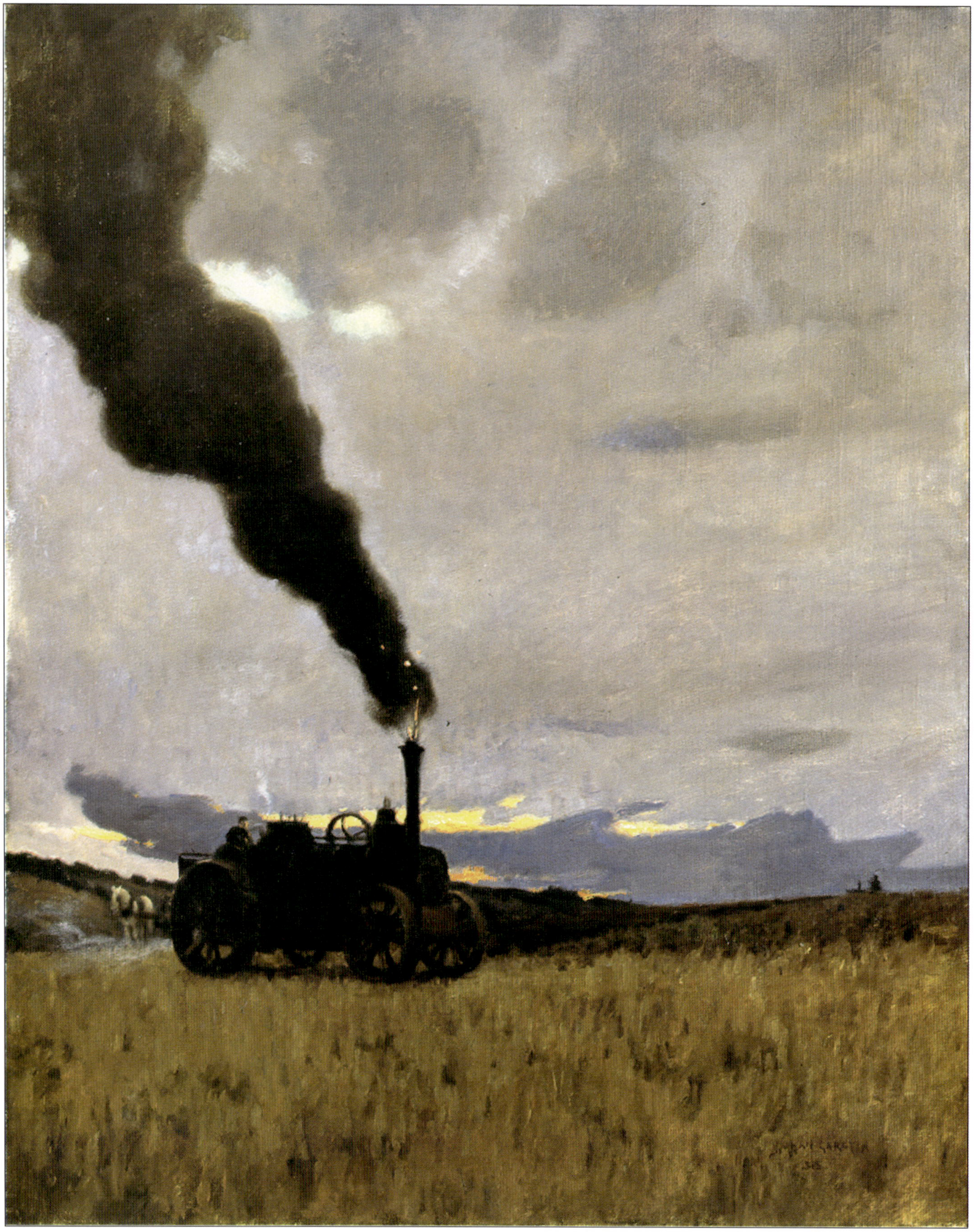

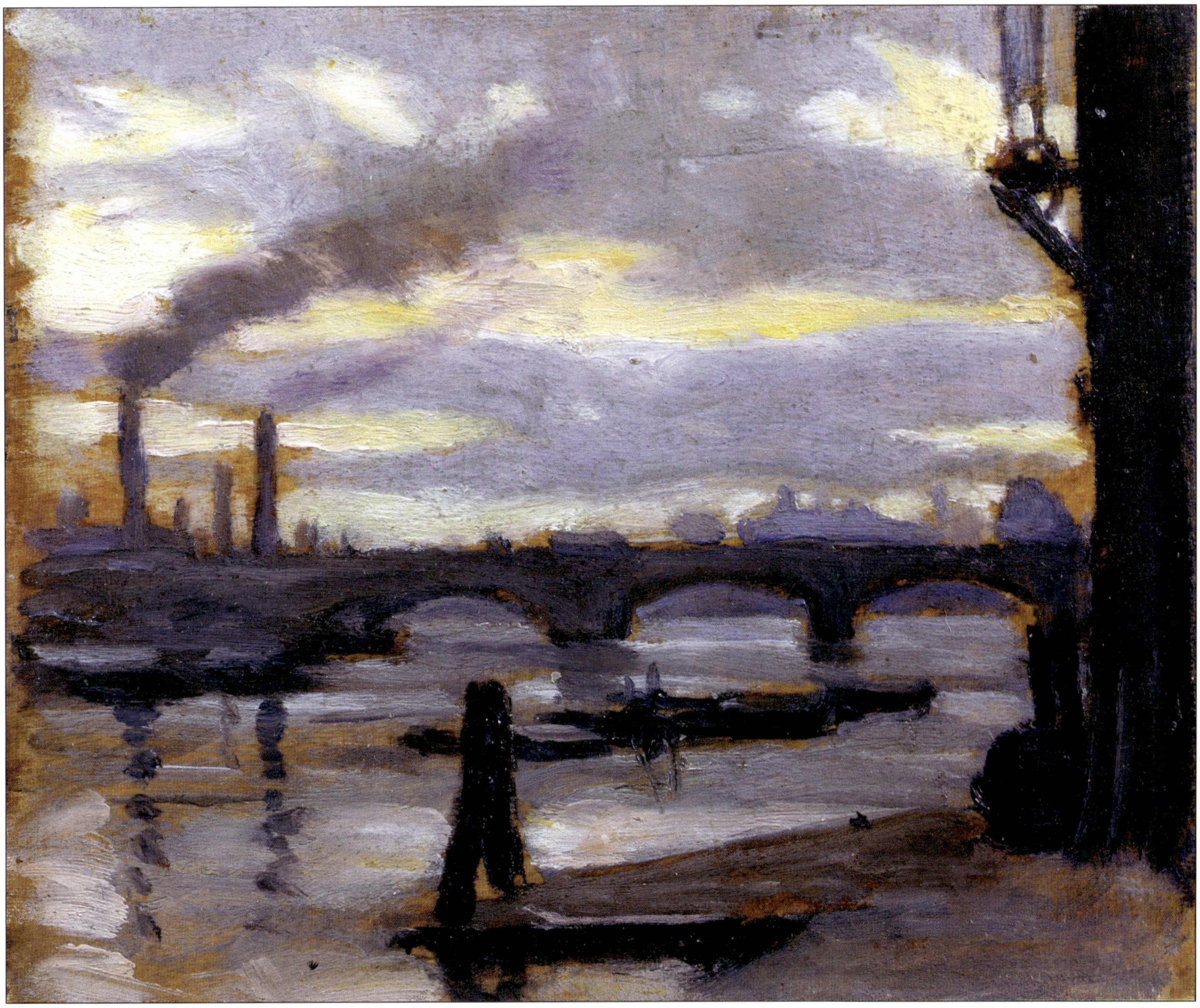

Back to the Continent and by the Orwell

In 1921 the first post-war summer school on the Continent took place at Wissant near Boulogne. There were further foreign painting parties in 1922 (Île-Tudy and then Daoulas, Brittany), 1923 (Semur, in Burgundy), 1924 (Giverny on the Seine) and, finally 1925 (probably at Montrésor, near Tours). Not long before his death Garstin went back to Venice, a trip that he had wanted to make for more than twenty years.

The foreign schools were, like their pre-war counterparts, both enjoyable and stimulating. Even allowing for some exaggeration, this is clear from the many letters of condolence after Garstin's death. One former student said that the schools at Semur and Giverny were the happiest summers she ever had, and Dochie thought that the final

Opposite:
Plate 51 *The Last Furrow*, 1918, oil, 50" x 40" (Kelvingrove Museum & Art Gallery, Glasgow).

Plate 52 *Battersea Bridge*, 1920, oil, 5" x 5.75" (York Art Gallery).

class was the most happy of them all. After Garstin's parties had ceased and he had turned elsewhere, Sir Henry Havelock Allen lamented the absence of the charabanc expeditions from which, after eating two largish meals and visiting numerous châteaux, they would return to a late supper. Garstin's ex-pupils were 'sheep without a shepherd'.[17]

Once again, Garstin found it stimulating to be abroad, although he may also have liked the Orwell area. He did not like Île Tudy at first, but the inhabitants soon caught his fancy, particularly the men, 'in their wonderful patchwork of blues and reds', and the women in black.[18] He painted them in the watercolours *The Hub of Île Tudy* (Plate 56) and *A Little Breton Port* (1924). As these paintings indicate, he employed an exceptionally bright palette, including some striking blues and oranges. There was now a dramatic rise in his output of small paintings. In 1924 he had a joint show with Alethea at Walker's Galleries, where he appears to have exhibited 50 watercolours. Although there were some old works, most seem to have been painted during the foreign painting parties of 1922 and 1923. *The Times*, in a complimentary review, observed:

> Garstin is at his best when he has least in the way of subject: a marsh, a reedy river bank, or a stretch of shore providing him with a few tinted greys for adjustment in a cunning pattern ... He is, before everything, a subtle artist, whether in composition or gradation of tone.[19]

Such landscapes of river and shore seem to have been a new development. Although they were not unknown, pure landscapes had not previously formed any great part of Garstin's output. None of the pictures to which *The Times* referred have, as yet, come to light, but there is a picture of lonely countryside that has similar characteristics, and which was exhibited at Walker's. It is called *Glowing Evening*, and is reproduced in Plate 58. The tones are warm and harmonious, with the tops of the stacks and the barn a most beautiful orange brown. The latter and the upper field, which are in the sun, are in nice contrast to the foreground, which is in shadow. There is also a pleasing contrast between the roofs and the trees, which are almost purple. The differing shapes of the barn and the stacks also provide interest, and the long low barn gives the picture a horizontal emphasis, and enhances the feeling of emptiness. Although this is an economical painting without unnecessary detail, it is also a piece of subtle observation, as shown by the slightly darker section of the barn where the wall is particularly high. *Landscape with Pools of Water* (1922), which is reproduced in Plate 57, is another fine piece of work. There is a marked contrast between the blue pool and the

I glanced at the window of Bridger

I glanced at the window of Bridger his shop
and what I caught sight of compelled me to
stop.

For there was a book by an artist of note
who pictures the things that the author chaps
wrote;

But now in this volume he turns it about
with other men's pictures while he does the
shout.

To be equal in practice and theory too
is a rare combination and given to few!
Yet this rare combination we're giving to
you!

Our poor little daughter we know is a duffer
so with practice and theory we're trying to
stuff her.

Norman to Alethea, Xmas 1921.

gentle surrounding greens; and the lively colour of the pool, together with the big sky, convey a feeling of freedom and joy. Attention is concentrated on the pool, with its well-executed reflections and bank, and the viewer is drawn into the picture.

As the Île Tudy pictures show, Garstin did not stop producing townscapes and other scenes with figures, and one of his last works, which must have been painted during his trip to Venice, is of a piazza. However, during his final years, he produced very few major works. One of his last was *Market Jew Street* (1922). He had particular difficulty painting this, complaining he had 'done quite a number of small sketches, but, when I come to doing them out on a large scale, I find they are not full enough, and my memory is not retentive enough'.[20] Despite his belief that it was not very good, it was hung on the line at the RA. If he was having particular difficulty painting large pictures, this seems to have been the only sign of failing powers. His last picture at the Royal Academy, *A Breton Fete,* was hung, and well hung, in 1923.

Garstin is known to have painted 660 works but, allowing for those that have not yet come to light, the total rises to about 835. This, however, includes studio pictures as well as many small watercolours. The number of major works that can be identified was 112, and in addition he painted 21 portraits of unknown size, most of which were probably largish. How did Garstin's output compare with that of comparable artists? For most the only information is the number of works exhibited at major galleries, and because pictures were often exhibited more than once this includes duplication. Garstin's figure (529 exhibits) is much higher than those for the other leading Newlyn artists, viz Frank Bramley (188), Chevallier Tayler (243), Elizabeth Forbes (257), Walter Langley (321), Stanhope Forbes (329) and Gotch (357). Nor would the picture change if leading Realists, such as La Thangue (274) and Osborne (292), were to be included.[21] Clausen alone seems to have been more prolific (1160), and he had a very long life. Numerous other qualifications and explanatory factors could be given. Suffice it to say that there is no reason to believe that Garstin was, despite his late start, unproductive.

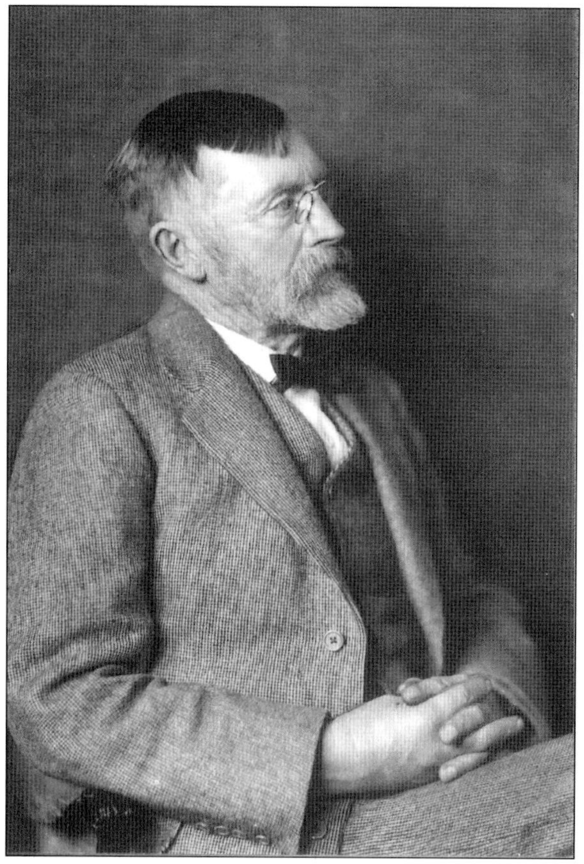

Garstin in old age.

Sadness below the Surface

Although Garstin appears to have enjoyed his continental summer schools, there seems, during his last years, to have been an undertow of sadness and lack of resilience. This is shown by two letters to Alethea in April 1923 about the selection of pictures by the Royal Academy. In the first he wrote that, 'chance, prejudice, fashion and habit govern the decisions. Dear me what a long experience of disappointment I have had, but I must not let it worry me'.[22] But it did worry him for in a second letter he speaks of

Right:
Plate 53 *Across the River, St Paul's*, 1920, oil, 5.6" x 5" (Ashmolean Museum, Oxford).

Below:
Plate 54 *St Mary-le-Strand*, 1920, oil, 6" x 5.25" (Ashmolean Museum, Oxford).

Opposite:
Plate 55 *Wren's Monument*, 1921, oil, 40" x 50" (Graves Art Gallery, Sheffield).

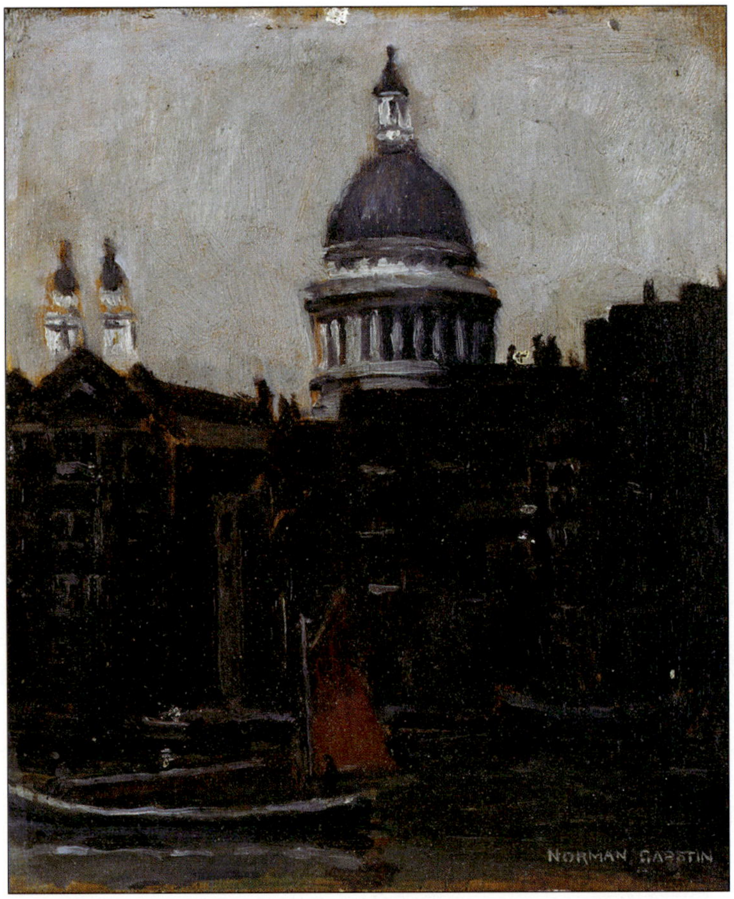

the fog of depression that seemed to surround us. I don't mean that anything else is wrong but the damned RA somehow seems to kick over one's sense of artistic rights and wrong, and it is always some time before one crawls from under the debris to start once more with less belief in one's own ideas or in anyone else's.[23]

He wrote this even though he was expecting one of his two submissions to be selected, and he did not revise what he had already written when he learned that *A Breton Fete* had indeed been nicely placed.

Garstin was now an old man and this inevitably meant decay and disappointment. He was becoming deaf and his friends were dying:

> I feel very sad and sorry to-day [in August 1922] at the death of old Hudson [i.e. W. H. Hudson, the naturalist and author] ... his death kills a deal of interest and pleasure in my life. I enjoyed talking with him over many things that not many of my friends care for, and his knowledge and keen vitality were so stimulating.[24]

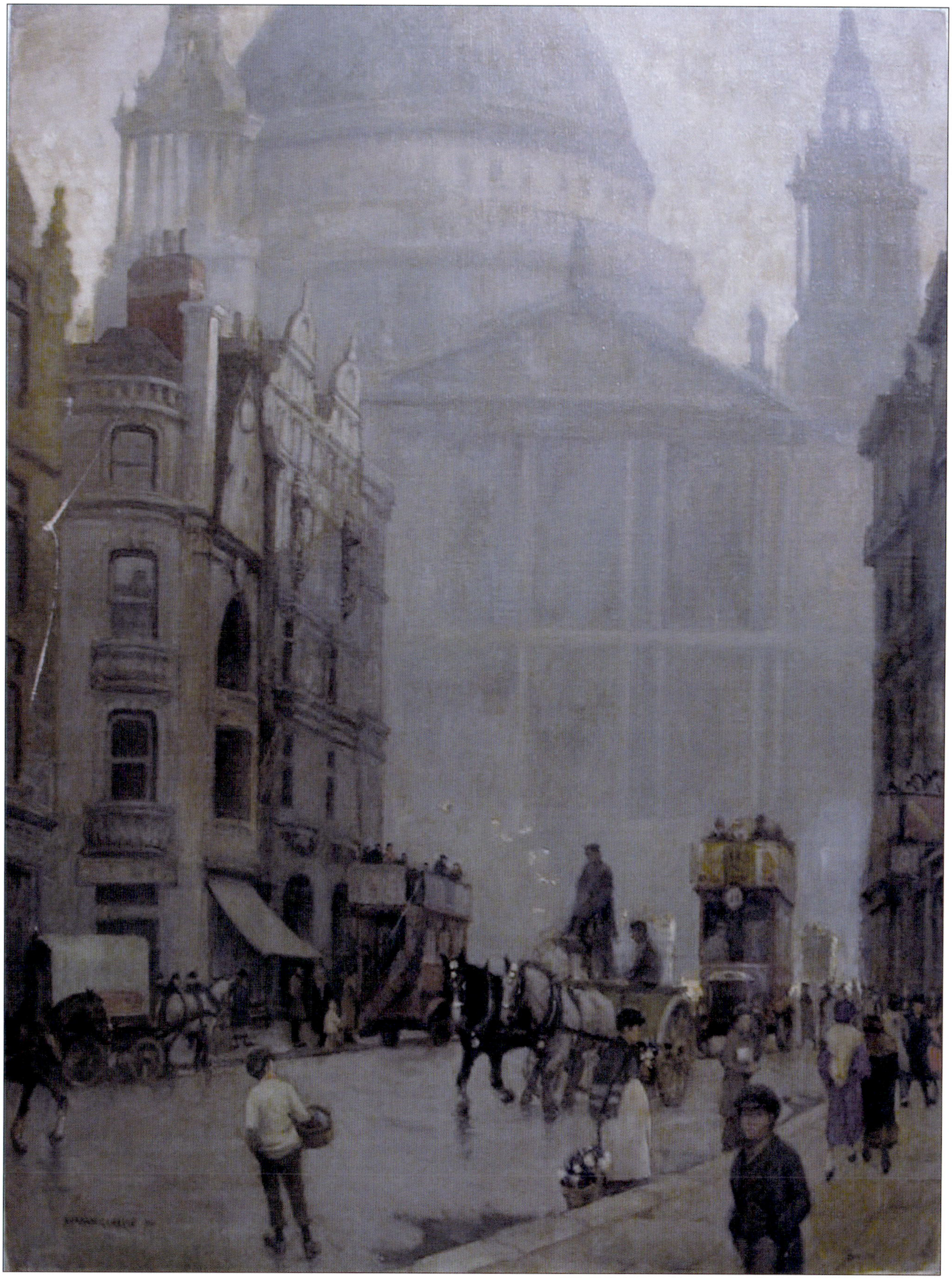

Nevertheless Garstin's sight continued to be fairly good, and, even in 1925, at the age of 78, he was in reasonably good health. There were more fundamental reasons for Garstin's sadness. They were both personal and political. His relations with Crosbie continued to be strained, because, as he recognised, of their incompatible attitudes:

> Of course [he wrote] it is impossible for us two to agree we are made so different. He has a barrack square point of view, not only on things military but in everything discipline, authority, prerogative, and his ideals. Whereas mine are freedom and all that makes for, his mind works backward – tradition, old customs, established institutions. I look forward, change, betterment, etc.[25]

He also seems to have been worried about Alethea's lack of success as an artist, and no doubt he was concerned at her failure to marry. He had no heart-warming grandchildren. Moreover he would still have been grieving for Denis, and he edited and introduced a further selection of his letters. Although he supported Irish independence and recognised the weaknesses and illusions of the Anglo-Irish class to which he belonged, he nevertheless had feelings of sadness and sympathy for it. Above all he was concerned about the danger of war.

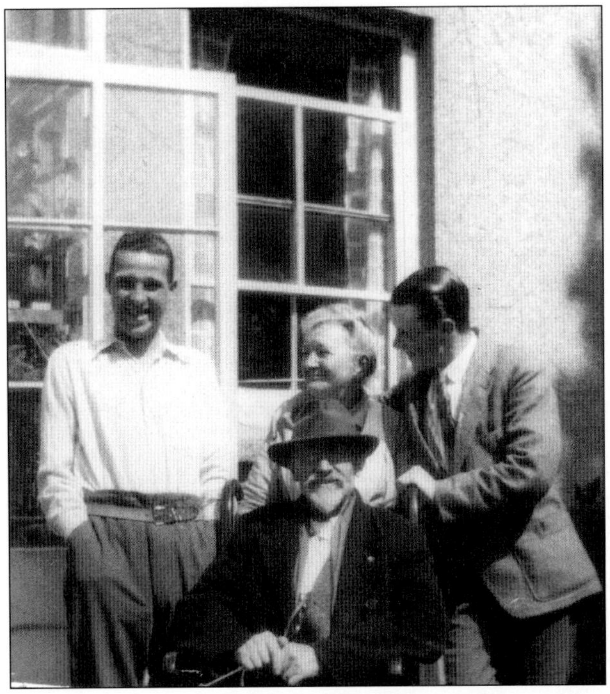

Garstin with friends outside Wellington Terrace shortly before his death.

Death and Remains

In late February 1926 Garstin became seriously ill with endocarditis, which is inflammation of the membranes in the heart. There then followed an agonising period of recoveries, relapses, and premature deathbed farewells. 'When they think I am better I am not so well as they think I am', Garstin observed, 'but when one gets to a certain point one wonders if it is worth while to get back again'.[26] To discover whether his abilities had completely deserted him he asked his nurse for a pencil. She was the vicious and bigoted Annie King, who was later to hound Bernard Walke: the pencil was refused, together with permission to smoke. Fortunately Garstin was able to let others know what was happening, and King was dismissed.[27] One of Garstin's requests demonstrates the extent of his political commitment: he asked that money be given to the Independent Labour Party after his death.

At 12.30 on Tuesday 22 June Stanhope Forbes, who had been visiting his old friend, called at Wellington Terrace and heard that there had been another relapse; at 4.30 he learned that Garstin had died an hour before. Ichabod: for the glory had departed. Three days later the funeral was conducted by Bernard Walke at the church of St Hilary. The beauty of this ancient country church had been enhanced, not long before, with paintings of the Cornish saints by the Newlyn artists. The panel depicting the charming, funny story of

St Buriena was by that outstanding, but comparatively little known and already semi-forgotten painter, Norman Garstin.

There were fairly short obituary notices in *The Telegraph* and *The Times*. The latter damned Garstin with faint praise, describing him as 'a man of general artistic and intellectual ability rather than a powerful artist, though his work, in several mediums, was remarkable for sensitive feeling and decorative charm'.[28] To deny that an artist who had painted *The Rain it Raineth* and *The Last Furrow* was powerful was foolish, to suggest that he was a painter of pretty pictures was nonsense. No article on his life and work appeared in *The Studio* or in any other journal. Nor was there a retrospective exhibition at a gallery of importance.

Garstin was to live on in the memory of his friends, that temporary immortality which is the best for which most of us can hope. Even when due allowance is made for permissible overstatement, the letters of condolence received by Dochie and Alethea were impressive testimony of the regard with which Garstin was held, and the affection he inspired. Father Andrew told Dochie that 'There was much about your Norman that was greatly akin to Christ and I have often seen a very sweet and tender look of sympathy transfigure his face'.[29] Many years after his death, Alethea was still receiving letters in which his kindness was recalled. Over seventy five years later Joan Manning-Sanders, who had met him as a young girl, had a clear impression of his persona. He was 'good and superior to most people', and not, unlike many artists, somebody who showed off or loudly voiced his opinions.[30] The most impressive evidence of esteem was the way in which a substantial fund was raised by his students and friends during, and perhaps after, his last illness. This appears to have totalled over £400, of which £210 was absorbed by medical expenses, and about £200 devoted to buying his works for galleries. What appears to have happened is that the money was given to Dochie who, in turn, presented pictures that Garstin had never sold to a selection of galleries throughout the British Isles.

In this way some of the best of Garstin's major works are to be found in public galleries, including, *The Last of the Fair* at the National Gallery of Ireland, *The Card Players* at Manchester, *The Last Furrow* at Glasgow, *Sunshine in the Beguinage* at Cork, and *Moulin de la Ville* at Brighton. These works were all painted after 1900, but Garstin had himself presented two of his earlier works to galleries, namely *The Rain it Raineth*, which is now at Penlee House in Penzance, and *A Stranger*, which is at the Hugh Lane in Dublin. Much later a large number of pictures by Garstin passed into the hands of galleries after the death of his daughter in 1978. Although a mixed bag, they include a substantial number of first rate, but small,

Above:
Plate 56 *The Hub of Île Tudy*, 1924, watercolour, 9.5" x 11.5" (private collection, auctioned as *At the Quayside*).

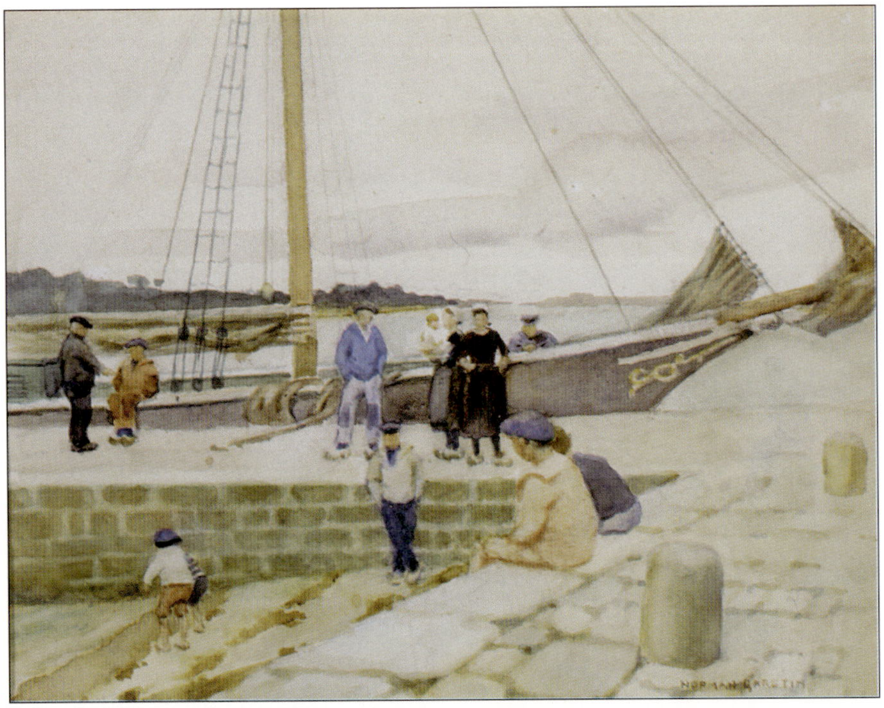

Plate 57 *Landscape with Pools of Water*, 1922, watercolour, 9.5" x 11.5" (private collection).

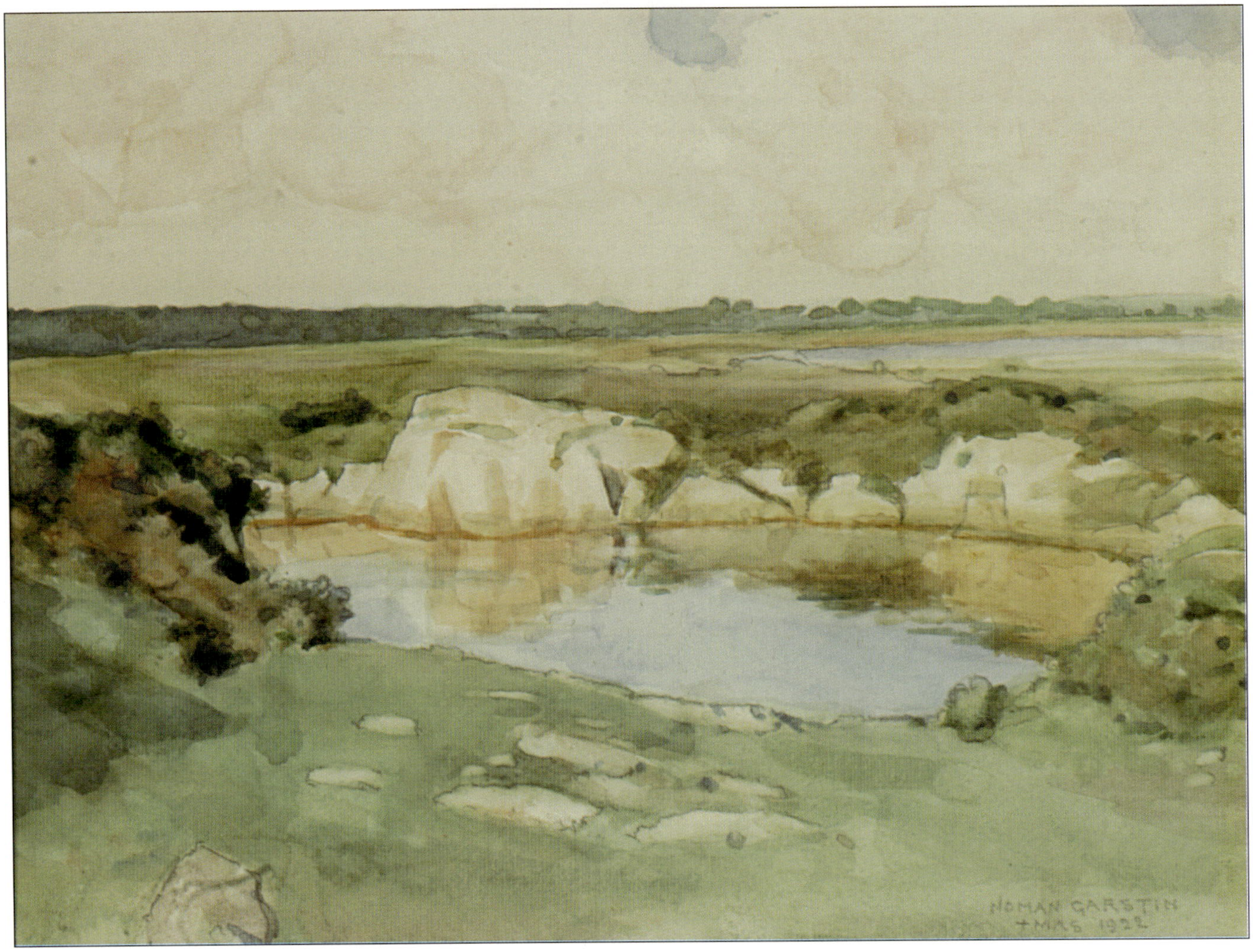

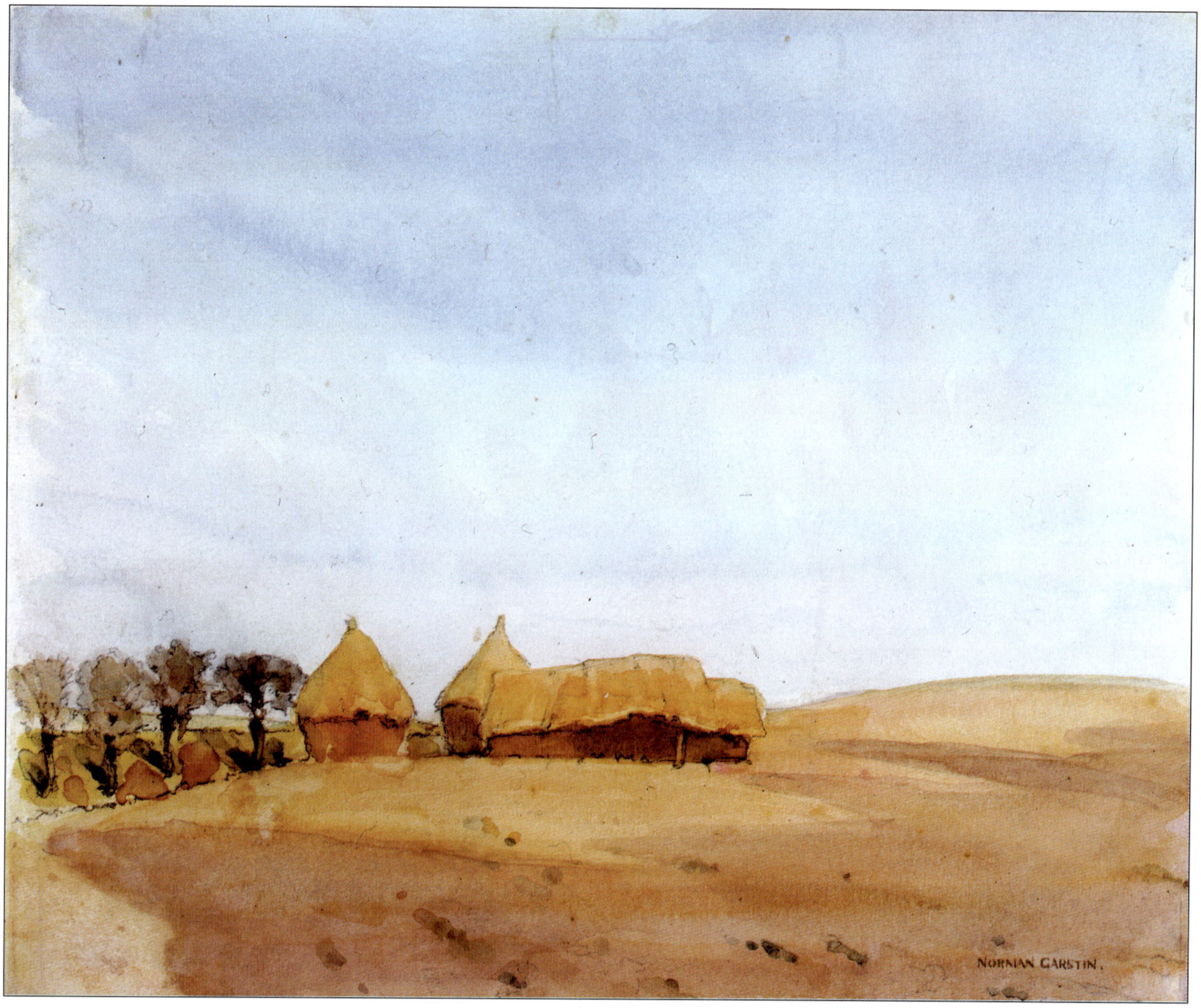

Plate 58 *Glowing Evening*, 1924, watercolour, 10.1" x 12.5" (V&A, London).

pictures. Hence Garstin has that form of immortality that is given to artists because their works continue to exist, though many of his best pictures are still in limbo and languishing in reserve collections, and two of his paintings have been lost.

Private collectors have shown greater perception than galleries, and Garstin's canvases were, by the end of 2003, fetching as much as £120,000 in New Bond Street and £43,000 at auctions in Dublin. Here his pictures often sell for high prices because of his connection with Ireland. It is ironic that the market, which Garstin so distrusted, should value his works more highly than the public galleries of which he approved. Nevertheless, Garstins can still be picked up for relatively small amounts, and his pictures are cheap in comparison with works of no higher quality by Stanhope Forbes or Walter Osborne.

Judging According to Merit

To know Garstin was to love him, and to know his work is to love it. As knowledge of his pictures increases, so his reputation will surely grow. On the artistic stock exchange the reputations of artists, and the prices of their pictures, rise and fall, but in the long run merit will out and fundamentals count. Why (to vary the analogy) should the Great Goddess of Painting, endowed with the power of judging between the incommensurable, find Garstin's best work of less merit, when she comes to make a final determination, than that of his major contemporaries, such as the Impressionists? This question cannot be answered: there is no way of judging between the chalk of Naturalism and the cheese of Impressionism. They are, as we have, seen different ways of viewing reality, corresponding to different parts of the field of vision.

My seemingly fanciful reference to a Goddess of Painting deciding the rival merits of artists does, however, provoke a question that can be answered, namely what the strengths of a particular artist were, and what contribution he or she made. In Garstin's case his principal strength and contribution was, I believe, the ability, time and again, to paint pictures with an absorbative power so intense that the viewer is drawn through the frame, and into the picture; or what I have called an *à travers* effect. It is for the reader, having carefully studied those of Garstin's works where this effect appears to be most marked, and then looked at some of the originals, to decide the degree to which I am correct in my estimate of his merits.

Chapter 7

'Golden lads and girls all must/As chimney sweepers come to dust'

Garstin's story is reminiscent of a novel of the Victorian or Edwardian eras. Trollope and other authors of the period frequently concluded their works by briefly telling the reader about the subsequent careers of their heroes and heroines. Garstin died at the end of the last chapter and about him there is nothing more to say, but readers may like to know what happened to his children, especially as Alethea became a painter and both Crosbie and Denis were authors and artists with words. The Garstins seem, despite some tensions, to have been an exceptionally happy, close and devoted family. Norman went so far as to say 'you children are our real selves'.[1] To avoid the risk of wearying the reader, my account will, however, be short, though both Crosbie and Alethea deserve more extensive treatment than will be given here. Denis, who was the most heroic and died first, has pride of place.

Denis Garstin in Peace

Born in 1890, Denis was a sensitive and imaginative child, dwelling much in a land of make believe and very afraid of the dark. His early education at Penzance High School was a misery. However, there was then a change and his father felt that 'he, more or less deliberately, set to work to build up a working philosophy of life as he meant to live it – he would enjoy his days and laugh through them, and this verily he did!'[2] After attending prep school, Denis went in 1904 to Blundell's, the Devon public school, with a house scholarship. In 1909, having gained an Exhibition (scholarship), he entered Sidney Sussex College, Cambridge, where he began by reading for the Classical Tripos, but ultimately obtained a joint degree in Classics and military subjects. While at Cambridge he

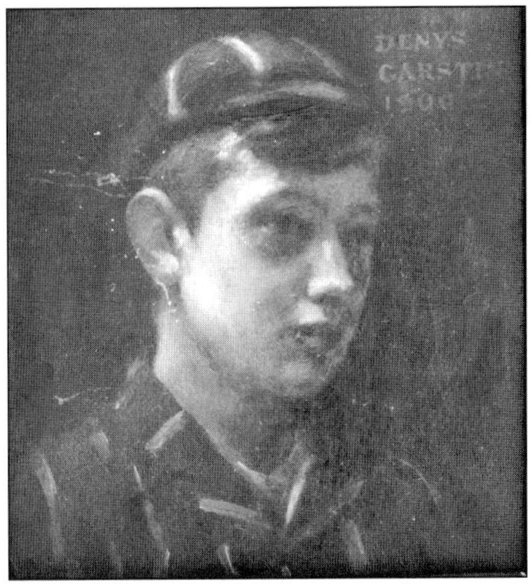

Portrait of Denys Garstin, 1906, oil, 8.75" x 8.1" (University of Hull). He was christened Denys. but called himself Denis

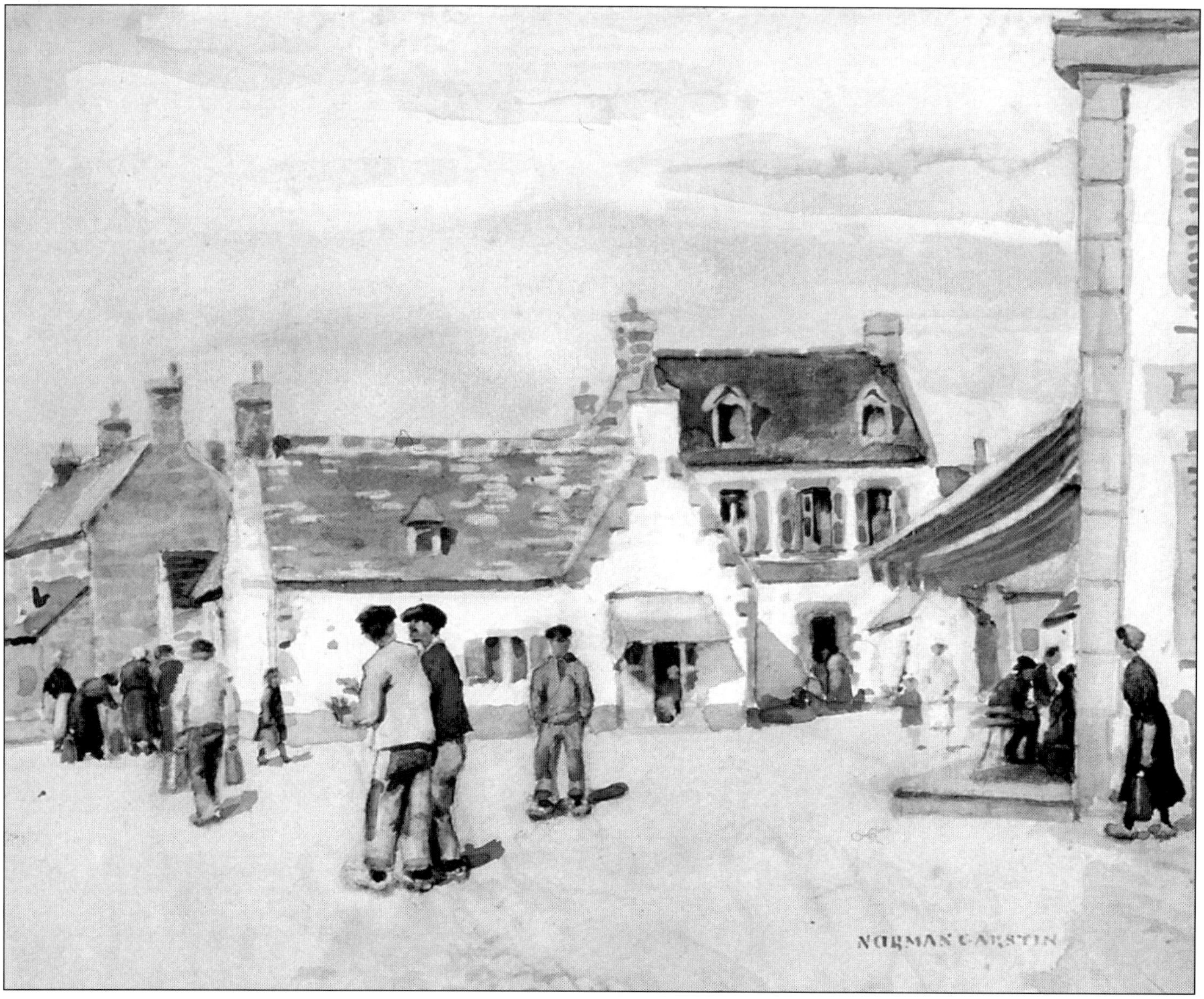

A Little Breton Port [Île Tudy], 1924, watercolour, 9.5" x 11.5" (private collection, auctioned as *Figures in a Village Street*).

rowed, played rugger, hunted, spent more than he could afford, and had little time for work.

In the summer of 1910 his father reported that, 'Dennie came up to town, very much of a swell – top hat, light waistcoat *dernier mode* – and pranced about the RA. He has a wonderful good eye for a picture and spotted all the best'.[3] But it would be wrong to jump to the conclusion that he was simply a dilettante youth in a gilded age. As Garstin recalled, when a suffragette attacked Sargent's portrait of Henry James at the Academy's opening day in 1913,

> an indignant crowd gathered around her somewhat menacingly. Denis ranged himself beside the woman and faced the hostile circle. Afterwards, when she wished to thank him, he wouldn't have that either: 'It isn't you I'm for', he said, 'it's the crowd I'm against'.[4]

These incidents reflect the two sides of his character and career. Denis was outgoing, confident and eager for enjoyment, but he was also perceptive, earnest and courageous. Although he skimped his academic studies at Cambridge, he did not waste his time: he embarked on journalism by editing the student magazine *Granta* and contributing to *Punch*; he became a trooper in the Cambridge Officer Training Corps; and, after spending six weeks of training in the summer of 1911, he was commissioned in the 18th Hussars.

After Cambridge, in 1912 Denis went to the Crimea, where he acted as tutor to a Russian family. Characteristically he made the most of his opportunities, learning to speak the language by talking to the servants, and writing a series of sketches that appeared in the *Daily News*, and other papers. On his return, he vacillated between journalism and the Indian army, but was forced through lack of money to give up the idea of a military career, where a private income was still necessary, especially in cavalry regiments. Then one night at a dinner party, he impressed a director of the West End department store Marshall and Snelgrove, who promptly offered him the job of publicity organizer. He decided to opt for what his father described as 'the drapery bird in the hand', and worked for the firm with enthusiasm and success until the outbreak of war.[5] 'I can't get it [the job] out of my head for a second', he told his sister. 'Wish I could sometimes, that's why I enjoy dances so much'.[6]

Denis at War

Being at the right place at the right time was a feature of Denis's life – until Luck finally deserted, and he was in the wrong place at the wrong time. The start of the First World War found him in Russia, where he had gone on holiday with the idea of writing some articles. After reaching Moscow and seeing Russia mobilize with apparent efficiency, he went to St Petersburg and was part of the great crowd when the German Embassy was sacked. He would, he thought, have enjoyed the French Revolution.[7] After a long and adventurous journey back to England through Finland, Sweden and Denmark – promptly described in an article for the *Daily News* – He enlisted. Denis, his father reported, 'is not keen about fighting but says he wants to do the right thing and says he is an efficient Officer'.[8] He was soon posted to the 18th and then the 10th Hussars. While in training, he wrote further articles and produced a book, *Friendly Russia*, which largely consists of his previous articles on the Crimea.

Although it contains colourful descriptions of incidents and characters, moistened by much conversation, *Friendly Russia* is for the most part somewhat lightweight, betraying its journalistic origins. Only when Denis turns to his recent experiences in Russia, and comes to describe the popular enthusiasm at the outbreak of War, the great crowds and their participants, does the book take on some of the qualities of a newsreel and become memorable in the manner of John Reed. When he returned to Russia, Denis found it 'simmering with discontent', but was then impressed by the upsurge of enthusiasm for the regime as war approached. The rank and file soldier, he concluded, 'will obey, they will follow, they will die, and die gamely'.[9] Despite its weaknesses, *Friendly Russia* was widely and, with a few exceptions, favourably reviewed. That the Russians were not barbarous or downtrodden was a welcome message about a new ally. The diary that Denis kept during his journey confirms that he was an intrepid and resourceful traveller. One aspect of his *joie de vivre* was his interest in pretty women and his flirtatiousness. He records, for instance, that in the Tivoli gardens at Copenhagen one young woman 'smiles and nestles confidingly and we waltz together so delightfully'.[10]

Denis went to France in the spring of 1915 and, despite belonging to a machine gun corps, survived the great battles at Ypres, Thiepval, Albert and Loos. His second book, *The Shilling Soldiers* published in 1918, is an account of his experiences in the trenches. It is a rich melange consisting of sections of diary, pen portraits, conversations, descriptions, and what are, in effect, short stories. The writing is spare and, for the most part, low key and thereby, as the following passage shows, all the more effective:

> Beyond the parapet the world is, more or less, unknown. You have the feeling that your trench is the limit of your nation and its power – an outpost of empire. There is a little strip of No-Man's-Land, and then the enemy in his outpost of empire. If you show yourself, he kills you; so you don't show yourself. You live most of your days seeing only the two walls of the trench and the sky, and when you do look over, or go out at nights to see your little world, your horizon even then is only some hundred yards away.
>
> You see by day a ragged field, pitted with shell-holes, in each of which there is always a bully-beef tin. The grass is lank and untidy, where it has been allowed to grow. There are some bodies lying stiffly about, the skin dark brown from exposure, and the clothes rotten. There is a look of a refuse heap about the field. Even the barbed wire, mended and strengthened in the darkness, helps the impression of disuse. Beyond this No-Man's-Land you see a low line of sand-bags – coloured sand-bags. And that is all.[11]

One of the book's strongest features is the way in which it shows how he, and other soldiers, responded to fear and the horrors of trench warfare. He says that his mind was unable to remain for long

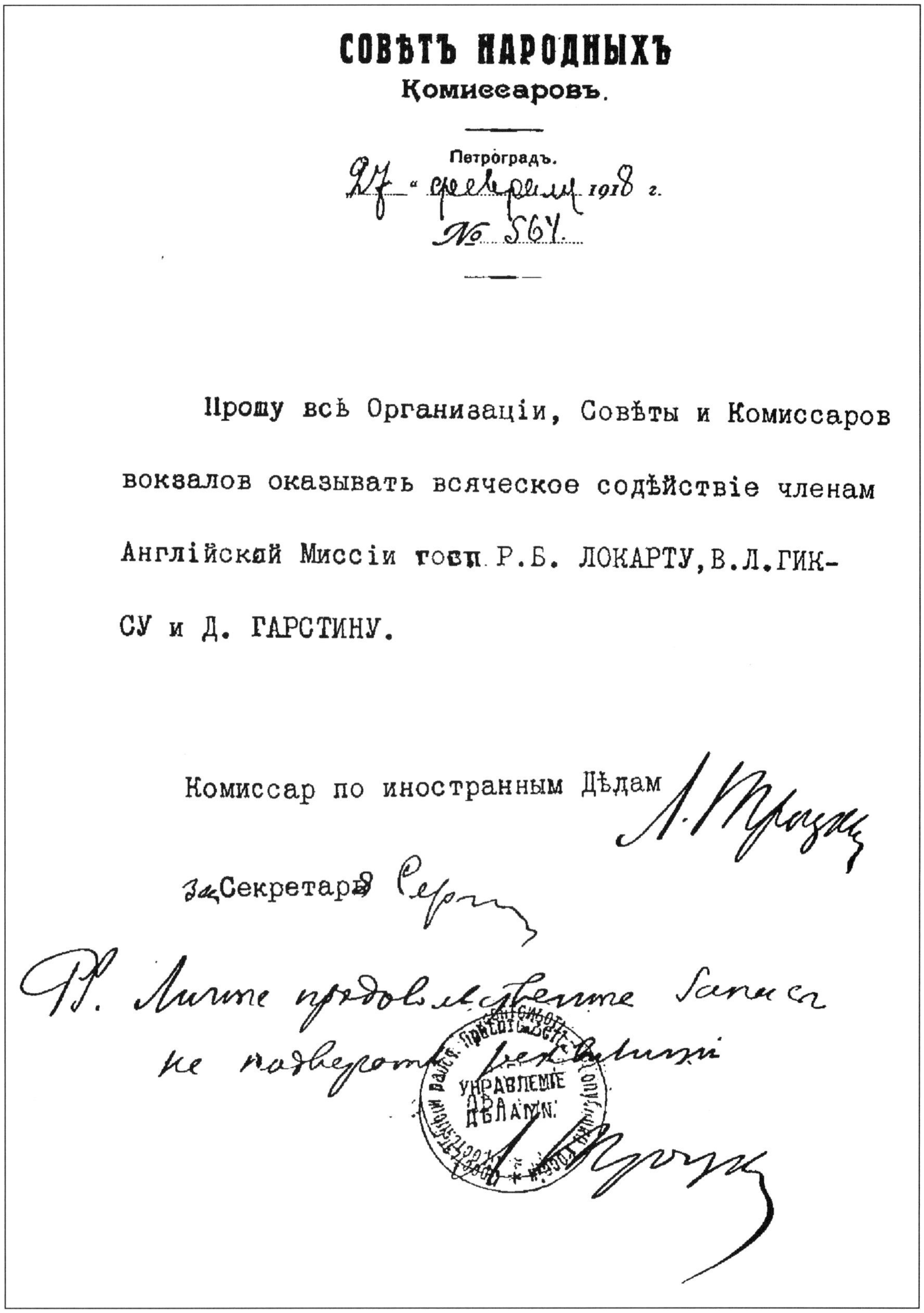

СОВѢТЪ НАРОДНЫХЪ
Комиссаровъ.

Петроградъ.
27 " февраля 1918 г.
№ 564.

Прошу всѣ Организаціи, Совѣты и Комиссаров вокзалов оказывать всяческое содѣйствіе членам Англійской Миссіи госп. Р.Б. ЛОКАРТУ, В.Л. ГИКСУ и Д. ГАРСТИНУ.

Комиссар по иностранным Дѣлам

За Секретаря

P.S. Личные продовольственные запасы не подвергать реквизиции

Travel permit for Denis Garstin and two others signed by Leon Trotski, Petrograd 27 Feb. 1918, who 'requests all Organisations, Soviets and Commissars of Railway Stations to give every assistance to' Garstin and his fellow travellers - Bruce Lockhart and V. L. Hicks. (Source: R. H. Bruce Lockhart, *Memoirs of a Secret Agent* (Putnam, 1932), following p. 272).

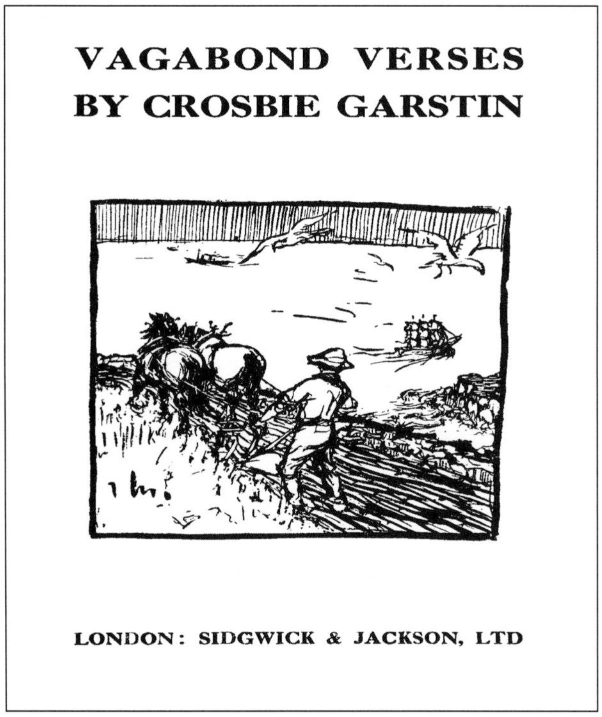

VAGABOND VERSES
BY CROSBIE GARSTIN

LONDON: SIDGWICK & JACKSON, LTD

Above: Title page of *Vagabond Verses* with illustration by Alethea Garstin.
Below: Crosbie Garstin in uniform.

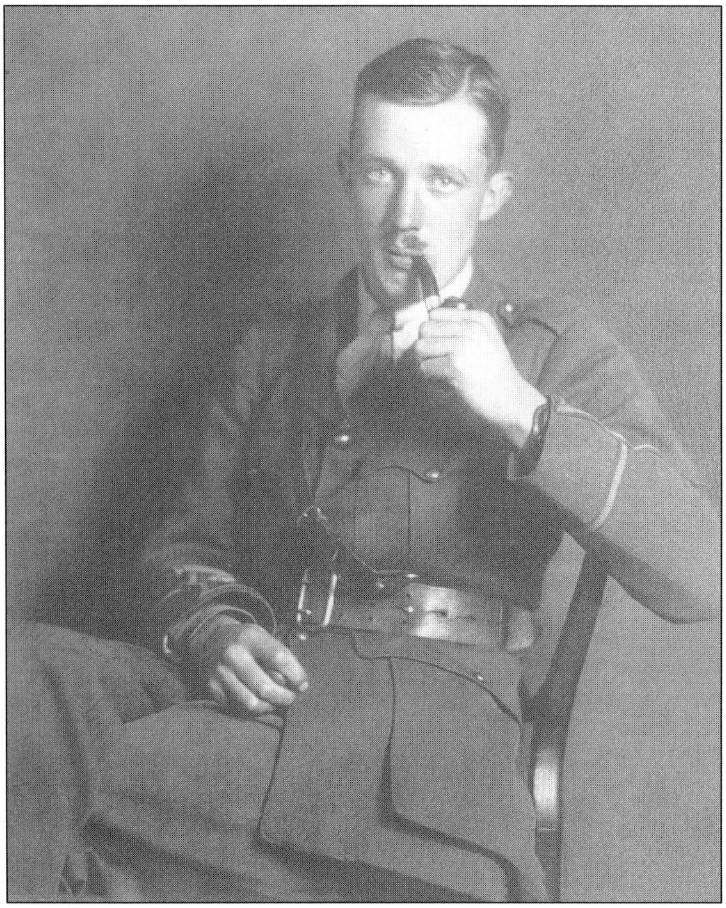

in the grip of any emotion and would pass rapidly from sickness, at the thought of death, to euphoria and gladness. The very carnage of battle made death more bearable:

> everywhere [he writes in his description of the battlefield at Loos] were bodies. Some were too hopelessly distorted to remind us that yesterday they were alive as we ourselves; but others – a boy lying, as a sleeping child, with his hand beneath his cheek, or a Highlander hanging doubled up on some uncut wire, like a rag-doll – these gave one terribly to feel.[12]

The Shilling Soldiers appears to have received universal, and deserved, critical acclaim.

In September 1916 Denis was, to his fury, transferred out of the trenches and sent to St Petersburg, where he laboured hard and effectively on propaganda work. When the Embassy closed in February 1918, Denis, who was by now a captain, volunteered to stay in Russia and join the staff of Bruce Lockhart who, having transferred to Moscow, was in charge of a shadow unit. Here Denis was a member of a committee of Allied officers formed to advise Trotsky on the training of the Red Army. It was hoped that in this way the Bolsheviks might be drawn into co-operation, but the French government vetoed the attempt. Denis was also engaged on coding and decoding messages to and from the Foreign Office. He put in so much effort that his health suffered and, with the permission of Lenin whom he knew, he went to a sanatorium for a rest.

It was characteristic of Denis that he had remained optimistic about the eventual success of the Revolution longer than his colleagues. However, even he became more and more depressed both with his work and with the deteriorating political scene. 'I'm sick of political situations', he told Alethea in September 1918. 'Sick to death of all this circus life and uniforms and saying the right thing, and compiling information and distributing it, and being perpetually British'.[13] After the October revolution, his political disillusionment was complete. When in January 1918 the Bolsheviks stopped the Constituent Assembly from meeting, he concluded that despotism was returning and that Russia had no instinct for liberty. By mid-1918, with Russia starving, he did not think that the Bolsheviks would retain power. 'It's evolution with a vengeance', he wrote in his final letter. 'But one gets parlous weary of the vengeance part of it'.[14] He had just described how a young man in a family he knew had been executed.

In July 1918 Denis was ordered to leave Moscow clandestinely and join the British Expeditionary Force in Archangel that was assisting the White Russians. After perilous escapes and adventures, he arrived safely and threw himself into the fray. On 15 August, on what he thought would be 'A nice quiet little expedition', he captured an armoured car by his own efforts, but was killed attempting to secure another.[15] For these exploits he received the MC and DSO, as well as two Russian medals.

The anti-war song that Denis, in the company of Bruce Lockhart, heard at a Moscow cabaret – illegal, but not yet closed by the Bolsheviks – might serve as his epitaph:

> I do not know why
> Or for what purpose.
> Who sent them to death
> With relentless, untrembling hand.
> Only it was so useless,
> So pitiless …[16]

But it would perhaps be wrong to conclude on such a dispiriting note. Although his death may have been pointless, his life was not: the only purposeless lives are those that have no significance for those who live them. Brief though it was, Denis's life was one of joy, or as much of this as any man can hope for.[17] His brother's verdict was that he 'had a very happy life and died at its zenith, before anything had soured'. Denis himself concluded the diary of his Russian trip in 1914 with the thought that, 'if I go out to the war and get done in, I shall have plenty of amusing things to look back on from that Elysium where I shall chew the cud of my life'.[18]

Crosbie's Early Career

Crosbie Garstin, the eldest child, was born in May 1887. After attending Penzance High School, he was sent to a prep school in Cheltenham, and then to a navy crammer. However, he failed to pass the exams necessary to enter the Navy and went instead to the County School, Bedford. Elstow, as it also called itself, was a minor public school where, according to its prospectus, pupils were educated 'at moderate cost'.[19] Crosbie was a poor student. His father described him

The Figure Head

There was an ancient carver who fashioned a saint;
But the parson wouldn't have it, so he took a pot of paint,
And changed its angel-garments for a dashing soldier–rig,
And said it was a figure-head and sold it to a brig.

The brig hauled her mainsail to an off-shore draught,
Then she shook her snowy royals and the Scillies went abaft,
And cloudy with her canvas she ran before the Trade,
Till she came to the Equator where she struck a merry-maid.

A string of pearls and conches were all of her togs,
But the porpoises and flying-fish they followed her like dogs;
She had a voice of silver and lips of coral red;
She climbed the dolphin-striker and kissed the figure-head.

The captain wore his blue coat with buttons of brass;
The mate he greased his forelock at the cabin looking-glass;
The bosu'n paced the fo'castle and coughed 'Ah ha, ahem!' –
But the merry-maid she turned her back and wouldn't look at them.

And every starry evening she'd swim in the foam
About the bows a-singing like a nightingale at home.
She'd call to him and sing to him as sweetly as a bird,
But the wooden-headed effigy he never said a word.

And every starry evening in the Doldrum calms
She'd wriggle up the bob-stay and throw her tender arms
About his scarlet shoulders, and fondle him and cry,
And stroke his curly whiskers, but he never winked an eye.

She couldn't get an answer to her tears or moans,
So she went and told her daddy, told the ancient Davy Jones.
Old Davy damned his eyesight, and puzzled of his wits –
Then he whistled up his hurricanes and tore the brig to bits.

Down on the ocean-bed, green fathoms deep,
Where the wrecks lie rotting and the great sea-serpents creep,
In a gleaming grotto all built of sailors' bones
Sits the handsome figure-head, listening to Miss Jones.

Songs o' love she sings him the live-long day,
And she hangs upon his bosom and sobs the night away,
But he never, never answers, for beneath his soldier paint
The wooden-headed lunatic still thinks that he's a saint.

Crosbie Garstin, *Vagabond Verses*

Picket

The clouds stampede across the moon.
Like mad grey mares. Along the plain
Sweep the chill lances of the rain.
Drear in the trees the night-winds rune.

The white sword of a searchlight splits
The sky in twain, then, quivering, falls
On a black waste of shattered walls
Of bare-rib roofs and crater-pits.

For in the north the guns begin
To grumble. Up the leaden sky,
Ashen of face and bleared of eye,
Dawn, like a ghost, creeps shivering in.

Flanders

Crosbie Garstin, *Vagabond Verses*

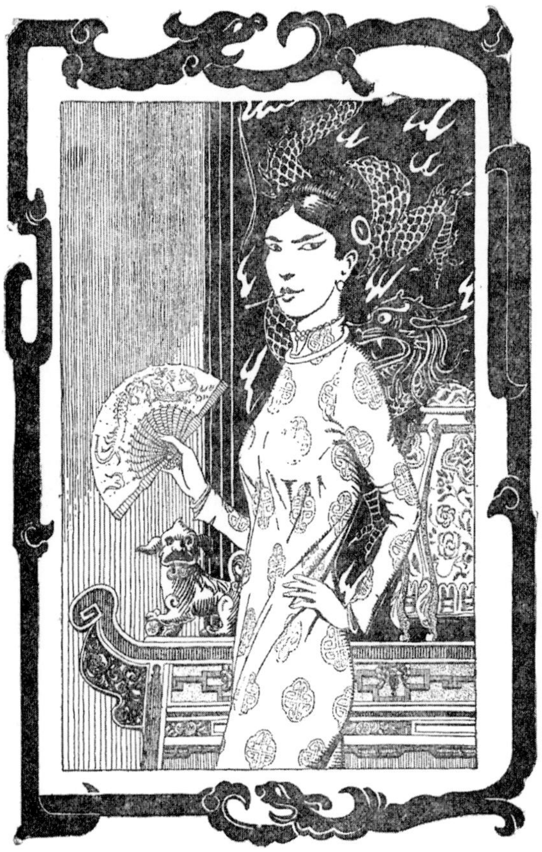

as being 'practically imune' to education, and Crosbie himself says that he 'broke all records for consistency in work by being bottom of one form for four years without a single interruption'.[20] He was, however, a notable sportsman – champion athlete and captain of the rugger and swimming teams – and he became head boy. His wit and humour were already of note, as were the verses and cartoons he contributed to the school magazine.

A high-spirited but over-assertive Crosbie makes a brief but dramatic appearance in a letter by Frances Hodgkins. At a summer school in Holland in 1903 Crosbie, together with Denis, organised a boat race against some American artists. Hodgkins, who was cox, took her crew on the river 'under Crosbie's kind if abusive wing'. When one of the crew caught a crab, and rolled into the bottom of the boat, 'Crosbie told her she was no more use than a dead kipper. She got offended and we had to row her back to shore'.[21]

After school, and a period knocking about the Continent, Crosbie followed in the footsteps of young men of good family for whom there was no obvious career: he went to the 'colonies'. In America and Canada, he worked as a horse breaker on western ranches, as a thresher, as a sawyer in the lumber camps of British Columbia, and as a miner on the Pacific coast. Later he went to Africa and became a ranger in Matabeleland and the manager of a cattle ranch in Bechuanaland. This was where he must have contracted the malaria from which he was to suffer for the rest of his life.

On the outbreak of the War he returned to England, enlisted in the King Edward's Horse and, in 1915, was awarded a field commission in France. He survived ten days on a cavalry manoeuvre, 'without much hope of coming back'. Just before leaving on one particularly nasty stunt he received his first book: 'I pushed one copy into my saddle wallets, and rode into action cheerfully, crooning a sort of "Nunc Dimittis" to myself – I had seen my first book'.[22] During 1916 he was in Ireland where he was, as an intelligence officer, involved in the military operations after the Easter Rising.

> I never [he wrote] saw such a miserable crowd in my life, looked like a bunch of pickpockets, miserable stinking degenerate lot ... They are a rotten bunch, they looted wholesale, fired buildings and shot at almost any darn thing they saw, civilians and all – shot 'em with lead elephant bullets, buckshot and other foul stuff we would shoot one of our own men for using on the Germans.[23]

Later Crosbie returned to the Western Front.

Crosbie the Writer

The war was a turning point in Crosbie's career: it saw his

emergence as a journalist and author. In 1917 a collection of poetry that had previously appeared in *Punch*, the *Pall Mall Gazette* and other places was published as *Vagabond Verses*; and in 1918 a series of war sketches from *Punch* were brought together in *The Mud Larks*. These books were followed by *The Sunshine Settlers* (1918), which contained reminiscences of his African adventures, and *The Mud Larks Again* (1919), which was a further series of war sketches. In *The Ballad of the Royal Ann* (1922) he returned to poetry and in *The Coasts of Romance* (1922) to travel.

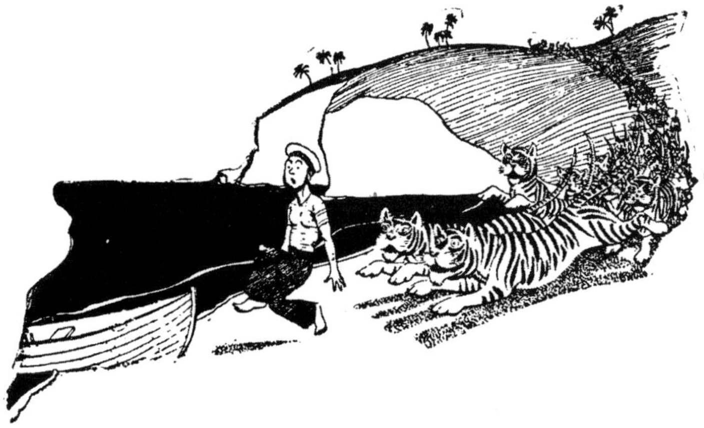

Numerous Tigers: illustration by Crosbie for *The Dragon and the Lotus* (London, 1928), p. 299.

Vagabond Verses are for the most part unashamedly light poetry characterised by insistent metre and strong rhyme, and even those poems that were written during, and deal with, the Great War cannot, with the possible exceptions of 'Picket' and 'The Flying Man', be described as serious. Only occasionally does Crosbie move beyond entertainment and produce poems that, like 'Alone' and 'Fog' that are more memorable. The two Mud Larks books are notable for their bantering humour. Crosbie is often extremely funny, but his facetious humour can become wearing. He refuses to take the war seriously, and his treatment of its more distressing aspects is shown by the beginning of one sketch: 'When we have finished slaying for the day, have stropped our gory sabres, hung our horses up to dry and are sitting about after mess ...'.[24] Humour was how Crosbie coped with horror but, although it is one method, his approach was less mature than that of his younger brother.

Crosbie's first novel, written jointly with Mrs Cecily Sidgwick, was *The Black Knight*, which appeared in 1920. Here Crosbie drew on his experiences of the timber regions of North America. He then turned to historical romance and between 1923 and 1926 his trilogy of novels about Ortho Penhale came out, beginning with *The Owls' House*, followed by *High Noon* (1925) and concluding with *The West Wind*. In 1928 Crosbie again turned to travel with *The Dragon and the Lotus*, which was an account of a journey to the Far East. Finally, there were to be two more novels *Houp La!* (1929) and *China Seas* (1930).

The Penhale novels were long in the making. Their germ was a short story of 1909 but, as Crosbie wrote, he realised that a novel was called for. However, he was too busy to start writing until 1922. The story was based on the legends and stories that he had heard in his boyhood. Ortho Penhale is the offspring of a steady farmer and an earthy gypsy girl, and his character reflects his parentage. After a tempestuous childhood, he becomes involved in a smuggling gang, commanded by a Methodist preacher (who really existed). This launches Ortho on a series of adventures, beginning with slavery on

Opposite:
A Lady of Hué: illustration by Crosbie for *The Dragon and the Lotus* (London, 1928), p. 197.

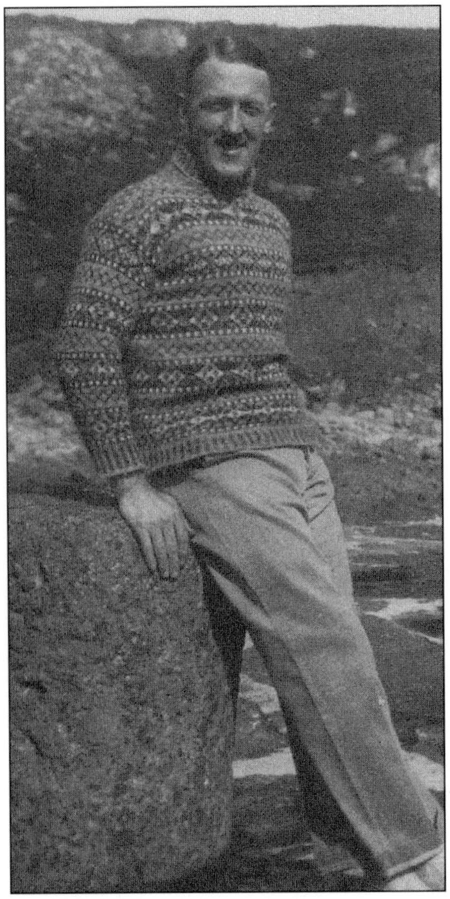

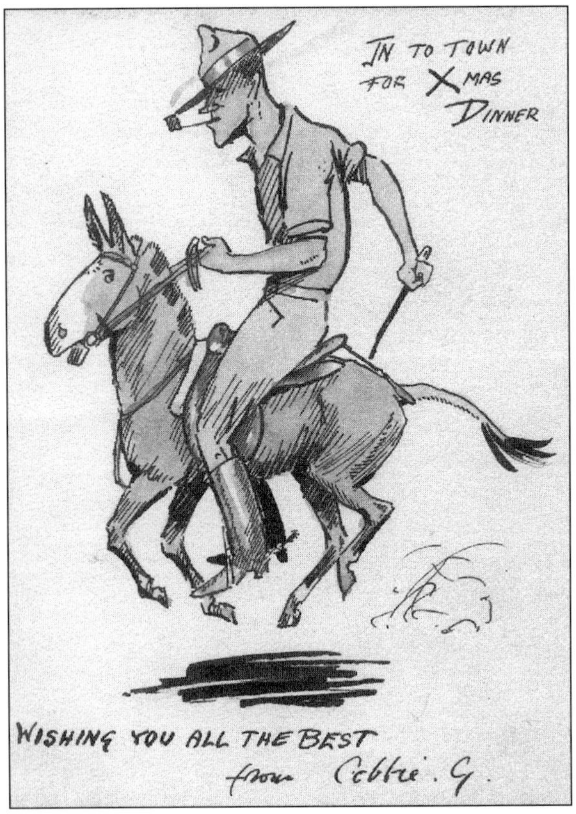

the Barbary Coast. He is an eighteenth-century James Bond: tall, dark, handsome, seductive and forever falling into, and out of, the hands of enemies. Ortho ends by returning to Cornwall lame and no longer young, and gives up his life, by diving into a boiling sea, to save others and avoid his own capture. Crosbie's writing is as spirited as Ortho's life: the Penhale novels are masterly adventure writing.

Crosbie's work received high acclaim from the critics, especially the Penhale novels. *The Observer*, for instance, described *The Owl's House* as 'the most emphatically enthralling yarn of eighteenth-century adventure that has been written for years', and the *New Statesman*, reviewing all three volumes, declared that 'Crosbie Garstin ... has genius'.[25] To judge from the number of new impressions, reprints, popular editions and American issues, his latter works were widely read. Although none of his novels are now in print, it can only be a matter of time before they are re-discovered.

Crosbie the Man

Between Crosbie as an author and Crosbie as a person there was a gulf; there was a chasm between Crosbie, as he would have us see him, and the man himself. The author that we are supposed to see is imperturbable, has a strong and wry sense of humour, and does not concern himself with social, political or moral questions. Interest in such matters would be incompatible with total detachment. The real Crosbie had strong opinions and prejudices, and possessed what was described as an 'ardent Celtic temperament'.[26] He could be moody, sullen and angry, as well as highly entertaining and excellent company. The overlap between Crosbie as an author and Crosbie as a real person was his sense of humour, this was the buckle which jointed the person and the persona. Alethea after his death observed, 'There are few people who caused so much laughter'.[27]

Crosbie's opinions and prejudices were, as his father saw, those of the barrack square, not only on things military but in everything: discipline, authority, prerogative, and general ideals. With a romantic view of the past, he valued tradition, old customs and established institutions. Crosbie believed in the Empire and loathed 'oily politicians', describing them as 'a hypocritical crowd of liars and time servers'.[28] The Liberals were anti-imperialist populists and the Unionists were, with the exception of Carson, stupid. Loggers and troopers were to his taste, and among gentlemen he was at ease, but he had little liking for those in between and had a distaste for trade and commerce.

After the death of Denis, he gave his parents this advice concerning the Court Circular: 'I don't want to be a snob but I don't think I should mention Marshall and Snelgroves. It was clean out of Denis' line ... I didn't care for it much'.[29] Not only was he a snob, he was also racist. In a letter to his parents he expressed humorous outrage that his sister was pleased at 'the defeat of a white man by an oily nigger' in a recent boxing match.[30] There was an accompanying drawing that was clever but distasteful.

That Crosbie could be sullen, angry and bullying was shown by his relations with his father. It is not surprising that, during the war, their relations were difficult. But much later, in 1922, Norman reported that, 'the peace has been kept between Crosbie and me – just kept! … I had to point out that his tone and manner were bullying, and then somehow we go on better; nothing is so bad as a rigid silence, it is so chilling! … But, of course, there were bursts of anger …'.[31] On the other hand, Crosbie's letters to his sister and his parents, whom he addressed as 'Darlings' display great affection, and *The West Wind* is dedicated 'To Norman Garstin Dearest of Fathers, Wittiest of Companions, Best of Friends'.

In 1924 Crosbie married Lilian Barkworth, though he had earlier been in love with Fryn Tennyson Jesse and possibly also with her sister Stella. There were no children and one gains the impression from what scraps of evidence there are that the relationship with Lilian was not a happy one. Before writing *The Dragon and the Lotus* Crosbie made a lengthy journey without her to the United States, Japan, the Chinese coast, Indo-China and Siam.

In April 1930 Crosbie went on a yachting trip with friends. Lilian was not there, but with a friend, earlier referred to by Crosbie as 'The elusive Martin Ingram', with whom she was planning to go to the races.[32] On Saturday 20 the party went ashore, dined at the Salcombe Hotel, and joined in a dance with other visitors. After midnight, Crosbie with a Miss Drake whom he had met, were being rowed over to the yacht. There was a choppy sea and the boat overturned. The boatman swam ashore for help, and Drake told Crosbie she too would swim to land. Crosbie was last seen swimming towards a boat.

Drake was later rescued but Crosbie drowned. As there was a strong ebb tide, conditions were not easy, but it seems unlikely that Crosbie would have drowned if he had been wholly sober. There was a strange similarity – and dissimilarity – between Crosbie's death and that of his hero Ortho Penhale, who died in a raging sea bringing others to safety.

Crosbie provided his own memorial notice at the time of his brother's death: 'I've had a perfectly splendid time, always enjoyed myself every moment … By golly I don't know anyone who has had the fun I've had, except Denis'.[33] Every moment must be an exaggeration, and by 1930 Crosbie had known sorrow, but the thrust is surely correct.

Opposite:
Crosbie, *c.*1925, and a Christmas card by Crosbie.

Alethea' s Upbringing

Alethea, the last of Garstin's children, was born in June 1894. Among family and friends she was known as Rikki but, when young, she was called 'the Pig' because of her hearty appetite. When she was eight Norman wrote that 'she shot up about an inch on the morning of her birthday and another inch was put on at lunch, but this was round her waist'.[34] She appears to have been a happy child, and to have been both spoilt and teased by her brothers.

Her father was extraordinarily fond of her and his letters often begin with extravagant and fanciful terms of endearment. For instance in 1913, when she was nineteen, he wrote to his 'turtle-tiger and lion-lamb, my chocolate cream-acid drop, my fearful-joy. We are all very sad because you are not here. Mother and I go down to meet every train hoping that you will come back, and then we return home very sad and wretched, only to start again for the next'.[35] In his letters to her during the early twenties, Garstin constantly bewails her absence and expresses the hope that she will soon come back. The illustrations that he frequently included were another token of his affection.

The bonds between father and daughter would have been particularly close because Alethea was from childhood interested in painting, and because, in contrast to her brothers, she did not go away to a prep school at an early age. She had lessons with the Bolitho governess and went on to the Penzance High School. Only then did she attend a boarding school in London, where she was far from happy. Garstin wryly observes of his children that, 'Naturally in an artists' colony they saw and heard much of painting and, naturally, regarded it as a dull occupation'.[36] He must have been referring to his sons, because Alethea began to join lessons in her father's classes as a very small girl. Dressed in one of the student's aprons, she would solemnly sit on a high stool paying careful attention to everything he said. Alethea also had the benefit of attending the summer schools, despite the disadvantage of having to occupy accommodation so poor that others had turned it down.

After such a training, her school visits to the National Gallery seemed very dull:

> We were taken in eleven horse carriages ... by drivers in uniforms green with age. We had to walk in threes – not allowed to go near the artists who were copying pictures – they were men! I wasn't allowed to look at the things I wanted to, either – it always had to be pictures of Saints – Lawrence with his frying pan – that sort of thing. I went to the matron and said 'Pictures make me feel ill.' After that I didn't have to go any more.[37]

Alethea already had a keen eye for humorous detail.

Alethea as a young woman.

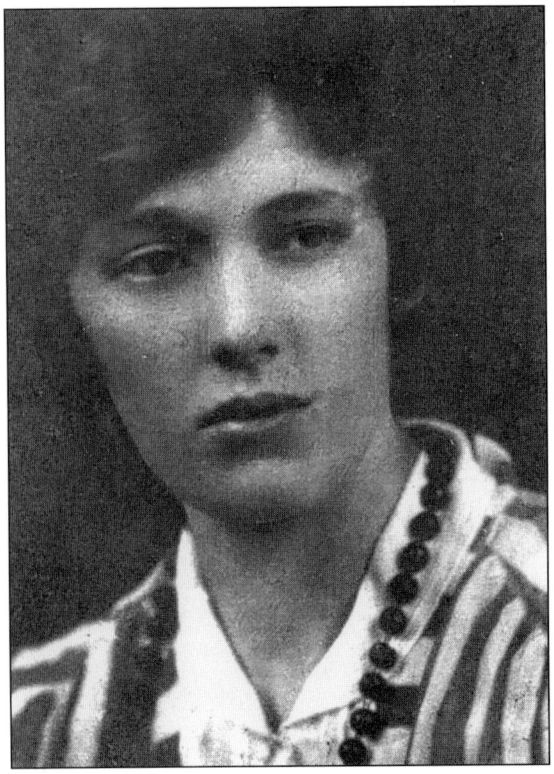

Alethea the Painter

Garstin was to be her only teacher and, although she attended Heatherly's School of Art for a short time to study life drawing, she received no tuition there. Alethea started painting seriously at the age of sixteen and, when she was not quite eighteen, had her first work, *The Chair-makers* (1912), accepted by the RA, making her one of the youngest persons to have work hung. It was admired by Sir Edward Poynter, the President of the Royal Academy, who asked to meet her and, when he did, offered his congratulations.

This was the auspicious start to Alethea's career as a painter, which did not finally close until her death in January 1978. It would be tedious to chronicle the events of a long life, and a synoptic view of her career is both more interesting and more useful. Her work as an artist was only interrupted during the two World Wars. After training as a nurse in 1915, she looked after convalescent soldiers in an English hospital and then, in 1917, went to France and worked in a home for refugee children run by the Quakers. The work and the conditions were hard and in the spring of 1918 Alethea became seriously ill with osteitis, which is inflammation of the bone, and she suffered from bouts of sinusitis for the rest of her life. During the Second World War she again looked after children, this time five evacuees, who came to live with her and her mother at Wellington Terrace. Their care and that of Dochie, who was becoming increasingly forgetful, filled her time and she did not get back to painting until after her mother's death in 1945.

Except for the war years, Alethea devoted her life to painting and travel, and they were joint activities: she painted wherever she went. Patrick Heron, the celebrated artist and critic, who did so much to promote her work, provided this verdict:

> She was, like her father … an impressionist – though her scope was wider, her sensibility gayer and, of course, closer to the painting of the present century … she was destined to miss – perhaps by a hairsbreadth – the acclaim her painting merited. … comparisons with [early and] middle period Vuillard; with Sickert at his best; and even with early Matisse … have already been penned, and many now believe they are not merely extravagant claims … [38]

Because of Heron's authority, this is the necessary starting point for the evaluation of Alethea's painting. Nevertheless it is only a point of departure. Alethea was not an Impressionist but, if anything, a Post-Impressionist. They repudiated illusionism and perspective, and enthusiastically embraced the negative concept that pictures were and should look flat, and the positive idea that painting was about form, by which was meant heightened and unnatural colour (Bonnard and Denis), shape and pattern (Cézanne), or the creation

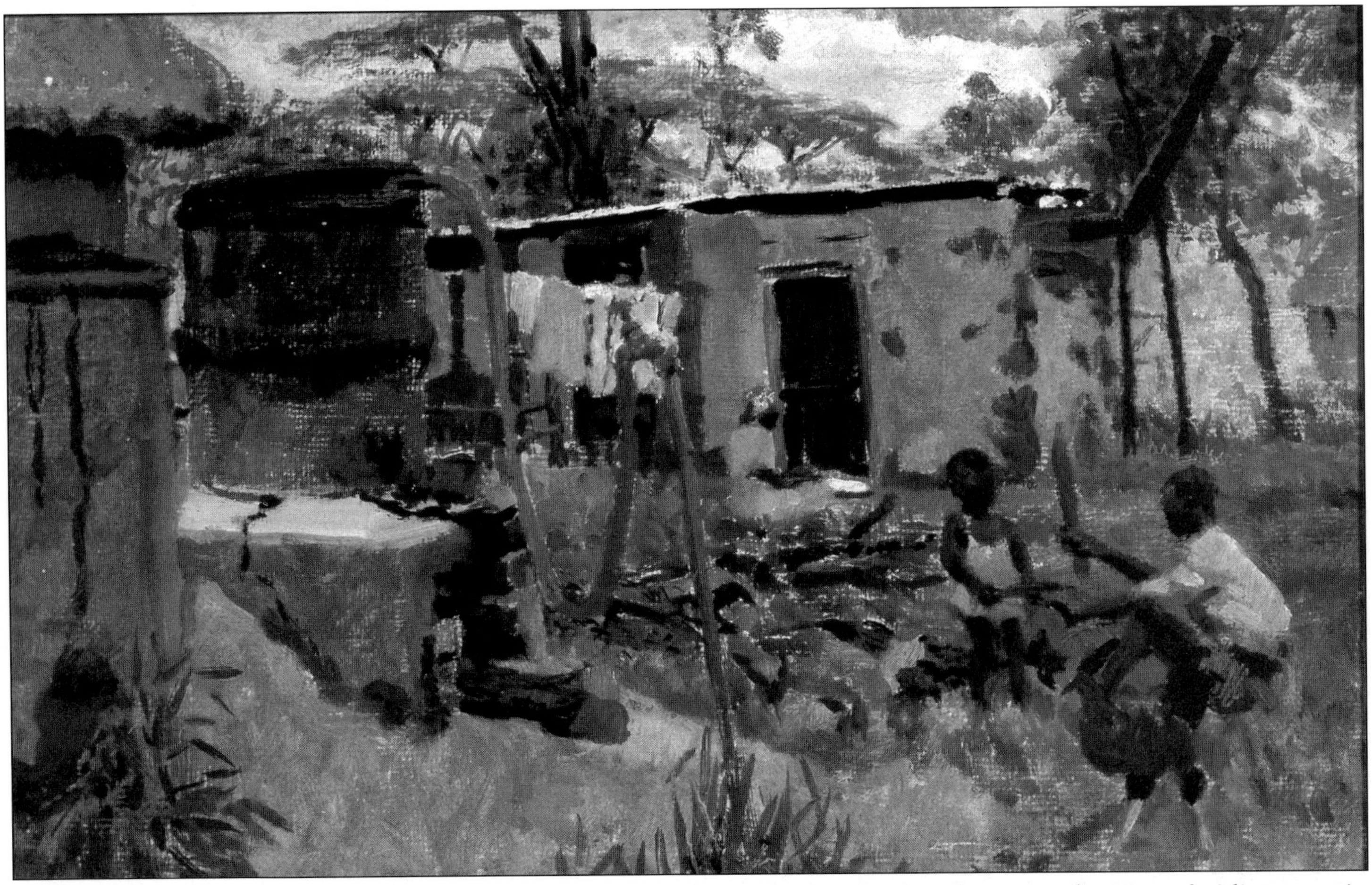

Alethea Garstin, *West Indian Village Scene*, oil, 8.5" x 12" (private collection).

of decorative works (Vuillard and Bonnard). Heron's idiosyncratic definition of impressionism was the recording of the thing seen, which is confusingly wide, though not broad enough to fit Vuillard and Matisse, who were not Realists.[39]

It is, once again, important to look at the strengths and weaknesses of the artist in question. Likening Alethea to Vuillard, Sickert and Matisse heightens expectations to such an extent that they are almost sure to be disappointed and, in reaction, her considerable, but not towering, merits overlooked. The great bulk of Alethea's pictures are landscapes and town scenes and, apart from the occasional portrait, her pictures are small and were painted *plein air*. Her scope was therefore somewhat narrow and she did not, like Vuillard, paint interiors. In general her works lack depth, and here she had an affinity with the Post-Impressionists, though as her pictures were not invariably flat one has the feeling the absence of depth was not a matter of deep conviction. The attraction of her pictures lies in their spontaneity: they were obviously painted quickly and on the spot. According to Canney, she seldom worked in the studio and, when she did try to improve her works at home, it was not a success.[40] Her pictures are characterised by sunlight, bold colours, humour and joy. They may not be profound but they are a pleasure. In order that the reader can judge for him or herself, two of Alethea's best paintings are reproduced here.

Alethea: Personality and Peregrinations

Alethea's painting reflected her personality and her travel. In 1913 Alethea went to Florence on what appears to have been the first of her numerous far-flung expeditions to foreign countries. After the war she not only visited the distantly related Garstins who lived at Braganstown, but spent much of 1920-2 in Portugal and Italy. Between 1927, when she learned to drive, and 1939 she went on

Alethea Garstin, *Harbour, Trinidad, West Indies,* oil, 12.5" x 15" (private collection).

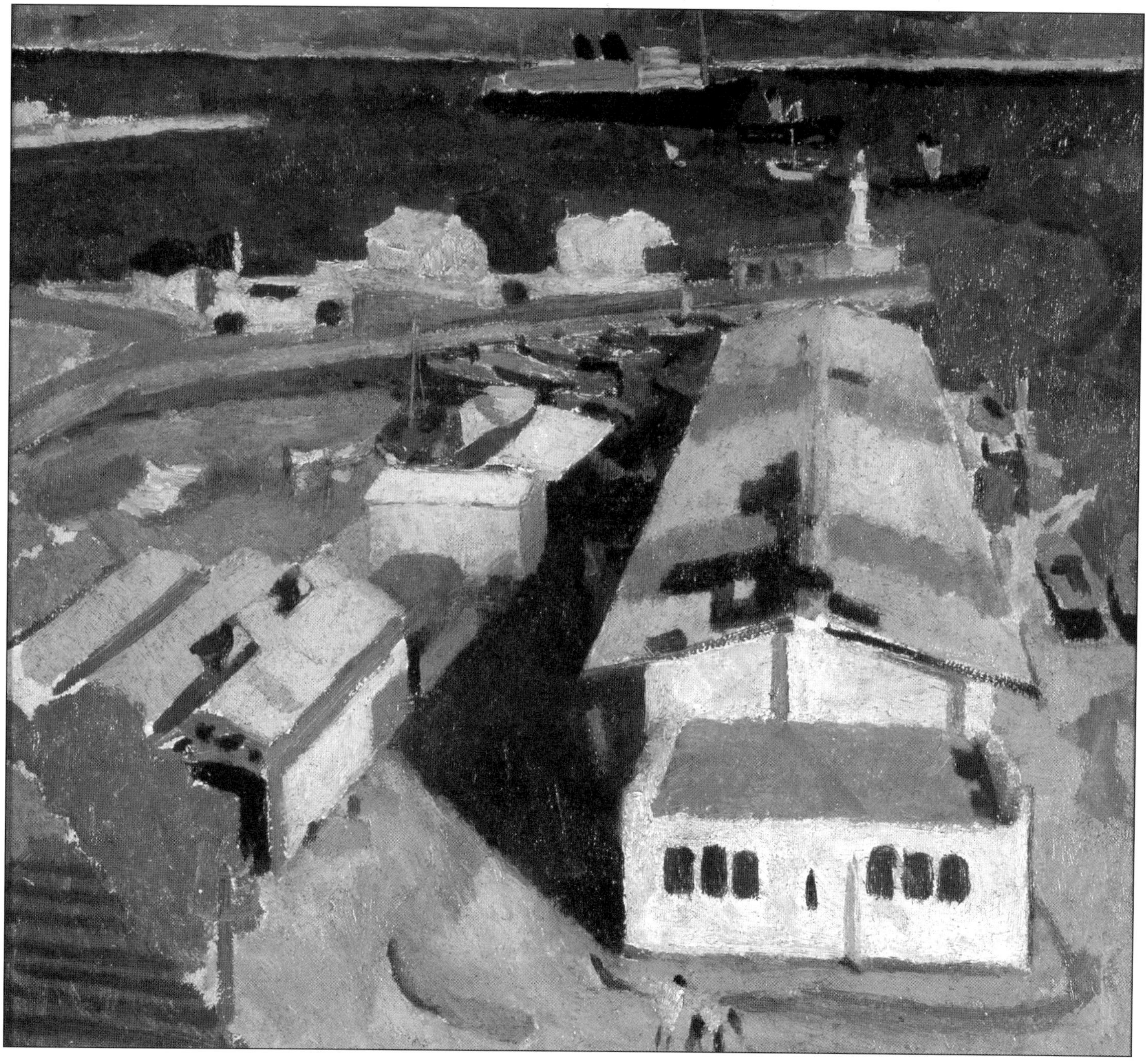

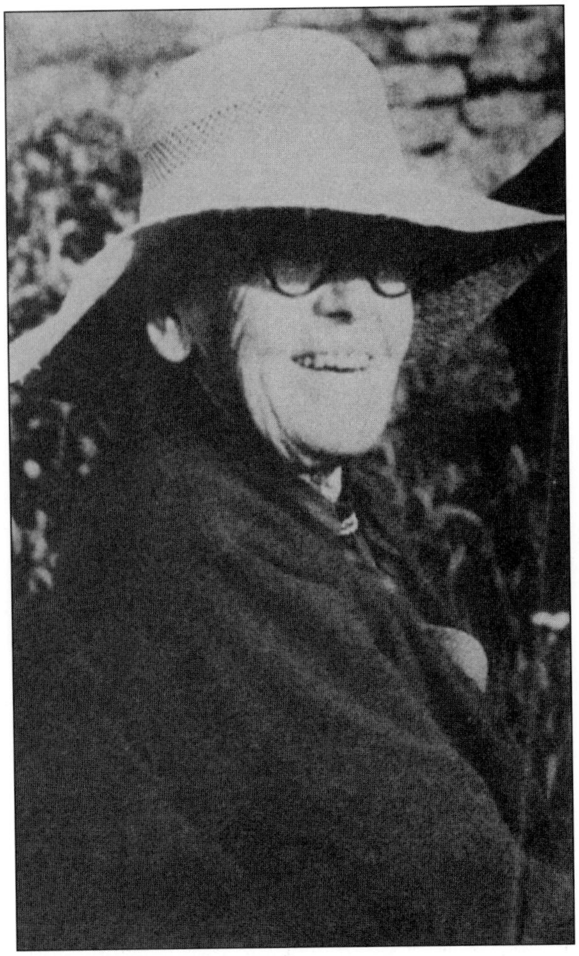

Alethea aged about 78, still jolly and jaunty.

numerous trips to Morocco, where on one occasion she drove her mother – by then in her eighties – through the desert; she also visited Spain, Egypt and Austria and, of course, France. After the Second World War, her trips were, if anything, more exotic. She went to Turkey, Tanganyika, Kenya, Indonesia, Australia, the Pacific Islands, the West Indies and the United States; as well as Ireland, France, Belgium, Spain, Switzerland, Italy, Tunisia and Egypt.

Bubbling is the word that best describes Alethea. She had a fine sense of humour; she was lively and outgoing; she was keenly interested in whatever was happening; she had remarkable energy; and, like her father and Denis, a gift for friendship. Her energy was displayed not only by her travel but also by her attendance, up to a late age, at local dances, where she would partner farmers. She hugely enjoyed parties, conversation and gardening. Unlike her father, she was not an intellectual and had no theories about painting; nor was she very interested in politics, though left-inclined; and she was not a great walker.[41] She travelled far and wide in her famous little Morris, and bought her last car at the age of 82. Her humour and kindness were shown by the way she treated her mother. When, in old age, Dochie was losing her memory, Alethea treated this as a laughing matter, but she laughed with her and not at her.

She had a wide circle of friends and they ranged from artists, including the naïve painter Alfred Wallis, to the upper class (Lady Mary Palairet and Princess Marthe Bibesco); though she was in no way snobbish. For many years Alethea was a close friend of the Newlyn artist Dod Procter (1892-1972), but ultimately their friendship cooled, after Dod proved difficult on a trip the Caribbean and took charge of clearing the studio at Wellington Terrace, when to Alethea's great distress the council decide to acquire the site, by compulsory purchase, for a (dismal) car park. This led to the loss of valuable records and caused Alethea to move to Zennor, near St Ives, where she became great friends with the Herons, who were her neighbours and landlords. Patrick's regard for Alethea no doubt explains his somewhat exaggerated respect for her work.

Alethea was throughout her life popular with men: at the Chelsea Arts Ball in 1914 every dance was booked. In 1927 or 1928 she became friends with the South African painter Edward Wolfe and, through him, with Edward Moorland Lewis (1903-43), who had been a pupil of Sickert. Her relationship with Lewis was, as his letters testify, intimate yet Platonic: 'here I am', he wrote in 1939, 'sitting down smoking a pipe and thinking how fortunate I am and blessing the day we spoke to each other ... Ever since then I have loved you very dearly with a love free from the complexity of sex'.[42] Why did Alethea never marry? The death of so many young men of her generation during the First World War may well be one reason, and she probably never found any one who lived up to the expectations her father had created.

Alethea had 29 pictures accepted by the Royal Academy and, besides the early joint exhibitions with her father, had a single person show at the Adams Gallery, Pall Mall, in April 1940. She participated in a group exhibition at the Redfern Gallery in 1954. Nevertheless her work received very little and probably declining attention during her lifetime. She exhibited nothing at the Academy after 1945, and only five pictures after 1932. West End galleries are, however, now starting to ask relatively large sums for her pictures.

Her work, like that of her father, lives on and, together with the books of her brothers, gives an enduring life to a brilliant family which, with her death, passed so sadly into history. The graveyard memorial that Alethea erected at St Hilary bears the inscription, 'In memory of Norman and Dochie Garstin so dearly loved and admired by their children Crosbie, Denis and Alethea, Amavimus, Amamus, Amabimus' – we have loved, we love, we shall love.

Notes

Introduction

[1] See p. 34, 35 below for a definition and discussion of Realism.

[2] Joanna Lace, *Norman Garstin and the Newlyn School* (BA Dissertation, Cambridge 1973), pp. 4-7, 26-32.

[3] Patrick Heron and Michael Canney, *Norman and Alethea Garstin: Two Impressionists - Father and Daughter* (Penwith Society of Arts, 1978).

[4] Quotation from Julian Campbell, *The Irish Impressionists: Irish Artists in France and Belgium 1850-1914* (National Gallery of Ireland, 1984), p. 86.

[5] James Thompson, *The East Imagined, Experienced, Remembered: Orientalist Nineteenth Century Painting* (National Gallery of Ireland, 1988).

[6] For a recent short life see Nic Hale, *Norman and Alethea Garstin* (Helston, An Lyverji Kernewek, 1999).

Chapter 1

[1] For Garstin's ancestry see *Burke's Landed Gentry*; James B. Leslie, *History of the Kilsaran Union of Parishes in the County of Louth* (Dundalk, William Tempest, 1908); Representative Church Body Library, Dublin. Henceforth, wherever it is not indicated, the place of publication is London.

[2] GP (for Garstin Papers at Morrab Library, Penzance), N (for Norman), A (for Alethea), Dp (for Deposit) 6, B (for Box) 7, 1670/6. Henceforth, all such references will be given in abbreviated form. Elsewhere C stands for Crosbie, D for Dochie and W for Wallet. There is little or no punctuation in Garstin's letters and lectures and it has, where necessary, been inserted.

[3] For William see National Archives, WO 25/801; *Hart's Army List*; George Brenton Laurie, *History of the Royal Irish Rifles* (Gale and Polden, 1914), p. 215.

[4] Heron and Canney [Introduction, note 3] p. 27. The portrait is inscribed Ann Fitzgerald (sic), who on a label is described as 'Ann Crosbie [Frend], later Ann Fitzgerald'. Although this was written by Garstin himself, it is wrong. There was no Ann Crosbie Fitzgerald, née Frend. As Census details show, the person in the portrait can only have been Ann Minnitt Fitzgerald.

[5] Alexander Mann Papers, N to Mrs Mann, 20 February 1909; FP (for FitzGerald Papers), N to Ada, 26 March 1916.

[6] Philip Ahier, *A Short History of Secondary Grammar Education in Jersey, as Exemplified in the Story of Victoria College Jersey* (University of London MA Thesis, 1963), p. 157.

[7] GP, D to C, 23 October 1891, Dp3 B3, 0006.

[8] GP, N to Denis, 20 July 1911, Dp6 B9, 1723/3.

[9] For the Church of Ireland see James Godkin, *Ireland and Her Churches* (Chapman and Hall, 1867); Desmond Bowen, *The Protestant Crusade in Ireland, 1800-70* (Gill and Macmillan, 1978); W. R. Le Fanu, *Seventy Years of Irish Life* (Edward Arnold, 1893), p. 158.

[10] GP, N to Lady Kimberley, 1925 or early 1926, Dp6 B8, 1683/8.

[11] Norman Garstin, 'The Work of Stanhope A. Forbes, A. R. A.', *The Studio*, 23 July 1901.

[12] GP, Dp6 B7, N to A, 1670/6.

[13] For Victoria College see D. J. Cottrill, *Victoria College Jersey, 1852-1972* (Chichester, Phillimore, 1977).

[14] *Cornishman,* 27 April 1921.

[15] Walter Shaw-Sparrow, *John Lavery and his Work* (Kegan Paul, 1911), p. 26.

[16] *Cornish Post and Mining News*, 1 October 1896, p. 8.

[17] Basil H. Jackson (editor), *Recollections of Thomas Graham Jackson* (OUP, 1950), pp. 115, 116.

[18] 'The March Hare Interviews Norman Garstin', *Paper Chase,* Summer Number 1909, p. 34.

[19] *Cornish Post and Mining News,* 1 October 1896.

[20] 'A now well-known artist', who can only be Garstin, quoted in Sir Lewis Michell, *The Life of the Rt Hon. Cecil John Rhodes 1853-1902* (Edward Arnold, 1910), Vol. 1, p. 41.

[21] Norman Garstin, 'Prehistoric Rhodes', *Black and White,* 5 December 1896, p. 728.

[22] Michell [note 20] p. 46.

[23] *Black and White* [note 21] p. 729.

[24] GP, D6 B8, 1681.
[25] William Charles Scully, *Reminiscences of a South African Pioneer* (T. Fisher Unwin, 1913), p. 146.
[26] Dochie Garstin, untitled biographical note on Garstin.
[27] GP, D to C, 23 October 1891, Dp3 B3, 0006.
[28] *Paper Chase* [note 18].
[29] 'Echoes from Home', *The Lantern,* 1 December 1877.
[30] Ibid., 11 May 1878.
[31] 'Our Surplus Women', *The Lantern,* 23 November 1878.
[32] 'Echoes from Home', *The Lantern,* 11 May 1878.
[33] 'Echoes from Erin', *The Lantern,* 25 May 1878.
[34] 'Our Surplus Women' [note 31].
[35] *Paper Chase* [note 18].
[36] Heron and Canney [Introduction, note 3] p. 19.
[37] 'Echoes from Home', *The Lantern,* 9 February 1878.

Chapter 2
[1] For the Antwerp Academy see Jeanne Sheehy, 'British Artists at the Antwerp Academy', *Art History.* Vol. 20, No 1, March 1997.
[2] For Verstraete see Lucien Solvay, *Le Paysage et les Paysagistes: Theodore Verstraete* (Brussels, Emile Bruylant, 1897).
[3] Linda Nochlin, *Realism* (Penguin, 1990), p. 13.
[4] For the development and divisions of realism see Gabriel P. Weisberg, *The Realist Tradition: French Painting and Drawing 1830-1900* (Cleveland Museum of Art, 1980), and Adrian Jenkins, *Painters and Peasants: Henry La Thangue and British Rural Naturalism 1880-1905* (Bolton Museum and Art Gallery, 2000).
[5] *Times Literary Supplement*, 4 June 1954, p. 368.
[6] Robert Emmons, *Life and Opinions of Walter Richard Sickert* (Faber and Faber, 1941), p. 63.
[7] See Preface for the steps taken to view pictures and find colour reproductions.
[8] *Paper Chase* [Chapter 1, note 18].
[9] Shaw-Sparrow [Chapter 1, note 15] pp. 40, 41.
[10] *The Minute,* 2 June 1896, p. 796.
[11] Caroline Fox, *Stanhope Forbes and the Newlyn School* (Newton Abbot, David and Charles, 1993), p. 12.
[12] Norman Garstin, 'Alexander Mann: An Appreciation', *The Studio*, 46, 1909, p. 302.
[13] For the ateliers and Carolus-Duran see H. Barbara Weinberg, *The Lure of Paris: Nineteenth Century American Painters and their French Teachers* (Abbeville Press, 1991).
[14] Eliot Gregory, *The Ways of Men* (New York, Charles Scribner's, 1900), p. 108.
[15] Will H. Low, *A Chronicle of Friendships 1873-1900* (Hodder and Stoughton, 1908), p. 23; Gregory, idem.
[16] H. Wayne Morgan, *An American Art Student in Paris: The Letters of Kenyon Cox 1877-1882* (Kent State University Press, 1986), pp. 14, 40, 49, 64, 65, 136.
[17] See *Carolus-Duran 1837-1917*, (Lille Palais des Beaux-Arts, 9 mars-9 juin 2003).
[18] *Paper Chase* [Chapter 1, note 18].
[19] Evan Charteris, *John Sargent* (Heinemann, 1927), p. 29.
[20] Ibid., pp. 27, 28. My translations.
[21] R. A. M. Stevenson, *Velasquez* (George Bell, 1902), p. 106.
[22] Low [note 15] p. 15.
[23] Garstin [note 12] pp. 302, 305.
[24] Norman Garstin, 'Édouard Manet', *Art Journal,* 1884, p. 110.
[25] Ibid., pp. 110, 111.
[26] See Fox [note 11] p. 12.

[27] GP, Clara to D, 17 April 1884, Dp3 B3, 0020.
[28] Betsy Cogger Rezelman, *The Newlyn Artists and their Place in Late-Victorian Art* (Indiana University PhD thesis, 1984), p. 111.
[29] It is difficult to be certain about the order and dates of Garstin's movements, and, in particular, whether he went home in the spring of both 1884 and 1885, or only in 1884.
[30] Norman Garstin, 'Tangier as a Sketching Ground', *The Studio,* 11, 1897, p. 177.
[31] GP, N to D, Dp3 B4, 0409.
[32] Garstin [note 30].
[33] Rezelman [note 28] p. 114.
[34] Heron and Canney [Introduction, note 3] p. 14.

Chapter 3
[1] GP, Dochie's Diary 1886, Dp3 W17, 0739.
[2] Caroline Fox and Francis Greenacre, *Artists of the Newlyn School 1880-1900* (Newlyn Orion Galleries, 1979), p. 209.
[3] Heron and Canney [Introduction, note 3] p. 23.
[4] *The Paper Chase* [Chapter 1, note 18] p. 35.
[5] Fox and Greenacre [note 2] p. 211.
[6] SFP (for Stanhope Forbes Papers at Tate), untitled talk at Passmore Edwards Gallery re early history of Newlyn Art Colony, p. 10.
[7] Bernard Walke, *Twenty Years at St. Hilary* (Anthony Mott, 1982), p. 200.
[8] GP, N to D, Dp6 B7, 1665/1.
[9] SFP, letter to mother, 7 November 1886.
[10] Linda Gill (editor), *Letters of Frances Hodgkins* (Auckland University Press, 1993), p. 92.
[11] SFP, ibid.
[12] GP, Dp6 B8, 1676.
[13] Norman Garstin, manuscript lecture beginning 'What is our Art?', GP, Dp6 B8, 1678.
[14] Alice Meynell, 'Newlyn', *Art Journal,* 1889, p. 140.
[15] Heron and Canney [Introduction, note 3] p. 12.
[16] GP, Dp6 B8, 1678.
[17] Heron and Canney [Introduction, note 3], p. 12.
[18] Michael Fried, *Absorbtion and Theatricality: Painting and the Beholder in the Age of Diderot* (Berkeley, University of California Press, 1980), p. 130.
[19] Ibid., p. 99.
[20] E. H. Gombrich, *Art and Illusion* (Phaidon, 2002), p. 236.
[21] Fried [note 18] pp. 130, 227-8.
[22] Walter Pater, *The Renaissance: Studies in Art and Poetry* (Macmillan, 1910 edition), pp. 238-9.
[23] See Catalogue Raisonné 2.
[24] Rezelman [Chapter 2, note 28] p. 219.
[25] Lace [Introduction, note 2] p. 32.
[26] *Cornish Telegraph,* 28 March 1889.
[27] Fox [Chapter 2, note 11] p. 39.
[28] FP, Mag Fulton to Ada, 12 September [1887].
[29] SFP, letter to Liz, 25 April 1887.
[30] Fox and Greenacre [note 2] p. 212.

Chapter 4
[1] Fox and Greenacre, [Chapter 3, note 2] p. 228.

[2] Ibid., p. 213; Hugh Lane note on Norman Garstin.
[3] Lace [Introduction, note 2] p. 32.
[4] *The Grosvenor Gallery 1890, An Illustrated Catalogue of the Summer Exhibition with Notes by Henry Blackburn* (Grosvenor Gallery, 1890), p. 15.
[5] FP, Mag Fulton to Ada, May [1891].
[6]GP, N to D, 29 May 1891, Dp3 B4, 0412.
[7] Canadian Pacific Archives, letter received 4 July 1891, R61.A.50747.
[8] GP, N to D, 30 July 1891, Dp3 B4, 0410.
[9] FP, Norman to Ada, 18 September 1891, addition.
[10] FP, to Ada. Undated but must be June 1892.
[11] James Ross, *A Treatise of Disorders of the Nervous System* (J. & A. Churchill, 1883), Vol. 2, p. 648.
[12] Heron and Canney [Introduction, note 3] p. 15.
[13] Norman Garstin, 'In C-P-Railia', *Art Journal,* 1892, pp. 175-6.
[14] GP, 'Painters and Painting', Dp6 B8, 1673, pp. 10, 13.
[15] GP, Dp6 B8, 1678.
[16] Pater [Chapter 3, note 22] p. 239.
[17] GP, Dp6 B8, 1678.
[18] Idem.
[19] *Cornishman,* 28 March 1901.
[20] Roger Fry, *Vision and Design* (OUP, 1981), pp. 117-18.
[21] See the Annex for details.
[22] For these developments see Laura Wortley, *British Impressionism: A Garden of Bright Images* (*The* Studio, Fine Art Publications, 1988).
[23] Garstin [Chapter 2, note 12] pp. 300, 301.
[24] For the Victorian art market see Paula Gillett, *The Victorian Painter's World* (Gloucester, Alan Sutton, 1990).
[25] Caroline Dakers *The Holland Park Circle: Artists and Victorian Society* (Yale University Press, 1999), pp. 4-5.
[26] Alexander Mann Papers, Mann to Kate, 12 May 1892.

Chapter 5
[1] Heron and Canney [Introduction, note 3] p. 21.
[2] Gill [Chapter 3, note 10] p. 133.
[3] Ibid., p. 92.
[4] FHP (for Frances Hodgkins letters at Alexander Turnbull Library, MS Papers 85) 28 July 1902, Folder 12.
[5] Gill [Chapter 3, note 10] p. 171.
[6] FHP 4 August 1903, Folder 15.
[7] Gill [Chapter 3, note 10] p. 92.
[8] Butler Diary (at Trinity College, Dublin), 8 August 1894.
[9] GP, Becca to A, 21 May 1954, Dp3 B8, 1684/8.
[10] Gill [Chapter 3, note 10] p. 94; FHP, 30 September 1902, Folder 12.
[11] GP, N to D, Dp6 B 7, 1665/7.
[12] GP, N to D, 10 October 1910, Dp6 B7, 1665/6.
[13] GP, N to A, [1912] Dp3 B4, 0246.
[14] GP, 'A Comedy of Commerce', Dp6 W19, 1650/8, p. 12.
[15] GP, N to D, 17 October [1905], Dp6 B7, 1665/5.
[16] Gill [Chapter 3, note 10] p. 133.
[17] *Paper Chase* [Chapter 1, note 18].
[18] *The Times,* 3 May 1909, p. 6.

[19] *Cornish Telegraph,* 25 March 1909, p. 6.
[20] *The Observer*, 30 April 1911.
[21] GP, Dp3 W14, 1551A; *The Times,* 10 May 1911.
[22] *Evening Standard,* 4 May 1910.
[23] Gill [Chapter 3, note 10] pp. 137, 229.
[24] FHP 2 May 1907, Folder 18.

Chapter 6
[1] Gill [Chapter 3, note 10] pp. 288, 289.
[2] CP (for Courtney Papers at LSE) N to Lady Courtney, 18 May 1918.
[3] G. P. Gooch, *Life of Lord Courtney* (Macmillan, 1920), pp. 579-82.
[4] GP, loose sheets accompanying four books On Civilization, Dp6 W19, 1650/15.
[5] GP, N to A, 5 August [1915?], Dp6 B7, 1669/4.
[6] Gill [Chapter 3, note 10] p. 300.
[7] Rev. E. M. Burgess, *Life of Bernard Walke,* unpublished typescript.
[8] *Daily Telegraph* as quoted in *Cornish Telegraph,* 30 June 1926.
[9] GP, N to A, 12? 1916, Dp3 B4, 0273.
[10] ZP (for Zennor Papers), D to N, undated but June or July 1917.
[11] GP, N to A, 22 June 1919, Dp3 B4, 0269.
[12] FP, N to Ada, 26 March 1916.
[13] CP, N to Lady Courtney [November 1915]; FP, idem.
[14] Philip Hills (editor), *Fellowship of Peace: Lily Collier, her Diaries 1917-1924* (Philip Hills, 1999), pp. 30, 31.
[15] GP, N to A, 30 March 1920, Dp3 B4, 0433.
[16] See Catalogue Raisonné 2.
[17] GP, 14 Sept 1926, Henry Havelock Allen to A, Dp6 B8, 1671/13.
[18] GP, N to A, 26 July 1922, Dp3 B5, 05873.
[19] *The Times,* 27 March 1924.
[20] GP, N to A, 20 March 1922, Dp6 B9, 1762/2.
[21] J. Johnson and A. Greutzner, *The Dictionary of British Artists 1880-1940* (Woodbridge, Antique Collectors' Club, 1976); my figure for Garstin's exhibits.
[22] GP, N to A, Dp3 B5, 0457.
[23] GP, N to A, 26 April 1923, Dp3 B5, 0441.
[24] GP, N to A, 22 August 1922, Dp6 B9, 1727/3.
[25] GP, N to A, 12 May 1922, Dp3 B4, 0437.
[26] FHP 26 June 1926, Folder 42.
[27] Philip C. Hills (editor), *Recordings: Alethea Garstin – BBC,* p. 173.
[28] *The Times,* 25 June 1926.
[29] GP, Dp3 B8, 1671/14.
[30] Joan Manning-Sanders, interview, January 2000.

Chapter 7
[1] GP, N to D, 7 July 1912, Dp6 B9, 1723/5.
[2] G, Dp6 W19, 1650/13.
[3] GP, N to A, 6 May 1910, Dp3 B4, 0267.
[4] GP, Dp6 W19, 1650/13
[5] ZP, Norman Garstin, preface to Denis's letters (unpublished), p. 5.
[6] ZP, D to A, undated.

[7] Denis Garstin, *Friendly Russia* (T. Fisher Unwin, 1915), p. 224.
[8] GP, N to A, 20 August 1914, Dp6 B7, 1666/5.
[9] Denis Garstin [note 7] pp. 215, 242.
[10] GP, Diary 18 July to 14 August 1914, Dp6 W18, 1555.
[11] Denis Garstin, *The Shilling Soldiers* (Hodder and Stoughton, 1918), pp. 71-2.
[12] Ibid., p.103.
[13] ZP, D to A, 14 September 1918.
[14] ZP, D to A, 21 June 1918.
[15] Denis Garstin [note 11] p. vi.
[16] R. H. Bruce Lockhart, *Memoirs of a British Agent* (Putnam, 1932), p. 261.
[17] GP, C to N and D, 5 September 1918, Dp3 B3, 0218.
[18] GP, Dp6 W18, 1555.
[19] GP, Dp3 B3, 0059.
[20] Garstin [note 5] p. 2; GP, unidentified cutting, Dp1 W18, 0763.
[21] FHP 4 August 1903, Folder 15.
[22] GP, unidentified cutting, Dp1 W18, 0763.
[23] GP, C to D, 5 May 1916, Dp3 B3, 0159.
[24] Crosbie Garstin, *The Mud Larks Again* (Methuen, 1919), p. 28.
[25] *New Statesman,* 9 October 1926, p. 740.
[26] *Cornishman,* 24 April 1930.
[27] GP, A to D, 27 April 1930, Dp3 B4, 0319.
[28] ZP, C to N and D, 29 April 1914; C to N and D undated.
[29] GP, C to N and D, 5 September 1918, Dp3 B3, 0218.
[30] GP, C to N and D, almost certainly 1910, Dp3 B4, 0362.
[31] GP, N to A, 12 May 1922, Dp3 B4, 0437.
[32] GP, C to A, Dp3 B4, 0333.
[33] GP, C to N and D, 5 September 1918, Dp3 B3, 0218.
[34] GP, N to D, June 1902, Dp3 W7 B3, 0050.
[35] GP, N to A, 9 June 1913, Dp3 B4, 0422.
[36] Garstin [note 5] p. 1.
[37] Heron and Canney [Introduction, note3] p. 21.
[38] *The Times*, 7 March 1978.
[39] Heron and Canney [Introduction, note 3] p. 4.
[40] Ibid., p. 22.
[41] Although Garstin denied having any theory about painting (Chapter 1, note 18), he had, as we have seen, a carefully thought-out position.
[42] Hale [Introduction, note 6] p. 38.

Other items from the Garstin Papers (GP) used
Dp2 W10 1482.
Dp3 B3 0049, 0069, 0078, 0132; **B4** 0261, 0273, 0297, 0314, 0354, 0372, 0411, 0419, 0438; **B5** 0443, 0452, 0465, 0473, 0537; **W11** 1486, 1507, 1513/10-15; **W14** 1554A; **W17** 0738, 0743, 0745-0747, 0755.
Dp4 W12 1527
Dp6 B7 1651/3, 1652/1, 1666/4, 1668/4, 1669/4, 1669/5, 1669/7, 1669/12; **B8** 1672/2 /37, 1682/4; **B9** 1723 /6, /8.

Catalogue Raisonné

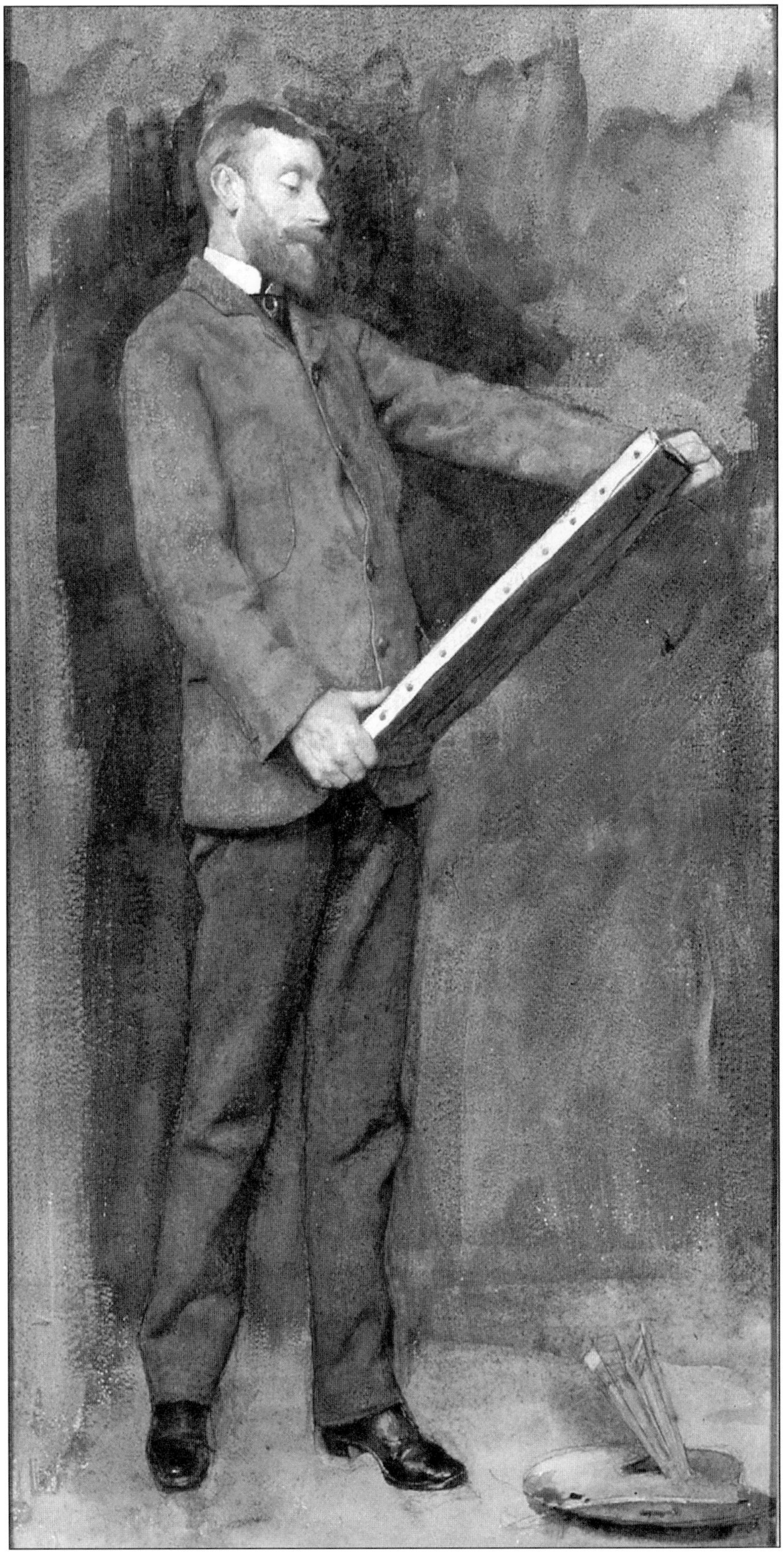

William John Wainwright, *Norman Garstin,* 1881, watercolour, private collection). This was painted when Garstin and Wainwright were both students of the Royal Academy, Antwerp.

Catalogue Raisonné 1: Garstin's Known Works in Date Order

Name of work (in order of preference: Garstin's name, what picture is now called, the subject; major works in bold)	Date first shown/ Gallery or *Place*	Medium (WC= Water colour)	Dimensions (side first in inches, rounded to nearest tenth for eights)	Price (£ or £ and s)	Sold (S) or Never Sold (NS) or Not for Sale (NFS)	Gallery/ availability of reproduction (R= available) or description (Des)
	1882					
Portrait of an Elderly Woman Wearing a Bonnet	*Jas Adam 06*	Oil	10.25x7			
Fierce Cat and Cowardly Dog	*Gift*	Litho			NS	R
Seated Dog	*Gift*	Litho			NS	R
Bird Nesting	Liverpool	Oil		15		
Little Gibionite, A	Liverpool	Oil		15.15s		
Trouble	RSocBritArt			15		
Trophies of the Port	Southport	Oil		17		
	1883					
Fashionable Parisien Stood on a Doorstep, A	*Bonhams 04*	Oil	21x13.75			R
Ireland	Dudley	Oil		12		
Looking for Windfalls	Dudley	Oil		8		
Artichokes, Hyères	*House*	Oil	5.5x9.25		NS	Bristol/R
Gardener's Daughter, The	Liverpool	Oil	19x24	25		R
Portrait of Dochie's Sister Maria	*Private*					
Philoméne	RA	Oil		15	S	
Glimpse of Rye, A	RB'ham	Oil		8		
Way to the Town is to Cross the River, The	RB'ham	Oil		10		
Shelter, The	*Sotheby's 89*	Oil	15.5x12.4			R
	1884					
Land in which it seemed always Afternoon, A	Liverpool	Oil		50		
Venetian Well, The	RSocBritArt	Oil		8		
	1885					
Back Street, Tangier	*de Veres 96*	Oil	9x5			R
Garden Gate, Tangier, A	Dudley	Oil				
Karbah, Tangier	Dudley	Oil				
Arabs [3 in street], Tangier	*House*	Oil	9.5x5.5		NS	Belfast/R
Coast, Tangier	*House*	Oil	9.5x5.5		NS	TePapa
Moroccan Woman in White Traditional Dress	*House*	Oil	9.5x5		NS	
On the Sands, Tangier [2 children, sea, coast]	*House*	Oil	9.5x5.5		NS	York/R
Ravine and Bridge, Spain	*House*	Oil	9.4x5.4		NS	Plymouth/R
Saint House and Field, Tangier	*House*	Oil	5.5x9.5		NS	Plymouth/R
Street and Trees	*House*	Oil	5.1x6		NS	Hull

Tangier Landscape	*House*	Oil	5.4x9.5		NS	Bristol
Islam	Newlyn 26	Oil	Small		NS	
Glimpse of Bay, Tangiers	*Phillips 97*	Oil	9x5.25			R
Che Belle Fiori!	RA	Oil		75	S	
Sunshine and Blossom -Venice	RA	Oil		60		
Public Salesman, Tangiers	RInstOilPnts	Oil		(8)		
From a Street Corner, Tangier	RSocBritArt	Oil		30		
His Latest Bride	RSocBritArt	Oil		35		
Israel in Morocco	RSocBritArt	Oil	9x5.25	8		R
Old Sam	*Sotheby's 85*	Oil	20x16			R
Near Tangier [figure & barn]	*The Studio*	Oil				R
Tangerine Beggar, A	*The Studio*	Oil				R
Tangier [2 figures, sea, headland]	*The Studio*	Oil				R
	1886					
Summer in Winter/Alienis Mensibus Aestas	Aberdeen	Oil	23x31	45		R
Courtyard in the Alhambra, Grenada, A	Aberdeen	Oil		8		
Gateway in the Alhambra	Aberdeen	Oil		8		
Street Scene in Tangier, A	Aberdeen	Oil		8		
Seated Arab, Tangier	*Catalogue*	Oil	12.5x19.5			R
Fishing Village in Normandy, A	*de Veres 01*	Oil	10.75x15			R
Haycocks and Sun	*House*	Oil	8.25x10.75		NS	Tate/R
Tale of Conquest, A	Liverpool	Oil		50		
Tangier Sands Evening	Liverpool	Oil		40		
Portrait of Mrs Anderson	*Private*			10	S	
In a Weary Land	RA	Oil		100		
Camel Driver, A	RInstOilPnts	Oil				
Day After, The	RScottishA					
As the Twig is Bent the Tree is Inclined	RSocBritArt	Oil		40		
Lumps of Delight	RSocBritArt	Oil		30	S £20	
	1887					
Breton Peasant Girl	*Christie's 86*	Oil	24x20			R
Hale Bar	Aberdeen	Oil		5		
In the Cottage by the Sea	Aberdeen	Oil	14x18	15	NS	Penzance/R
Scraps	Aberdeen	Oil		15		
September [1887]	Aberdeen	Oil		7		
Portrait of Crosbie Garstin	*House*	Oil	10x8	NFS	NS	Penzance
Arts from Italy, The	Liverpool	Oil		50		
To Wait for an Answer	Liverpool	Oil		30		
Troubadour, A	Liverpool	Oil		40		
Boys!	Manchester	Oil		25		
Hasty One!, A	Manchester	Oil		50		
Marazion	NEAC	Oil		5	S	
Painter's Wife, The/ Portrait, A	NEAC	Oil	28x20		NS	NGIreland/R
On revient toujours a ses premiers armours	RB'ham	Oil		30		
Portrait of Anne FitzGerald	*The Studio*	Oil	7.75x6	NFS	NS	R
	1888					
Nasty One, A	Aberdeen					

From Door to Door	Liverpool	Oil	22x16	60		R
Among the Flowers of May	Manchester	Oil		10		
Iron Master, An	NEAC	Oil		(100)		R
Progress and Poverty	RA	Oil	44x35	42		R
Oh Look There!	RSocBritArt	Oil	8.75x11.75	20		R
Temptation	RSocBritArt	Oil	32x25	25		R
Towards the Sun-Setting, Newlyn	RSocBritArt	Oil	20x24	25		R
	1889					
Ancient Mariner, An	*Dunedin*	Oil		12		
Song of the Sea, The	Grosvenor	Oil		(30)		
Rain it Raineth Every Day, The	Liverpool	Oil	37x64	75	NS	Penzance/R
Two Heads are Better than One	Liverpool	Oil	16.5x19	15		R
Overdue [at Penzance station]	NEAC	Oil	26.5x35.5	50		R
Farmer and his Daughter	*Phillips 87*	Oil	25x18			R
Portrait of R. R. Fulton, Esq	RHAA	Oil		NFS		
Ruby	RHAA	Oil		10		
Steady Drizzle, A [ie Penzance Market House]	RInstOilPnts	Oil	35.5x27.5	(25)	NS	Truro/R
	1890					
August	RCornwall	Oil		3		
In Newlyn Town	RCornwall	Oil		6		
Maids of the Mill	RCornwall	Oil		9		
Inflated Stock, An (The Balloon)	Dod&Dod	Oil				
Other People's Dinners	Dod&Dod	Oil	16x14	15		
To Cheat Surprise and Prying Eyes	Dod&Dod	Oil		50		Des
What the Moon Saw	Grosvenor					
Stranger, A	RA	Oil	53x83	250	NS	Hugh Lane/R
	1891					
Burrard's Inlet, Vancouver	*Art Journal*	Oil				R
China Town, Victoria, Vancouver Island	*Art Journal*	Oil				R
Crooked Lake, Assiniboine River	*Art Journal*	Oil				R
Greater Glacier of the Selkirks, The	*Art Journal*	Oil				R
Home in the North-West, A	*Art Journal*	Oil				R
In the Rocky Mountain Park, Banff	*Art Journal*	Oil				R
North-West Shanties	*Art Journal*	Oil				R
Settler's 'Shack', A	*Art Journal*	Oil				R
Coast Guard, The	Dundee	Oil		10		
[Portrait of] Ann Crosbie Frend, later Ann Fitzgerald	*House*	Oil	6.25x4.8	NFS	NS	
[Portrait of] Elizabeth Frend	*House*	Oil	10x8.5	NFS	NS	Tate/R
Canadian Landscape with Rising Moon	*House*	Oil	7.75x10.5		NS	York/R
Hell Gate Canyon, Fraser River, near Yale	*House*	Oil	8.25x10.5		NS	Hull/R
December and May	Leeds	Oil		10.10s		
Cotillon, The	Liverpool	Oil	49x38	200		R
Rude Valentine, A	RB'ham	Oil		25		
Canadian Mountain Scene	*The Studio*	Oil	8.5x10.5	NFS	NS	R
	1892					
Her Signal	RA	Oil	61.5x44.25	150	S	Truro/R

What's News?	RScottishA	Oil	14x20			R
	1893					
Hollyhocks and Lilies	Liverpool	Oil		35		
Aurora Borealis on the Prairie	RCornwall	Oil		5		R
Cul-de-Sac	RCornwall	Oil		5		
Great Lone Land, The	RCornwall	Oil		5		
Prairie Town, A	RCornwall	Oil		5		R
Sunset on the Rockies	RCornwall	Oil		5		
[Portrait of] Dr Carne Ross	Manchester	Oil		NFS	S	
[Portrait of] Mrs Carne Ross	Manchester	Oil		NFS		
Tryst, A	Manchester	Oil	36x24	35		R
Portrait of a Boy [in 18th-century costume]	RA	Oil	60x37	NFS		R
	1894					
Gleaners	Manchester	Oil		15		R
Last Dance, The	Manchester	Oil	53x35	125		R
Twin Moons	Manchester	Oil		15		Des
	1895					
Garden Gates	*Gift, Jas Adam 04*	WC	11.75x8.5	NFS	NS	R
[Portrait of] Miss Nancy Howell	Manchester	Oil		NFS	S	R
All in a Garden Fair	Newlyn					Des
Evening	Newlyn					Des
Home from School	Newlyn			6.6s	S	
In Spring	Newlyn					Des
Park Corner	Newlyn			5.5s	S	
Penzance from Newlyn	Newlyn			5.5s	S	
Trengwainton	*Yellow Book*					R
	1896					
Leaning against His Spade He Gazed at Me	*Black&W*	Oil				R
Newlyn from 'The Meadow'	*House*	Oil	15x9			R
Girl amongst Poppies, Bateman's Meadow, Newlyn	*Lay 89*	WC	10x6.5			R
Poppies	Manchester	Oil	28x16	20		R
Bit of Old Penzance, A	Newlyn					
Harvest Moon	Newlyn			4.4s	S	
Newlyn through Trees	Newlyn					
Scarlet Letter, The	RA	Oil	60x42	NFS		R
Moorish Bride, A	Southport	Oil		20		
Bit of Helston, A [alleyway and 2 children]	*The Studio*	Oil				R
Bit of Helston, A [river scene]	*The Studio*	Oil				R
Furry Dance at Helston, The	*The Studio*	Oil				R
Woman in Traditional Costume	*The Studio*	Litho				R
	1897					
Mullion Valley	RCornwall	Oil		3.3s		
Piece of Silver that was Lost, The	Manchester	Oil	41x47	150		R
Chequered Shade	Newlyn			5.5s	S	
Mount's Bay in June	Newlyn	Oil	10x7.5	6.6s	S	Penzance/R

Near Helston	Newlyn			3.3s	S	
Spoils of the Hedge, The	Newlyn			6.6s	S	
	1898					
[Portrait of] Mary Dochie Alethea Garstin	*House*	Oil	10.25x8	NFS	NS	Bristol/R
Mount's Bay and Tolcarne from Trewidden Farm Footpath with Alethea and Her Mother.	*House*	Oil	8x10	NFS	NS	Tate/R
Bon Jour Madame	Newlyn			10	S	
Near Mount's Bay	Newlyn			5.5s	S	
Water Gate	Newlyn			4.4s	S	
Danger	RA	Oil		105		R
Autumn Garden, An	RB'ham	Oil		26.5s		
Cornish Upland, A	RB'ham			4.4s		
Cornish Village, A	RB'ham			10.10s		
	1899					
XMAS 99 MY 3 [children]	*Gift*	Stencil	14x10.5	NFS	NS	R
Corner of the Common, A	Newlyn				S	
Portrait of Miss W. Nichalls	Newlyn		Smallish			
Portrait of Mr Edmund Carlyon [of St Austell]	Newlyn	Oil	48x28		S	R
Portrait of Mrs David Howell	Newlyn		Large			
Two Jews, The ?	Newlyn			10.10s	S	
Young Boy Looking Out to Sea/Solitude	*Phillips 99*	WC	10x7			R
[Portrait of] Denys Garstin [in Georgian costume]	RA	Oil		NFS		Des
Little Bethel, The	York	Oil		63		Des
	1900					
Caudebec, pictures of	Newlyn	WC		8.8s	S	
Fête Nationale Caudebec, Un	Newlyn			2.2s	S	
On the Road to Mousehole	Newlyn			2.2s	S	
Orchard	Newlyn	WC		5.5s	S	
Rose and the Ring, The	RA	Oil		NFS (63)		R
	1901					
Mill of les Gorets, Quimperlé	Hull	WC		12		
Place St Michel, Quimperlé	Hull	Oil	35.25x35.25	35	NS	Plymouth/R
Town Bridge Quimperlé, The	Liverpool	Oil		63		
Moulin de la Ville Quimperlé, Le	NEAC	Oil	26.5x36	30	NS	Brighton/R
Bridge on the Isole, A	Newlyn					Des
Caudebec	Newlyn			5.10s	S	
Fowl Market, The	Newlyn			3.10s	S	
Look of Beauty, A	Newlyn					Des
[Portrait of] John B. Cornish	Newlyn			NFS		
St Ives Bay	Newlyn			3.12s	S	
Stencil	Newlyn	Stencil		2.2s	S	
Mill of les Gouls Quimperlé, The	RB'ham	WC		12.12s		
Old Bridge of Lovignon, The	RB'ham	Oil		52.10s		
Water Gate, The	RB'ham	Oil		15.15s		

	1902					
Some … Friends	Newlyn			4.4s	S	
Wolf in the Fold, A	RInstOilPnts	Oil		63		Des
Dividing Waters	Southport	Oil		50		
Old House on the Elbe, An	Whitechapel					
	1903					
[Portrait of] A Wicked Little Girl [Alethea]	Newlyn					
[Portrait of] Dorothy Kate Richmond	*Private*	Oil	31.75x25.75			TePapa/R
Little Show, The	RInstOilPnts	Oil		63		
	1904					
Café Rose [Dinan]**, Le**	City London	Oil	36x36.5	(75)		
Tregenier, Brittany	*Dunedin*	WC	4.5x6.5		S	Dunedin
Among the Pots [Water colour]	*FineArtSoc*	WC		6.6s	S	
At the Back of the New Church, Delft	*FineArtSoc*	WC		15.15s		
At the Foot of the Gardens, Caudebec	*FineArtSoc*	WC		21		
At the Gate of the Cordelliers, Dinan	*FineArtSoc*	WC		6.6s	S	
Bend of the Seine	*FineArtSoc*	WC		10.10s		
Bouille, on the Seine, La	*FineArtSoc*	WC		12.12s		
Boulangerie, Dinan, La	*FineArtSoc*	WC		6.6s	S	
Breezy Morning, Holland, A	*FineArtSoc*	WC		12.12s		
Bric-à-brac at Bruges	*FineArtSoc*	WC		6.6s		
Bright October, Delft	*FineArtSoc*	WC	21x15	21		R
By Nôtre Dame, Bruges	*FineArtSoc*	WC		10.10s		
By the Fountain, Falaise	*FineArtSoc*	WC		8.8s		
By the Rance	*FineArtSoc*	WC		5.5s	S	
Café by the Rance	*FineArtSoc*	WC		6.6s		
Canal near Bruges, A	*FineArtSoc*	WC		10.10s		
Château by the River [Ellé], Quimperlé, A	*FineArtSoc*	WC	14.25x7	9.9s	S	R
Château Garden, The	*FineArtSoc*	WC	14x10.5	7.7s		R
Château Moat, Normandy	*FineArtSoc*	WC		5.5s	S	
Church of the Beguinage, Bruges	*FineArtSoc*	WC		5.5s	S	
Cirque Anglais at Dinan, Le	*FineArtSoc*	WC		6.6s		
Clock Tower. Vire, The	*FineArtSoc*	WC		8.8s	S	
Corner Stall, Dinan, A	*FineArtSoc*	WC		12.12s		
Cottage Garden, Holland, A	*FineArtSoc*	WC		21		
Dark Water, Vire	*FineArtSoc*	WC		10.10s		
Different Opinions. Pig Market, Dinan	*FineArtSoc*	WC		12.12s		
Dutch Village, A	*FineArtSoc*	WC		10.10s		
Evening by the Vire, St Lô	*FineArtSoc*	WC		12.12	S	
Féte de la Republique	*FineArtSoc*	WC		6.6s		
Fish Stall, Les Andelys, A	*FineArtSoc*	WC		6.6s		
Flower Market, Dinan	*FineArtSoc*	WC		6.6s		
Flower Stall, Bruges, A	*FineArtSoc*	WC		12.12s		
For the Oven, Mortain	*FineArtSoc*	WC		6.6s	S	
For Winter Fuel, Dinan	*FineArtSoc*	WC		6.6s		
Fourteenth of July, Dinan	*FineArtSoc*	WC		10.10s		

Fruit Stall, Dinan, The	*FineArtSoc*	WC		15.15s		
Garden of the Sluggard, Dinan	*FineArtSoc*	WC		8.8s	S	
Gate of the Beguinage	*FineArtSoc*	WC		5.5s		
Goddes Huis [Almshouse] Bruges, A	*FineArtSoc*	WC		15.15s		
Green Alley by the Seine, A	*FineArtSoc*	WC		10.10s		
Green-Grocery, Dinan, A	*FineArtSoc*	WC		6.6s	S	
Greetings	*FineArtSoc*	Stncl		3.3s		
Home upon the Waters, Holland	*FineArtSoc*	WC		21		
In a Flax Barn, Holland	*FineArtSoc*	WC		8.8s		
In Mortain	*FineArtSoc*	WC		6.6s	S	
In the Eye of the Sun, Delft	*FineArtSoc*	WC		10.10s	S	
In the Fish Market, Bruges	*FineArtSoc*	WC	7x5	6.6s		R
In the Turf Market, Delft	*FineArtSoc*	WC	12x9.5	10.10s		R
Jour Maigre, Bruges	*FineArtSoc*	WC	18x12	6.6s		R
Lace and Lilies, Bruges	*FineArtSoc*	WC		15.15s	S	R
Last of the Light, Holland	*FineArtSoc*	WC		6.6s		
Little Purchase, Dinan, A	*FineArtSoc*	WC		12.12s		
Lower Town, Dinan, The	*FineArtSoc*	WC		12.12s		
Marche aux Chiffons, Bruges	*FineArtSoc*	WC		6.6s		
Market by the Seine	*FineArtSoc*	WC		6.6s		
Market Day, Dinan	*FineArtSoc*	WC		6.6s	S	
Market Place, St Lô, The	*FineArtSoc*	WC	11.5x9	12.12s	S	R
Market. Caudebec, The	*FineArtSoc*	WC	6.75x5	6.6s		R
Mauvais Temps, Dinan	*FineArtSoc*	WC		12.12s	S	
Mère Duval	*FineArtSoc*	WC		6.6s	S	
Milk Stall, Dinan, The	*FineArtSoc*	WC		15.15s	S	
Moorland Mill, Normandy, A	*FineArtSoc*	WC		5.5s		
Near Rançon, Normandy	*FineArtSoc*	WC		10.10s	S	
Normandy Meadows	*FineArtSoc*	WC		9.9s		
Oddments, The Dyver, Bruges	*FineArtSoc*	WC		12.12s		
Old Caudebec	*FineArtSoc*	WC	11.5x9.25	12.12s		R
Old Dinan	*FineArtSoc*	WC		6.6s	S	
Pig Market, Dinan	*FineArtSoc*	WC		6.6s		
Pigs and Peasants, Dinan	*FineArtSoc*	WC		6.6s	S	
Pink Café, Dinan, The	*FineArtSoc*	WC		8.8s	S	
Place du Guesclin, Dinan	*FineArtSoc*	WC		21		
Pont Flamand, Bruges, Le	*FineArtSoc*	WC		10.10s		
Purple and Gold, Delft	*FineArtSoc*	WC	22x14.5	26.5s		Dunedin/R
Reach of the Rance, A	*FineArtSoc*	WC		6.6s	S	
Rue de la Boucherie, Caudebec	*FineArtSoc*	WC		15.15s		
Saturday, Holland	*FineArtSoc*	WC		15.15s		
School Hour, Petit Andelys	*FineArtSoc*	WC	6.75x4.75	6.6s	S	R
Seeding Flax, Holland	*FineArtSoc*	WC		8.8s		
Shady Walk, St Lô, A	*FineArtSoc*	WC		6.6s		
Silver Mist, Delft	*FineArtSoc*	WC		5.5s		
Street of Curiosity Shops, Dinan	*FineArtSoc*	WC		12.12s		
Summer's Evening, Holland	*FineArtSoc*	WC		15.15s		
Sun and Wind, Near Delft	*FineArtSoc*	WC		5.5s	S	
Sunday Morning, St Lô	*FineArtSoc*	WC		6.6s		
Sunny Morning in Delft, A	*FineArtSoc*	WC		12.12s	S	
Terrace by the Seine, A	*FineArtSoc*	WC		18.18s	S	
Twilight in the Garden, Caudebec	*FineArtSoc*	WC		10.10s		
Two Mounts	*FineArtSoc*	Stncl		3.3s	S	
Universal Panacea, The	*FineArtSoc*	WC		6.6s		

Vendredi, Bruges	*FineArtSoc*	WC		6.6s		R
Waiting for their Master	*FineArtSoc*	WC		7.7s		
Water Gate by the Ellé, A	*FineArtSoc*	WC		9.9s		
Wet Day, Dinan, A	*FineArtSoc*	WC		6.6s	S	
Wood Choppers, Dinan	*FineArtSoc*	WC		6.6s		
Worsted Sellers, Bruges	*FineArtSoc*	WC		10.10s		
[Portrait of] Mrs Walter St John Mildmay	Newlyn			NFS		
Rim Gate, The	Newlyn			5.5s	S	
Prentice, The	RA	Oil	39x29	78.15s		R
In the Heat of the Day [Caudebec]	Southport	Oil	31.75x39.5	52.10s		R
	1905					
Church Door, A	Newlyn	WC				
Tea Room ...	Newlyn			4.4s	S	
Breton Market, A	RA	Oil		(50)		
For the Fête	RInstPntWC	WC		15.15s		
	1906					
Day's Work o'er	RCornwall	WC		15.15s		
Portrait of Denys Garstin	*House*	Oil	8.75x8.1	NFS	NS	Hull
Portrait of Dr Macnamara	Munster			NFS		
Portrait of Dr O'Dwyer	Munster			NFS		
Portrait of Dr Young	Munster			NFS		
Portrait of Mrs Davidson	Newlyn			NFS		
New Moon, Gravelines, The	RA	Oil		20		Des
Evening in a Little Bourg, Montreuil Sur Mer	RInstOilPnts	Oil		52.10s		Des
	1907					
Wellington Ter Pensance [sic]	*Gift*	Woodct	4x2	NFS	NS	R
Xmas Card [18th-century rider]	*Gift*	Stncl		NFS	NS	
Xmas Card [man and horse]	*Gift*	Stncl		NFS	NS	
Farmyard in Picardy	Hull	WC		(10)		
Moonlight Number Two [on lake]	Newlyn	WC	9.25x13.25	(13.13s)	S	R
Moonlight, Lamplight, and Sunlight	Newlyn			(13.13s)	S	
Watch Tower in the Low Countries, A [La Grand Place, Furnes]	RA	Oil		100		R
Evening Meal, The	RHibernian	Oil		60		Des
Quarry in Normandy	*Sotheby's 86*	WC	15x10			
	1908					
First and Last [St Just stagecoach]	*Gift*	Woodct	4x6	NFS	NS	R
Grandpère, Le	RA	Oil		26.15s		
Chalk Quarry, The	Ridley	Oil	36x28	31.10s		R
Landing Stage	Ridley			12.12s		
Other Days Other Manners	Ridley	WC		15.15s		
	1909					
Xmas, 1909, Diest	*Gift*	Woodct		NFS	NS	R
[Portrait of] Nina Birch	Newlyn	Oil	29.5x19.25	NFS		R
Card Players, The/In a Flemish Hospice	RA	Oil	30.5x36.25	50	NS	Manchester/R

S. Nicholas: Furnes	RB'ham			20		
Lacemaker, The	RHibernian	Oil		31.10s		
Late Load, A	RInstOilPnts	Oil		100	NS	Des
New Bridge	*The Studio*					R
[Portrait of] Alethea Garstin	WalkersGal			NFS		
[Portrait of] Crosbie Garstin, Esq	WalkersGal			NFS		
14 Juillet, Le	WalkersGal			5.5s		
Abbey, The	WalkersGal			9.9s		
At the Green Post	WalkersGal			7.7s		
At the Window	WalkersGal			10.10s		
Bargain, A	WalkersGal			7.7s		
Bark Mill, The	WalkersGal			15.15s		
Barrow Load, The	WalkersGal			15.15s		
Beguinage, Dixmude, The	WalkersGal			9.9s		
Bishop's Wood, The	WalkersGal			15.15s		
Bric-à-Brac	WalkersGal			10.10s		
By the Little Shrine	WalkersGal			9.9s		
Carrousel, Le	WalkersGal			7.7s		
Cassel from the Sand Pits	WalkersGal			12.12s		
Cathedral Door, Trèguier, The	WalkersGal	WC	12x9.5	9.9s		R
Corner of the Farm, A	WalkersGal			9.9s		R
Cottage in Picardy, A	WalkersGal	WC	11x9	9.9s		R
Crockery Stall, The	WalkersGal			7.7s		
Day after the Dance, The	WalkersGal			63		
Drinking Pool, The	WalkersGal			15.15s		
Duck Pond, The	WalkersGal			9.9s		
Dunes, The	WalkersGal			10.10s		
Evening on the Dunes	WalkersGal			12.12s		
Flemish Market Place, A	WalkersGal			16.16s		
Garden Gate, The	WalkersGal			12.12s		
Home of Rest, A	WalkersGal			15.15s		
Hospice, the Men's Room, The	WalkersGal			15.15s		
Hospice, the Women's Room, The	WalkersGal			15.15s		
House with Green Shutters. The	WalkersGal			21		
In the Hospice Garden	WalkersGal			15.15s		
Kermersse, La	WalkersGal	WC		7.7s		
Little Sweetie Shop, The	WalkersGal			10.10s		
Marchande de Chouxfleurs, La	WalkersGal			9.9s		
Market Place, Cassel, The	WalkersGal	WC	9x11.5	9.9s		R
Market Place, Montreuil-sur-Mer,	WalkersGal			9.9s		
Market Place, Trèguier	WalkersGal			9.9s		
Market Stall, A	WalkersGal			4.4s		
Milking Time	WalkersGal			9.9s		
Mills, Montreuil-sur-Mer, The	WalkersGal	WC	10x7	7.7s		
Monsieur le Curé	WalkersGal			15.15s		
Mower, The	WalkersGal			7.7s		
Musée, Cassel, Le	WalkersGal			9.9s		
Nieuport	WalkersGal			10.10s		
Our Little Terrace	WalkersGal			9.9s		
Over the Flemish Plain	WalkersGal			12.12s		
Passing the Time of Day	WalkersGal			15.15s		
Pet Rabbit, The	WalkersGal	WC	11x8.75	10.10s		R
Picardy Homestead, A	WalkersGal			11.11s		R
Picture Dealer, The	WalkersGal			7.7s		

Portrait of Henry Kneeshaw Esq [of North Wales]	WalkersGal			NFS		
Procession, The	WalkersGal	WC	9x5	6.6s		
Roundabout, The	WalkersGal			7.7s		
Salt House, St Valéry-sur-Somme, The	WalkersGal			9.9s		
Sea Lavender	WalkersGal			9.9s		
Sunshine in the Beguinage	WalkersGal			9.9s		
Sweetmeat Stall, The	WalkersGal			7.7s		
Tannery Yard, The	WalkersGal			15.15s		
Turkeys	WalkersGal			15.15		
Twins, The	WalkersGal			7.7s		
Windmill in Picardy, A	WalkersGal			15.15s		
Woodland Path, A	WalkersGal			4.4s		
White Horse, The	WalkersGal			7.7s		
	1910					
Greetings from Garstins [artist painting horse]	*Gift*	Stencl	5.5x4.5	NFS	NS	R
Xmas 1910, Newlyn [rider & another horse]	*Gift*	Woodct	5x7.5	NFS	NS	R
Among the Pots [preliminary study]	*House*	Oil	21.1x17.1		NS	R
Oudenarde, Canal, Timber Barge and House	*House*	Oil	6.25x 8.6		NS	Exeter/R
Wet Passage, The: Small Version	*House*	Oil	10.6x8.5		NS	Penzance/R
Garden Fete, The	Newlyn					Des
Portrait of Mr Roddie Black	Newlyn	Oil	22x18			
Sunshine in the Beguinage/ Beguinage, Le	RA	Oil	35.75x 29.75	73.10s	NS	Cork/R
Wet Sunday, The [Diest]	RA	Oil		73.10s		Des
[Portrait of] The Late Mrs Kneeshaw	RCambrian			NFS		
In the Shadow of the Church	Ridley			10.10s		
Blacksmith's Workshop	*Ross 03*	Oil	10x14			
	1911					
Greetings for Xmas 1911 Josselin [citadel]	*Gift*	Litho	8.25x5.5	NFS	NS	R
Among the Pots [Oil]	RA	Oil	50x40	150	NS	Plymouth/R
Wet Passage, The	Ridley	Oil		42		Des
	1912					
Xmas Greetings from the Garstins, Milk Sellers, Guémené	*Gift*	Litho	6.75x5.5	NFS	NS	R
Beganier Garden, Josselin	Newlyn	Oil	10.5x8	8.8s	S	R
Market Day. Josselin (1)	Newlyn			8.8s	S	
Cabaret, The	RA	Oil		80	S	Des
[Portrait of] Maynie	Ridley	Oil				
Breton Needlewomen	Ridley	Oil	36x30	60		R
Breton Needlewomen, A.[preliminary study]	Studio	Oil	12x9.5	NFS	NS	R
Breton Pardon, A [preliminary study]	Studio	Oil	23.25x28.5	NFS	NS	R
After Mass, Diest	WalkersGal	Oil				
Almshouses. Diest, The	WalkersGal	Oil				
Ancient Grandeur	WalkersGal	Oil				

Beguines Garden. Oudenarde	WalkersGal	Oil				
Butter and Eggs	WalkersGal	Oil				
Carrousel. Oudenarde, The	WalkersGal	Oil				
Château Josselin	WalkersGal	WC				
Church of the Beguinage. Diest, The	WalkersGal	Oil	10.5x8.25		NS	Sheffield
Cloister and the Hearth	WalkersGal	Oil		4.4s		
Convent Gate. Evening, The	WalkersGal	Oil	18x15.5			R
Deserted Abbey, The	WalkersGal	Oil				
Duchess's Garden, The	WalkersGal	Oil				
Earthenware	WalkersGal	Oil	10.5x8.25			R
Evening Fête. Diest, The	WalkersGal	Oil	21.75x18.25			R
Farmhouse on the Hill. Josselin, The	WalkersGal	Oil				
Flemish Farm, A	WalkersGal	WC				
Foot-bridge. Oudenarde, The	WalkersGal	Oil				
Harvest Field. Oudenarde, The	WalkersGal	WC				
Hayfield, The	WalkersGal	Oil				
Holy Well, The [Josselin]	WalkersGal	Oil	11x8.5			R
Horse Fair. Oudenarde	WalkersGal	Oil				
House of St Joseph, The	WalkersGal	Oil				
In the Estaminet	WalkersGal	Oil	8.25x10.5			R
Joy Riders	WalkersGal	Oil				
Kermesse. Diest	WalkersGal	WC	9.1x11.5			V&A/R
Lilies [Big]	WalkersGal	Oil	20x30			
Little Brother. Diest, The	WalkersGal	Oil			(20)	
Little Lane, The	WalkersGal	Oil	7.75x10.5		NS	Plymouth
Little Rose Garden, A	WalkersGal	Oil				
Little Shrine. Diest, The	WalkersGal	Oil				
Little Street. Diest, The	WalkersGal	Oil				
Lower Town. Josselin, The	WalkersGal	Oil				
Madonna Lilies	WalkersGal	Oil	10.6x8.25			R
Main Street. Diest, The	WalkersGal	Oil				
Mallows, The	WalkersGal	Oil				
Market Day. Josselin (2)	WalkersGal	Oil	10x8			R
Market Stall. Josselin	WalkersGal	Oil				
Market. Oudenarde	WalkersGal	Oil				
Mill Gate. Oudenarde, The	WalkersGal	Oil				
Mill Race. Oudenarde, The	WalkersGal	Oil				
Morning Post (Portrait)	WalkersGal	Oil				
Oudenarde, from the Scheld	WalkersGal	Oil				
Pig Market. Josselin, The	WalkersGal	Oil	8.75x11.25			
Pottery Market, Oudenarde	WalkersGal	Oil		21		
Poultry Market. Josselin	WalkersGal	Oil		(8.8s)		
Red Houses, The	WalkersGal	Oil	23.5x19			R
Roundabout. Night. Diest, The	WalkersGal	Oil	8.25x10.5		NS	Belfast/R
Saint Croix. Josselin	WalkersGal	Oil				
Saturday [Josselin]	WalkersGal	Oil	9x6			R
Street Near the Ramparts. Diest, A	WalkersGal	Oil				
Stubble Field. Oudenarde	WalkersGal	WC	10x6			
Sunflecks. Diest	WalkersGal	Oil				
Under the Shrine	WalkersGal	Oil				
Water Garden, The	WalkersGal	WC	13.25x9			R
White House. Josselin, The	WalkersGal	Oil				

1913

Greetings for Xmas 1913, Le Faouët	*Gift*	Litho	8x5	NFS	NS	R
Shrine, The	Liverpool	Oil		100		Des
Breton Pardon, A	RA	Oil		150		
Road over the Hill, The	Ridley			10.10s		
September [1913]	Ridley			10.10s		
Worsted Seller	Ridley			10.10s		
	1914					
Pardon of St Barbe, Brittany [Chapelle Ste Barbe, Le Faouët]	*House*	Oil	8.75x6.4		NS	Exeter/R
Portrait of Mrs Venning [of Penzance]	*Letter*					
Cornishman, The [engine]	Newlyn	Oil				Des
Tea at the [castle] **Ruins**	RA	Oil		50		Des
From my Window [Hotel Croix d'Or, Le Faouët]	Ridley	Oil	21x16	25		R
Last of the Fair, The	Ridley	Oil	30x25.5	50	NS	NGIreland/R
Who Comes There	Ridley	Oil		25		
	1915					
Old Parsonage, The [WC]	*Gift*	WC		NFS	NS	
Black Bear, Wareham	Ridley	Oil	12x10	10.10s		
East Street, Wareham	Ridley	Oil	12x10	10.10s		
Old Parsonage, The [Oil]	*Studio*	Oil	8.25x10.75	NFS	NS	R
	1916					
Burford [with church to left]	*Christie's 03*	Oil	17x20.75			R
Bull Hotel, Burford, The	*House*	Oil	8.25x10.5		NS	Tate/R
Burford from West Hall Hill Farmyard	*House*	Oil	16.5x20.5		NS	TePapa
Near Burford	*House*	Oil	5x6		NS	TePapa/ R
Burford [with church to right]	*House*	Oil	19.9x23.9		NS	Norwich
Indulgence, An	RA	Oil		30		
View of a Village	*Sotheby's 87*	WC	14x12			
	1917					
Big Pots	IntSociety	Oil				
In August Month	RA	Oil		52.10s		
Sculptor, The/ Workshop, The	RA	Oil	28x23	42	S	R
	1918					
Last Furrow, The	RBritColonl	Oil	50x40	(75)	NS	Glasgow/R
	1919					
From the Butter Cross, Ludlow	RA	Oil		63		
	1920					
Across the River, St Paul's	*House*	Oil	5.6x5		NS	Oxford/R
Battersea Bridge	*House*	Oil	5x5.75		NS	York/R
King's Bench Walk	*House*	Oil	5.9x5		NS	Belfast
London Church	*House*	Oil	6x5		NS	
Ludgate Hill	*House*	Oil	6x5		NS	Oxford/R
St Mary-le-Strand	*House*	Oil	6x5.25		NS	Oxford/R
St Paul's Churchyard	*House*	Oil	6x5		NS	R
St Paul's Cross	*House*	Oil	5.9x5.1		NS	York

Thames Scene	*House*	Oil	5x6		NS	
Wren's Monument: Small Version	*House*	Oil	6x5		NS	R
Green Cottage, Pin Mill [Suffolk]	Ipswich			26.5s		
Burford Bridge	RA	Oil		42		
	1921					
Market Jew Street, Penzance	*House*	Oil	5x6		NS	Penzance
Fleet Street	*Letter*	Oil			S	
Wells [Cathedral]	RA	Oil		75		Des
Street in the Cotswolds, Burford	Ridley			21		
Our Garden, Burford	Sheffield	WC				
Wren's Monument	Sheffield	Oil	40x50	45	S	Sheff'd/R
	1922					
Landscape with Pools of Water	*Gift*	WC	9.5x11.5	NFS	NS	R
Market Jew Street [Penzance]	RA	Oil		40		
	1923					
Breton Fete, A	RA	Oil		52.10		Des
	1924					
St Buriena	*Gift*	Oil	14x25	NFS	NS	St Hilary
Over the Vale of Evesham	Newlyn	WC				Des
Semur en Auxois	Sheffield	WC		15.15s		
Across the Avenue	WalkersGal	WC		14		
Bathing Hour, The	WalkersGal	WC		9		
Blue Day, A	WalkersGal	WC		14		
Bluebell Wood	WalkersGal	WC		9		
Boglands – Île Tudy	WalkersGal	WC		14		
Burgundy	WalkersGal	WC		16		
Butt and Oyster [Inn, Pinn Mill, Suffolk]	WalkersGal	WC	14.9x18.1	14		R
Chemineux, Burgundy	WalkersGal	WC		14		
Daoulas	WalkersGal	WC		14		
Down the River	WalkersGal	WC		14		
Dragon , A	WalkersGal	WC		16		
Dunes Wissant, The	WalkersGal	WC		16		
Estuary – Brittany, An	WalkersGal	WC		14		
Flemish Garden, A	WalkersGal	WC		15		
Glowing Evening	WalkersGal	WC	10.1x12.5	16		V&A/R
Grey Evening	WalkersGal	WC		16		
Hawthorn	WalkersGal	WC		16		
Hedgerow	WalkersGal	WC		14		
Hub of Île Tudy, The	WalkersGal	WC	9.5x11.5	14		R
In Shropshire	WalkersGal	WC		14		
In the Eye of the Wind	WalkersGal	WC		14		
Little Breton Port [Île Tudy], A	WalkersGal	WC	9.5x11.5	14		R
Ludford Bridge	WalkersGal	WC	14.5x12	14		R
Old Citadel, The	WalkersGal	WC		10		
Picardy	WalkersGal	WC		9		
Plane Trees and Firs	WalkersGal	WC		14		
Reeds in the River	WalkersGal	WC		14		
Rooster, A	WalkersGal	WC		14		
Sand Crater, A	WalkersGal	WC		14		

Screen of Trees – Daoulas, A	WalkersGal	WC		14		
Shining Sands	WalkersGal	WC		9		
Silver Grey Marshes	WalkersGal	WC		16		
Soeurs de Charité	WalkersGal	WC		10		
Still Lagoon, A	WalkersGal	WC		14		
Thistles and Ragwort	WalkersGal	WC		14		
Towards the Sun	WalkersGal	WC		10		
Upland Furrow, An	WalkersGal	WC		10		
Wayside Cross, A	WalkersGal	WC		14		
White Horse	WalkersGal	WC	9.5x11.75	14		R
White Road in Picardy, A	WalkersGal	WC		16		
Wind-clouds	WalkersGal	WC		14		
Wissant	WalkersGal	WC		14		
Wooden Horses, The	WalkersGal	WC		14		
	1925					
In France	*House*	Oil	8.75x6.75		NS	Hull
Montrésor	Newlyn 26	WC			NS	Des
Venetian Scene, A	*Studio*	Oil		NFS	NS	
View of an Italian Piazza, A	*Studio*	WC	22x15	NFS	NS	R
	1926					
Calm Evening, A	Newlyn					
Heart of London, The	Ridley			31.10s		
	1927					
View over Penzance	*Catalogue*	Oil	10.5x9			
Appleblossom	*House*	Oil	6.25x8.75		NS	
At the Fair	*House*	Oil	5x6		NS	Belfast
Bulls and Cows	*House*	Oil	5x5.9		NS	Hull
Canal	*House*	Oil	5.5x7		NS	Hull
Cart and Classical Building	*House*	Oil	6x5		NS	Hull
Fair, The	*House*	Oil	6.25x8.75		NS	
French House and Figures Late Evening	*House*	Oil	8x6		NS	
Houses and Boats, Newlyn	*House*	Oil	9.4x5.4		NS	Penzance/R
Landscape	*House*	Oil	5x6		NS	Hull
Ponies under Trees	*House*	Oil	5x6		NS	
Rider and Horses under Trees	*House*	Oil	5.6x6		NS	
Seated Brown Dog Facing Left	*House*	Oil	9x10.5		NS	
Seated Dog Facing Right	*House*	WC	3.5x4.75		NS	
Sketch of a Red-brown Horse Facing Right	*House*	Oil	7.5x9		NS	
Sketch of a Brown Horse Facing Left	*House*	Oil	9x9		NS	
Sketch of Two Horses and Plough	*House*	Oil	21x14.75		NS	
Swan on Trengwainton Ponds	*House*	Oil	10.5x7.9		NS	
Taking the Fence	*House*	Oil	5x6		NS	York
Threshing by Steam Traction Engine	*House*	Oil	15x19.5		NS	
Two Horses and a Man	*House*	Oil	4.75x5.25		NS	
Two Swans	*House*	Oil	10.5x8		NS	
Wellington Terrace. View from the Studio	*House*	Oil	10x12		NS	
Self-portrait	*Limerick*	Chalk	5x4	NFS	NS	Limerick/R
Portrait of C. W. Raxworthy	*Private*					

April in England	*Studio*	WC		NFS	NS	
Before the Start, Point to Point, Brittany	*Studio*	WC	18x21	NFS	NS	
Breton Village, A	*Studio*	WC	11.75x10.25	NFS	NS	R
Cart Horses and Figures in a Village Square	*Studio*	WC	14.5x10.5	NFS	NS	R
Coastal View with a Harbour in the Distance, A	*Studio*	Oil	11.5x9.5	NFS	NS	R
Dark Chestnuts, The	*Studio*	WC	15x10.75	NFS	NS	R
English Landscape with Church and Trees, An	*Studio*	WC	10.75x15.5	NFS	NS	
Figures by a Fountain, Brussels	*Studio*	WC	7x4.75	NFS	NS	
Garden Scene, A	*Studio*	WC		NFS	NS	
Hayrick in a Landscape	*Studio*	WC		NFS	NS	
Horsefair, A	*Studio*	WC		NFS	NS	
Landscape with a Blossom Tree in the Foreground	*Studio*	Oil	15.75x9.5	NFS	NS	
Landscape with a Study of Horses verso	*Studio*	WC		NFS	NS	
Landscape of Wild Flowers	*Studio*	WC	10.75x11.25	NFS	NS	R
Mountain View with Cherry Trees in Blossom	*Studio*	Oil	6.25x8.75	NFS	NS	
Point to Point [jump] (No 889)	*Studio*	Oil	10.5x11.5	NFS	NS	R
Point to Point [gathering], A (No 890)	*Studio*	Oil	9.75x9.75	NFS	NS	R
River Landscape, Autumn	*Studio*	WC	6.75x11.5	NFS	NS	
Sailors in a Gale	*Studio*	WC		NFS	NS	
Souvenir [river landscape]	*Studio*	WC	9.75x13.25	NFS	NS	
Street Scene	*Studio*	WC		NFS	NS	
Study of a Child	*Studio*	WC	6.75x4.75	NFS	NS	R
Study of a Cottage with landscape verso	*Studio*	WC		NFS	NS	
Study of a Horse, Brittany	*Studio*	WC	9x9.5	NFS	NS	
Study of a Horse and Cart (No 1210)	*Studio*	WC	9.5x13.5	NFS	NS	R
There was an Old Man of Bude	*Studio*	WC		NFS	NS	R
There was an Old Man of Porthgwarra	*Studio*	WC		NFS	NS	
There was an Old Man of St Ives	*Studio*	WC		NFS	NS	
Two Coastal Scenes (No 893)	*Studio*	WC		NFS	NS	
Two Coastal Scenes (No 888)	*Studio*	WC	9.75x11.5	NFS	NS	
Two Landscapes (No 888)	*Studio*	Oil		NFS	NS	
View Along the River Bank	*Studio*	WC	11x13.5	NFS	NS	R
View of a Lake with Sailing Boats	*Studio*	WC	9.5x12	NFS	NS	R
Wooded Landscape, A	*Studio*	Oil		NFS	NS	
	1978					
Lilies [Small]	*Sotheby's 78*	Oil	10x7			
Washing Day	*Christie's 82*	Oil	20x16			
Autumn	*Sotheby's 82*	Oil	29.5x24.5			R
[Portrait of] Nora Downing	*Sotheby's 86*	Oil	10.75x8			R
Young Girl Reading, A	*Christie's 87*	Oil	10.25x7			R
Hollyhocks [& river]	*Sotheby's 87*	WC	15x11			R
Cornish Toast, A	*Lay 88*	Oil	17.75x13.5			R
Fishwives of Newlyn	*Sotheby's 88*	Oil	15x21			
Harbour at Dawn	*Lay 89*	WC	5x7			R
Boats in Newlyn Harbour from the						

Meadows on Chywoone Hill	*Lane 91*	WC	10x9	
Permearmans from the Sandhills	*Lane 94*	WC	6x9	
Street. Peel [Isle of Man]	*Christie's 97*	WC	7x10	R
Grey Horse, The	*Sotheby's 97*	WC	9x11	
Stroll in the Garden, A/Mrs Bolitho	*Sotheby's 98*	Oil	26.75x20	R
Morning in the Creek	*Moran 99*	Oil	28x36	R
His Favourite Pastime - Bubbles!	*WhittonL 01*	Oil	16x11	R
View of a Treelined Footpath Leading to a Distant Sculpture	*BiddleW 03*	Oil	7.75x5.75	R
Street Leading to the Harbour, Par, Cornwall, A	*Lane 03*	WC	10.5x7.5	R
Hayle Estuary	*Lay 03*	WC	9.5x11.5	R
St Mary's Church, Penzance	*Lay 04*	WC	7.5x5	R

Major works are canvases where the initial price was £25 or more and/or one side is 20 inches or more, excluding preliminary works that do not appear to have been intended for sale.

Where picture names are in italics there is some doubt about whether Norman or Alethea was the painter.

Date First Shown is, in order of precedence, the year of first exhibition by Garstin; the known or probable year of painting; 1927 for pictures never sold or sold privately, 1978 for pictures auctioned

Gallery or *Place* is, in order of precedence, the gallery where Garstin first exhibited (except at Newlyn, if exhibited elsewhere); the publication in which the picture is reproduced (e.g. *Black&W*=Black and White); *House* for pictures owned by Alethea and listed in Canney (pp. 26, 27) and/or in a private collection; *Studio* for a studio picture sold at Sotheby's (23 October 2000 or 23 May 2001) and re-sold at de Veres (6 March 2001, 20 November 2001, 26 November 2002) or the Gorry Gallery (14 June 2001); the auctioneer; *Private* for unexhibited portraits; and *Gift* for probable gifts. Abbreviations include Dod&Dod=Dowdeswell and Dowdeswell; *FineArtSoc*=Fine Art Society; NEAC=New English Art Club; RB'ham=Royal Birmingham Society of Artists; RCornwall=Royal Cornwall Polytechnic Society; WalkersGal=Walkers Galleries, Bond Street. A =Academy, R=Royal.

NB: this Catalogue Raisonné is based on the best information that is now available. As new material comes to light, it will almost certainly be necessary to revise a few entries and become possible to add further pictures.

Catalogue Raisonné 2: Summary of Works, and Estimated Earnings, by Year

Year	Major	Portraits, excluding known small works	Other Oils	Water-Colours	Other & Unknown Media	Total	Estimated Earnings at Catalogue Prices (£)
1882	--	--	3	--	4	7	32
1883	2	1	7	--	--	10	100
1884	1	--	1	--	--	2	27
1885	5	--	18	--	--	23	226
1886	6	1	7	--	1	15	234
1887	8	--	7	--	--	15	236
1888	5	--	3	--	--	8	208
1889	5	1	3	--	--	9	314
1890	2	--	5	--	1	8	74
1891	2	--	15	--	--	17	84
1892	2	--	--	--	--	2	200
1893	3	2	5	--	--	10	114
1894	1	--	2	--	--	3	114
1895	--	1	--	1	7	9	78
1896	2	--	6	1	4	13	149
1897	1	--	2	--	3	6	66
1898	2	--	2	--	5	9	117
1899	3	1	--	1	4	9	195
1900	1	--	--	2	2	5	221
1901	4	1	1	2	6	14	82
1902	2	--	--	--	2	4	45
1903	2	1	--	--	--	3	118
1904	3	1	--	93	3	100	1013
1905	1	--	--	2	1	4	122
1906	1	4	2	1	--	8	138
1907	2	--	--	3	4	9	144
1908	2	--	--	1	2	5	224
1909	5	3	--	7	55	70	874
1910	4	1	3	--	4	12	275
1911	2	--	--	--	1	3	298
1912	5	1	51	6	1	64	825
1913	2	--	--	--	4	6	189
1914	5	1	1	--	--	7	158
1915	--	--	3	--	1	4	109
1916	4	--	2	1	--	7	83
1917	2	--	1	--	--	3	113
1918	1	--	--	--	--	1	149
1919	1	--	--	--	--	1	58
1920	2	--	10	--	--	12	34
1921	2	--	2	1	1	6	252
1922	1	--	--	1	--	2	74
1923	1	--	--	--	--	1	60
1924	1	--	--	45	--	46	602

1925	--	--	2	2	--	4	24
1926	1	--	--	--	1	2	103
1927	--	1	30	30	1	62	--
1978 etc.	5	--	6	9	--	20	--
Total known	112	21	200	209	118	660	8955
Undiscovered						175	
Total, including Undiscovered						835	

Major includes portraits known to be major, and Other includes known oils of unknown size and value. For the purpose of estimating Garstin's earnings it has been assumed that pictures (excluding those not sold in Garstin's lifetime) were, in order of declining preference, disposed of when they are known to have been sold, when they were last exhibited, or when they were painted. Hence Garstin's income is likely to be overstated in 1904, 1909, 1912 and 1924 when major exhibitions were held, and to be understated in subsequent years when unsold works were disposed of. The value of those works that cannot be dated (included at 1927 or 1978 etc) has been spread evenly over Garstin's working life in the case of oils (£4.38 per year), and over the period 1900-26 for watercolours (£3.59 per annum). Pictures were priced at their last exhibition value or, where this was not known, at 4.25p per square inch for major works of known size; at £9.70 each for most watercolours; and at £10.75 for other works, except Canadian pictures (£5) and portraits (£25). These average prices were, in turn, derived from the exhibition prices of similar works, apart from portraits where an arbitrary value (£25) had to be used. The number of undiscovered pictures was estimated from previously known paintings that have come up for sale etc (87), from previously unknown works (36), and from previously known works which were sold during Garstin's lifetime and have not yet been re-sold (401; which divided by 87 equals 4.61, and when this is multiplied by 36 gives 175). The value of known works, at actual or estimated catalogue prices, will tend on the one hand to understate net income because of unknown works, but on the other hand to overstate it because of the commission payable to galleries (usually 5-15%), because artists cut prices to make sales (typically by around 40%), and because of the cost of framing, transport and materials. On balance, Garstin's net earnings are likely to have been significantly smaller than catalogue values suggest.

Annex: Reproductions of Garstin's Oils and Watercolours during his Lifetime, excluding those appearing in his own articles

Picture	Gallery/author	Publisher/Journal	Short Title	Date	Page
Progress and Poverty	RA	Chatto & Windus	*Academy Notes*	1888	64
An Iron Master	New English Art Club	*Pall Mall Gazette Extra*	Pictures of 1888	1888	86
An Iron Master	New English Art Club	Henry Blackburn (editor)	*Academy Sketches*	1888	193
An Iron Master	Alice Meynell	*Art Journal*	'Newlyn'	1889	140
Overdue	New English Art Club	*Pall Mall Gazette Extra*	Pictures of 1889	1889	
A Stranger	RA	*Magazine of Art*	Royal Academy Pictures	1890	77
A Stranger	RA	*Pall Mall Gazette*	Pictures of 1890	1890	43
A Stranger	RA	Chatto & Windus	*Academy Notes*	1890	83
A Stranger	The Walker		*The Walker*	1890	114
Her Signal	RA	*Pall Mall Gazette*	Pictures of 1892	1892	63
Her Signal	RA	*Magazine of Art*	Royal Academy Pictures	1892	127
Her Signal	RA	*Black & White*	*Handbook to the Royal Academy*	1892	137
Her Signal	The Walker		*The Walker*	1892	62
The Cotillon	RA	Chatto & Windus	*Academy Notes*	1892	130
Portrait of a Boy	RA	*Magazine of Art*	Royal Academy Pictures	1893	
Portrait of a Boy	RA	*Pall Mall Gazette*	Pictures of 1893	1893	
Portrait of a Boy	RA	*Black & White*	*Handbook to the Royal Academy*	1893	142
The Last Dance	RA	*Pall Mall Gazette*	Pictures of 1895	1895	44
The Last Dance	RA	Chatto & Windus	*Academy Notes*	1895	115
The Last Dance	The Walker		*The Walker*	1895	65
The Scarlet Letter	RA	Chatto & Windus	*Academy Notes*	1896	115

The Scarlet Letter	RA	*Black & White*	*Black & White*	1896	632 16 May
The Scarlet Letter	RA	*Black &White*	*Handbook to the Royal Academy*	1896	58
The Piece of Silver that was Lost	RA	Chatto & Windus	*Academy Notes*	1898	51
Danger	RA	*The Studio*	*The Studio*	1898	134
The Rose and the Ring	RA	Chatto & Windus	*Academy Notes*	1900	112
The Rose and the Ring	RA	*Black & White*	*Handbook to the Royal Academy*	1900	44
Edmund Carlyon Esq	?	*Black & White*	*Handbook to the Royal Academy*	1900	83
Lace and Lilies	Fine Art Society	*The Studio*	Studio-Talk	1904	74
Vendredi, Bruges	Fine Art Society	*The Studio*	Studio-Talk	1904	74
Prentices	The Walker		*The Walker*	1906	123
A Watch Tower in the Low Countries	RA	Wells Gardner, Darton	*Academy Notes*	1907	
A Corner of the Farm (A Village Corner, Picardy)	Walkers Gallery	*The Studio*	Studio-Talk	1909	227
A Picardy Homestead (A Farm Entrance, Picardy)	Walkers Gallery	*The Studio*	Studio-Talk	1909	227
Among the Pots	The Walker		*The Walker*	1911	112

Index of Garstin's Works

References in **bold** are to pages with illustrations

General Index

References in **bold** are to pages with illustrations